# Contents



Moon Palace . . . . . . . . . . . . . . . . . . . . . . . . . . 5

Additional material . . . . . . . . . . . . . . . . . . . . . 345

*Nothing can astound an American.*
Jules Verne

# 1

It was the summer that men first walked on the moon. I was very young back then, but I did not believe there would ever be a future. I wanted to live dangerously, to push myself as far as I could go, and then see what happened to me when I got there. As it turned out, I nearly did not make it. Little by little, I saw my money dwindle to zero; I lost my apartment; I wound up living in the streets. If not for a girl named Kitty Wu, I probably would have starved to death. I had met her by chance only a short time before, but eventually I came to see that chance as a form of readiness, a way of saving myself through the minds of others. That was the first part. From then on, strange things happened to me. I took the job with the old man in the wheelchair. I found out who my father was. I walked across the desert from Utah to California. That was a long time ago, of course, but I remember those days well, I remember them as the beginning of my life.

I came to New York in the fall of 1965. I was eighteen years old then, and for the first nine months I lived in a college dormitory. All out-of-

**Nothing can astound an American** from the beginning of the third chapter of Jules Verne's *De la terre à la lune (From the Earth to the Moon)* first published in 1867. The novel portrays Americans as lovers of technology and war. **men first walked on the moon** On July 20, 1969 the Americans Neil Armstrong and Edwin Aldrin were the first people to walk on the moon. This achievement was seen by Americans as proof that the American economic system was superior to that of the Soviet Union. It was also at a time when there was great opposition to the Vietnam war. **to dwindle to zero** to slowly run out of s.th. until nothing is left **the desert** Auster probably means the Mojave desert east of Los Angeles **college dormitory** building on a university campus where students can live

town freshmen at Columbia were required to live on campus, but once the term was over I moved into an apartment on West 112th Street. That was where I lived for the next three years, right up to the moment when I finally hit bottom. Considering the odds against me, it was a miracle I lasted as long as I did.

I lived in that apartment with over a thousand books. They had originally belonged to my Uncle Victor, and he had collected them slowly over the course of about thirty years. Just before I went off to college, he impulsively offered them to me as a going-away present. I did my best to refuse, but Uncle Victor was a sentimental and generous man, and he would not let me turn him down. "I have no money to give you," he said, "and not one word of advice. Take the books to make me happy." I took the books, but for the next year and a half I did not open any of the boxes they were stored in. My plan was to persuade my uncle to take the books back, and in the meantime I did not want anything to happen to them.

As it turned out, the boxes were quite useful to me in that state. The apartment on 112th Street was unfurnished, and rather than squander my funds on things I did not want and could not afford, I converted the boxes into several pieces of "imaginary furniture." It was a little like working on a puzzle: grouping the cartons into various modular configurations, lining them up in rows, stacking them one on top of another, arranging and rearranging them until they finally began to resemble household objects. One set of sixteen served as the support for my mattress, another set of twelve became a table, others of seven became chairs, another of two became a bedstand, and so on. The overall effect was rather monochromatic, what with that somber light brown everywhere

**freshman** first year student **Columbia** Columbia University to the northwest of Central Park in Manhattan near the Hudson River—it is one of the top universities in America—Auster received a B.A. and M.A. at Columbia with an emphasis on comparative literature. **on campus** within the grounds of the university **term** a school year, like 2 semesters at a German university **to hit bottom** (coll) to reach the lowest point possible **the odds against me** i.e. how bad the situation appeared to be **Uncle Victor** Auster's uncle gave him a collection of world literature **unfurnished** without furniture **to squander** to waste **modular configurations** way of putting together the individual modules or units to form a new and larger unit, also a reference to the lunar module that was used to bring Armstrong and Aldrin to the surface of the moon **to stack** to pile, to put one thing on top of the other **bedstand** nightstand, small table next to a bed **monochromatic** only black and white and shades of gray **somber** dark, gloomy, shadowy

you looked, but I could not help feeling proud of my resourcefulness. My friends found it a bit odd, but they had learned to expect odd things from me by then. Think of the satisfaction, I would explain to them, of crawling into bed and knowing that your dreams are about to take place on top of nineteenth-century American literature. Imagine the pleasure of sitting down to a meal with the entire Renaissance lurking below your food. In point of fact, I had no idea which books were in which boxes, but I was a great one for making up stories back then, and I liked the sound of those sentences, even if they were false.

My imaginary furniture remained intact for almost a year. Then, in the spring of 1967, Uncle Victor died. This death was a terrible blow for me; in many ways it was the worst blow I had ever had. Not only was Uncle Victor the person I had loved most in the world, he was my only relative, my one link to something larger than myself. Without him I felt bereft, utterly scorched by fate. If I had been prepared for his death somehow, it might have been easier for me to contend with. But how does one prepare for the death of a fifty-two-year-old man whose health has always been good? My uncle simply dropped dead one fine afternoon in the middle of April, and at that point my life began to change, I began to vanish into another world.

There is not much to tell about my family. The cast of characters was small, and most of them did not stay around very long. I lived with my mother until I was eleven, but then she was killed in a traffic accident, knocked down by a bus that skidded out of control in the Boston snow. There was never any father in the picture, and so it had just been the two of us, my mother and I. The fact that she used her maiden name was proof that she had never been married, but I did not learn that I was illegitimate until after she was dead. As a small boy, it never occurred to me to ask questions about such things. I was Marco Fogg, and my mother was Emily Fogg, and my uncle in Chicago was Victor Fogg. We were all Foggs, and it made perfect sense that people from the same family should have the same name. Later on, Uncle Victor told me that his father's name had originally been Fogelman, but someone in the immigration offices at

**resourcefulness** ability to find ways of getting out of a difficult situation **to lurk** to stay hidden until ready to attack or appear (lauern) **in point of fact** in fact **bereft** here: feeling sad and lonely because of having lost s.o. **scorched** with the surface burned and damaged (versengt), here: completely left alone without help (im Stich gelassen) **to contend with s.th.** to deal with **to skid out of control** to slide suddenly because the driver has lost control of a car, bus, truck, etc. **illegitimate** [ˌɪl.ɪˈdʒɪt.əmət] born of parents who were not married

Ellis Island had truncated it to Fog, with one g, and this had served as the family's American name until the second g was added in 1907. *Fogel* meant bird, my uncle informed me, and I liked the idea of having that creature embedded in who I was. I imagined that some valiant ancestor of mine had once actually been able to fly. A bird flying through fog, I used to think, a giant bird flying across the ocean, not stopping until it reached America.

I don't have any pictures of my mother, and it is difficult for me to remember what she looked like. Whenever I see her in my mind, I come upon a short, dark-haired woman with thin child's wrists and delicate white fingers, and suddenly, every so often, I can remember how good it felt to be touched by those fingers. She is always very young and pretty when I see her, and that is probably correct, since she was only twenty-nine when she died. We lived in a number of small apartments in Boston and Cambridge, and I believe she worked for a textbook company of some sort, although I was too young to have any sense of what she did there. What stands out most vividly for me are the times we went to the movies together (Randolph Scott Westerns, *War of the Worlds, Pinocchio*), and how we would sit in the darkness of the theater, working our way through a box of popcorn and holding hands. She was capable of telling jokes that sent me into fits of raucous giggling, but that happened only rarely, when the planets were in the right conjunction. More often than not she was dreamy, given to mild sulks, and there were times when I felt a true sadness emanating from her, a sense that she was battling

**Ellis Island** processing center on an island in New York Harbor for newly arrived immigrants (1892-1954) **to truncate** to make shorter especially by cutting off the end with a knife **to embed** to fix deep and firmly into s.th. **valiant** brave, courageous **ancestor** people in your family who lived before you **Cambridge** small city to the northwest of Boston where Harvard University and M.I.T. are located **Randolph Scott** (1898-1987) American actor who usually played the honest but misunderstood hero in mostly mediocre westerns in the 40s, 50s, and 60s **War of the Worlds** One of the better science fiction films (1953) that were so popular in America at the height of the Cold War in the 1950s when a nuclear war seemed possible. It is based on the novel by the English writer H.G. Wells, in which Martians threaten to destroy the world. **Pinocchio** 1940 Disney cartoon film based on Collodi novel—Auster discusses the themes of seeking identity and the search for one's father in Collodi's novel in "The Book of Memory." **to work one's way through** (coll) here: to slowly eat up until nothing is left **fit** Anfall **raucous** [ˈrɑː.kəs] unpleasantly loud **to giggle** to laugh in a nervous and silly way **given to sulks** often in a bad mood **to emanate** to come or flow from

against some vast and internal disarray. As I grew older, she left me at home with baby-sitters more and more often, but I did not understand what these mysterious departures of hers meant until much later, long after she was dead. With my father, however, all was a blank, both during and after. That was the one subject my mother refused to discuss with me, and whenever I asked the question, she would not budge. "He died a long time ago," she would say, "before you were born." There was no evidence of him anywhere in the house. Not one photograph, not even a name. For want of something to cling to, I imagined him as a dark-haired version of Buck Rogers, a space traveler who had passed into the fourth dimension and could not find his way back.

My mother was buried next to her parents in Westlawn Cemetery, and after that I went to live with Uncle Victor on the North Side of Chicago. Much of that early period is lost to me now, but I apparently moped around a lot and did my fair share of sniffling, sobbing myself to sleep at night like some pathetic orphan hero in a nineteenth-century novel. At one point, a foolish woman acquaintance of Victor's ran into us on the street and started crying when she was introduced to me, dabbing her eyes with a handkerchief and blubbering on about how I must be poor Emmie's love child. I had not heard that term before, but I could tell that it hinted at gruesome and unfortunate things. When I asked Uncle Victor to explain it to me, he invented an answer I have always remembered.

**disarray** state of not being properly organized, confusion **all was a blank** here: there was no way to get information **to budge** here: to change one's attitude or opinion **Buck Rogers** science fiction hero in the 1930s, at first in comics, then later as a film and radio series **fourth dimension** i.e. time **Westlawn Cemetery** there is actually a cemetery with this name in Chicago and near Boston **North Side** residential area to the north of Chicago that includes areas of lower and upper income people **to mope around** to walk around feeling sad and full of pity for oneself **did my share fair share of sniffling** i.e. I often cried to myself (habe ich häufig geschluchzt) **to sob oneself to sleep** to cry noisily with great sadness until one falls asleep **orphan** child who has lost his or her parents—allusion to the extremely successful novels of Horatio Alger (1832-1899), which reflect the zeitgeist of America in the late 19th century—Most of Alger's heroes were poor virtuous boys, often orphaned, who became successful by hard and honest work. Luck played a role as well; cf. also Charles Dicken's *David Copperfield* and the 18th century novel *Tom Jones* by Henry Fielding **to run into s.o.** to meet s.o. by chance **to dab** to press against s.th. lightly and gently several times **to blubber** to cry noisily and unpleasantly **love child** euphemism for illegitimate child **gruesome** causing one to feel horror or disgust

"All children are love children," he said, "but only the best ones are ever called that."

My mother's older brother was a spindly, beak-nosed bachelor of forty-three who earned his living as a clarinetist. Like all the Foggs, he had a penchant for aimlessness and reverie, for sudden bolts and lengthy torpors. After a promising start as a member of the Cleveland Orchestra, these traits eventually got the better of him. He overslept rehearsals, showed up at performances without his tie, and once had the effrontery to tell a dirty joke within earshot of the Bulgarian concertmaster. After he was sacked, Victor bounced around with a number of lesser orchestras, each one a little worse than the one before, and by the time he returned to Chicago in 1953, he had learned to accept the mediocrity of his career. When I moved in with him in February of 1958, he was giving lessons to beginning clarinet students and playing for Howie Dunn's Moonlight Moods, a small combo that made the usual rounds of weddings, confirmations, and graduation parties. Victor knew that he lacked ambition, but he also knew that there were other things in the world besides music. So many things, in fact, that he was often overwhelmed by them. Being the sort of person who always dreams of doing something else while occupied, he could not sit down to practice a piece without pausing to work out a chess problem in his head, could not play chess without thinking about the failures of the Chicago Cubs, could not go to the ballpark without considering some minor character in Shakespeare, and then, when he finally got home, could not sit down with his book for more than twenty minutes without feeling the urge to play his clarinet. Wher-

**spindly** tall and thin **beak-nosed** having a long curved nose like the mouth of a bird **penchant for aimlessness and reverie** ['rev.ər.i] tending to have no direction or purpose and often day-dreaming **sudden bolt** sudden burst of energy **torpor** ['tɔːpər] state of little or no energy (Apathie) **the Cleveland Orchestra** one of the top American orchestras in Cleveland, Ohio **trait** a characteristic in a person's personality **to get the better of s.o.** here: to dominate, to take control of **rehearsal** Probe **effrontery** rude behavior without feeling ashamed (Unverschämtheit) **within earshot** still close enough to be heard **to sack** (BE coll) to dismiss from a job, to fire **to bounce around** (coll.) to travel around **lesser** less important **mediocrity** quality of not being very good (Mittelmäßigkeit) **mood** state of one's feelings (Laune) **chess** Schach **Chicago Cubs** baseball team in Chicago that indeed played very poorly in the 1950s and early 1960s **ballpark** (USA) baseball stadium **cluttered** here: disorderly, chaotic, untidy

ever he was, then, and wherever he went, he left behind a cluttered trail of bad chess moves, of unfinished box scores, and half-read books.

It was not hard to love Uncle Victor, however. The food was worse than it had been with my mother, and the apartments we lived in were shabbier and more cramped, but in the long run those were minor points. Victor did not pretend to be something he was not. He knew that fatherhood was beyond him, and therefore he treated me less as a child than as a friend, a diminutive and much-adored crony. It was an arrangement that suited us both. Within a month of my arrival, we had developed a game of inventing countries together, imaginary worlds that overturned the laws of nature. Some of the better ones took weeks to perfect, and the maps I drew of them hung in a place of honor above the kitchen table. The Land of Sporadic Light, for example, and the Kingdom of One-Eyed Men. Given the difficulties the real world had created for both of us, it probably made sense that we should want to leave it as often as possible.

Not long after I arrived in Chicago, Uncle Victor took me to a showing of the movie *Around the World in 80 Days*. The hero of that story was named Fogg, of course, and from that day on Uncle Victor called me Phileas as a term of endearment—a secret reference to that strange moment, as he put it, "when we confronted ourselves on the screen." Uncle Victor loved to concoct elaborate, nonsensical theories about things, and he never tired of expounding on the glories hidden in my name. Marco Stanley Fogg. According to him, it proved that travel was in my blood, that life would carry me to places where no man had ever been before. Marco, naturally enough, was for Marco Polo, the first

**trail** Spur **chess move** a change of position of a chesspiece **box score** a table into which the score, the performance of the individual players, and other statistics of a baseball game can be written or is already printed in a newspaper **cramped** with very little space for people **fatherhood was beyond him** He could never be a father. **diminutive** small **much-adored** much loved **crony** close friend who will even help to do s.th. dishonest **to overturn** to reverse, to completely change so that everything is the opposite **sporadic** happening only occasionally **given** considering **showing** an occasion when a film can be seen **Around the World in 80 Days** a very costly but successful American film made in 1956 based on the novel of the same name by the French writer Jules Verne (1828-1905)—The hero, an Englishman, Phileas Fogg bets he can go around the world in 80 days. In spite of a number of hair-raising adventures he wins the bet. **term of endearment** name or expression used for s.o. one loves **to concoct** to invent s.th. that is clearly not true or absurd **to expound on** to explain s.th. in detail **Marco Polo** (1254-1324), famous Renaissance adventurer and writer who traveled to the Far East and reported about it.

European to visit China; Stanley was for the American journalist who had tracked down Dr. Livingstone "in the heart of darkest Africa"; and Fogg was for Phileas, the man who had stormed around the globe in less than three months. It didn't matter that my mother had chosen Marco simply because she liked it, or that Stanley had been my grandfather's name, or that Fogg was a misnomer, the whim of some half-literate American functionary. Uncle Victor found meanings where no one else would have found them, and then, very deftly, he turned them into a form of clandestine support. The truth was that I enjoyed it when he showered all this attention on me, and even though I knew his speeches were so much bluster and hot air, there was a part of me that believed every word he said. In the short run, Victor's nominalism helped me to survive the difficult first weeks in my new school. Names are the easiest thing to attack, and Fogg lent itself to a host of spontaneous mutilations: Fag and Frog, for example, along with countless meteorological references: Snowball Head, Slush Man, Drizzle Mouth. Once my last name had been exhausted, they turned their attention to the first. The o at the end of Marco was obvious enough, yielding epithets such as Dumbo, Jerko, and

**Stanley** In November 1871 the Anglo-American explorer Sir Henry Morton Stanely (born as John Rowlands) (1841-1904), hired by an American newspaper, finally found the long lost explorer and missionary Dr. David Livingstone near Lake Tanganyika. **to track down** to finally find s.o. after searching in several different places **"in the heart of darkest Africa"** expression used for Zaire (formerly the Congo) Until the end of the 19th century Africa was known as "the dark continent," cf. Joseph Conrad's novel *Heart of Darkness* **to storm around** to move about in a noisy and fast way **misnomer** wrong or unsuitable name **whim** sudden decision made without any particular reason **half-literate** poorly educated **functionary** government worker whose job is not very important, here: a functionary at Ellis Island **deftly** skilfully, cleverly **clandestine** [klæn'des.tɪn] secret **bluster** speaking in an angry and loud way that seems threatening **nominalism** i.e. giving things a name, an allusion to Nominalism, one of two schools of thought in the Middle Ages—They believed that only a particular object or event has true reality—the opposite of Plato **to lend itself to** to be especially suitable for **host** a large number **spontaneous** not planned **mutilation** changing or damaging s.th. so that it is completely ruined **fag** (USA slang) homosexual man **slush** partly melted snow **drizzle** slight rain (Sprühregen) **to yield** to produce a result **epithet** ['ep.ɪ.θet] adjective or short phrase used to describe s.o. **Dumbo** derived from the word "dumb"—also a reference to the Disney cartoon film (1941) "Dumbo," a flying elephant who is at first treated as an outcast **jerko** from "jerk," (American slang), annoyingly foolish and stupid person

Mumbo Jumbo, but what they did in other ways defied all expectations. Marco became Marco Polo; Marco Polo became Polo Shirt; Polo Shirt became Shirt Face; and Shirt Face became Shit Face—a dazzling bit of cruelty that stunned me the first time I heard it. Eventually, I lived through my schoolboy initiation, but it left me with a feeling for the infinite fragility of my name. This name was so bound up with my sense of who I was that I wanted to protect it from further harm. When I was fifteen, I began signing all my papers M. S. Fogg, pretentiously echoing the gods of modern literature, but at the same time delighting in the fact that the initials stood for *manuscript*. Uncle Victor heartily approved of this about-face. "Every man is the author of his own life," he said. "The book you are writing is not yet finished. Therefore, it's a manuscript. What could be more appropriate than that?" Little by little, Marco faded from public circulation. I was Phileas to my uncle, and by the time I reached college, I was M. S. to everyone else. A few wits pointed out that those letters were also the initials of a disease, but by then I welcomed any added associations or ironies that I could attach to myself. When I met Kitty Wu, she called me by several other names, but they were her personal property, so to speak, and I was glad of them as well: Foggy, for example, which was used only on special occasions, and Cyrano, which developed for reasons that will become clear later. Had Uncle Victor lived to meet her, I'm sure he would have appreciated the fact that Marco, in his own small way, had at last set foot in China.

**mumbo jumbo** meaningless words used in a ritual **to defy** to be so unusual or extreme that is difficult to understand **dazzling** extremely impressive **to stun** to shock or surprise **initiation** period of time when s.o. new is introduced to a group often with a special ceremony **fragility** state of not being strong and thus easily broken or damaged **to be bound up with** to be closely connected with **M.S.** allusion to the short story "MS in a Bottle" by Edgar Allan Poe (1809-1849) **pretentiously** trying to seem more important than one really is **gods of modern literature** for example such writers of the 20th century as: T.S. Eliot (1888-1965), E.E. Cummings (1894-1962), J.D. Salinger (1919-) **to delight in** to find great joy in **to fade from public circulation** (to fade: to slowly disappear) here: to slowly no longer be used in public **a disease** i.e. multiple sclerosis **Cyrano** ['sɪr.ə.noʊ] a reference to Edmond Rostands drama *Cyrano de Bergerac* (1897) The hero is the French soldier, poet, and writer (1619-1655) that bears the name of the drama. Because of his large nose he feels himself too ugly to reveal his feelings to the woman he loves. Only by providing his witless rival with witty and elegant poetry and letters can he gain her indirect love. There was a historical Cyrano.

The clarinet lessons did not go well (my breath was unwilling, my lips impatient), and I soon wormed my way out of them. Baseball proved more compelling to me, and by the time I was eleven I had become one of those skinny American kids who went everywhere with his glove, pounding my right fist into the pocket a thousand times a day. Baseball no doubt helped me over some hurdles at school, and when I joined the local Little League that first spring, Uncle Victor came to nearly all the games to cheer me on. In July of 1958, however, we moved abruptly to Saint Paul, Minnesota ("a rare opportunity," said Victor, referring to some job he had been offered to teach music), but by the following year we were back in Chicago. In October, Victor bought a television set and allowed me to stay home from school to watch the White Sox lose the World Series in six games. That was the year of Early Wynn and the go-go Sox, of Wally Moon and his moon-shot home runs. We pulled for Chicago, of course, but we were both secretly glad when the man with the bushy eyebrows hit one out in the last game. With the start of the next season, we went back to rooting for the Cubs—the bumbling, sad-sack Cubs, the team that possessed our souls. Victor was a staunch advocate of daytime baseball, and he saw it as a moral good that the chewing gum king had not succumbed to the perversion of artificial lights. "When I go

**to worm one's way out of s.th.** to find dishonest excuses for not doing s.th. **compelling** extremely attractive **skinny** a bit too thin **glove** heavy leather glove used to catch a baseball **pocket** part of the baseball glove between the bottom of the fingers and thumb where the baseball is normally caught **hurdle** a difficulty or problem that must be overcome **Little League** baseball team for boys or girls aged 8 to 12 sponsored by a local firm **White Sox lose the World Series** In 1959 the Chicago White Sox lost to the Los Angeles Dodgers in the World Series, the most important series of games in a baseball season, which is played in autumn **go-go Socks** nickname given to this team because they were fast and young **moon-shot home run** a point was made for the team by hitting the ball high and wide—Wally Moon was not known for hitting many home runs, but they were called "moon-shots" **to pull for** (coll) to support **man with the bushy eyebrows** i.e. Chuck Essegian, who played for the Dodgers **to hit one out** to hit the ball so wide and far that a point could be made **to root for** (coll) to support **Cubs** i.e. the Chicago cubs **bumbling** careless and making a lot of mistakes—at the end of the 50s and beginning of the 60s the Cubs really did play badly **sad-sack** incompetent—from the cartoon character Sad-Sack created during World War II, for whom everything seemed to go wrong **staunch advocate** very firm and strong supporter **chewing gum king** i.e. Philip Wrigley of chewing-gum fame, whose firm owned the Chicago Cubs **to succumb to** to give in to, to allow to do because you are not strong enough to continue to oppose s.th.

to a game," he would say, "the only stars I want to see are the ones on the diamond. It's a sport for sunshine and wooly sweat. Apollo's cart hovering at the zenith! The great ball burning in the American sky!" We had lengthy discussions during those years about such men as Ernie Banks, George Altman, and Glen Hobbie. Hobbie was a particular favorite of his, but in keeping with his view of the world, my uncle declared that he would never make it as a pitcher, since his name implied unprofessionalism. Crackpot remarks of this sort were essential to Victor's brand of humor. Having developed a true fondness for his jokes by then, I understood why they had to be delivered with a straight face.

Shortly after I turned fourteen, the household population expanded to three. Dora Shamsky, née Katz, was a stout, mid-fortyish widow with an extravagant head of bleached blond hair and a tightly girdled rump. Since the death of Mr. Shamsky six years before, she had been working as a secretary in the actuarial division of Mid-American Life. Her meeting with Uncle Victor took place in the ballroom of the Featherstone Hotel, where the Moonlight Moods had been on hand to provide musical entertainment for the company's annual New Year's Eve bash. After a whirlwind

**the diamond** the baseball field because the four bases joined together look like a diamond **wooly sweat** sweat that results from watching an exciting game even when the weather has become cool **Apollo's cart** Apollo was also known as the god of light in Greek mythology; he was said to pull the sun along in a chariot **to hover** to stay in one place in the air **great ball** i.e., the sun—also used to describe the explosion of the first atomic bomb in New Mexico on July 16, 1945 **Ernie Banks, George Altman, Glen Hobbie** They actually played for the Chicago Cubs. **in keeping with** in agreement with **to make it** to succeed **pitcher** person on the baseball team on the field who throws the ball to a batter (Schläger) on the opposing team **implied unprofessionalism** i.e. the name Hobbie reminded Uncle Victor of the word "hobby," i.e. the baseball player played baseball as if it were his hobby and not his profession **crackpot** (coll) crazy **brand of humor** kind of humor **to deliver** to tell **with a straight face** with a serious expression on one's face **Shamsky** sham: a person who pretends to be something other than she/he is **née** family name a woman is born with **Katz** in America considered to be a typically Jewish name **stout** (ironic) rather fat **to bleach** to make a lighter color with chemicals **tightly girdled rump** i.e. She wore a tight girdle (Mieder) around the middle of her body. **actuarial division** department in an insurance company that deals with statistics **Mid-American Life** a life insurance company that exists **Featherstone Hotel** never existed **to be on hand** to be present **New Year's Eve** the evening of December 31 **bash** (slang) party, celebration **whirlwind** here: rapid and rushed

courtship, the couple tied the knot in March. I saw nothing wrong with any of this per se and proudly served as best man at the wedding. But once the dust began to settle, it pained me to notice that my new aunt did not laugh very readily at Victor's jokes, and I wondered if that might not indicate a certain obtuseness on her part, a lack of mental agility that boded ill for the prospects of the union. I soon learned that there were two Doras. The first was all bustle and get-up-and-go, a gruff, mannish character who stormed about the house with sergeantlike efficiency, a bulwark of brittle good cheer, a know-it-all, a boss. The second Dora was a boozy flirt, a tearful, self-pitying sensualist who tottered around in a pink bathrobe and puked up her binges on the living room floor. Of the two, I much preferred the second, if only because of the tenderness she seemed to show for me then. But Dora in her cups posed a conundrum that I was quite at a loss to untangle, for these collapses of hers made Victor morose and unhappy, and more than anything else in the world, I hated to see my uncle suffer. Victor could put up with the sober, nagging Dora, but her drunkenness brought out a severity and impatience in him that struck me as unnatural, a perversion of his true self. The good and the bad were therefore constantly at war with each other. When Dora was good, Victor was bad; when Dora was bad, Victor was good. The good Dora created a bad Victor, and the good Victor returned only when Dora was bad. I remained a prisoner of this infernal machine for more than a year.

Fortunately, the bus company in Boston had made a generous settlement. By Victor's calculations, there would be enough money to pay for

**courtship** time when a man seeks to get a woman to marry him **per se** [ˌpɜːˈseɪ] (Latin) in itself **best man** the man who helps the man about to get married at a wedding (Trauzeuge) **obtuseness** inability to understand s.th. **agility** quickness of thought **to bode ill** to be a bad sign for the future **bustle** busy activity **get-up-and-go** (coll) energy **gruff** rough (schroff) **bulwark** [ˈbʊl.wək] Bollwerk **brittle** showing no warm feelings **boozy flirt** (coll) i.e. when she was drunk she liked to flirt with other men **sensualist** only interested in sensual pleasure **to totter around** to walk about unsteadily **to puke** (coll) to vomit (sich übergeben) **binge** a short time of excessive eating and drinking **in one's cups** (coll) drunk **to pose a conundrum** [kəˈnʌn.drəm] to be a puzzle or riddle to s.o. **to be at a loss** to be unable to **to untangle** here: to understand (entwirren) **morose** in a bad mood, unhappy and silent **sober** not drunk **to nag** to continuously complain about another person's behavior **severity** a state of being strict or harsh (Härte, Strenge) **infernal machine** (ironic) a hidden bomb that should harm or destroy such as used by anarchists **settlement** a legal financial agreement (Abfindung)

four years of college, modest living expenses, and something extra to carry me into so called real life. For the first few years he kept this fund scrupulously intact. He fed me out of his own pocket and was glad to do so, taking pride in his responsibility and showing no inclination to tamper with the sum or any part of it. With Dora now on the scene, however, Victor changed his plan. Withdrawing the interest that had accumulated on the lump, along with certain bits of the something extra, he enrolled me in a private boarding school in New Hampshire, thinking in this way to reverse the effects of his miscalculation. For if Dora had not turned out to be the mother he had been hoping to provide for me, he saw no reason not to look for another solution. Too bad for the something extra, of course, but that could not be helped. When faced with a choice between the now and the later, Victor had always gone with the now, and given that his whole life was bound up in the logic of this impulse, it was only natural that he should opt for the now again.

I spent three years at Anselm's Academy for Boys. When I returned home after the second year, Victor and Dora had already come to a parting of the ways, but there did not seem to be any point in switching schools again, and so I went back to New Hampshire when summer vacation was over. Victor's account of the divorce was fairly muddled, and I could never be sure of what really happened. There was some talk about missing bank accounts and broken dishes, but then a man named George was mentioned, and I wondered if he wasn't involved in it as well. I did not press my uncle for details, however, since when all was said and done, he seemed more relieved than stricken to be alone again. Victor had survived the marriage wars, but that did not mean he had no wounds to show for it. His appearance was disturbingly rumpled (buttons missing, collars soiled, the cuffs of his pants frayed), and even his jokes had begun to take on a wistful, almost poignant quality. Those signs were bad

**scrupulously** extremely carefully **to tamper with** here: to make use of s.th. without authority **to withdraw** to take money out of a bank account **interest** Zinsen **to accumulate** to become more and more **lump** (coll) the money that one has put in the bank **to enroll** to officially arrange for s.o. to join a school **to opt for** to choose, to decide on **Anselm's Academy** never existed—Anselm (1033-1109) a saint who was one of founders of scholasticism **to come to a parting of the ways** to decide to separate **muddled** confusing, unclear **stricken** seriously affected by s.th. unpleasant **rumpled** disorderly **soiled** dirty **cuff** (AE) the end of a pair of trousers that is turned up **frayed** thin and worn from frequent use **wistful** sad and thoughtful especially when thinking of what could have happened in the past **poignant** [ˈpɔɪ.njənt] making one sad and full of pity

enough, but more troubling to me were the physical lapses. There were moments when he stumbled as he walked (a mysterious buckling of the knees), knocked into household objects, seemed to forget where he was. I knew that life with Dora had taken its toll, but there must have been more to it than that. Not wanting to increase my alarm, I managed to convince myself that his troubles had less to do with his body than with his state of mind. Perhaps I was right, but looking back on it now, it is difficult for me to imagine that the symptoms I first saw that summer were not connected to the heart attack that killed him three years later. Victor himself said nothing, but his body was speaking to me in code, and I did not have the wherewithal or the sense to crack it.

When I returned to Chicago for Christmas vacation, the crisis seemed to have passed. Victor had recovered much of his bounce, and great doings were suddenly afoot. In September, he and Howie Dunn had disbanded the Moonlight Moods and started another group, joining forces with three younger musicians who took over at drums, piano, and saxophone. They called themselves the Moon Men now, and most of their songs were original numbers. Victor wrote the lyrics, Howie composed the music, and all five of them sang, after a fashion. "No more old favorites," Victor announced to me when I arrived. "No more dance tunes. No more drunken weddings. We've quit the rubber chicken circuit for a run at the big time." There was no question that they had put together an original act, and when I went to see them perform the next night, the songs struck me as a revelation—filled with humor and spirit, a boisterous form of mayhem that mocked everything from politics to love. Victor's lyrics had a jaunty, dittylike flavor to them, but the underlying tone was almost Swiftian in its effect. Spike Jones meets Schopenhauer, if

**lapse** unusual or abnormal behavior caused by a lack of concentration **to take its toll** to cause damage or injury **wherewithal** here: ability, knowledge that allows one to cope with s.o. **to crack** to decode **bounce** liveliness, energy **afoot** planned **to disband** to break up **after a fashion** in a manner **rubber chicken circuit** i.e. at show business, political, or business club meetings where speeches or lectures are given—meals of tasteless chicken are often served **run** an attempt **the big time** (coll) opportunity where a lot of money can be made **act** show **revelation** a surprising fact that until now had been unknown **boisterous** noisy and full of energy **mayhem** chaos **jaunty** cheerful and full of confidence **dittylike** like a short simple song **Swiftian** like Jonathan Swift (1667-1745) English satirist known for his *Gulliver's Travels* **Spike Jones** (1911-1965) American bandleader famous for his absurd versions of popular songs; pistols and cowbells were used—especially popular in the 1940s and 50s **Schopen-**

such a thing is possible. Howie had swung the Moon Men a booking in one of the downtown Chicago clubs, and they wound up performing there every weekend from Thanksgiving to Valentine's Day. By the time I came back to Chicago after high school graduation, a tour was already in the works, and there was even some talk of cutting a record with a company in Los Angeles. That was how Uncle Victor's books entered the story. He was going on the road in mid-September, and he didn't know when he would be back.

It was late at night, less than a week before I was supposed to leave for New York. Victor was sitting in his chair by the window, working his way through a pack of Raleighs and drinking schnapps from a dime-store tumbler. I was sprawled out on the couch, floating happily in a stupor of bourbon and smoke. We had been talking about nothing in particular for three or four hours, but now the conversation had hit a lull, and each of us was drifting in the silence of his own thoughts. Uncle Victor sucked in a last drag from his cigarette, squinted as the smoke curled up his cheek, and then snuffed out the butt in his favorite ashtray, a souvenir from the 1939 World's Fair. Studying me with misty affection, he took another sip from his drink, smacked his lips, and let out a deep sigh. "Now we come to the hard part," he said. "The endings, the farewells, the famous last words. Pulling up stakes, I think they call it in the Westerns. If you don't

**hauer** (1788-1869) German philosopher strongly influenced by Kant and eastern philosophies: Life is a struggle of the intellect against sexual desire. **to swing** (coll) to manage to get s.th. **to wind up** to arrive in a situation **in the works** (coll) already planned **to cut a record** to make a recording on a record (Schallplatte) **to work one's way through** here: to slowly smoke all the cigarettes in a pack **Raleighs** [ˈrɔː.liz] a brand of American cigarettes that actually existed, cf. Sir Walter Raleigh **dime-store** a shop that sells cheap goods **tumbler** drinking glass with straight sides **to sprawl** to lie lazily with the arms and legs stretched out **stupor** state of not being able to think clearly because of too much alcohol **to hit a lull** [ʌ] to no longer continue, to become inactive **drag** the act of sucking in the smoke from the end of a cigarette **to squint** to look at s.th. with the eyes partially closed **to curl up** to move up making circles **to snuff out** here: to press the burning end of a cigarette on a surface to put out the fire **butt** [ʌ] what is left of a cigarette after most of it has been smoked **1939 World's Fair** fair that took place in Queens, New York City with the war in Europe soon to break out **misty** with tears **sip** a small amount of s.th. to drink **to smack your lips** to make a short loud noise with your lips as when you are hungry **to pull up stakes** to pull up a short pointed piece of metal or wood that is used to hold down a rope connected to a tent, i.e. to leave a place for a new one

hear from me often, Phileas, remember that *you're* in my thoughts. I wish I could say I know where I'll be, but new worlds suddenly beckon to us both, and I doubt there will be many chances for writing letters." Uncle Victor paused to light another cigarette, and I could see that his hand trembled as he held the match. "No one knows how long it will last," he continued, "but Howie is very optimistic. The bookings are extensive so far, and no doubt others will follow. Colorado, Arizona, Nevada, California. We'll be setting a westerly course, plunging into the wilderness. It should be interesting, I think, no matter what comes of it. A bunch of city slickers in the land of cowboys and Indians. But I relish the thought of those open spaces, of playing my music under the desert sky. Who knows if some new truth will not be revealed to me out there?"

Uncle Victor laughed, as though to undercut the seriousness of this thought. "The point being," he resumed, "that with so much distance to be covered, I must travel light. Objects will have to be discarded, given away, thrown into the dust. Since it pains me to think of them vanishing forever, I have decided to hand them over to you. Who else can I trust, after all? Who else is there to carry on the tradition? I begin with the books. Yes, yes, all of them. As far as I'm concerned, it couldn't have come at a better moment. When I counted them this afternoon, there were one thousand four hundred and ninety-two volumes. A propitious number, I think, since it evokes the memory of Columbus's discovery of America, and the college you're going to was named after Columbus. Some of these books are big, some are small, some are fat, some are thin—but all of them contain words. If you read those words, perhaps they will help you with your education. No, no, I won't hear of it. Not one peep of protest. Once you're settled in New York, I'll have them shipped to you. I'll keep the extra copy of Dante, but otherwise you must have them all. After that, there's the wooden chess set. I'll keep the magnetic one, but the wood must go with you. Then comes the cigar box with the baseball autographs. We have nearly every Cub of the past two decades, a few

**to plunge** here: to suddenly move into s.th. unkown **bunch** large number **city slicker** (coll) here: a person who has always lived in a big city and knows little about life in the country **to relish** [ˈrel.ɪʃ] to enjoy, to look forward to **to undercut** here: to reduce the importance of s.th. **to discard** to get rid of s.th. **propitious** likely to bring about good results **to evoke the memory** here: to cause s.th. to remember s.th. **peep** any kind of sound **Dante** (1265-1321) first important author to write in Italian, famous for his *Divine Comedy* **Cub** i.e. the Chicago Club player

stars, and numerous lesser lights from around the league. Matt Batts, Memo Luna, Rip Repulski, Putsy Caballero, Dick Drott. The obscurity of those names alone should make them immortal. After that, I come to various trinkets, doo-dads, odds and ends. My souvenir ashtrays from New York and the Alamo, the Haydn and Mozart recordings I made with the Cleveland Orchestra, the family photo album, the plaque I won as a boy for finishing first in the statewide music competition. That was in 1924, if you can believe it—a long, long time ago. Finally, I want you to have the tweed suit I bought in the Loop a few winters back. I won't be needing it in the places I'm going to, and it's made of the finest Scottish *wool*. I've worn it just twice, and if I gave it to the Salvation Army, it would only wind up on the back of some besotted creature from Skid Row. Much better that you should have it. It will give you a certain distinction, and there's no crime in looking your best, is there? We'll go to the tailor first thing tomorrow morning and have it altered.

"That takes care of it, I think. The books, the chess set, the autographs, the miscellaneous, the suit. Now that my kingdom has been disposed of, I feel content. There's no need for you to look at me like that. I know what I'm doing, and I'm glad to have done it. You're a good boy, Phileas, and you'll always be with me, no matter where I am. For the time being, we move off in opposite directions. But sooner or later we'll meet again, I'm sure of it. Everything works out in the end, you see, everything connects. The nine circles. The nine planets. The nine innings. Our nine lives.

**lesser lights** i.e. those of less importance **from around the league** i.e. in other teams in the National league, one of the two leagues in professional baseball **Mat Batts, etc....** all these players actually existed **obscurity** quality of being unkown **immortal** here: never forgotten, everlasting **trinkets** small pretty objects not worth much **doo-dads** (coll) unimportant objects the name of which cannot be remembered **odds and ends** other objects that cannot be classified **the Alamo** small church in Texas in which Americans unsuccessfully defended themselves against Mexican soldiers in the Texas rebellion against Mexico (1836) It is still a popular tourist attraction. **plaque** [ɑː] a small decorated plate or disk given to s.o. who has won a competition **tweed** a rough woolen cloth used for suits and coats **the Loop** the center of Chicago with many department stores and shops, by the 1960s it had gone into decline **Salvation Army** an international religious group founded to help the poor in cities **besotted** in a state of confusion because of too much alcohol **Skid Row** (slang) poor area in a town where the homeless gather **distinction** a special quality **tailor** Schneider **to alter** to make a piece of clothing longer or wider, etc. **That takes care of it.** That's everything. **to dispose of** to get rid of **nine circles** the Greek hell, Styx, was said to have nine circles or areas, also the nine circles of Dante's *Divine Comedy* **nine innings** A baseball game is divided into nine innings.

Just think of it. The correspondences are infinite. But enough of this blather for one night. The hour grows late, and sleep is calling to us both. Come, give me your hand. Yes, that's right, a good firm grip. Like so. And now shake. That's right, a shake of farewell. A shake to last us to the end of time."

Every week or two, Uncle Victor would send me a postcard. These were generally garish, full-color tourist items: depictions of Rocky Mountain sunsets, publicity shots of roadside motels, cactus plants and rodeos, dude ranches, ghost towns, desert panoramas. Salutations sometimes appeared within the borders of a painted lasso, and once a mule even spoke with a cartoon bubble above his head: Greetings from Silver Gulch. The messages on the back were brief, cryptic scrawls, but I was not hungry for news from my uncle so much as an occasional sign of life. The real pleasure lay in the cards themselves, and the more inane and vulgar they were, the happier I was to get them. I felt that we were sharing some private joke each time I found one in my mailbox, and the very best ones (a picture of an empty restaurant in Reno, a fat woman on horseback in Cheyenne) I even went so far as to tape to the wall above my bed. My roommate understood the empty restaurant, but the horseback rider baffled him. I explained that she bore an uncanny resemblance to my uncle's ex-wife, Dora. Given the way things happen in the world, I said, there was a good chance that the woman was Dora herself.

Because Victor did not stay anywhere very long, it was hard for me to answer him. In late October I wrote a nine-page letter about the New York City blackout (I had been trapped in an elevator with two friends), but I did not mail it until January, when the Moon Men began their three week stint in Tahoe. If I could not write often, I nevertheless managed to

**correspondence** relationship or connection between two or more ideas or facts **blather** silly talk **grip** Griff **garish** unpleasantly colored or decorated **depiction** picture **dude ranch** a place to spend your vacation that is like a western ranch **salutations** greetings **borders** here: the edge of the lasso **mule** Maultier **Silver Gulch** made up name of a ghost town—gulch = Schlucht **cryptic** with a hidden meaning, mysterious **scrawls** hurried writing **inane** silly **Cheyenne** probably Cheyenne in Wyoming **to baffle** to be difficult to understand **to bear an uncanny resemblance to** to seem to be very similar to s.th. or s.o. in a way that is rather strange or difficult to explain **New York City blackout** the sudden loss of electricity in all of northeastern America on November 9, 1965—Manhattan had no electricity for 14 hours. **stint** here: performance **Tahoe** [ˈtɑːhoʊ] town in Idaho

stay in spiritual contact with him by wearing the suit. Suits were hardly in fashion for undergraduates back then, but I felt at home in it, and since for all practical purposes I had no other home, I continued to wear it every day, from the beginning of the year to the end. At moments of stress and unhappiness, it was a particular comfort to feel myself swaddled in the warmth of my uncle's clothes, and there were times when I imagined the suit was actually holding me together, that if I did not wear it my body would fly apart. It functioned as a protective membrane, a second skin that shielded me from the blows of life. Looking back on it now, I realize what a curious figure I must have cut: gaunt, disheveled, intense, a young man clearly out of step with the rest of the world. But the fact was that I had no desire to fit in. If my fellow students pegged me as an oddball, that was not my problem. I was the sublime intellectual, the cantankerous and opinionated future genius, the skulking Malevole who stood apart from the herd. It almost makes me blush to remember the ridiculous poses I struck back then. I was a grotesque amalgam of timidity and arrogance, alternating between long, awkward silences and blazing fits of rambunctiousness. When the mood came upon me, I would spend whole nights in bars, smoking and drinking as though I meant to kill myself, quoting verses from minor sixteenth-century poets, making obscure references in Latin to medieval philosophers, doing everything I could to impress my friends. Eighteen is a terrible age, and while I walked around with the conviction that I was somehow more grown-up than my classmates, the truth was that I had merely found a different way of being young. More than anything else, the suit was the badge of my identity, the emblem of how I wanted others to see me.

**undergraduate** student at a university or college for the first four years of study **swaddled** wrapped up tightly, usually when talking about a baby **to cut a figure** to create an impression on other people **gaunt** very thin **disheveled** untidy **to peg s.o. as** (coll AE) to classify s.o. as **oddball** (coll) strange person **sublime** most excellent, perfect **cantankerous** tending to get into arguments about unimportant matters **opinionated** having very strong opinions that one doesn't want to change **skulking** moving about secretly with plans to do s.th. bad **Malevole** [ˌmæləˈvoʊlə] character in a satirical play *The Malcontent* (1604) who plays the cynical observer of life—by John Marston (1575-1634) **to strike a pose** to act in an unnatural way that should impress other people **amalgam** [əˈmæl.gəm] combination **timidity** being easily frightened **blazing** extreme **fit** sudden attack (Anfall) **rambunctiousness** (AE) highly excited behavior **obscure** [əbˈskjʊər] not clearly understandable **conviction** strong belief **badge** here: special feature or sign that shows a quality

Objectively considered, there was nothing wrong with the suit. It was a dark greenish tweed with small checks and narrow lapels—a sturdy, well-made article of clothing—but after several months of constant wear, it began to give a haphazard impression, hanging on my skinny frame like some wrinkled afterthought, a sagging turmoil of wool. What my friends didn't know, of course, was that I wore it for sentimental reasons. Under my nonconformist posturing, I was also satisfying the desire to have my uncle near me, and the cut of the garment had almost nothing to do with it. If Victor had given me a purple zoot suit, I no doubt would have worn it in the same spirit that I wore the tweed.

When classes ended in the spring, I turned down my roommate's suggestion that we share an apartment the following year. I liked Zimmer well enough (he was my best friend, in fact), but after four years of roommates and dormitories, I could not resist the temptation to live alone. I found the place on West 112th Street and moved in on June fifteenth, arriving with my bags just moments before two burly men delivered the seventy-six cartons of Uncle Victor's books that had been sitting in storage for the past nine months. It was a studio apartment on the fifth floor of a large elevator building: one medium-size room with a kitchenette in the southeast corner, a closet, a bathroom, and a pair of windows that looked out on an alley. Pigeons flapped their wings and cooed on the ledge, and six dented garbage cans stood on the ground below. The air was dim inside, tinged gray throughout, and even on the brightest days it

**with small checks** mit einem kleinen Karomuster **lapel** Revers **sturdy** strong, not easily broken **haphazard** careless, disorderly **frame** here: body **wrinkled** zerknittert **afterthought** a comment or thought that one thinks of afterwards **to sag** to hang down because of the weight of s.th. **turmoil** a state of uncertainty or confusion because of a crisis **posturing** unnatural behavior to attract attention **garment** article of clothing **zoot suit** a suit popular with young men in the early 1940s with a long coat, wide lapels, and padded shoulders **Zimmer** also the name of the family—including the daughter—in Tübingen that took care of Friedrich Hölderlin (German poet 1770-1843) in the last years of his life when he went insane—Auster discusses Hölderlin and Zimmer in his *The Invention of Solitude* **burly** heavily built **in storage** in a warehouse **studio apartment** (AE) small one-room apartment **kitchenette** open kitchen that is part of the living-room/bedroom **alley** narrow path between buildings **to flap** to move up and down quickly **ledge** Fenstersims **dented** a part of the surface that has been pushed in because of being hit **to tinge** to give s.th. a small amount of a color

did not exude more than a paltry radiance. I felt some pangs at first, small thumps of fear about living on my own, but then I made a singular discovery that helped me to warm up to the place and settle in. It was my second or third night there, and quite by accident I found myself standing between the two windows, positioned at an oblique angle to the one on the left. I shifted my eyes slightly in that direction, and suddenly I was able to see a slit of air between the two buildings in back. I was looking down at Broadway, the smallest, most abbreviated portion of Broadway, and the remarkable thing was that the entire area of what I could see was filled up by a neon sign, a vivid torch of pink and blue letters that spelled out the words MOON PALACE. I recognized it as the sign from the Chinese restaurant down the block, but the force with which those words assaulted me drowned out every practical reference and association. They were magic letters, and they hung there in the darkness like a message from the sky itself. MOON PALACE. I immediately thought of Uncle Victor and his band, and in that first, irrational moment, my fears lost their hold on me. I had never experienced anything so sudden and absolute. A bare and grubby room had been transformed into a site of inwardness, an intersection point of strange omens and mysterious, arbitrary events. I went on staring at the Moon Palace sign, and little by little I understood that I had come to the right place, that this small apartment was indeed where I was meant to live.

I spent the summer working part-time in a bookstore, going to the movies, and falling in and out of love with a girl named Cynthia, whose face has long since vanished from my memory. I felt more and more at home in my new apartment, and when classes started again that fall, I threw myself into a hectic round of late-night drinking with Zimmer and my friends, of amorous pursuits, and long, utterly silent binges of reading

**to exude** to flow out slowly and steadily **paltry** too small to be important or useful **radiance** a soft shining or glowing light **pang** sudden sharp feeling of pain **thump** heavy blow **singular** unusual, remarkable **oblique** schräg **to shift** to change the direction or focus **slit** a long narrow hole or cut **abbreviated** made shorter **Broadway** street than runs north and south in Manhattan **torch** (fig) a stick with a burning fire at the end to produce a light **Moon Palace** name of a Chinese restaurant that actually existed on 112th Street and Broadway, but closed down at the end of the 1980s **down the block** i.e. on Broadway **to assault** here: to strongly affect one's emotions **grubby** rather dirty **omen** any sign of what will happen in the future **arbitrary** happening by chance **Cynthia** another name for the goddess of the moon Diana **amorous pursuits** (formal, ironic) i.e. trying to find a girlfriend

and studying. Much later, when I looked back on those things from the distance of years, I understood how fertile that time had been for me.

Then I turned twenty, and not many weeks after that I received a long, almost incomprehensible letter from Uncle Victor written in pencil on the backs of yellow order blanks for the Humboldt Encyclopedia. From all that I could gather, hard times had hit the Moon Men, and after a lengthy run of bad luck (broken engagements, flat tires, a drunk who bashed in the saxophonist's nose), the group had finally split up. Since November, Uncle Victor had been living in Boise, Idaho, where he had found temporary work as a door-to-door encyclopedia salesman. But things had not panned out, and for the first time in all the years I had known him, I heard a note of defeat in Victor's words. "My clarinet is in hock," the letter said, "my bank statement reads nil, and the residents of Boise have no interest in encyclopedias."

I wired money to my uncle, then followed it with a telegram urging him to come to New York. Victor answered a few days later to thank me for the invitation. He would wrap up his affairs by the end of the week, he said, and then catch the next bus out. I calculated that he would arrive on Tuesday, Wednesday at the latest. But Wednesday came and went, and Victor did not show up. I sent another telegram, but there was no response. The possibilities for disaster seemed infinite to me. I imagined all the things that can happen to a man between Boise and New York, and suddenly the American continent was transformed into a vast danger zone, a perilous nightmare of traps and mazes. I tried to track down the owner of Victor's rooming house, got nowhere with that, and then, as a last resort, called the Boise police. I carefully explained my problem to the sergeant at the other end, a man named Neil Armstrong. The following day, Sergeant Armstrong called back with the news. Uncle Victor

**order blank** a printed form on which a customer can order s.th. **Humboldt Encyclopedia** an Auster joke—Humboldt (famous German naturalist and explorer, 1769-1859) did publish a kind of encyclopedia *Kosmos* 1845-1862—that included the latest scientific information about the world, but that would hardly be the kind of encyclopedia sold in America in the 1960s **run** here: period **to pan out** here: to develop as hoped **in hock** (coll. AE) verpfändet **bank statement** Kontoauszug **nil** with nothing **to wrap up** (coll) to finish up **perilous** ['per.əl.əs] (formal) very dangerous **trap** Falle **maze** any confusing network of streets, pathways, etc., labyrinth **rooming house** a house with individual furnished rooms or flats for renting **last resort** the last possible course of action open to one **Neil Armstrong** also: American astronaut, the first man on the moon in 1969

had been found dead at his lodgings on North Twelfth Street—slumped in a chair with his overcoat on, a half-assembled clarinet locked in the fingers of his right hand. Two packed suitcases had been standing by the door. The room was searched, but the authorities had turned up nothing to suggest foul play. According to the medical examiner's preliminary report, heart attack was the probable cause of death. "Tough luck, kid," the sergeant added, "I'm really sorry."

I flew out West the next morning to make the arrangements. I identified Victor's body at the morgue, paid off debts, signed papers and forms, prepared to have the body shipped home to Chicago. The Boise mortician was in despair over the state of the corpse. After languishing in the apartment for almost a week, there wasn't much to be done with it. "If I were you," he said to me, "I wouldn't expect any miracles."

I set up the funeral by telephone, contacted a few of Victor's friends (Howie Dunn, the broken-nosed saxophonist, a number of former students), made a half-hearted attempt to reach Dora (she couldn't be found), and then accompanied the casket back to Chicago. Victor was buried next to my mother, and the sky pelted us with rain as we stood there watching our friend disappear into the earth. Afterward, we drove to the Dunns' house on the North Side, where Mrs. Dunn had prepared a modest spread of cold cuts and hot soup. I had been weeping steadily for the past four hours, and in the house I quickly downed five or six double bourbons along with my food. It brightened my spirits considerably, and after an hour or so I began singing songs in a loud voice. Howie accompanied me on the piano, and for a while the gathering became quite raucous. Then I threw up on the floor, and the spell was broken. At six o'clock, I said my good-byes and lurched out into the rain. I wandered

**lodgings** rented room or rooms in which one lives **to slump** to sink or fall heavily and suddenly **foul play** criminal or violent action **preliminary report** the first incomplete report before the final one **tough luck** (coll) bad luck **morgue** a building where dead bodies are kept before burial **debts** [dets] money that is still owed **mortician** (AE) undertaker—a person whose profession is the preparation of the dead for burial and the management of funerals (Beisetzung) **corpse** dead body **casket** (AE) a box in which a corpse is buried **to pelt** to throw down with force **North Side** area of Chicago to the north of the center **modest** not very much, not very expensive **spread** (coll) variety, range **cold cuts** cooked meats sliced and served cold **to down** (coll) to drink **to brighten one's spirits** to put one in a better mood **to throw up** (coll) to vomit (sich erbrechen) **to break the spell** spell: a state as if under the influence of magic (den Bann brechen) **to lurch** to walk suddenly forwards or from side to side

blindly for two or three hours, threw up again on a doorstep, and then found a thin, gray-eyed prostitute named Agnes standing under an umbrella on a neon-lit street. I accompanied her to a room in the Eldorado Hotel, gave her a brief lecture on the poems of Sir Walter Raleigh, and then sang lullabies to her as she took off her clothes and spread her legs. She called me a lunatic, but then I gave her a hundred dollars, and she agreed to spend the night with me. I slept badly, however, and at four a.m. I slipped out of bed, climbed into my wet clothes, and took a taxi to the airport. I was back in New York by ten o'clock.

In the end, the problem was not grief. Grief was the first cause, perhaps, but it soon gave way to something else something more tangible, more calculable in its effects, more violent in the damage it produced. A whole chain of forces had been set in motion, and at a certain point I began to wobble, to fly in greater and greater circles around myself, until at last I spun out of orbit.

The fact was that my money situation was deteriorating. I had been aware of this for some time, but until now the threat had loomed only in the far distance, and I had not given it any serious thought. On the heels of Uncle Victor's death, however, and the thousands of dollars I had spent during those terrible days, the budget that was supposed to see me through college had been blown to smithereens. Unless I did something to replace the money, I would not make it to the end. I computed that if I went on spending at my current rate, my funds would be exhausted by November of my senior year. And by that I meant everything: every nickel, every dime, every penny right down to the bottom.

**Agnes** name from the Greek meaning pure, untouched sexually **Eldorado Hotel** does not exit, Eldorado: mythical area full of riches and gold thought to exist in the New World by 16th and 17th Europeans, now used to mean any place where one can become rich **Sir Walter Raleigh** (1554-1618) English adventurer, pirate, (who also believed in an Eldorado) writer, a favorite of Queen Elizabeth I. **lullaby** [ˈlʌl.ə.baɪ] a quiet song to put a child to sleep **lunatic** a crazy person (*luna*, Latin word for moon) **grief** great sadness, especially after s.o. has died **tangible** having real substance **to wobble** to move from side to side in an unsteady way **to spin** to turn rapidly around a central point **orbit** path taken by a planet or moon around another object **to deteriorate** to make or become worse or lower in quality, value, character, etc. **to loom** to appear as a large shape that is threatening **on the heels** following closely **to blow to smithereens** to completely destroy **senior year** normally the fourth year of studying

My first impulse was to quit college, but after toying with the idea for a day or two, I thought better of it. I had promised my uncle that I would graduate, and since he was no longer around to approve any change of plans, I did not feel at liberty to break my word. On top of that, there was the question of the draft. If I left college now, my student deferment would be revoked, and I did not welcome the thought of marching off to an early death in the jungles of Asia. I would remain in New York, then, and continue with my classes at Columbia. That was the sensible decision, the proper thing to do. After such a promising start, it would not have been difficult for me to go on acting sensibly. All kinds of options were available to people in my situation—scholarships, loans, work-study programs—but once I began to think about them, I found myself stricken with disgust. It was a sudden, involuntary response, a jolting attack of nausea. I wanted no part of those things, I realized, and therefore I rejected them all—stubbornly, contemptuously, knowing full well that I had just sabotaged my only hope of surviving the crisis. From that point on, in fact, I did nothing to help myself, refused even to lift a finger. God knows why I behaved like that. I invented countless reasons at the time, but in the end it probably boiled down to despair. I was in despair, and in the face of so much upheaval, I felt that drastic action of some sort was necessary. I wanted to spit on the world, to do the most outlandish thing possible. With all the fervor and idealism of a young man who had thought too much and read too many books, I decided that the thing I should do was nothing: my action would consist of a militant refusal to take any action at all. This was nihilism raised to the level of an aesthetic

**to toy with** to play with **to feel at liberty** to feel free **draft** the selection by the U.S. government of men to serve in the armed forces, in the second half of the 1960s, when the Vietnam war was at its height, more and more men between 18 and 26 were being selected to serve in Vietnam **student deferment** students at a college or university were allowed to complete their studies before having to serve in the armed forces, deferment = the act of allowing s.th. to happen later **to revoke** to take back or withdraw; cancel **scholarship** Stipendium **loan** money you can borrow from a bank **disgust** a strong dislike because of s.th. sickening **involuntary** done without intention **jolting** sudden, surprising, shocking **nausea** [ˈnɔː.si.ə] a sick feeling before one vomits **stubborn** refusing to give in, to agree, or change one's action **comtemptuous** with an attitude showing that others are completely worthless and cannot be respected **full well** exactly, precisely **to boil down to** to have as the most basic factor **upheaval** a strong, sudden, or violent disturbance, as in politics, social conditions, etc. **to spit** spucken **outlandish** extremely strange **fervor** intense feeling or belief

proposition. I would turn my life into a work of art, sacrificing myself to such exquisite paradoxes that every breath I took would teach me how to savor my own doom. The signs pointed to a total eclipse, and grope as I did for another reading, the image of that darkness gradually lured me in, seduced me with the simplicity of its design. I would do nothing to thwart the inevitable, but neither would I rush out to meet it. If life could continue for the time being as it always had, so much the better. I would be patient, I would hold fast. It was simply that I knew what was in store for me, and whether it happened today, or whether it happened tomorrow, it would nevertheless happen. Total eclipse. The beast had been slain, its entrails had been decoded. The moon would block the sun, and at that point I would vanish. I would be dead broke, a flotsam of flesh and bone without a farthing to my name.

That was when I started reading Uncle Victor's books. Two weeks after the funeral, I picked out one of the boxes at random, slit the tape carefully with a knife, and read everything that was inside it. It proved to be a strange mixture, packed with no apparent order or purpose. There were novels and plays, history books and travel books, chess guides and detective stories, science fiction and works of philosophy—an absolute chaos of print. It made no difference to me. I read each book to the end and refused to pass judgment on it. As far as I was concerned, each book was equal to every other book, each sentence was composed of exactly the right number of words, and each word stood exactly where it had to be. That was how I chose to mourn my Uncle Victor. One by one, I

**proposition** a proposal or topic presented for consideration **to savor** (fig) to enjoy the taste or smell of s.th. **doom** death or a terrible fate **eclipse** Mond-/Sonnenfinsternis **to grope** to search uncertainly or with difficulty (for a solution, answer, etc.) **reading** interpretation **to lure** to attract s.o. by the promise of some kind of reward **to seduce** to persuade s.o. to do s.th. he or she normally wouldn't do **to thwart** to oppose successfully or prevent **the inevitable** s.th. unavoidable, sure to happen, certain **so much the better** then that is even better **in store** what should happen in the future **slain** (archaic) killed in a violent way **entrails** ['en.treɪlz] the internal organs of a person or animal **to decode** to analyze so as to make predictions as was done by priests in ancient times **dead broke** completely without any money **flotsam** parts of a ship wreck found floating in the water **farthing** a former British bronze coin worth a quarter of an old penny, i.e. a coin worth very little **at random** in a purposeless fashion, not following any prearranged order **to pass judgment on s.th.** to declare a judgment on **to be composed of** to consist of **to mourn** to feel or express sadness for the death or loss of s.o. or s.th.

would open every box, and one by one I would read every book. That was the task I set for myself, and I stuck with it to the bitter end.

Each box contained a jumble similar to the first, a hodgepodge of high and low, heaps of ephemera scattered among the classics, ragged paperbacks sandwiched between hardbound editions, potboilers lying flush with Donne and Tolstoy. Uncle Victor had never organized his library in any systematic way. Each time he had bought a book, he had put it on the shelf next to the one he had bought before it, and little by little the rows had expanded, filling more and more space as the years went by. That was precisely how the books had entered the boxes. If nothing else, the chronology was intact, the sequence had been preserved by default. I considered this to be an ideal arrangement. Each time I opened a box, I was able to enter another segment of my uncle's life, a fixed period of days or weeks or months, and it consoled me to feel that I was occupying the same mental space that Victor had once occupied—reading the same words, living in the same stories, perhaps thinking the same thoughts. It was almost like following the route of an explorer from long ago, duplicating his steps as he thrashed out into virgin territory, moving westward with the sun, pursuing the light until it was finally extinguished. Because the boxes were not numbered or labeled, I had no way of knowing in advance which period I was about to enter. The journey was therefore made up of discrete, discontinuous jaunts. Boston to Lenox, for example. Minneapolis to Sioux Falls. Kenosha to Salt Lake City. It didn't matter to me that I was forced to jump around the map. By the end, all the blanks would be filled in, all the distances would be covered.

**jumble** disorderly mass **hodgepodge** a number of things mixed in no particular order **heap** a collection of articles or mass of material gathered together in one place **ephemera** [ɪˈfəm.ər.ə] things that are short-loved **scattered** thrown about in different directions **ragged** in bad condition **hardbound edition** book with hard covers **potboiler** poorly written literary work made to make money **flush** at the same level as the surface of s.th. else **Donne** John Donne (1572-1631) major metaphysical poet in England known for his erotic and religious poems **Tolstoy** (1828-1910) major Russian novelist (*War and Peace*) and moral philosopher **by default** because no particular action was taken **to console** to serve as a source of comfort to s.o. after a lose or disappointment **to thrash** to move forward in a violent way **virgin** undiscovered, untouched **to extinguish** to put out **to label** to put a piece of paper on s.th. to identify it **discrete** separate **discontinuous** with interruptions **jaunt** short excursion **Lenox** town in Massachusetts, near which there are famous concerts of classical music **Sioux** [su:] **Falls** city in South Dakota **Kenosha** city in Wisconsin **blank** empty spaces

I had read many of the books before, and still others had been read out loud to me by Victor himself: *Robinson Crusoe, Doctor Jekyll and Mr. Hyde, The Invisible Man*. I did not let that stand in my way, however. I plowed through everything with equal passion, devouring old works as hungrily as new. Piles of finished books rose in the corners of my room, and whenever one of these towers seemed in danger of falling, I would load up two shopping bags with the threatened volumes and take them along with me on my next visit to Columbia. Directly across from the campus on Broadway was Chandler's Bookstore, a cramped and dusty rathole that did a brisk trade in used books. Between the summer of 1967 and the summer of 1969 I made dozens of appearances there, and little by little I divested myself of my inheritance. That was the one action I allowed myself—making use of what I already owned. I found it wrenching to part with Uncle Victor's former possessions, but at the same time I knew that he would not have held it against me. I had somehow discharged my debt to him by reading the books, and now that I was so short of money, it seemed only logical that I should take the next step and convert the books into cash.

The problem was that I couldn't earn enough. Chandler drove hard bargains, and his understanding of books was so different from mine that I barely knew what to say to him. For me, books were not the containers of words so much as the words themselves, and the value of a given book was determined by its spiritual quality rather than its physical condition. A dog-eared Homer was worth more than a spanking Virgil, for example;

**Robinson Crusoe** novel by Daniel Defoe ( 1660-1731) English novelist, pamphleteer, and journalist **The Invisible Man** novel by the Afro-American writer Ralph Ellison (1914-1994) about a black man's search for identity **to plow through** here: to read through slowly and carefully BE: plough **to devour** here: to read eagerly, with great interest **Chandler's Bookstore** There never was a bookstore with this name. Raymond Chandler (1888-1959) wrote high quality detective stories usually set in California. **cramped** with very little space to move about **to do a brisk trade** to sell a lot of things **to divest yourself of s.th.** to get rid of **inheritance** money or property you get as the result of the death of s.o. **wrenching** painful **to discharge a debt** to pay a debt **to drive a hard bargain** to insist on the best possible price or deal **dog-eared** with the corner of the page folded down **Homer** ['hoʊ.mər] c. 800B.C., blind Greek poet said to have written *The Iliad* and *The Odyssey.* **spanking** normally: spanking new, i.e. completely new **Virgil** ['vɜː.dʒɪl] (70-19 BC) major Roman poet

three volumes of Descartes were worth less than one by Pascal. Those were essential distinctions for me, but for Chandler they did not exist. A book was no more than an object to him, a thing that belonged to the world of things, and as such it was not radically different from a shoebox, a toilet plunger, or a coffeepot. Each time I brought in another portion of Uncle Victor's library, the old man would go into his routine. Fingering the books with contempt, perusing the spines, hunting for marks and blemishes, he never failed to give the impression of someone handling a pile of filth. That was how the game worked. By degrading the goods, Chandler could offer rock-bottom prices. After thirty years of practice, he had the pose down pat, a repertoire of mutterings and asides, of wincings, tongue-clicks, and sad shakes of the head. The act was designed to make me feel the worthlessness of my own judgment, to shame me into recognizing the audacity of having presented these books to him in the first place. Are you telling me you want money for these things? Do you expect money from the garbage man when he carts away your trash?

I knew that I was being cheated, but I seldom bothered to protest. What was I to do, after all? Chandler dealt from a position of strength, and nothing would ever change that—for I was always desperate to sell, and he was always indifferent to buy. Nor was there any point in feigning indifference to sell. The sale would simply not be made, and no sale was finally worse than being cheated. I discovered that I tended to do better when I brought in small doses of books, no more than twelve or fifteen at a time. The average price per volume seemed to go up ever so slightly

**Descartes** ['deɪ.kɑːt] (1596-1650) René Descartes, French philosopher and mathematician. He is considered the father of modern philosophy. He believed the perceived world was true and not an illusion and the mind and the real world were completely separate. **Pascal** (1623-62) Blaise Pascal, French philosopher, mathematician, and physicist **distinction** a characteristic that makes s.th. different **plunger** a stick with a rubber cup at the end used to clear a stuck toilet **contempt** an attitude that other people are completely worthless and should not be respected **to peruse** to examine with care **spine** back **blemish** small mark or defect that spoils the appearance of s.th. **to degrade** to reduce in worth **rock-bottom** very lowest **pose** certain way of behavior to produce an effect **to have s.th. down pat** (AE) to be able to do s.th. so perfectly you don't have to think about it **aside** remark made in a soft voice so that only certain people should hear it **wincing** a sudden expression on the face that expresses pain **tongue-click** a hard sound made with the tongue to show your disapproval **audacity** boldness, fearlessness **to cart away** to carry away on an open vehicle with wheels **trash** (AE) rubbish **to bother** to make an effort, to take the trouble to do s.th. **to feign** [feɪn] to pretend **ever so slightly** just a little bit

then. But the smaller the exchange, the more often I would have to return, and I knew that I had to keep my visits to a minimum—for the more I dealt with Chandler, the weaker my position would grow. No matter what I did, therefore, Chandler was bound to win. As the months went by, the old man made no effort to talk to me. He never said hello, he never cracked a smile, he never even shook my hand. His manner was so blank that I sometimes wondered if he remembered me from one visit to the next. As far as Chandler was concerned, I might have been a new customer each time I came in—a collection of disparate strangers, a random horde.

As I sold off the books, my apartment went through many changes. That was inevitable, for each time I opened another box, I simultaneously destroyed another piece of furniture. My bed was dismantled, my chairs shrank and disappeared, my desk atrophied into empty space. My life had become a gathering zero, and it was a thing I could actually see: a palpable, burgeoning emptiness. Each time I ventured into my uncle's past, it produced a physical result, an effect in the real world. The consequences were therefore always before my eyes, and there was no way to escape them. So many boxes were left, so many boxes were gone. I had only to look at my room to know what was happening. The room was a machine that measured my condition: how much of me remained, how much of me was no longer there. I was both perpetrator and witness, both actor and audience in a theater of one. I could follow the progress of my own dismemberment. Piece by piece, I could watch myself disappear.

* * *

Those were difficult days for everyone, of course. I remember them as a tumult of politics and crowds, of outrage, bullhorns, and violence. By

**to be bound** to be certain **to crack a smile** (coll) to break into a smile **blank** showing no expression **disparate** completely different **random** without any plan or arrangement **horde** a vast crowd, mob **to dismantle** to take apart **to shrink/shrank/shrunk** to become or cause to become smaller in size **to atrophy** to become weak because of a lack of use **gathering zero** oxymoron: increasing to nothing **palpable** easily perceived by the senses or the mind, obvious **to burgeon** to develop, to grow, to flourish **to venture** to risk going somewhere where it could be dangerous **perpetrator** the person responsible for performing a crime, etc. **dismemberment** the act of cutting a body apart **tumult** [ˈtjuː.mʌlt] state of confusion, noise, and great excitement—the 1960s in America and Europe were a time of protest again authority, political unrest, and especially in America a time of division because of the Vietnam war. **outrage** a feeling of great anger and shock **bullhorn** (AE) a device held to the mouth to

the spring of 1968, every day seemed to retch forth a new cataclysm. If it wasn't Prague, it was Berlin; if it wasn't Paris, it was New York. There were half a million soldiers in Vietnam. The president announced that he wouldn't run again. People were assassinated. After years of fighting, the war had become so large that even the smallest thoughts were now contaminated by it, and I knew that no matter what I did or didn't do, I was as much a part of it as anyone else. One evening, as I sat on a bench in Riverside Park looking out at the water, I saw an oil tank explode on the other shore. Flames suddenly filled the sky, and as I watched the chunks of burning wreckage float across the Hudson and land at my feet, it occurred to me that the inner and the outer could not be separated except by doing great damage to the truth. Later that same month, the Columbia campus was turned into a battleground, and hundreds of students were arrested, including daydreamers like Zimmer and myself. I am not planning to discuss any of that here. Everyone is familiar with the story of that time, and there would be no point in going over it again. That does not mean I want it to be forgotten, however. My own story stands in the

make one's voice louder—associated with the police chief of Birmingham (Alabama) "Bull" Connor, who used a bullhorn and police dogs to stop Martin Luther King's demonstration against segregation and the bombing of black churches in 1963 **to retch forth** to vomit out **cataclysm** [ˌkæt.ə.klɪ.zəm] violent and sudden event or change **Prague** the Soviet Union marched into Prague in August 1963 to remove the liberal government **Berlin** during a demonstration against the German government one of the leaders of the student leftist movement Rudi Dutschke was shot at (April 11, 1968) and seriously injured **Paris** in Paris in May 1968 there were massive student demonstrations against De Gaulle and the educational system **New York** There were race riots in New York in 1967 and a year later after Martin Luther King was killed. **president** President Johnson announced on March 31, 1968 that he would not run for president again, after it became obvious he would have no chance of being reelected because of the Vietnam war. **to assassinate** to kill for political reasons—John Kennedy was assassinated in 1963, his brother Robert Kennedy and Martin Luther King in 1968, and the radical black political leader, Malcolm X. **to contaminate** to make impure, esp. by touching or mixing, pollute **Riverside Park** a narrow park along the west bank of Manhattan **oil tank explode** An oil tank on the New Jersey side of the Hudson really did burn, but did not explode in the way Auster describes. **chunk** a thick solid piece, as of meat, wood, etc. **Columbia campus…battleground** There was a protest at Columbia University in the spring of 1968 (especially April 23-30) against firms that were involved in the Vietnam war that wanted to hire students from Columbia.

rubble of those days, and unless this fact is understood, none of it will make sense.

By the time I had started classes for my third year (September 1967), my suit was long gone. Battered by the soaking it had taken in Chicago, the seat of the pants had worn through, the jacket had split along the pockets and vent, and I had finally abandoned it as a lost cause. I hung it in my closet as a souvenir of happier days and went out and bought myself the cheapest, most durable clothes I could find: work boots, blue jeans, flannel shirts, and a secondhand leather jacket from an Army surplus store. My friends were startled by this transformation, but I said nothing about it, since what they thought was finally the least of my concerns. The same with the telephone. I did not have it disconnected in order to isolate myself from the world, but simply because it was an expense I could no longer afford. When Zimmer harangued me about it one day in front of the library, grumbling about how difficult it had become to reach me, I dodged the question of my money problems by sailing into a long song and dance about wires, voices, and the death of human contact. "An electrically transmitted voice is not a real voice," I said. "We've all grown used to these simulacra of ourselves, but when you stop and think about it, the telephone is an instrument of distortion and fantasy. It's communication between ghosts, the verbal secretions of minds without bodies. I want to be able to see the person I'm talking to. If I can't, I'd rather not talk at all." Such performances were becoming

**rubble** (fig) pieces of broken stones, bricks, etc **to batter** to damage **soaking** becoming totally wet **seat** the part of trousers you sit on **to split** zerreißen **vent** the narrow straight opening at the bottom of a jacket or coat **durable** long-lasting **Army surplus store** store that sells clothes that the Army can't use any more **to harangue** [həˈræŋ] to make a loud aggressive speech that criticizes or blames s.o. or tries to persuade people about s.th. **to grumble** to keep complaining **to dodge** to avoid by using tricks **to sail into s.th.** (fig) to begin quickly and smoothly with s.th. **song and dance** (AE) a very complicated explanation or excuse for s.th. you have done **simulacrum** (sing) **simulacra** (plural) (defined by Auster in his novel *Leviathan* as an illusion of reality) any image or representation of something—First used by Plato to mean a poor copy of s.th., it has been adopted by postmodernist theorists such as the French social critic Jean Baudrillard (cf. *Simulacra et Simulation*, 1981) to mean the reality that is created in films, videos, and TV. **distortion** changing the appearance, sound, or shape of something so that it becomes strange or unclear **verbal** using words **secretion** a substance, usually liquid, produced by part of a plant or animal

more and more typical of me—the excuses, the double-talk, the odd theories I propounded in response to perfectly reasonable questions. Because I did not want anyone to know how hard up I was, I saw no choice but to lie my way out of these scrapes. The worse off I was, the more bizarre and contorted my inventions became. Why I had stopped smoking, why I had stopped drinking, why I had stopped eating in restaurants—I was never at a loss to devise some preposterously rational explanation. I wound up sounding like an anarchist hermit, a latter-day crank, a Luddite. But my friends were amused, and in that way I managed to protect my secret. Pride no doubt played a role in these shenanigans, but the crucial thing was that I didn't want anyone to interfere with the course I had set for myself. Talking about it would only have led to pity, perhaps even to offers of help, and that would have botched the whole business. Instead, I walled myself up in the delirium of my project, clowned at every possible opportunity, and waited for time to run out.

The last year was the hardest. I stopped paying my electricity bills in November, and by January a man from Con Edison had come to disconnect the meter. For several weeks after that, I experimented with a variety of candles, investigating each brand for its cheapness, luminosity, and long-lastingness. To my surprise, Jewish memorial candles turned out to be the best bargain. I found the flickering lights and shadows extremely beautiful, and now that the refrigerator had been silenced (with its fitful, unexpected shudderings), I felt that I was probably better off without

**double-talk** talk that fools people into thinking it is reasonable but is full of contradictions and nonsense **to propound** to suggest for others to think about **scrape** (coll) an embarrassing situation **contorted** twisted out of shape, i.e. completely illogical **to be at a loss** to be uncertain what to do **preposterous** absurd **hermit** person living completely alone separated from the rest of society **latter-day** present-day **crank** (AE) a person who is usually in a bad mood **Luddite** ['lʌd.aɪt] any of the textile workers opposed to mechanization who rioted and organized machine-breaking between 1811 and 1816 **shenanigan** slightly dishonest activity **to botch** (coll) to do something badly, because you have been careless or because you didn't have the training **to clown at s.th.** to not take s.th. seriously **Con Edison** the company that supplies electricity in New York City **meter** here: the device that measures the amount of electricity used **luminosity** brightness **Jewish memorial candles** candles that are used for a menorah, a candlestick with seven parts during Hanukkah, the feast of light **bargain** something bought cheaply or for less than its usual price **to flicker** to shine with an unsteady light that goes on and off quickly **fitful** happening irregularly for short periods of time **shuddering** shaking or trembling suddenly and violently

electricity anyway. Whatever else might have been said about me, I was resilient. I sought out the hidden advantages that each deprivation produced, and once I learned how to live without a given thing, I dismissed it from my mind for good. I knew that the process could not go on forever, that eventually there would be things that could not be dismissed, but for the time being I marveled at how little I regretted the things that were gone. Slowly but surely, I discovered that I was capable of going very far, much farther than I would have thought possible.

After I paid the tuition for my final semester, I was down to less than six hundred dollars. A dozen boxes remained, as well as the autograph collection and the clarinet. To keep myself company, I would sometimes put the instrument together and blow into it, filling the apartment with weird ejaculations of sound, a hurly-burly of squeaks and moans, of laughter and plaintive snarls. In March, I sold the autographs to a collector named Milo Flax, an odd little man with a nimbus of curly blond hair who advertised in the back pages of *The Sporting News*. When Flax saw the array of Cub signatures in the box, he was awe-struck. Studying the papers with reverence, he looked up at me with tears in his eyes and boldly predicted that 1969 would be the Cubs' year. He was almost right, of course, and if not for a late-season slump, combined with the lightning surge of the ragtag Mets, it surely would have happened. The autographs

**resilient** recovering easily and quickly from shock, illness, hardship, etc **deprivation** something you need or usually have that you are prevented from having **to dismiss from your mind** to put out of your mind, to refuse to think about any more **to marvel at s.th.** to be filled with surprise about s.th. **tuition** [tju'ɪʃ.ᵊn] payment made to a college or university to study there **to keep oneself company** here: to keep oneself busy so as not to feel lonely **weird** strange **ejaculation** here: sudden outburst of noise **hurly-burly** a lot of busy, noisy activity **squeak** a high shrill sound **moan** low long mournful sound expressing suffering or pleading **plaintive** expressing melancholy; mournful, sad **snarl** speaking in a nasty angry way **Milo** 1. Greek athlete in Olympic games (500 B.C.) 2. Roman politician (95 B.C.-47 B.C.) **flax** plant used for making cloth **nimbus** a bright circle of light found around the head of a holy person **The Sporting News** American magazine that reports about football, baseball, basketball, etc. **array** an impressive display or collection **awe-struck** full of overwhelming wonder, admiration, respect **reverence** great respect and admiration for s.o. or s.th. **bold** courageous, confident, and fearless **Cub's year** i.e., the year when the Chicago Cubs would win the World Series **slump** a sudden or marked decline or failure, as in progress or achievement; collapse **surge** here: sudden success **ragtag** disorderly **Mets** New York Mets—baseball team founded in 1962; they finally won the World Series in 1969.

fetched one hundred and fifty dollars, which covered more than a month's rent. The books kept me in food, and I managed to squeeze through April and May with my head above water, finishing up my schoolwork with a flurry of candlelight cramming and typing. At that point I sold my typewriter for twenty-six dollars, which enabled me to rent a cap and gown and attend the countercommencement that had been organized by the students to protest the official university ceremonies.

I had done what I had set out to do, but there was no chance to savor my triumph. I had come to my last hundred dollars, and the books had dwindled to three boxes. Paying the rent was out of the question now, and though the security deposit would see me through another month, I was bound to be evicted after that. If the notices started in July, then the crunch would come in August, which meant that I would be out on the street by September. From the vantage of June first, however, the end of the summer was light-years away. The problem was not so much what to do after that, but how to get there in the first place. The books would bring in approximately fifty dollars. Added to the ninety-six I already had, that meant there would be a hundred and forty-six dollars to see me through the next three months. It hardly seemed enough, but by restricting myself to one meal a day, by ignoring newspapers, buses, and every kind of frivolous expense, I figured I might make it. So began the summer of 1969. It seemed almost certain to be the last summer I spent on earth.

Throughout the winter and early spring, I had stored my food on the windowledge outside the apartment. A number of things had frozen solid during the coldest months (sticks of butter, containers of cottage cheese),

**to squeeze through** here: to survive **flurry** mass **to cram** to study for an examination by hastily memorizing **cap and gown** a black flat cap and long piece of clothing worn for special ceremonies such as a graduation (special ceremony at a school or university for those who have just completed their studies.) **countercommencement** June 4, 1968: At the same time as the official commencement (graduation ceremony) many students decided to hold an alternative or countercommencement because of internal political conflicts, conflicts with the school administration, and divided opinion about the Vietnam war. **to savor** to fully enjoy **to dwindle** to grow or cause to grow less in size, intensity, or number **security deposit** Kaution **to be bound to do th.** to be certain or sure to do s.th. **to evict** to force to leave because of not paying the rent, etc. **crunch** (coll) the critical moment or situation **vantage** position, point of time **approximately** about **frivolous** [ˈfrɪv.əl.əs] not serious or sensible

but nothing that was not edible after it had thawed. The main problem had been guarding against soot and pigeon shit, but I soon learned to wrap my provisions in a plastic shopping bag before leaving them outside. After one of these bags was blown off the ledge in a storm, I began anchoring them with a string to the radiator in the room. I grew quite adept at managing this system, and because the gas was mercifully included in the rent (which meant that I did not have to worry about losing my stove), the food situation seemed well under control. But that was during the cold weather. The season had changed now, and with the sun lingering in the sky for thirteen or fourteen hours a day, the ledge did more harm than good. The milk curdled; the juice turned rank; the butter melted into glistening pools of yellow slime. I suffered through a number of these disasters, and then I began to overhaul my diet, realizing that I had to shun all goods that perished in the heat. On June twelfth, I sat down and charted out my new regimen. Powdered milk, instant coffee, small packages of bread—those would be my staples—and every day I would eat the same thing: eggs, the cheapest, most nutritious food known to man. Now and then I would splurge on an apple or an orange, and if the craving ever got too strong, I would treat myself to a hamburger or a can of stew. The food would not spoil, and (theoretically at any rate) I would not starve. Two eggs a day, soft-boiled to perfection in two and a half minutes, two slices of bread, three cups of coffee, and as much water as I could drink. If not inspiring, the plan at least had a certain geometrical elegance. Given the paucity of options to choose from, I tried to take heart from this.

I did not starve, but there was rarely a moment when I did not feel hungry. I often dreamt about food, and my nights that summer were

**edible** can be eaten **to thaw** to become or cause to become unfrozen **provisions** food **radiator** Heizkörper **adept** good **mercifully** fortunately **to linger** here: to stay for what seems like a long time **to curdle** to become thick and sour **rank** having a very strong and unpleasant smell or taste **to glisten** to gleam, to shine **to overhaul** here: to completely change **to shun** to avoid deliberately; keep away from **to perish** to become destroyed so that it can no longer be used **to chart out** to make a detailed plan **regimen** here: diet **staple** main or basic food **nutritious** full of the natural substances that your body needs to stay healthy or to grow properly **to splurge** to spend more money than you can afford **craving** an extremely strong desire for something **to treat yourself to s.th.** to give yourself s.th. enjoyable that you pay for yourself **to spoil** to become useless so that it can't be used any more **paucity** smallness of quantity; insufficiency, lack of **to take heart** to feel encouraged

filled with visions of feasts and gluttony: platters of steak and lamb, succulent pigs floating in on trays, castlelike cakes and desserts, gigantic bowls of fruit. During the day, my stomach cried out to me constantly, gurgling with a rush of unappeased juices, hounding me with its emptiness, and it was only through sheer struggle that I was able to ignore it. By no means plump to begin with, I continued to lose weight as the summer wore on. Every now and then, I would drop a penny into a drugstore Exacto scale to see what was happening to me. From 154 in June, I fell to 139 in July, and then to 123 in August. For someone who measured slightly over six feet, this began to be dangerously little. Skin and bone can go just so far, after all, and then you reach a point when serious damage is done.

I was trying to separate myself from my body, taking the long road around my dilemma by pretending it did not exist. Others had traveled this road before me, and all of them had discovered what I finally discovered for myself: the mind cannot win over matter, for once the mind is asked to do too much, it quickly shows itself to be matter as well. In order to rise above my circumstances, I had to convince myself that I was no longer real, and the result was that all reality began to waver for me. Things that were not there would suddenly appear before my eyes, then vanish. A glass of cold lemonade, for example. A newspaper with my name in the headline. My old suit lying on the bed, perfectly intact. Once I even saw a former version of myself blundering around the room, searching drunkenly in the corners for something he couldn't find. These hallucinations lasted only an instant, but they would continue to resonate inside me for hours on end. Then there were the periods when I simply lost track of myself. A thought would occur to me, and by the time I fol-

**gluttony** the bad habit of eating and drinking too much **platter** large plate **succulent** [ˈsʌk.jə.lənt] juicy and delicious **to gurgle** to make low bubbling noises when s.th. liquid is flowing **unappeased** not satisfied **to hound** to be constantly chased, here: to persecute, to plague **plump** a bit too fat **to wear on** to pass on very slowly **Exacto** American company that makes scales for drugstores **others** cf. Diogenes (412-323 B.C.) Greek philosopher who lived an extremely simple life, Knut Hamsun's (Norwegian novelist, 1859-1952) *Hunger* (1890) as mentioned by Auster in his essay "The Art of Hunger," Kafka's *A Hungerartist*. Auster himself almost starved to death in France. **to waver** to become uncertain or unsteady **to blunder** to move in an unsteady way, as if you cannot see properly **to resonate** to make a strong deep sound that you continue to hear for a while **to lose track of s.th.** to fail to pay attention to s.th. so you don't know where you are

lowed it to its conclusion, I would look up and discover that it was night. There was no way to account for the hours I had lost. On other occasions, I found myself chewing imaginary food, smoking imaginary cigarettes, blowing imaginary smoke rings into the air around me. Those were the worst moments of all, perhaps, for I realized then that I could no longer trust myself. My mind had begun to drift, and once that happened, I was powerless to stop it.

Most of these symptoms did not appear until mid-July. Prior to that, I dutifully read through the last of Uncle Victor's books, then sold them off to Chandler up the street. The closer I got to the end, however, the more trouble the books gave me. I could feel my eyes making contact with the words on the page, but no meanings rose up to me anymore, no sounds echoed in my head. The black marks seemed wholly bewildering, an arbitrary collection of lines and curves that divulged nothing but their own muteness. Eventually, I did not even pretend to understand what I was reading. I would pull a book from the box, open it to the first page, and then move my finger along the first line. When I came to the end, I would start in on the second line, and then the third line, and so on down to the bottom of the page. That was how I finished the job: like a blind man reading braille. If I couldn't see the words, at least I wanted to touch them. Things had become so bad for me by then, this actually seemed to make sense. I touched all the words in those books, and because of that I earned the right to sell them.

As chance would have it, I took the last ones up to Chandler on the same day the astronauts landed on the moon. I received a little more than nine dollars from the sale, and as I walked back down Broadway afterward, I decided to stop in at Quinn's Bar and Grill, a small local hangout that stood on the southeast corner of 108th Street. The weather was extremely hot that day, and there didn't seem to be any harm in splurging on a couple of ten-cent beers. I sat on a stool at the bar next to three or four of the regulars, enjoying the dim lights and the coolness of the air

**to account for s.th.** to be the explanation of s.th. **prior to** before **bewildering** totally confusing **arbitrary** happening by chance rather than a plan **to divulge** to give s.o. information, especially about s.th. that is secret **muteness** inability to speak or make a sound **braille** [breɪl] a form of printing with raised parts that a blind person can read by touching the paper with their fingers **Quinn's Bar and Grill** bar and grill = a pub where you can also get grilled food—a bar of this name never existed on 108th Street, Quinn is the name of a detective in Auster's *The City of Glass* **stool** a seat with just three or four legs **regulars** i.e. regular customers

conditioning. The big color television set was on, glowing eerily over the bottles of rye and bourbon, and that was how I happened to witness the event. I saw the two padded figures take their first steps in that airless world, bouncing like toys over the landscape, driving a golf cart through the dust, planting a flag in the eye of what had once been the goddess of love and lunacy. Radiant Diana, I thought, image of all that is dark within us. Then the president spoke. In a solemn, deadpan voice, he declared this to be the greatest event since the creation of man. The old-timers at the bar laughed when they heard this, and I believe I managed to crack a smile or two myself. But for all the absurdity of that remark, there was one thing no one could challenge: since the day he was expelled from Paradise, Adam had never been this far from home.

For a short time after that, I lived in a state of nearly perfect calm. My apartment was bare now, but rather than discourage me as I had thought it would, this emptiness seemed to give me comfort. I am quite at a loss to explain it, but all of a sudden my nerves became steadier, and for the next three or four days I almost began to recognize myself again. It is curious to use such a word in this context, but for that brief period following the sale of Uncle Victor's last books, I would even go so far as to call myself *happy*. Like an epileptic on the brink of a seizure, I had entered that strange half-world in which everything starts to shine, to give off a new and astonishing clarity. I didn't do much during those days. I paced around my room, I stretched out on my mattress, I wrote down my thoughts in a notebook. It didn't matter. Even the act of doing nothing seemed important to me, and I had no qualms about letting the

**eerily** mysteriously, weirdly, strangely **rye** whisky made from rye (Roggen) **padded** filled with a soft material to make it thicker **figures** i.e. Neil Armstrong and "Buzz" Aldrin; the former was the first to step on the moon at 10:56 p.m. New York time. Auster is talking about the Apollo 11 mission. **to bounce** to move like a ball hitting s.th. hard **golf cart** i.e., special vehicle that was built for riding around the moon. It was not used on the Apollo 11 mission. **a flag** i.e. the American flag, but flags of other countries were brought to the moon and brought back to earth **lunacy** mental illness that was often thought to be caused by a full moon (Luna = Latin word for moon) **radiant** bright, shining **Diana** the Roman goddess of the hunt and the moon—Venus is usually considered the goddess of love **president** i.e. President Nixon (1969-1974) President Nixon is incorrectly quoted by Auster **deadpan** seeming to be completely serious **steady** stable **on the brink of** just about to start with s.th. **seizure** a sudden attack of an illness **clarity** state of being clear—as Saint Francis of Assisi (1182-1226) after fasting for 40 days **to pace** to walk with regular slow or fast steps **qualms** doubts

hours pass in idleness. Every now and then, I would plant myself between the two windows and watch the Moon Palace sign. Even that was enjoyable, and it always seemed to generate a series of interesting thoughts. Those thoughts are somewhat obscure to me now—clusters of wild associations, a rambling circuit of reveries—but at the time I felt they were terribly significant. Perhaps the word *moon* had changed for me after I saw men wandering around its surface. Perhaps I was struck by the coincidence of having met a man named Neil Armstrong in Boise, Idaho, and then watching a man by the same name fly off into outer space. Perhaps I was simply delirious with hunger, and the lights of the sign had transfixed me. I can't be sure of any of it, but the fact was that the words *Moon Palace* began to haunt my mind with all the mystery and fascination of an oracle. Everything was mixed up in it at once: Uncle Victor and China, rocket ships and music, Marco Polo and the American West. I would look out at the sign and start to think about electricity. That would lead me to the blackout during my freshman year, which in turn would lead me to the baseball games played at Wrigley Field, which would then lead me back to Uncle Victor and the memorial candles burning on my windowsill. One thought kept giving way to another, spiraling into ever larger masses of connectedness. The idea of voyaging into the unknown, for example, and the parallels between Columbus and the astronauts. The discovery of America as a failure to reach China; Chinese food and my empty stomach; thought, as in food for thought, and the head as a palace of dreams. I would think: the Apollo Project; Apollo, the god of music; Uncle Victor and the Moon Men traveling out West. I would think the West; the war against the Indians; the war in Vietnam, once called Indochina. I would think weapons, bombs, explosions; nuclear clouds in the deserts of Utah and Nevada; and then I would ask

**idleness** wasting time not doing anything **to plant oneself** to stand firmly somewhere **to generate** to produce or bring into being, create **obscure** vague, indefinite **cluster** group **rambling** disconnected **circuit** here: series **reverie** ['rev.ər.i] the act of daydreaming **delirious** in a state of a delirium **to transfix** to make motionless, esp. with horror or shock **to haunt** to repeatedly come back to s.o.'s mind because it is impossible to forget **freshman** student in the first year at a college or university **Wrigley Field** baseball stadium in Chicago where the Chicago Cubs usually play **windowsill** Fenstersims **food for thought** a common expression in English: an idea that is worth thinking about **Apollo Project** the moon project of the U.S. in the 1960s and 70s **Apollo** also the god of light and healing **nuclear clouds** Auster is talking about the nuclear bomb tests that took place above the ground in the 1940s and 50s in Nevada, New Mexico, and the Pacific, not in Utah.

myself—why does the American West look so much like the landscape of the moon? It went on and on like that, and the more I opened myself to these secret correspondences, the closer I felt to understanding some fundamental truth about the world. I was going mad, perhaps, but I nevertheless felt a tremendous power surging through me, a gnostic joy that penetrated deep into the heart of things. Then, very suddenly, as suddenly as I had gained this power, I lost it. I had been living inside my thoughts for three or four days, and one morning I woke up and found that I was somewhere else: back in the world of fragments, back in the world of hunger and bare white walls. I struggled to recapture the equilibrium of the previous days, but I couldn't do it. The world was pressing down on me again, and I could barely catch my breath.

I entered a new period of desolation. Stubbornness had kept me going until then, but little by little I felt my resolve weaken, and by August first I was ready to cave in. I did my best to contact a number of friends, fully prepared to ask for a loan, but nothing much came of it. A few exhausting walks in the heat, a pocketful of squandered dimes. It was summer, and everyone seemed to have left the city. Even Zimmer, the one person I knew I could count on, had strangely vanished from sight. I walked up to his apartment on Amsterdam Avenue and 120th Street several times, but no one answered the bell. I slipped messages into the mailbox and under the door, but still there was no response. Much later, I learned that Zimmer had moved to another apartment. When I asked him why he hadn't given me his new address, he said that I had told him I was spending the summer in Chicago. I had forgotten this lie, of course, but by then I had made up so many lies, I could no longer keep track of them.

Not knowing that Zimmer was gone, I kept going to the old apartment and leaving messages under the door. One Sunday morning in early August, the inevitable finally happened. I rang the bell, fully expecting no

**correspondence** similarity or analogy **to surge** to rush forward **gnostic** ['nɑːstɪk] having to do with the religious movement Gnosticism in the 2nd century A.D. They believed that only they had mystical knowledge of Christ and God. The body was seen as the enemy of spiritual life. **desolation** feeling of loneliness and being abandoned **stubbornness** unwilling to change your mind even when it's unreasonable **resolve** strong determination to succeed in doing something **to cave in** to stop doing s.th. because the pressure is too great **loan** money lent for a period of time **to squander** to spend wastefully **dime** (AE) a ten cent coin **Amsterdam Avenue** street parallel with Broadway **to keep track of s.th.** to follow the course or progress of s.th. **inevitable** s.th. sure to happen or unavoidable

one to be there, even turning to leave as I pushed the button, when I heard movement from within the apartment the scraping of a chair, the thump of footsteps, a cough. A flood of relief washed through me, but all came to nothing an instant later when the door opened. The person who should have been Zimmer was not. It was someone else entirely: a young man with a dark, curly beard and hair that hung down to his shoulders. I gathered that he had just woken up, since he didn't have anything on but a pair of undershorts. "What can I do for you?" he asked, studying me with a friendly if somewhat puzzled expression, and at that moment I heard laughter from the kitchen (a mixture of male and female voices) and realized that I had walked in on some kind of party.

"I think I'm in the wrong place," I said. "I was looking for David Zimmer."

"Oh," said the stranger, not missing a beat, "you must be Fogg. I was wondering when you'd turn up again."

It was a brutal day outside—scalding, dog-day heat—and the walk had nearly done me in. As I stood in front of the door now, with sweat dripping into my eyes and my muscles feeling all spongy and stupid, I wondered if I had heard the stranger correctly. My impulse was to turn around and run away, but I suddenly felt so weak that I was afraid of passing out. I put my hand on the doorframe to steady myself and said, "I'm sorry, but would you say that again? I don't think I caught it the first time."

"I said you must be Fogg," the stranger repeated. "It's really quite simple. If you're looking for Zimmer, then you must be Fogg. Fogg was the one who left all the messages under the door."

"That's very astute," I said, letting out a small fluttering sigh. "I don't suppose you know where Zimmer is now."

"Sorry. I don't have the slightest idea."

Again, I began mustering my courage to leave, but just as I was about

**to scrape** to produce a harsh sound when moving along a rough surface **thump** the sound of a heavy object hitting or pounding a comparatively soft surface **relief** a feeling of cheerfulness that follows the removal of anxiety, pain **to gather** to conclude, to assume **to not miss a beat** to notice every little detail **scalding** very hot like being burnt with boiling water **dog-day** from "dog-days," the hottest days in the summer **to do s.o. in** (coll) to completely exhaust **spongy** like a sponge (Schwamm) **to pass out** to become unconscious, faint **to catch** to understand **astute** able to understand situations or behavior very well and very quickly, clever **to flutter** to move lightly and quickly (flattern) **to muster** to succeed in getting

to turn away, I saw that the stranger was staring at me. It was an odd and penetrating look, aimed directly at my face. "Is something wrong?" I asked him.

"I was just wondering if you're a friend of Kitty's."

"Kitty?" I said. "I don't know anyone named Kitty. I've never met anyone named Kitty in my life."

"You're wearing the same shirt she is. It made me think you must be connected to her somehow."

I looked down at my chest and saw that I had a Mets T-shirt on. I had bought it at a rummage sale earlier in the year for ten cents. "I don't even like the Mets," I said. "The Cubs are the team I root for."

"It's a weird coincidence," the stranger continued, paying no attention to what I had said. "Kitty is going to love it. She loves things like that."

Before I had a chance to protest, I found myself being led by the arm into the kitchen. There I came upon a group of five or six people sitting around the table eating Sunday breakfast. The table was crowded with food: bacon and eggs, a full pot of coffee, bagels and cream cheese, a platter of smoked fish. I had not seen anything like this in months, and I scarcely knew how to react. It was as though I had suddenly been put down in the middle of a fairy tale. I was the hungry child who had been lost in the woods, and now I had found the enchanted house, the cottage built of food.

"Look everyone," announced my grinning, bare-chested host. "It's Kitty's twin brother."

At that point I was introduced around the table. Everyone smiled at me and said hello, and I did my best to smile back. It turned out that most of them were students at Juilliard—musicians, dancers, singers. The host's name was Jim or John, and he had just moved into Zimmer's old apartment the day before. The others had been out partying that night,

**odd** strange **penetrating** durchdringend **rummage sale** (AE) an event at which old clothes, toys etc are sold as a way of getting money, for example to help a school or church **coincidence** a surprising instance of events happening at the same time **bagel** ['beɪg.əl] hard bread roll in the shape of a ring that was originally eaten by Jews in New York, but has become popular with the general public in America **cream cheese** Doppelrahmfrischkäse **enchanted** changed by magic so that it has special powers **cottage** Hütte, cf. Grimm fairytale "Hänsel und Gretel" **bare-chested** without wearing anything about the waist **Juillard** The Juillard School, one of the most renowned music schools in America that trains professional musical performers and dancers—it was for many years located near Columbia University until 1969.

someone said, and instead of going home afterward, they had decided to burst in on Jim or John with an impromptu housewarming breakfast. That explained his lack of clothing (he had been asleep when they ran the bell) and the abundance of food I saw before me. I nodded politely when they told me all this, but I only pretended to be listening. The fact was that I couldn't have cared less, and by the time the story was over, I had forgotten everyone's name. For want of anything better to do, I studied my twin sister, a small Chinese girl of nineteen or twenty with silver bracelets on both-wrists and a beaded Navaho band around her head. She returned my look with a smile—an exceptionally warm smile, I felt, filled with humor and complicity—and then I turned my attention back to the table, powerless to keep my eyes off it for very long. I realized that I was on the verge of embarrassing myself. The smells from the food had begun to torture me, and as I stood there waiting for them to invite me to sit down, it was all I could do not to grab something off the table and shove it in my mouth.

Kitty was the one who finally broke the ice. "Now that my brother is here," she said, obviously entering into the spirit of the moment, "the least we can do is ask him to join us for breakfast." I wanted to kiss her for having read my mind like that. An awkward moment followed, however, when no extra chair could be found, but again Kitty came to the rescue, gesturing for me to sit between her and the person to her right. I promptly wedged myself into the spot, planting one buttock on each chair. A plate was set before me along with the necessary accoutrements: knife and fork, glass and cup, napkin and spoon. After that, I entered a miasma of feeding and forgetting. It was an infantile response, but once

**impromptu** [ɪmˈprɒmp.tjuː] spontaneous, without preparation **housewarming** given after moving into a new home **abundance** great amount or supply **I couldn't care less** I was totally indifferent **bracelet** a band or chain that you wear around your wrist or arm as a decoration **beaded** made with beads (one of a set of small, usually round pieces of glass, wood, plastic etc, that you can put on a string) **Navaho** [ˈnæv.ə.hoʊ] a group of Native Americans that lives in Arizona, New Mexico, and Utah **complicity** the action of taking part with another person in a crime or some kind of wrongdoing **on the verge of** on the point of, just about to **to grab** to take hold of s.o. or s.th. with a sudden or violent movement **to shove** to push or thrust **awkward** embarrassing **to gesture** to express yourself using your hands or bodily movements **to wedge yourself** to squeeze yourself into a narrow space **buttock** Gesäßbacke **accoutrements** [əˈkuː.trə.mənts] equipment **miasma** in a state as if under a corrupting influence **infantile** typical of the behavior of a child

the food entered my mouth, I wasn't able to control myself. I chomped down one dish after another, devouring whatever they put in front of me, and eventually it was as though I had lost my mind. Since the generosity of the others seemed infinite, I kept on eating until everything on the table had disappeared. That is how I remember it, in any case. I gorged myself for fifteen or twenty minutes, and when I was done, the only thing left was a pile of whitefish bones. Nothing more than that. I search my memory for something else, but I can never find it. Not one morsel. Not even a crust of bread.

It was only then that I noticed how intently the others were staring at me. Had it been as bad as that? I wondered. Had I slobbered and made a spectacle of myself? I turned to Kitty and gave her a feeble smile. She did not seem disgusted so much as stunned. That reassured me somewhat, but I wanted to make amends for any offense I might have caused the others. That was the least I could do, I thought: sing for my grub, make them forget I had just licked their plates clean. As I waited for an opportunity to enter the conversation, I became increasingly aware of how good it felt to be sitting next to my long-lost twin. From the drift of the talk around me, I gathered that she was a dancer, and there was no question that she did a lot more for her Mets T-shirt than I did for mine. It was hard not to be impressed, and as she went on chatting and laughing with the others, I kept on sneaking little glances at her. She wore no makeup and no bra, but there was a constant tinkling of bracelets and earrings as she moved. Her breasts were nicely formed, and she displayed them with an admirable nonchalance, neither flaunting them nor pretending they were not there. I found her beautiful, but more than that I liked the way

**to chomp down** to chew noisily **to devour** to swallow or eat up greedily **generosity** willingness in giving away one's money, time, etc. **to gorge yourself** to eat until you are too full to eat any more **whitefish** freshwater American fish similar to salmon (Lachs) **morsel** small piece **crust** the hard brown outer surface of bread **intently** with great concentration **to slobber** sabbern **to make a spectacle of yourself** to behave in a way that others think you are making a fool of yourself **feeble** extremely weak **disgusted** sickened because of s.th. unpleasant **stunned** shocked, very surprised **to make amends** to say you are sorry for the harm you have caused and try to make things better **offense** an illegal action or a crime, a wrongdoing **grub** (slang) food **to lick** to move your tongue across the surface of s.th. so as to eat it **drift** the general meaning of what is being said **to sneak** here: to do s.th. secretly so as not to be noticed **to tinkle** to make light ringing sounds **nonchalance** [ˌnaːn.ʃəˈlaːnts] calm behavior that shows one is not worried about anything **to flaunt** to display on purpose, to show off

she held herself, the way she did not seem to be paralyzed by her beauty as so many beautiful girls did. Perhaps it was the freedom of her gestures, the blunt, down-to-earth quality I heard in her voice. This was not a pampered, middle-class kid like the others, but someone who knew her way around, who had managed to learn things for herself. The fact that she seemed to welcome the nearness of my body, that she did not squirm away from my shoulder or leg, that she even allowed her bare arm to linger against mine—these were things that drove me to the point of foolishness.

I found an opening into the conversation a few moments later. Someone started talking about the moon landing, and then someone else declared that it had never really happened. The whole thing was a hoax, he said, a television extravaganza staged by the government to get our minds off the war. "People will believe anything they're told to believe," that person added, "even some rinky-dink bullshit filmed in a Hollywood studio." That was all I needed to make my entrance. Jumping in with the most outrageous remark I could think of, I calmly asserted that not only had last month's moon landing been genuine, it was by no means the first time it had happened. Men had been going to the moon for hundreds of years, I said, perhaps even thousands. Everyone tittered when I said that, but then I launched into my best comico-pedantic style, and for the next ten minutes I showered them with a history of moon lore, replete with references to Lucian, Godwin, and others. I wanted to impress them with how much I knew, but I also wanted to make them laugh. Intoxicated by the meal I had just finished, determined to prove to

**blunt** direct and to the point **down-to-earth** sensible, practical, realistic **pampered** spoiled, looked after too much **to know your way around** to be able to deal with situations because of having the necessary experience **to squirm away** here: to move slightly away **hoax** s.th. done to make people believe it is true, a joke **extravaganza** an elaborately staged event **rinky-dink** (AE coll.) cheap and of poor quality **bullshit** (slang) nonsense **to make an entrance** normally: to make an appearance on the stage and begin to perform **outrageous** shocking, extremely unusual **to assert** to state, to declare **genuine** real, authentic **to titter** to give a short nervous laugh **comico-pedantic** in a comic way showing how much academic knowledge one has **lore** body of knowledge or tradition **replete with** with a full supply of **Lucian** (120 B.C. to about 180 B.C.) Greek satirist—in one of his works he describes a trip to the moon **Godwin** Godwin, Francis (1562-1633) English bishop and historian who wrote the first story of space travel in English literature, *The Man in the Moone: or A Discourse of a Voyage Thither by Domingo Gonsales, the Speedy Messenger.* **intoxicated** drunk

Kitty that I was not like anyone she had ever met, I worked myself into top form, and my sharp, staccato delivery soon had them all in stitches. Then I began to describe Cyrano's voyage to the moon, and someone interrupted me. Cyrano de Bergerac wasn't real, the person said, he was a character in a play, a make-believe man. I couldn't let this error go uncorrected, and so I made a short digression to tell them the story of Cyrano's life. I sketched out his early days as a soldier, discussed his career as a philosopher and poet, and then dwelled at some length on the various hardships he encountered over the years: financial troubles, an agonizing bout with syphilis, his battles with the authorities over his radical views. I told them how he had finally found a protector in the Duc d'Arpajon, and then, just three years later, how he had been killed on a Paris street when a building stone fell from a rooftop and landed on his head. I paused dramatically to allow the grotesqueness and humor of this tragedy to sink in. "He was only thirty-six at the time," I said, "and to this day no one knows if it was an accident or not. Had one of his enemies murdered him, or was it simply a matter of chance, of blind fate pouring destruction down from the sky? Alas, poor Cyrano. This was no figment, my friends. He was a creature of flesh and blood, a real man who lived in the real world, and in 1649 he wrote a book about his trip to the moon. Since it's a firsthand account, I don't see why anyone should doubt what he says. According to Cyrano, the moon is a world like this one. When seen from that world, our earth looks just like the moon does from here. The Garden of Eden is located on the moon, and when Adam and Eve ate from the Tree of Knowledge, God banished them to the earth. Cyrano

**staccato** short and abrupt **delivery** manner of speaking in public **in stitches** laughing uncontrollably **Bergerac** French writer who lived from 1619 to 1655. He was the subject of the play *Cyrano de Bergerac* (1897) by Edmond Rostand **make-believe** unreal, imagined **digression** the act of moving away from the main subject that you are talking or writing about **to sketch out** to make a brief description **to dwell on** to talk or write about s.th. for a rather long time **hardship** s.th. that causes difficulties or suffering in life **to encounter** to be faced with **agonizing** causing terrible pain and suffering **bout** a short period of time during which you suffer from an illness **syphilis** a disease transmitted by sexual contact—There is, however, no proof that Cyrano actually had syphilis. **Duc d'Arpajon** He actually existed. **stone** It actually was a wooden beam. Otherwise the description of Bergerac's life is by and large correct. **figment** fantastic or imagined idea **1649** *L'Histoire comique des états et empires de la lune*—a novel that combines science fiction with social criticism—it was published after Bergerac's death in 1655. The description of the plot given in the novel is for the most part correct. **to banish** to no longer allow s.o. to stay in a certain place

first attempts to travel to the moon by strapping bottles of lighter-than-air dew to his body, but after reaching the Middle Distance, he floats back to earth, landing among a tribe of naked Indians in New France. There he builds a machine that eventually takes him to his destination, which no doubt goes to show that America has always been the ideal place for moon launchings. The people he encounters on the moon are eighteen feet tall and walk on all fours. They speak two different languages, but neither language has any words in it. The first, used by the common people, is an intricate code of pantomime gestures that calls for constant movement from all parts of the body. The second language is spoken by the upper classes, and it consists of pure sound, a complex but unarticulated humming that closely resembles music. The moon people do not eat by swallowing food but by smelling it. Their money is poetry—actual poems, written out on pieces of paper whose value is determined by the worth of the poem itself. The worst crime is virginity, and young people are expected to show disrespect for their parents. The longer one's nose, the more noble one's character is considered to be. Men with short noses are castrated, for the moon people would rather die out as a race than be forced to live with such ugliness. There are talking books and traveling cities. When a great philosopher dies, his friends drink his blood and eat his flesh. Bronze penises hang from the waists of men—in the same way that seventeenth-century Frenchmen used to carry swords. As a moon man explains to the befuddled Cyrano: Is it not better to honor the tools of life than the tools of death? Cyrano spends a good part of the book in a cage. Because he is so small, the moon people think he must be a parrot without feathers. In the end, a giant black man throws him back to earth with the Anti-Christ."

I rattled on like that for several more minutes, but all the talk had worn me down, and I could feel my inspiration beginning to flag.

**to strap** to fasten s.th. onto s.th. with a narrow band of strong material **dew** Tau **New France** what is today Quebec in Canada, a French colony until 1763 **destination** place one wants to go to **intricate** with many small parts that fit together, complicated **unarticulated** not clear or easily understood **to hum** to sing a song by making a continuous sound with the lips closed **to resemble** to be similar to **value** the amount that s.th. is worth **virginity** condition of never having had sex **noble** edel **to castrate** to remove the sexual organs **befuddled** completely confused **to rattle on** to talk about s.th. not especially interesting for a long time **to wear s.o. down** to cause s.o. to become increasingly tired **to flag** to become tired or weak

Midway through my last speech (on Jules Verne and the Baltimore Gun Club), it abandoned me entirely. My head shrank, then grew enormously large; I saw peculiar lights and comets darting behind my eyes; my stomach began to rumble, to bulge with dagger-thrusts of pain, and suddenly I felt I was going to be sick. Without a word of warning, I broke off from my lecture, stood up from the table, and announced that I had to leave. "Thank you for your kindness," I said, "but urgent business calls me away. You are dear, good people, and I promise to remember you all in my will." It was a deranged performance, a madman's jig. I staggered out of the kitchen, knocking over a coffee cup in the process, and groped my way to the door. By the time I got there, Kitty was standing next to me. To this day, I still don't understand how she managed to get there before I did.

"You're a very strange brother," she said. "You look like a man, but then you turn yourself into a wolf. After that, the wolf becomes a talking machine. It's all mouths for you, isn't it? First the food, then the words—into the mouth and out of it. But you're forgetting the best thing mouths are made for. I'm your sister, after all, and I'm not going to let you leave without kissing me good-bye."

I started to apologize, but then, before I had a chance to say anything, Kitty stood on her toes, put her hand on the back of my neck, and kissed me—very tenderly, I felt, almost with compassion. I didn't know what to make of it. Was I supposed to treat it as a genuine kiss, or was it just one more part of the game? Before I could decide, I accidentally leaned my back against the door, and the door opened. It felt like a message to me, a secret cue that things had come to an end, and so, without another word, I continued backing out the door, turned as my feet crossed the sill, and left.

**Jules Verne** 1828-1905, French writer, esp. of science fiction, such as *Twenty Thousand Leagues under the Sea* (1870) and *Around the World in Eighty Days* (1873) **the Baltimore Gun Club** a club in Verne's novel *From the Earth to Moon* that planned a trip to the moon with a cannon in 1865 **peculiar** strange **to dart** to move or throw swiftly and suddenly **to rumble** to make a loud sounding noise **to bulge** to stick out in a round shape **dagger-thrusts** Dolchstöße **deranged** crazy, mad **jig** a kind of quick dance **in the process** while doing s.th. **to grope one's way** to try to find your way with your hands when unable to see properly **tenderly** gently **compassion** strong feeling of sympathy for s.o. who is suffering **to make of s.th.** to find a explanation for s.th. **to treat** to regard, to consider **cue** an action or event that provides a signal **sill** the part of a door frame under the door

After that, there were no more free meals. When the second eviction notice arrived on August thirteenth, I was down to my last thirty-seven dollars. As it turned out, that was the same day the astronauts came to New York for their ticker-tape parade. The sanitation department later reported that three hundred tons of trash were thrown to the streets during the festivities. It was an all-time record, they said, the largest parade in the history of the world. I kept my distance from such things. Not knowing where to turn anymore, I left my apartment as seldom as possible, trying to conserve whatever strength I still had. A quick jaunt down to the corner for supplies and then back again, nothing more than that. My ass became raw from wiping myself with the brown paper bags I carried home from the market, but it was the heat I suffered from most. The air in the apartment was intolerable, a sweatbox stillness that bore down on me night and day, and no matter how wide I opened the windows, I could not coax a breeze to enter the room. My pores gushed constantly. Even sitting in one place put me in a sweat, and when I moved in any way at all, it provoked a flood. I drank as much water as possible. I took cold baths, doused my head under the tap, pressed wet towels against my face and neck and wrists. This offered scant comfort, but at least I was able to keep myself clean. The soap in the bathroom had shrunk to a small white sliver by then, and I had to keep it in reserve for shaving. Because my stock of razor blades was also running low, I limited myself to two shaves a week, carefully scheduling them to fall on the days when I went out to

**eviction notice** a legal document that states s.o. must leave the apartment or house he or she is living in **to be down to** to be left with **ticker-tape parade** a parade along Broadway in lower Manhattan that is organized for Americans that have done s.th. heroic; paper is thrown out of office buldings. The ticker-tape parade for the two astronauts who landed on the moon actually took place on August 13, 1969. **sanitation department** the organization that removes waste from streets and people's homes **trash** waste material **festivities** things that are done to celebrate **jaunt** short journey for pleasure **ass** AE (slang) After **raw** wund **intolerable** very unpleasant **sweatbox** AE (slang) small room in which one sweats, especially a prison cell **to bear down on s.o.** to press down on s.o. **to coax** to work on s.th. carefully and patiently so that it functions properly **breeze** gentle wind **pore** small holes in the skin through which sweat can pass through **to gush** here: to allow sweat to pour out in large quantities **to douse** to cover with water **tap** Wasserhahn **scant** not enough, little **comfort** feeling physically good **sliver** very small thin piece of s.th. **stock** supply **razor blade** Rasierklinge

do my shopping. Although it probably didn't matter, it consoled me to think that I was managing to keep up appearances.

The essential thing was to plot my next move. But that was precisely what gave me the most trouble, the thing I could no longer do. I had lost the ability to think ahead, and no matter how hard I tried to imagine the future, I could not see it, I could not see anything at all. The only future that had ever belonged to me was the present I was living in now, and the struggle to remain in that present had gradually overwhelmed the rest. I had no ideas anymore. The moments unfurled one after the other, and at each moment the future stood before me as a blank, a white page of uncertainty. If life was a story, as Uncle Victor had often told me, and each man was the author of his own story, then I was making it up as I went along. I was working without a plot, writing each sentence as it came to me and refusing to think about the next. All well and good, perhaps, but the question was no longer whether I could write the story off the top of my head. I had already done that. The question was what I was supposed to do when the pen ran out of ink.

The clarinet was still there, sitting in its case by my bed. I am ashamed to admit it now, but I nearly buckled under and sold it. Worse than that, I even went so far as to take it to a music store one day to find out how much it was worth. When I saw that it wouldn't bring in enough to cover a month's rent, I abandoned the idea. But that was the only thing that spared me the indignity of going through with it. As time went on, I realized how close I had come to committing an unpardonable sin. The clarinet was my last link to Uncle Victor, and because it was the last, because there were no other traces of him, it carried the entire force of his soul within it. Whenever I looked at it, I was able to feel that force within myself. It was something to cling to, a piece of wreckage to keep me afloat.

Several days after my visit to the music store, a minor disaster nearly drowned me. The two eggs I was about to place in a pot of water and boil

**to console** to serve as a source of comfort to (someone) in disappointment, loss, sadness, etc **to keep up appearances** to continue to wear good clothes and behave as if you still had a lot of money **to plot your next move** to plan your next course of action **to unfurl** to open, to unroll like a flag or sail in the wind **blank** empty space, s.th. completely unknown **off the top my head** without any previous thought **to buckle under** to decide to do s.th. unpleasant because of being under great pressure **indignity** a situation that makes you feel ashamed or not respected **to cling to** to hold tightly to **afloat** on the surface of the water, not drowning **minor** insignificant

up for my daily meal slipped through my fingers and broke on the floor. Those were the last two eggs of my current supply, and I could not help feeling that this was the cruelest, most terrible thing that had ever happened to me. The eggs landed with an ugly splat. I remember standing there in horror as they oozed out over the floor. The sunny, translucent innards sank into the cracks, and suddenly there was muck everywhere, a bobbing slush of slime and shell. One yolk had miraculously survived the fall, but when I bent down to scoop it up, it slid out from under the spoon and broke apart. I felt as though a star were exploding, as though a great sun had just died. The yellow spread over the white and then began to swirl, turning into a vast nebula, a debris of interstellar gases. It was all too much for me—the last, imponderable straw. When this happened, I actually sat down and cried.

Struggling to get a grip on my emotions, I went out and splurged on a meal at the Moon Palace. It didn't help. Self-pity had given way to extravagance, and I loathed myself for surrendering to the impulse. To carry my disgust even further, I started off with egg drop soup, unable to resist the perversity of the pun. I followed it with fried dumplings, a plate of spicy shrimp, and a bottle of Chinese beer. The good this nourishment might have done me, however, was negated by the poison of my thoughts. I nearly gagged on the rice. This was no dinner, I told myself, it was a last meal, the food they serve up to a condemned man before they drag him

**splat** noise that s.th. wet makes when it hits a hard surface **to ooze** to flow slowly **translucent** not transparent but allowing light to pass through **innards** normally: the parts inside a body **crack** Spalt **muck** slimy dirt **to bob** to move up and down when floating on the surface of water **slush** here: a substance like a partly melted piece of ice **yolk** yellow part of an egg **to scoop up** to pick up with a spoon or the curved hand **to swirl** to quickly move in a twisting circle **nebula** a cloud of particles and gases or planets seen in the sky at night **debris** [ˈdeɪ.briː] pieces that are left after s.th. has been destroyed **interstellar** appearing between the stars **last straw** that last problem in a series of problems that makes you give up **imponderable** difficult to determine **to get a grip on s.th.** to start controlling s.th. **to splurge** to spend more money on s.th. than you can afford **to loathe** to feel strong hatred **to surrender** to allow yourself to be controlled or influenced by something **disgust** a feeling of annoyance and disappointment because of one's unacceptable behavior **egg drop soup** a soup in which a raw egg is put into hot soup **pun** Wortspiel, i.e. he is thinking of when he had dropped two eggs on the floor **dumpling** a small ball of dough (Teig) **spicy** stark gewürzt **nourishment** food that is needed to live, grow, and stay healthy **to negate** to make ineffective **to gag** to be unable to swallow s.th. so that it might come out of one's mouth again

off to the gallows. Forcing myself to chew it, to get it down my throat, I remembered a phrase from Raleigh's last letter to his wife, written on the eve of his execution: *My brains are broken.* Nothing could have been more apt than those words. I thought of Raleigh's chopped-off head, preserved by his wife in a glass box. I thought of Cyrano's head, crushed by the stone that fell on it. Then I imagined my head cracking open, splattering like the eggs that had fallen to the floor of my room. I felt my brains dribbling out of me. I saw myself in pieces.

I left an exorbitant tip for the waiter, then walked back to my building. When I entered the lobby, I made a routine stop by my mailbox and discovered there was something in it. Other than eviction notices, it was the first mail that had come for me that month. For a brief moment I fancied that some unknown benefactor had sent me a check, but then I examined the letter and saw that it was merely a notice of another kind. I was to report for my army physical on September sixteenth. Considering my condition at that moment, I took the news rather calmly. But by then it hardly seemed to matter where the stone fell. New York or Indochina, I said to myself, in the end they came to the same thing. If Columbus could confuse America with Cathay, who was I to quibble over geography? I entered my apartment and slipped the letter into Uncle Victor's clarinet case. Within a matter of minutes, I had managed to forget all about it.

I heard someone knocking at the door, but I decided it was not worth the effort to see who it was. I was thinking, and I did not want to be disturbed. Several hours later, I heard someone knock again. This second knocking was rather different from the first, and I did not think it could

**gallows** Galgen **eve** the evening before s.th. happens **...my brains are broken...** This phrase is contained in a letter to his wife that he wrote on March 22, 1618. **chopped-off head** head cut off with an ax—His wife is said to have carried his preserved head around with her until the day she died. **to splatter** to move or fall, especially a liquid, so that drops fall in many different directions **to dribble** to flow very slowly in small irregular drops **exorbitant** [ɪɡˈzɔːr.bətənt] much higher or greater than is reasonable **tip** Trinkgeld **lobby** a room or corridor used as an entrance hall **other than** besides **to fancy** to imagine **benefactor** a person who supports or helps a person, institution, etc., esp. by giving money **army physical** Musterung **Indochina** the peninsula in SE Asia that consists of Burma, Thailand, Laos, Kampuchea, Vietnam, and Malaysia—Auster is thinking more of Vietnam, in which the U.S.A. was involved in a war at the time. **Cathay** the name Marco Polo gave for China—indeed Columbus refused to believe he had found a completely new world **to quibble** to argue about small points or details that are completely unimportant

have been made by the same person. It was a coarse and brutal pounding, an angry fist that rattled the door on its hinges, whereas the other had been discreet, almost tentative: the work of a single knuckle, tapping its faint, intimate message on the wood. I turned these differences over in my mind—for several hours, pondering the wealth of human information that was buried in such simple sounds. If the two knocks had been made by the same person, I thought, then the contrast would seem to indicate a terrible frustration, and I was hard-pressed to think of anyone who was that desperate to see me. This meant that my original interpretation was correct. There had been two people. One had come in friendship, the other had not. One was probably a woman, the other was not. I continued thinking about this until nightfall. As soon as I was aware of the darkness, I lit a candle, then went on thinking about it until I fell asleep. In all that time, however, it did not occur to me to ask who those people might have been. Even more to the point, I did not make any effort to understand why I did not want to know.

The pounding started again the next morning. By the time I was sufficiently awake to know I was not dreaming it, I heard a jangle of keys out in the hall—a loud, percussive thunder that exploded in my head. I opened my eyes, and at that moment a key entered the lock. The latch turned, the door swung open, and into the room stepped Simon Fernandez, the building superintendent. Sporting his customary two-day beard, he was dressed in the same khaki pants and white T-shirt that he had been wearing since the beginning of summer—a dingy outfit by now, smudged with grayish soot and the drippings of several dozen lunches. He looked directly into my eyes and pretended not to see me. Ever since Christmas, when I had failed to give him his annual tip (another expense struck from the books), Fernandez had turned hostile. No more hellos,

**coarse** very impolite, showing poor taste **to pound** to hit s.th. making a loud sound **to rattle** to shake with quick repeated knocking noises **hinge** Angel **discreet** careful so that no-one gets upset or embarrassed **knuckle** Fingerknöchel **to tap** to hit lightly **faint** weak, difficult to see, hear, smell etc. **hard-pressed** in difficulties **nightfall** time just before it gets dark **to occur to s.o.** to suddenly think of s.th. **jangle** sound of metal objects hitting each other **percussive** as in the act of hitting or striking **latch** Riegel **Simon Fernandez** also the name of the pilot who sailed with Sir Walter Raleigh in his unsuccessful attempts to found a colony in Virginia at the end of the 16th century **building superintendent** (AE) Hausmeister **to sport** to wear in a proud way **customary** usual **dingy** dirty and in a bad condition **to smudge** to make a dirty mark on a surface **soot** [sʊt] black powder that is produced when something is burned **drippings** the liquid that fell from the food

no more talk about the weather, no more stories about his cousin from Ponce who almost made it as a short-stop with the Cleveland Indians. Fernandez had taken his revenge by acting as though I did not exist, and we had not exchanged a word in months. On this morning of mornings, however, there was an unexpected reversal of strategy. He sauntered around the room for several moments, tapping the walls as though inspecting them for damage, and then, passing by the bed for the second or third time, he stopped, turned, and did an exaggerated doubletake as he noticed me at last. "Jesus Christ," he said. "Are you still here?"

"Still here," I said. "In a manner of speaking."

"You gotta be out today," Fernandez said. "Apartment's rented for the first of the month, you know, and Willie's coming with the painters tomorrow morning. You don't want no cops dragging you out of here, do you?"

"Don't worry. I'll be out in plenty of time."

Fernandez looked around the room with a proprietary air, then shook his head in disgust. "You've got some place here, my friend. If you don't mind me saying so, it reminds me of a coffin. One of those pine boxes they bury bums in."

"My decorator has been on vacation," I said. "We were planning to do the walls in robin's egg blue, but then we weren't sure if it would match the tile in the kitchen. We agreed to give it a little more thought before taking the plunge."

"Smart college boy like you. You got some kinda problem or what?"

"No problem. A few financial setbacks, that's all. The market has been down lately."

**Ponce** a city in Puerto Rico **short-stop** a position in left field in the game of baseball **Cleveland Indians** professional baseball team in Cleveland, Ohio **to take one's revenge** sich rächen **reversal** a change that is the opposite of what was done before **to saunter** to walk along in a slow confident way **to tap** to hit s.th. lightly with your hand or fingers **to do a doubletake** to react to a surprise after a short delay because one didn't notice anything unusual at first **gotta** (AE) have got to, must **cop** (AE) a policeman **to drag out** here: to make s.o. leave by force **with a proprietary air** acting as if he were the owner **coffin** a long box in which a dead person is buried **pine** Kiefer **bum** (AE) a man who has no home or job and asks people for money **decorator** person who plans the wallpaper, curtains, and furniture, etc. for rooms **robin's egg blue** robin = Rotkelchen—light blue color **tile** Fliese **to take the plunge** to finally decide to do something, especially after worrying about it for a long time **kinda** (AE) kind of **setback** s.th. that stops the progress of s.th. (Rückschlag)

"You need money, you gotta work for it. The way I see it, you just sit around on your ass all day. Like some chimp in the zoo, you know what I mean? You can't pay the rent if you don't have no job."

"But I do have a job. I get up in the morning just like everyone else, and then I see if I can live through another day. That's full-time work. No coffee breaks, no weekends, no benefits or vacations. I'm not complaining, mind you, but the salary is pretty low."

"You sound like a fuck-up to me. A smart college boy fuck-up."

"You shouldn't overestimate college. It's not all it's cracked up to be."

"If I was you, I'd go see a doctor," said Fernandez, suddenly showing some sympathy. "I mean, just look at you. It's pretty sad, man. There ain't nothing there no more. Just a lot of bones."

"I've been on a diet. It's hard to look your best on two soft-boiled eggs a day."

"I don't know," said Fernandez, drifting off into his own thoughts. "Sometimes it's like everybody's gone crazy. If you wanna know what I think, it's those things they're shooting into space. All that weird shit, those satellites and rockets. You send people to the moon, something's gotta give. You know what I mean? It makes people do strange things. You can't fuck with the sky and expect nothing to happen."

He unfurled the copy of the *Daily News* he was carrying in his left hand and showed me the front page. This was the proof, the final piece of evidence. At first I couldn't make it out, but then I saw that it was an aerial photograph of a crowd. There were tens of thousands of people in the picture, a gigantic agglomeration of bodies, more bodies than I had

**ass** (AE slang) the part of the body you sit on **chimp** (coll) short for chimpanzee **benefit** additional service or payment for health insurance, pension, vacation, etc **a fuck-up** (AE slang) s.o. who has made a complete mess of his/her life **to overestimate** to judge something to be better than it really is **It's not all it's cracked up to be.** (coll) It's not as wonderful as many people think. **to drift off** to gradually move off to somewhere **wanna** (coll) want to **weird** [wɪrd] strange, bizarre **shit** (slang) here: things that one disapproves of **something's gotta give** (slang) s.th. has got to give—s.th. negative has to happen **to fuck** (slang) here: to play around with, to deal carelessly with **to unfurl** here: to open, to unfold **Daily News** in the late 60s the New York City newspaper with the largest circulation, an example of the popular press—still exists **evidence** fact or object that makes you believe s.th. is true **to make s.th. out** to be able to read **aerial** from a plane **agglomeration** a large collection of things that do not seem to belong together, a mass

ever seen in one place before. Woodstock. It had so little to do with what was happening to me just then, I didn't know what to think. Those people were my age, but for all the connection I felt with them, they might have been standing on another planet.

Fernandez left. I stayed where I was for several minutes, then climbed out of bed and put on my clothes. It did not take me long to get ready. I filled a knapsack with a few odds and ends, tucked the clarinet case under my arm, and walked out the door. It was late August, 1969. As I remember it, the sun was shining brightly that morning, and a small breeze was blowing off the river. I turned south, paused for a moment, and then took a step. Then I took another step, and in that way I began to move down the street. I did not look back once.

**Woodstock** legendary rock festival that took place in southeast New York in the summer of 1969 that is now seen as the climax of the youth counterculture of the 1960s **knapsack** a bag made of cloth or leather that you carry on your back **odds and ends** all kinds of small things that are not very valuable **to tuck** to put or push into a small space

# 2

From this point on, the story grows more complicated. I can write down the things that happened to me, but no matter how precisely or fully I do that, those things will never amount to more than part of the story I am trying to tell. Other people became involved, and in the end they had as much to do with what happened to me as I did myself. I am thinking of Kitty Wu, of Zimmer, of people who were still unknown to me at the time. Much later, for example, I learned that Kitty was the person who had come to my apartment and knocked on the door. She had been alarmed by my antics at that Sunday breakfast, and rather than go on worrying about me, she had decided to check in at my place to see if I was all right. The problem was finding out my address. She looked for it in the telephone book the next day, but since I had no telephone, there was no listing for me. That only made her more worried. Remembering that Zimmer was the name of the person I had been looking for, she started looking for Zimmer herself—knowing that he was probably the only person in New York who could tell her where I lived. Unfortunately, Zimmer did not move into his new apartment until the second half of August, a good ten or twelve days later. At approximately the same moment she managed to get his number from information, I was dropping the eggs on the floor of my room. (We worked this out almost to the minute, rehashing the chronology until every action had been accounted for.) She called Zimmer at once, but his line was busy. It took her several

**to amount to** to be equal to or add up to in effect, meaning, or quantity **antics** strange or silly behavior **to check in** (ironic) normally: to report at the main desk in a hotel or airport that you have arrived **listing** Eintrag **to rehash** to re-work or to repeat s.th. old **to account for** here: to determine **his line was busy** He was already on the phone with s.o. else.

minutes to reach him, but by then I was already sitting in the Moon Palace, falling to pieces in front of my food. After that, she took the subway to the Upper West Side. The journey dragged on for more than an hour, however, and by the time she got to my apartment, it was too late. I was lost in thought, and I did not answer her knock. She told me that she went on standing outside the door for five or ten minutes. She heard me talking to myself in there (the words were too muffled for her to make them out), and then, very abruptly, it seems that I started to sing—a crazy, tuneless kind of singing, she said—but I do not remember that at all. She knocked again, but again I stayed where I was. Not wanting to make a nuisance of herself, she finally gave up and left.

That was how Kitty explained it to me. It sounded plausible enough at first, but once I started to think about it, her story grew less convincing. "I still don't understand why you came," I said. "We had only met each other that one time, and I couldn't have meant anything to you then. Why would you go to all that trouble for someone you didn't even know?"

Kitty turned her eyes away from me and looked down at the floor. "Because you were my brother," she said, very quietly.

"That was just a joke. People don't put themselves out like that for the sake of a joke."

"No, I guess not," she said, giving a small shrug. I thought she was going to continue, but several seconds went by, and she did not say anything more.

"Well?" I said. "Why did you do it?"

She looked up at me for a brief moment, then fixed her eyes on the floor again. "Because I thought you were in danger," she said. "I thought you were in danger, and I had never felt so sorry for anyone in my life."

She went back to my apartment the following day, but I was already gone by then. The door was ajar, however, and as she pushed it open and stepped across the threshold, she found Fernandez whirling around the

**Upper West Side** the area of Manhattan from the west of Central Park (Central Park West) to the Hudson River **to drag on** to seem to continue for too long a time **muffled** difficult to understand or hear because of being behind a door or covered by s.th. **to make a nuisance of yourself** to behave in a way that annoys other people **plausible** reasonable or likely to be true **to put oneself out** to go to the trouble to do s.th., to make an effort to do s.th. **for the sake of** because of **shrug** Achselzucken **ajar** [əˈdʒɑːr] slightly open **threshold** doorway, entrance **to whirl around** to spin around quickly

room, angrily stuffing my things into plastic garbage bags and cursing under his breath. As Kitty described it, he looked like someone trying to clean out the room of a man who had just died of the plague: moving swiftly in a panic of revulsion, barely even touching my belongings for fear they might infect him. She asked Fernandez if he knew where I had gone, but there wasn't much he could tell her. I was a crazy, fucked-up son of a bitch, he said, and if he knew anything about anything, I was probably crawling off somewhere to look for a hole to die in. Kitty left at that point, went back down to the street, and called Zimmer from the first telephone booth she found. His new apartment was on Bank Street in the West Village, but when he heard what she had to tell him, he dropped what he was doing and rushed uptown to meet her. That was how I finally came to be rescued: because the two of them went out and looked for me. I was not aware of it at the time, of course, but knowing what I know now, it is impossible for me to look back on those days without feeling a surge of nostalgia for my friends. In some sense, it alters the reality of what I experienced. I had jumped off the edge of a cliff, and then, just as I was about to hit bottom, an extraordinary event took place: I learned that there were people who loved me. To be loved like that makes all the difference. It does not lessen the terror of the fall, but it gives a new perspective on what that terror means. I had jumped off the edge, and then, at the very last moment, something reached out and caught me in midair. That something is what I define as love. It is the one thing that can stop a man from falling, the one thing powerful enough to negate the laws of gravity.

I had no clear idea of what I was going to do. When I left my apartment on the first morning, I simply started walking, going wherever my steps decided to take me. If I had any thought at all, it was to let chance determine what happened, to follow the path of impulse and arbitrary

**to stuff** to fill s.th. in a quick and careless way **to curse** fluchen **under one's breath** speaking in a quiet way so nobody can hear you **the plague** die Pest **revulsion** a very strong feeling or dislike or shock **fucked-up** so confused as to no longer have life under control **son of a bitch** (AE slang) Scheißkerl **to crawl** kriechen **telephone booth** (AE) telephone box (BE) **Bank Street** street to the west of Greenwich Village in the southern part of Manhattan—At the beginning of the 19th century it was the center of banking. **the West Village** area to the west of Greenwich Village **surge** sudden increase **to alter** to change **gravity** the force that pulls everything to the center of the earth **arbitrary** happening by chance rather than planned

events. My first steps went south, and so I continued to go south, realizing after one or two blocks that it would probably be best to leave my neighborhood anyway. Note how pride weakened my resolve to stand aloof from my misery, pride and a sense of shame. A part of me was appalled by what I had allowed to happen to myself, and I did not want to run the risk of seeing anyone I knew. Walking north meant Morningside Heights, and the streets up there would be filled with familiar faces. If not friends, I was sure to bump into people who knew me by sight: the old crowd from the West End bar, classmates, former professors. I did not have the courage to withstand the looks they would give me, the stares, the mystified second glances. Worse than that, I was horrified by the thought of having to talk to any of them.

I headed south, and for the rest of my sojourn in the streets, I did not set foot on Upper Broadway again. I had something like sixteen or twenty dollars in my pocket, along with a knife and a ballpoint pen; my knapsack contained a sweater, a leather jacket, a toothbrush, a razor with three fresh blades, an extra pair of socks, skivvies, and a small green notebook with a pencil stuck in the spiral binding. Just north of Columbus Circle, less than an hour after I had launched out on my pilgrimage, an improbable occurrence took place. I was standing in front of a watch-repair shop, studying the mechanism of some ancient timepiece in the window, when I suddenly looked down and saw a ten-dollar bill lying at my feet. I was too shaken to know how to react. My mind was already in a tumult, and rather than simply call it a stroke of good luck, I persuaded myself that something profoundly important had just happened: a religious event, an out-and-out miracle. As I bent down to pick up the

**resolve** firm determination, firm purpose **to stand aloof** to distance yourself emotionally from problems or not care about them **appalled** [əˈpɔːld] very shocked **Morningside Heights** the area between Columbia University and the Hudson River to the west of Harlem **to bump into s.o.** (coll) to meet s.o. you know by chance **West End bar** bar between 111th and 115th Street on Broadway that still exists today **mystified** unable to explain or understand **glance** quick look **sojourn** a short stay somewhere **Upper Broadway** the part of Broadway that is to the north of the southern edge of Central Park **blade** Klinge **skivvies** men's underwear (trademark) **spiral binding** i.e. the pages and cover of the notebook are held together by a wire twisted into circles **Columbus Circle** a traffic circle at the southwest corner of Central Park **to launch** to start s.th. officially **pilgrimage** Pilgerfahrt **occurrence** incident **stroke of good luck** something lucky that happens to you unexpectedly **profoundly** extremely **out-and-out** complete

money and saw that it was real, I began to tremble with joy. Everything was going to work out, I told myself, everything was going to come out right in the end. Without pausing to consider the matter any further, I walked into a Greek coffee shop and treated myself to a farmer's breakfast: grapefruit juice, cornflakes, ham and eggs, coffee, the works. I even bought a pack of cigarettes after the meal was over and remained at the counter to drink another cup of coffee. I was seized by an uncontrollable sense of happiness and well-being, a newfound love for the world. Everything in the restaurant seemed wonderful to me: the steaming coffee urns, the swivel stools and four-slotted toasters, the silver milkshake machines, the fresh muffins stacked in their glass containers. I felt like someone about to be reborn, like someone on the brink of discovering a new continent. I watched the counterman go about his business as I smoked another Camel, then turned my attention to the frowsy waitress with the fake red hair. There was something inexpressibly poignant about both of them. I wanted to tell them how much they meant to me, but I couldn't get the words out of my mouth. For the next few minutes, I just sat there in my own euphoria, listening to myself think. My mind was a blithering gush, a pandemonium of rhapsodic thoughts. Then my cigarette burned down to a stub, and I gathered up my forces and moved on.

By midafternoon, the weather had become stifling. Not knowing what else to do with myself, I went into one of the triple-feature movie theaters on Forty-second Street near Times Square. It was the promise of air conditioning that lured me in, and I entered the place blindly, not even

**to treat yourself to s.th.** to buy s.th. special for yourself **the works** (coll) everything **urn** a metal container that holds a large amount of tea or coffee **swivel stool** a round stool on which you can turn **four-slotted toaster** a toaster in which you can put in four slices of bread at the same time **muffin** a cup-shaped kind of sweet bread often with pieces of fruit in it **counterman** the man behind the counter who takes the orders and serves the food **frowsy** not tidy, shabby **inexpressibly** with a feeling so strong that it cannot be expressed in words **poignant** making you feel sad or full of pity **blithering** foolish, stupid **gush** here: a sudden feeling or expression of emotion **pandemonium** wild confusion **rhapsodic** full of delight and joyous emotions **stub** the part of the cigarette that is left after it is smoked **to gather up one's forces** here: to try to get enough strength or energy to do s.th. **stifling** very hot and difficult to breathe in **triple-feature** showing three main films **Forty-second Street** a street on the west side that indeed has many movie theaters (cinemas) **Times Square** square in downtown New York around which there are many theaters and movie theaters **to lure** to attract s.o. with the promise of a reward

bothering to check the marquee to see what was playing. For ninety-nine cents, I was willing to sit through anything. I took a seat in the smoking section upstairs, then slowly worked my way through ten or twelve more Camels as I watched the first two films, the titles of which I now forget. The theater was one of those gaudy dream palaces built during the Depression: chandeliers hanging in the lobby, marble staircases, rococo embellishments on the walls. It was not a theater so much as a shrine, a temple built to the glory of illusion. Owing to the temperatures outside, the better part of New York's derelict population seemed to be in attendance that day. There were drunks and addicts in there, men with scabs on their faces, men who muttered to themselves and talked back to the actors on the screen, men who snored and farted, men who sat there pissing in their pants. A crew of ushers patrolled the aisles with flashlights, checking to see if anyone had fallen asleep. Noise was tolerated, but it was apparently against the law to lose consciousness in that theater. Each time an usher found a sleeping man, he would shine his flashlight directly in his face and tell him to open his eyes. If the man didn't respond, the usher would walk over to his seat and shake him until he did. The recalcitrant ones were ejected from the theater, often to loud and bitter protests. This happened half a dozen times throughout the afternoon. It didn't occur to me until much later that the ushers were probably looking for dead bodies.

I didn't let any of it bother me. I was cool, I was calm, I was content. Given the uncertainties that were waiting for me once I walked out of there, I had a remarkably firm grip on things. Then the third feature began, and all of a sudden I felt the ground shift inside me. It turned out

**to bother to do s.th.** to take the time or trouble to do s.th. **marquee** here: a large sign over the entrance of a movie theater that indicates what is being shown **gaudy** bright and colorful in a vulgar way **the Depression** the worldwide economic crisis of the early 1930s **chandelier** a large round structure for holding many light bulbs that hangs from the ceiling **embellishment** a detail or ornament that is added **shrine** a holy place of worship **owing to** because of **the better part of** most of **derelict** a person with no home or money who lives on the streets **to be in attendance** (formal) to be present at a certain event **scab** dried blood that forms over a cut or wound while it is healing **to snore** schnarchen **to fart** furzen **to lose consciousness** bewusstlos werden **recalcitrant** refusing to do what you are told to do, stubborn **to eject** to force s.o. to leave **to occur to s.o.** to suddenly think of s.th. **to bother** to upset or worry **content** happy and satisfied **given** considering **to have a firm grip on s.th.** to have s.th. under control **to shift** to move from one place or position to another

to be *Around the World in 80 Days*, the same movie I had seen with Uncle Victor back in Chicago eleven years before. I thought it would give me pleasure to see it again, and for a short time I considered myself lucky to be sitting in the theater on the precise day when this film was being shown—this film, of all the films in the world. It seemed as though fate was watching out for me, as though my life was under the protection of benevolent spirits. Not long after that, however, I discovered strange and unaccountable tears forming behind my eyes. At the moment when Phileas Fogg and Passepartout scrambled into the hot air balloon (somewhere in the first half-hour of the film), the ducts finally gave way, and I felt a flood of hot, salty tears burning down my cheeks. A thousand childhood sorrows came storming back to me, and I was powerless to ward them off. If Uncle Victor could have seen me, I thought, he would have been crushed, he would have been sick at heart. I had turned myself into a nothing, a dead man tumbling head-first into hell. David Niven and Cantinflas were gazing out from the carriage of their balloon, floating over the lush French countryside, and I was down in the darkness with a bunch of drunks, sobbing out my wretched life until I couldn't breathe anymore. I stood up from my seat and made my way for the exit downstairs. Outside, the early evening assaulted me with light, surrounded me with sudden warmth. This is what I deserve, I said to myself. I've made my nothing, and now I've got to live in it.

It went on like that for the next several days. My moods charged recklessly from one extreme to another, shunting me between joy and despair

**benevolent** [bɪˈnev.əl.ənt] kind, wishing well **spirits** Geister **unaccountable** difficult to explain **Phileas Fogg** the hero in the film and novel *Around the World in 80 Days* **Passepartout** the name of Phileas Fogg's servant who travels with him (the name also means a permit that allows one to pass through or enter any area) **to scramble** to climb with difficulty **duct** Tränenkanal **to give way** here: to allow the tears to begin to flow **sorrow** an event that makes you feel great sadness **to ward s.th. off** to prevent or stop s.th. harmful from happening to you **crushed** upset or shocked **to tumble** to fall quickly and suddenly downwards **David Niven** British actor (1910-1983) who played Phileas Fogg **Cantinflas** Mexican comedian and actor (1911-1993) who played Passepartout **to gaze** to look at someone or something for a long time **carriage** here: large basket hanging from a balloon that carries passengers **to float** to move slowly in the air or stay up in the air **lush** plentiful, thriving (satt, üppig) **bunch** group **to sob out** here: to cry or weep noisily until one is so tired that one can't continue **wretched** miserable **to assault** to attack **recklessly** without thinking about the possible bad or dangerous results of your actions **to shunt** to move from side to side

so often that my mind became battered from the journey. Almost anything could set off the switch: a sudden confrontation with the past, a chance smile from a stranger, the way the light fell on the sidewalk at any given hour. I struggled to achieve some equilibrium within myself, but it was no use: everything was instability, turmoil, outrageous whim. At one moment I was engaged in a philosophical quest, supremely confident that I was about to join the ranks of the illuminati; at the next moment I was in tears, collapsing under the weight of my own anguish. My self-absorption was so intense that I could no longer see things for what they were: objects became thoughts, and every thought was part of the drama being played out inside me.

It had been one thing to sit in my room and wait for the sky to fall on top of me, but it was quite another to be thrust out into the open. Within ten minutes of leaving the theater, I finally understood what I was up against. Night was approaching, and before too many more hours had passed, I would have to find a place to sleep. Remarkable as it seems to me now, I had not given any serious thought to this problem. I had assumed that it would somehow take care of itself, that trusting in blind dumb luck would be sufficient. Once I began to survey the prospects around me, however, I saw how dismal they really were. I was not going to stretch out on the sidewalk like some bum, I said to myself, lying there for the whole night wrapped in newspapers. I would be exposed to every madman in the city if I did that; it would be like inviting someone to slit my throat. And even if I wasn't attacked, I was sure to be arrested for vagrancy. On the other hand, what possibilities for shelter did I have?

**to set off** here: to cause to turn on **turmoil** violent or confused movement **outrageous** extremely shocking or unusual **whim** a sudden, passing idea, impulsive or irrational thought **to be engaged in** to be busy doing s.th. **quest** a long search for s.th. **supremely** very much **to join the ranks** to become a member of a group **illuminati** outstanding historical persons of great knowledge; also a religious sect at the end of the 18th century with ties to the Masons; Herder, Goethe, Mozart, etc. were members **anguish** mental or physical suffering resulting from extreme pain or worry **self-absorption** the state of only being concerned about yourself **to thrust out** to throw out **to survey** to consider all the possibilities carefully **prospects** chances of future success **dismal** here: hopeless **bum** (AE) s.o. who has no home or job, and who asks people for money **to be exposed to** to be not protected from attack **to slit** to make a long narrow cut **for vagrancy** for the crime of living on the streets and asking people for money **shelter** a place where one is protected from the wind, rain, and cold

The thought of spending the night in a flophouse repulsed me. I couldn't see myself lying in a room with a hundred down-and-outs, having to breathe their smells, having to listen to the grunts of old men buggering each other. I wanted no part of such a place, not even if I could get in for free. There were the subways, of course, but I knew in advance that I would never be able to close my eyes down there—not with the lurching and the noise and the fluorescent lights, not when I thought some transit cop might be coming along at any moment to crash his nightstick against the soles of my feet. I wandered around in a funk for several hours, trying to come to a decision. If I eventually chose Central Park, it was only because I was too exhausted to think of anything else. At about eleven o'clock I found myself walking down Fifth Avenue, absently running my hand along the stone wall that divides the park from the street. I looked over the wall, saw the immense, uninhabited park, and realized that nothing better was going to present itself to me at that hour. At the very worst, the ground would be soft in there, and I welcomed the thought of lying down on the grass, of being able to make my bed in a place where no one could see me. I entered the park somewhere near the Metropolitan Museum, trekked out toward the interior for several minutes, and then crawled under a bush. I wasn't up to looking any more carefully than that. I had heard all the horror stories about Central Park, but at that moment my exhaustion was greater than my fear. If the bush didn't keep me hidden from view, I thought, there was always my knife to defend myself with. I bunched up my leather jacket into a pillow, then squirmed around for a while as I tried to get comfortable. As soon as I stopped moving, I heard a cricket chirp in an adjacent shrub. Moments later, a small breeze began to rustle the twigs and slender branches around my

**flophouse** (AE, slang) a cheap hotel, that often has many beds in one room **down-and-out** s.o. who has no job, no money, and nowhere to live **grunt** Grunzen **to bugger** (slang) to have anal sex **to lurch** to move suddenly forwards or sideways (here in reference to the subway cars) **fluorescent light** [flɔːˈres.ənt] Neonlicht (used in the subway stations) **transit cop** (AE) a New York City subway policeman **nightstick** (AE) a short thick stick used as a weapon by policemen **sole** the bottom surface of the foot **Metropolitan Museum of Art** one of the major art museums in New York between 84th and 78th Street within Central Park on Fifth Avenue, the east edge of Central Park **to trek** to make a long difficult journey on foot **to bunch up** here: to press together **to squirm** to twist your body from side to side **cricket** Grille **to chirp** here: zirpen **adjacent** nearby **shrub** a large bush **to rustle** to cause to make a noise because of rubbing **twig** thin branch that grows out of a thicker branch **slender** thin

head. I didn't know what to think anymore. There was no moon in the sky that night, not a single star. Before I remembered to take the knife out of my pocket, I was fast asleep.

I woke up feeling as though I had slept in a boxcar. It was just past dawn, and my entire body ached, my muscles had turned into knots. I extricated myself gingerly from the bush, cursing and groaning as I moved, and then took stock of my surroundings. I had spent the night at the edge of a softball field, sprawled out in the shrubbery behind home plate. The field was situated in a shallow dip of land, and at that early hour a speckle of thin gray fog was hanging over the grass. Absolutely no one was in sight. A few sparrows swooped and chittered in the area around second base, a blue jay rasped in the trees overhead. This was New York, but it had nothing to do with the New York I had always known. It was devoid of associations, a place that could have been anywhere. As I turned this thought over in my mind, it suddenly occurred to me that I had made it through the first night. I would not say that I rejoiced in the accomplishment—my body hurt too much for that—but I knew that an important piece of business had been put behind me. I had made it through the first night, and if I had done it once, there was no reason to think I couldn't do it again.

I slept in the park every night after that. It became a sanctuary for me,

**boxcar** (AE) a railroad car with walls and a roof used for carrying freight **to extricate yourself from s.th.** to remove yourself from a place that is difficult to get out of **gingerly** carefully because you are afraid of hurting yourself **to groan** stöhnen **to take stock of** here: to closely examine a situation and then take action **softball** a game similar to baseball but with a larger, lighter ball **sprawled out** lying down with the legs and arms stretched out **shrubbery** group of large bushes planted together **home plate** the position in baseball/softball where the batter (Schläger) hits the ball, or a member of the opposite team passes over to score a point **shallow** not very deep **dip of land** an area of land that is lower than the surrounding area—There are several softball/baseball fields near the museum that are all slightly higher than the surrounding area. **speckle** small marks covering a background of a different color **sparrow** Sperling **to swoop** to move suddenly downwards in the air **to chitter** zwitschern **second base** the second of the four positions a baseball player has to run over to score a point for his team **blue jay** Eichelhäher **to rasp** krächzen **devoid of** completely lacking **to rejoice** to be very happy about s.th. **accomplishment** s.th. successful that has been achieved after a lot of effort **sanctuary** a place that is safe and provides protection

a refuge of inwardness against the grinding demands of the streets. There were eight hundred and forty acres to roam in, and unlike the massive gridwork of buildings and towers that loomed outside the perimeter, the park offered me the possibility of solitude, of separating myself from the rest of the world. In the streets, everything is bodies and commotion, and like it or not, you cannot enter them without adhering to a rigid protocol of behavior. To walk among the crowd means never going faster than anyone else, never lagging behind your neighbor, never doing anything to disrupt the flow of human traffic. If you play by the rules of this game, people will tend to ignore you. There is a particular glaze that comes over the eyes of New Yorkers when they walk through the streets, a natural and perhaps necessary form of indifference to others. It doesn't matter how you look, for example. Outrageous costumes, bizarre hairdos, T-shirts with obscene slogans printed across them—no one pays attention to such things. On the other hand, the way you act inside your clothes is of the utmost importance. Odd gestures of any kind are automatically taken as a threat. Talking out loud to yourself, scratching your body, looking someone directly in the eye: these deviations can trigger off hostile and sometimes violent reactions from those around you. You must not stagger or swoon, you must not clutch the walls, you must not sing, for all forms of spontaneous or involuntary behavior are sure to elicit stares, caustic remarks, and even an occasional shove or kick in the

**refuge** [ˌref.jʊˈdʒiː] a place that provides protection or shelter from danger **inwardness** concentrating on the mind and inner thoughts **grinding** oppressive (erdrückend) **demands** the difficult or tiring things that you are forced to do (Forderungen) **acre** 1 acre = 4047 square meters **to roam** to walk around without any clear purpose **gridwork** a system of straight streets decided on in 1811 that run parallel to each other from the west to east and the north to south **to loom** to appear threatening as a large, unclear shape **perimeter** [pəˈrɪm.ɪ.tər] the border around an enclosed area **solitude** the state of being alone especially when it is desired—cf the American writer Thoreau's (1817-1862) *Walden* and Paul Auster's *Ghosts* **commotion** noisy activity **to adhere to** to behave according to a particular rule **rigid** very strict and difficult to change **protocol** system of rules **to lag behind** to move more slowly than the others **to disrupt** to prevent s.th. from continuing in the usual way **glaze** a glassy film over the eyes **outrageous** very shocking **hairdo** the way a person's hair is cut or styled **utmost** greatest **odd** strange **deviation** here: behavior that is noticeably different from is expected **to trigger off** to make something happen very quickly **to stagger** to walk with difficulty almost falling **to swoon** to become unconscious and fall down **to clutch** to hold on tightly **for** here: denn **involuntary** done without intention **to elicit** to cause, to bring about **stare** a long steady look **caustic** very sarcastic **shove** a strong push

shins. I was not so far gone that I received any treatment of that sort, but I saw it happen to others, and I knew that a day might eventually come when I wouldn't be able to control myself anymore. By contrast, life in Central Park allowed for a much broader range of variables. No one thought twice if you stretched out on the grass and went to sleep in the middle of the day. No one blinked if you sat under a tree and did nothing, if you played your clarinet, if you howled at the top of your lungs. Except for the office workers who lurked around the fringes of the park at lunch hour, the majority of people who came in there acted as if they were on holiday. The same things that would have alarmed them in the streets were dismissed as casual amusements. People smiled at each other and held hands, bent their bodies into unusual shapes, kissed. It was live and let live, and as long as you did not actively interfere with what others were doing, you were free to do what you liked.

There is no question that the park did me a world of good. It gave me privacy, but more than that, it allowed me to pretend that I was not as bad off as I really was. The grass and the trees were democratic, and as I loafed in the sunshine of a late afternoon, or climbed among the rocks in the early evening to look for a place to sleep, I felt that I was blending into the environment, that even to a practiced eye I could have passed for one of the picnickers or strollers around me. The streets did not allow for such delusions. Whenever I walked out among the crowds, I was quickly shamed into an awareness of myself. I felt like a speck, a vagabond, a pox of failure on the skin of mankind. Each day, I became a little dirtier than I had been the day before, a little more ragged and confused, a little more different from everyone else. In the park, I did not have to carry around this burden of self-consciousness. It gave me a threshold, a boundary, a

**shin** the front part of your leg between your knee and your foot **range** Auswahl **variables** possibilities **to blink** here: to show surprise **to howl** [aʊ] to make a long loud cry because you are unhappy, in pain, or angry **to lurk** to wait somewhere quietly and secretly, to hide **fringe** edge **to dismiss** to not consider important **casual** without being planned **to do s.o. a world of good** (coll) to help s.o. very much **to loaf** to walk around lazily when one should be working **to blend** to fit in well with, to harmonize with **practiced** with a lot of experience, skilled **to pass for** to be considered the real thing although that is not the case **stroller** a person just walking about in a relaxed way **delusion** a mistaken belief or idea **to be shamed into s.th.** to be forced to do s.th. that makes one ashamed **awareness** being able to notice s.th. **speck** a very small mark, spot, or piece of something **pox** Pocken **ragged** with torn clothes, clothes in a bad condition **burden** Last **self-consciousness** being embarrassed because one is the object of the attention of others **threshold** starting point

way to distinguish between the inside and the outside. If the streets forced me to see myself as others saw me, the park gave me a chance to return to my inner life, to hold on to myself purely in terms of what was happening inside me. It is possible to survive without a roof over your head, I discovered, but you cannot live without establishing an equilibrium between the inner and outer. The park did that for me. It was not quite a home, perhaps, but for want of any other shelter, it came very close.

Unexpected things kept happening to me in there, things that seem almost impossible to me as I remember them now. Once, for example, a young woman with bright red hair walked up to me and put a five-dollar bill in my hand—just like that, without any explanation at all. Another time, a group of people invited me to join them on the grass for a picnic lunch. A few days after that, I spent the whole afternoon playing in a softball game. Considering my physical condition at the time, I turned in a creditable performance (two or three singles, a diving catch in left field), and whenever my team was at bat, the other players kept offering me things to eat and drink and smoke: sandwiches and pretzels, cans of beer, cigars, cigarettes. Those were happy moments for me, and they helped to carry me through some of the darker stretches when my luck seemed to have run out. Perhaps that was all I had set out to prove in the first place: that once you throw your life to the winds, you will discover things you had never known before, things that cannot be learned under any other circumstances. I was half-dead from hunger, but whenever something good happened to me, I did not attribute it to chance so much as to a special state of mind. If I was able to maintain the proper balance between desire and indifference, I felt that I could somehow will the universe to respond to me. How else was I to judge the extraordinary acts of generosity that I experienced in Central Park? I never asked anyone for any-

**to distinguish** to recognize the difference **in terms of** considering, regarding **equilibrium** balance **for want of** in the absence of, lacking **to turn in a creditable performance** to do well enough to deserve praise **single** in baseball: when the batter (Schläger) hits the ball in such a way that he can make it successfully to first base **diving catch** in baseball: when a player in the field successfully catches the ball hit by the batter just before the ball hits the ground, thus making it no longer possible for that batter to continue—for the moment—in the game **at bat** the turn of the baseball team to hit the ball while the other team is out on the field **stretch** period of time **to set out to do s.th.** to start to plan s.th., to achieve s.th. **to attribute to** to say that s.th. is caused by s.th.

thing, I never budged from my spot, and yet strangers were continually coming up to me and giving me help. There must have been some force emanating from me into the world, I thought, some indefinable something that made people want to do this. As time went on, I began to notice that good things happened to me only when I stopped wishing for them. If that was true, then the reverse was true as well: wishing too much for things would prevent them from happening. That was the logical consequence of my theory, for if I had proven to myself that I could attract the world, then it also followed that I could repel it. In other words, you got what you wanted only by not wanting it. It made no sense, but the incomprehensibility of the argument was what appealed to me. If my wants could be answered only by not thinking about them, then all thoughts about my situation were necessarily counterproductive. The moment I began to embrace this idea, I found myself staggering along an impossible tightrope of consciousness. For how do you not think about your hunger when you are always hungry? How do you silence your stomach when it is constantly calling out to you, begging to be filled? It is next to impossible to ignore such pleas. Time and again, I would succumb to them, and once I did, I automatically knew that I had destroyed my chances of being helped. The result was inescapable, as rigid and precise as a mathematical formula. As long as I worried about my problems, the world would turn its back on me. That left me no choice but to fend for myself, to scrounge, to make the best of it on my own. Time would pass. A day, two days, perhaps even three or four, and little by little I would purge all thoughts of rescue from my mind, would give myself up for lost. It was only then that any of the miraculous occurrences

**to budge** (coll) to move **spot** a certain place or area **to emanate** to flow or come from **reverse** opposite **consequence** something that happens as a result of a particular set of conditions **to repel** to force or drive back **incomprehensibility** being difficult or impossible to understand **to appeal** to attract, to please **wants** needs **to embrace** to accept a new idea eagerly **tightrope** a high wire or rope that is walked on in the circus, here: a very difficult situation where one must be very careful **consciousness** being very aware of one's surroundings and thoughts **to beg** to ask for s.th. eagerly that one needs very much **plea** [pli:] serious or urgent request **time and again** frequently **to succumb to** to stop being opposed to s.th. because the desire is so strong **inescapable** impossible to avoid **to fend for yourself** to support or provide for yourself without any outside help **to scrounge** (coll) to search about everywhere for what is needed, especially if one doesn't have to pay for it **to purge** to get rid of **miraculous** completely unexpected and resulting from extremely good luck **occurrence** s.th. that happens

ever took place. They always struck like a bolt from the blue. I could not predict them, and once they happened, there was no way I could count on seeing another. Each miracle was therefore always the last miracle. And because it was the last, I was continually being thrown back to the beginning, continually having to start the battle all over again.

I spent a portion of every day looking for food in the park. This helped to keep expenses down, but it also allowed me to postpone the moment when I would have to venture into the streets. As time went on, the streets were what I came to dread most, and I was willing to do almost anything to avoid them. The weekends were particularly helpful in that regard. When the weather was good, enormous numbers of people came into the park, and I soon learned that most of them had something to eat while they were there: all manner of lunches and snacks, stuffing themselves to their hearts' content. This inevitably led to waste, gargantuan quantities of discarded but edible food. It took me a while to adjust, but once I accepted the idea of putting things into my mouth that had already touched the mouths of others, I found no end of nourishment around me. Pizza crusts, fragments of hot dogs, the butt ends of hero sandwiches, partially filled cans of soda—the meadows and rocks were strewn with them, the trash bins were fairly bursting with the abundance. To undercut my squeamishness, I began giving funny names to the garbage cans. I called them cylindrical restaurants, pot-luck dinners, municipal care packages—anything that could deflect me from saying what they really were. Once, as I was rummaging around in one of them, a policeman

**bolt from the blue** s.th. that is totally unexpected **to predict** to say what will happen **portion** part of s.th. bigger **to postpone** to put off, to delay, to do at a later date **to venture** to go somewhere where it could be dangerous **to dread** to fear **in that regard** diesbezüglich **to one's heart's content** as much as one wants **inevitably** unavoidably **gargantuan** very large **to discard** to get rid of s.th. that is no longer wanted **to adjust** to get used to **crust** hard edge **butt end** the round end of French bread (Baguette) **hero sandwich** (AE) sandwich made with French bread **soda** (AE) Limonade **meadow** Wiese **strewn** covered from place to place with **trash bin** container for waste **fairly** more than a little **abundance** a great amount **to undercut** to destroy the effectiveness of s.th. **squeamishness** quality of being easily shocked **garbage can** (AE) dustbin (BE) **pot-luck dinner** a meal made up of dishes of food brought by many different people **municipal** having to do with the government of a town or city **care package** (AE) a package of food that is sent to someone living away from home; originally the packages of food and clothing that Americans sent to Europe after World War Two **to deflect** here: to cause to forget **to rummage** to search through while looking for s.th. often carelessly

came up to me and asked what I was doing. I stammered for a few moments, completely caught off guard, and then blurted out that I was a student. I was working on an urban studies project, I said, and had spent the entire summer doing statistical and sociological research on the contents of city garbage cans. To back up my story, I reached into my pocket and pulled out my Columbia I.D. card, hoping that he wouldn't notice it had expired in June. The policeman studied the picture for a moment, looked at my face, studied the picture again for comparison, and then shrugged. Just be sure you don't put your head in too far, he said. You're liable to get stuck in one if you don't watch out.

I don't mean to suggest that I found this pleasant. There was no romance in stooping for crumbs, and whatever novelty it might have had in the beginning quickly wore off. I remembered a scene from a book I had once read, *Lazarillo de Tormes*, in which a starving hidalgo walks around with a toothpick in his mouth to give the impression that he had just eaten a large meal. I began affecting the toothpick disguise myself, always making a point to grab a fistful of them when I went into a diner for a cup of coffee. They gave me something to chew on in the blank periods between meals, but they also added a certain debonair quality to my appearance, I thought, an edge of self-sufficiency and calm. It wasn't much, but I needed all the props I could find. It was especially difficult to approach a garbage can when I felt that others were watching me, and I always made an effort to be as discreet as possible. If my hunger generally won out over my inhibitions, that was because my hunger was simply

**to stammer** to speak with difficulty so that it is difficult to understand **off guard** unprepared **to blurt out** to say suddenly and involuntarily **I.D.** identity **to expire** to no longer be valid (gültig) after a certain date **to shrug** mit den Achseln zucken **liable** likely **to stoop** to bend down **crumb** very small piece of dry food, especially bread or cake **novelty** quality of being new or interesting **Lazarillo de Tormes** the first Spanish picaresque novel (Schelmenroman) written in 1554 by an unknown author **hidalgo** (Spanish) nobleman (Adliger)—There is indeed such a character in the novel. **toothpick** a thin piece of wood to get food out between the teeth **to affect** to pretend **disguise** s.th. you wear to change your appearance and hide who you are or s.th. you do **diner** (AE) a small inexpensive restaurant **blank** here: when there was nothing to eat **debonair** [ˌdeb.əˈner] stylish and confident **edge** certain amount, degree **self-sufficiency** being able to provide yourself with everything without outside help **prop** any movable object such as a book or knife used on the set of a stage play or film **inhibition** a feeling of worry or embarrassment that stops you from doing or saying what you'd really like to do

too great. On several occasions, I actually heard people laughing at me, and once or twice I saw small children pointing in my direction, telling their mothers to look at the silly man who was eating garbage. Those are things you never forget, no matter how much time has passed. I struggled to keep my anger under control, but I can recall at least one episode in which I snarled so fiercely at a little boy that he burst into tears. By and large, however, I managed to accept these humiliations as a natural part of the life I was living. In my strongest moods, I was able to interpret them as spiritual initiations, as obstacles that had been thrown across my path to test my faith in myself. If I learned how to overcome them, I would eventually reach a higher stage of consciousness. In my less exultant moods, I tended to look at myself from a political perspective, hoping to justify my condition by treating it as a challenge to the American way. I was an instrument of sabotage, I told myself, a loose part in the national machine, a misfit whose job was to gum up the works. No one could look at me without feeling shame or anger or pity. I was living proof that the system had failed, that the smug, overfed land of plenty was finally cracking apart.

Thoughts like these took up a large portion of my waking hours. I was always acutely conscious of what was happening to me, but no sooner would something happen than my mind would respond to it, blazing up with incendiary passion. My head burned with bookish theories, battling voices, elaborate inner colloquies. Later on, after I had been rescued, Zimmer and Kitty kept asking me how I had managed to do nothing for so many days. Hadn't I been bored? they wondered. Hadn't I found it tedious? Those were logical questions, but the fact was that I never became bored. I was subject to all kinds of moods and emotions in the

**to snarl** to say in an angry, nasty way **fiercely** strongly, violently **humiliation** a loss of pride because you have been made to look stupid or silly **spiritual** having to do with the mind or soul **initiation** a process or ceremony that one must go through before becoming a member or a club, secret society, etc. **obstacle** s.th. that blocks your way so you can't achieve s.th. **faith** trust or belief **exultant** very proud or happy because you have been successful **challenge** a questioning of the truth of s.th. **American way** the system of free enterprise—the American capitalist system **misfit** a person who does not conform to the rules of society **to gum up the works** (coll) to prevent everything from working properly **smug** being too satisfied with oneself **overfed** eating too much food **to crack apart** to break apart into little pieces **acutely** very much **to blaze up** (fig) to suddenly burn very brightly **incendiary** [ɪnˈsen.di.er.i] (fig) burning **elaborate** complicated **colloquy** [ˈkɑː.ləkwɪ] discussion **tedious** tiring, boring **to be subject to** einer Sache unterworfen sein

park, but boredom wasn't one of them. When I wasn't busy with practical concerns (looking for a place to sleep at night, taking care of my stomach), I seemed to have a host of other activities to pursue. By mid-morning, I was generally able to find a newspaper in one of the trash bins, and for the next hour or so I would assiduously comb its pages, trying to keep myself abreast of what was happening in the world. The war continued, of course, but there were other events to follow as well: Chappaquiddick, the Chicago Eight, the Black Panther trial, another moon landing, the Mets. I tracked the spectacular fall of the Cubs with special interest, marveling at how thoroughly the team had unraveled. It was difficult for me not to see correspondences between their plunge from the top and my own situation, but I did not take any of it personally. When it came right down to it, I was rather gratified by the Mets' good fortune. Their history was even more abominable than the Cubs', and to witness their sudden, wholly improbable surge from the depths seemed to prove that anything in this world was possible. There was consolation in that

**host** a large number **to pursue** to continue to try to do **assiduously** very carefully to make sure everything is done properly **to comb** to search through carefully **to keep abreast of** to make sure that one knows all the latest news **war** i.e. the Vietnam war **Chappaquiddik** [ˌʃæp.əˈkwɪd.ɪk] scandal surrounding the brother of John F. Kennedy, Edward Kennedy, who caused a car accident on Chappaquiddik Island in Massachusetts on July 18, 1969 that led to the death of a young woman who was in the car with him—as a result Edward Kennedy lost all hope of becoming a presidential candidate **Chicago Eight** later the Chicago Seven—a group of radicals who were brought to trial for trying to violently disrupt the 1968 Democratic National Convention—The trial started in September 1969, becoming an absurd conflict between the hippie generation of the 60s and the establishment. **the Black Panther trial** Auster is probably thinking of the trial of Bobby Seale in 1969—one of the leaders of the Black Panther Party, a black radical marxist party that often got into trouble with the police in the 60s and early 70s. **another moon landing** i.e. the Apollo 12 landing in November 1969 **to track** to closely follow **spectacular** unusually large **Cubs** i.e. the Chicago Cubs; indeed this team was one of the best teams in August only to become one of the worst teams by the end of September 1969 **to marvel** to feel great surprise **to unravel** here: to completely fall apart, to become a complete failure **correspondence** connection **plunge** sudden fall **when it came right down to it** after considering the situation **to be gratified** to feel pleased and satisfied **abominable** terrible **to witness** to experience **surge** here: sudden rise—The Mets, which had had a rather poor record, did extremely well in 1969 and even won the 1969 World Series

thought. Causality was no longer the hidden demiurge that ruled the universe: down was up, the last was the first, the end was the beginning. Heraclitus had been resurrected from his dung heap, and what he had to show us was the simplest of truths: reality was a yo-yo, change was the only constant.

Once I had pondered the news of the day, I usually spent some time ambling through the park, exploring areas I had not visited before. I enjoyed the paradox of living in a man-made natural world. This was nature enhanced, so to speak, and it offered a variety of sites and terrains that nature seldom gives in such a condensed area. There were hillocks and fields, stony outcrops and jungles of foliage, smooth pastures and crowded networks of caves. I liked wandering back and forth among these different sectors, for it allowed me to imagine that I was traveling over great distances, even as I remained within the boundaries of my miniature world. There was the zoo, of course, down at the bottom of the park, and the pond where people rented small pleasure boats, and the reservoir, and the playgrounds for children. I spent a good deal of time just watching people: studying their gestures and gaits, thinking up life stories for them, trying to abandon myself totally to what I was seeing. Often, when my mind was particularly blank, I found myself lapsing into dull and obsessive games. Counting the number of people who passed a given spot, for example, or cataloguing faces according to which animals they

**causality** the idea that an effect or result must have a direct cause—cf. the Scottish philosopher David Hume (1711-1776), who also has doubts about causality **demiurge** ['dem.i.ɜ:rdʒ] creator of the universe (according to Plato), or any creative force **Heraclitus** (535-474 BC) Greek philosopher who believed there was no permanent reality except the reality of change. **to resurect** to bring back to life from the dead **dung heap** (Misthaufen) It is said that Heraclitus buried himself in cow manure (Kuhmist) to regain his health. **to amble** to walk in a relaxed way **to enhance** to improve **terrain** a particular kind of land **condensed** reduced in size, made more compact **hillock** small hill **outcrop** a rock or a group of rocks above the surface of the earth **foliage** leaves **pasture** a field of grass for cattle or sheep **network** a system of things connected to each other **cave** Höhle—There are no real caves in Central Park. **sector** part **zoo** the Central Park Zoo **pond** Auster probably means the Lake in the southern part of Central Park where rowboats can be rented **reservoir** the Reservoir: the largest artificial lake in the center of Central Park for drinking water **gait** the way s.o. walks **to abandon oneself to** to allow your emotions to take complete control when doing s.th. **blank** with no ideas, unproductive **to laps into s.th.** to drift or slide into s.th. **dull** not interesting or exciting **obsessive** completely concentrating on s.th. in a way that is more than normal

resembled—pigs or horses, rodents or birds, snails, marsupials, cats. Occasionally, I jotted down some of these observations in my notebook, but for the most part I found little inclination to write, not wanting to remove myself from my surroundings in any serious way. I understood that I had already spent too much of my life living through words, and if this time was going to have any meaning for me, I would have to live in it as fully as possible, shunning everything but the here and now, the tangible, the vast sensorium pressing down on my skin.

I encountered dangers in there as well, but nothing truly calamitous, nothing I did not manage to run away from in the end. One morning, an old man sat down beside me on a bench, stuck out his hand, and introduced himself as Frank. "You can call me Bob if you want to," he said, "I'm not fussy. Just as long as you don't call me Bill, we'll get along fine." Then, with barely a pause, he launched into a complicated story about gambling, going on at great length about a thousand-dollar bet he had made in 1936 which involved a horse named Cigarillo, a gangster named Duke, and a jockey named Tex. I lost him after the third sentence, but there was something enjoyable about listening to his scattered, half-cocked tale, and since he seemed perfectly harmless, I didn't bother to walk away. About ten minutes into his monologue, however, he suddenly jumped up from the bench and grabbed the clarinet case that I was holding on my lap. He ran down the macadam footpath like some invalid jogger, moving with pathetic little shuffling steps, arms and legs shooting crazily in all directions. It wasn't hard for me to catch up to him. Once I did, I snagged his arm brusquely from behind, spun him around, and wrenched the clarinet case from his hands. He seemed surprised that I had bothered to go after him. "That's no way to treat an old man," he said, showing not the slightest remorse over what he had done. I felt a

**rodent** Nagetier **snail** Schnecke **marsupial** Beuteltier **to jot down** to write s.th. quickly **inclination** desire **to shun** to avoid **tangible** able to be felt **sensorium** here: everything that affects the sensual organs **to encounter** to experience, to be faced with **calamitous** [kəˈlæm.ɪ.təs] disastrous **fussy** concerned or worried about little details **barely** hardly **to launch into s.th.** to suddenly start with s.th. **Tex** a common nickname for s.o. from Texas **scattered** here: chaotic **half-cocked** so poorly told as to seem unbelievable **lap** Schoß **macadam** a road surface made of a mixture of broken stones and tar (Teer) **invalid** not able to use the body properly because of an illness **pathetic** jämmerlich **to shuffle** to walk very slowly without lifting one's feet **to shoot** here: to suddenly move outwards **to snag** to grab **brusquely** [brʌskli] quickly in a rude way

powerful urge to punch him in the face, but he was already trembling so hard with fear that I held myself back. Just as I was about to turn away, he gave me a frightened, contemptuous look, and then sent a large gob of spit flying in my direction. About half of it dribbled down his chin, but the rest of it landed on my shirt about chest high. I averted my eyes from him for a moment to inspect the damage, and in that split-second he scrambled away again, glancing back over his shoulder to see if I was coming after him. I thought that would be the end of it, but once he had put a safe distance between us, he stopped in his tracks, turned around, and started shaking his fist at me, jabbing the air with indignation. "Fucking commie!" he shouted. "Fucking commie agitator! You should go back to Russia where you belong!" He was taunting me to come after him, obviously hoping to keep our adventure alive, but I didn't fall into the trap. Without saying another word, I turned around and left him where he was.

It was a trivial episode, of course, but others had a more menacing air to them. One night, a gang of kids chased me across Sheep's Meadow, and the only thing that saved me was that one of them fell and twisted his ankle. Another time, a belligerent drunk threatened me with a broken beer bottle. Those were close calls, but the most terrifying moment came on a cloudy night toward the end, when I accidentally stumbled into a bush where three people were making love—two men and a woman. It was difficult to see much, but my impression was that they were all naked, and from the tone of their voices after they discovered I was there, I gathered they were also drunk. A branch snapped under my left foot, and then I heard the woman's voice, followed by a sudden thrashing of leaves and twigs. "Jack," she said, "there's some creep over there." Two

**urge** strong desire **to punch** to hit with the fist **contemptuous** showing that someone or something is not important and deserves no respect **gob of spit** mass of spit (Spucke) from the mouth **to avert** to turn away **split-second** very short time less than a second **to scramble away** here: to walk hurriedly away with some difficulty **to stop in one's tracks** to stop suddenly **to jab the air** to move one's hand with quick movements when excited **indignation** anger because you feel you have been unfairly treated **commie** (slang) Communist **to taunt** to try to make s.o. angry by making fun of the person **trivial** unimportant **menacing air** with a threatening appearance **Sheep's Meadow** the Sheep Meadow—meadow in the southern part of Central Park **belligerent** very unfriendly and ready to fight **close call** an incident that could have easily been a disaster **to stumble** to walk along and almost fall **to gather** to assume, to reach a conclusion **to snap** to break with a sudden loud noise **to thrash** to move about in a violent way **creep** (AE slang) a very unpleasant person

voices answered instead of one, both of them grunting with hostility, charged with a violence I had rarely heard before. Then a shadowy figure rose up and pointed what looked like a gun in my direction. "One word, asshole," he said, "and I'll give it back to you six times." I assumed he was talking about the bullets in the gun. If fear has not distorted what happened, I believe I heard a click at that point, the sound of the hammer being cocked into place. Before I understood how scared I was, I took off. I just turned on my heels and ran. If my lungs hadn't finally given out on me, I probably would have run until morning.

It's impossible to know how long I could have taken it. Assuming that no one had killed me, I think I might have lasted until the start of the cold weather. Aside from a few unexpected incidents, things seemed fairly well under control. I spent my money with excruciating care, never more than a dollar or a dollar and a half a day, and that alone would have deferred the moment of reckoning for some time. Even when my funds dipped perilously close to the bottom, something always seemed to turn up at the last minute: I would find money on the ground or some stranger would step forth and produce one of those miracles I have already discussed. I did not eat well, but I don't think I ever went an entire day without getting at least a morsel or two into my stomach. It's true that I was alarmingly thin by the end, just 112 pounds, but most of the weight loss occurred during the final days I spent in the park. That was because I came down with something—a flu, a virus, God knows what—and from then on I didn't eat anything at all. I was too weak, and every time I managed to put something into my mouth, it came right back up again. If my two friends hadn't found me when they did, I don't think there's any question that I would have died. I had run out of reserves, and there was nothing left for me to fight with.

The weather had been with me from the start, so much so that I had stopped thinking of it as a problem. Almost every day was a repetition of the day before: beautiful late-summer skies, hot suns parching the

**to grunt** grunzen **hostility** very unfriendly attitude **charged with a violence…** in a state in which a violent act seemed likely to happen **asshole** (slang) Arschloch **to distort** to change the appearance of s.th. so that it is strange or unclear **hammer** part of a pistol or rifle that falls on the back of a bullet causing it to explode and go through the barrel (Lauf) **to cock into place** to pull back the hammer so that it is ready to fall on the back of the bullet **aside from** except for **excruciating** very extreme **to defer** to postpone, to delay **reckoning** time when the results of your actions become clear **to dip** to go downward **perilously** dangerously **morsel** small piece of food **flu** Grippe **to parch** to dry out

ground, and the air then drifting into the coolness of cricket-filled nights. During the first two weeks, it hardly rained at all, and when there was rain, it never amounted to more than a sprinkle. I began pushing my luck, sleeping more or less out in the open, by now conditioned to believe that I would be safe wherever I was. One night, as I lay dreaming on a patch of grass, utterly exposed to the heavens, I finally got caught in a downpour. It was one of those cataclysmic rains: the sky suddenly splitting in two, buckets of water descending a prodigious fury of sound. I was drenched by the time I woke up, my whole body pummeled, the drops bouncing off me like buckshot. I started running through the darkness, frantically searching for a place to hide, but it took several minutes before I managed to find shelter under a ledge of granite rocks, and by then it hardly mattered where I was. I was as wet as someone who had swum across the ocean.

The rain continued until dawn, at times slackening to a drizzle, at times exploding with monumental bursts—screeching battalions of cats and dogs, pure wrath tumbling from the clouds. These eruptions were unpredictable, and I did not want to run the risk of getting caught in one. I clung to my tiny spot, dumbly standing there in my waterlogged boots, my clammy blue jeans, my glistening leather jacket. My knapsack had been subjected to the same soaking as everything else, and that left me with nothing dry to change into. I had no choice but to wait it out, shivering in the darkness like a stray mutt. For the first hour or two I did my best not to feel sorry for myself, but then I gave up the effort and let forth in a spree of shouting and cursing, putting all my energies into the most

**to drift** to move slowly in the air **sprinkle** (AE) a light rain **patch** small area **utterly** completely **exposed** unprotected **downpour** a lot of rain in a short time **cataclysmic** disastrous **prodigious** in large amount **fury** wild rage **drenched** completely wet **to pummel** [ʌ] to hit again and again **buckshot** grober Schrot **ledge** narrow flat surface of rock that sticks out **to slacken** to gradually become weaker **drizzle** a very light rain **to screech** to make a very unpleasant sound **battalion** a large unit of soldiers—cf. It's raining cats and dogs. **wrath** great anger **to tumble** to fall down quickly and suddenly **eruption** sudden violent burst **to cling/clung/clung** to remain close to **dumbly** unable to speak **waterlogged** completely full of water **clammy** wet and cold in an unpleasant way **to glisten** to shine because of being wet or oily **to be subjected to s.th.** to be forced to go through s.th. difficult **soaking** being made completely wet **to shiver** to shake because of being cold **stray** walking around because of having no home **mutt** a dog of no particular breed (Rasse) **to let forth** to begin to express loudly **spree** a short time when you do everything you have always wanted to do such as a spending spree or drinking spree

vile imprecations I could think of—putrid strings of invective, nasty and circuitous insults, bombastic exhortations against God and country. After a while, I had worked myself up to such a pitch that I was sobbing through my words, literally ranting and hiccuping at the same time, and yet through it all managing to summon up such artful and long-winded phrases that even a Turkish cutthroat would have been impressed. This continued for perhaps half an hour. Afterward, I was so spent that I fell asleep right where I was, still standing up. I dozed for several minutes, then was roused by another onslaught of rain. I wanted to renew my attack, but I was too tired and hoarse to scream anymore. For the rest of the night I just stood there in a trance of self-pity, waiting for the morning to come.

At six o'clock I walked into a hash house on West Forty-eighth Street and ordered a bowl of soup. Vegetable soup, I think it was, with greasy chunks of celery and carrots bobbing in a yellowish broth. It warmed me to a certain extent, but with my wet clothes still plastered to my skin, the dampness was penetrating too deeply for the soup to have any permanent effect. I went downstairs to the men's room and dried off my head under the nozzle of an electric sani-blower. To my horror, the gusts of hot wind puffed up my hair into a ridiculous tangle, and I wound up looking like a

**vile** very unpleasant, nasty **imprecation** words or phrases that are meant to get other persons angry **putrid** awful, disgusting **string** a group of similar things **invective** rude and insulting words that are meant to get others angry **circuitous** [sə'kjuː.ɪ.təs] lengthy, complicated **exhortation** a speech that should persuade others **to work yourself up to s.th.** here: to develop, to increase one's emotions **pitch** extreme excitement **to sob** to cry noisily **to rant** to talk or complain in a loud, excited, and rather confused way **to hiccup** den Schluckauf haben **to summon up** to make a great effort to use s.th. **artful** clever at tricking people **long-winded** using too many words in a way that bores people **cutthroat** murderer **spent** exhausted **to doze** to sleep lightly for a short time **to rouse** to wake up **onslaught** (fig) strong attack **hoarse** with a sore throat that makes it difficult to speak **trance** in a dreamlike state **hash house** (slang) a cheap restaurant **West Forty-eighth Street** probably near the Hudson River where ships still docked until the beginning of the 70s **greasy** oily **chunk** large piece **to bob** to move up and down on the surface of a liquid **broth** thin, clear soup **plastered to** here: spread very close to **dampness** condition of being slightly wet **penetrating** durchdringend **men's room** (AE) men's toilet **nozzle** Düse **sani-blower** a machine that blows out hot air to dry one's hands **gust** sudden strong movement of wind **to puff up** to make s.th. bigger with air **ridiculous** silly, absurd **tangle** twisted mass **to wind up** (coll) to end up in a certain state

gargoyle, a crazed figure jutting from the bell tower of some Gothic cathedral. Desperate to undo the mess, I impulsively loaded my razor with a fresh blade, the last one in my knapsack, and started hacking off my wild serpent locks. By the time I was finished, my hair was so short that I scarcely recognized myself anymore. It accentuated my thinness to an almost appalling degree. My ears stuck out, my Adam's apple bulged, my head seemed no bigger than a child's. I'm starting to shrink, I said to myself, and suddenly I heard myself talking out loud to the face in the mirror. "Don't be afraid," my voice said. "No one is allowed to die more than once. The comedy will be over soon, and you'll never have to go through it again."

Later that morning, I spent a couple of hours in the reading room of the public library, counting on the stuffiness of the place to help dry out my clothes. Unfortunately, once the clothes began to dry in earnest, they also began to smell. It was as if all the folds and crevices of my garments had suddenly decided to tell their secrets to the world. This had never happened before, and it shocked me to realize that such a noxious odor could be coming from my person. The mixture of old sweat and rainwater must have produced some bizarre chemical reaction, and as my clothes grew progressively drier, the smell became uglier and more overpowering. Eventually, it got so bad that I could even smell my feet—a horrific stench that came right through the leather of my boots, invading my nostrils like a cloud of poison gas. It didn't seem possible that this was happening to me. I continued thumbing through the pages of the *Encyclopaedia Britannica*, hoping that no one would notice the smell, but these prayers soon came to naught. An old man sitting across the table

**gargoyle** a monstrous figure on the outside of Gothic churches that carries water out **crazed** having become crazy **to jut** to stick out **to hack off** to cut off roughly **serpent** large snake **lock** Locke—cf. Medusa, a woman in Greek mythology whose hair was changed to serpents **to accentuate** to emphasize **appalling** shocking **to bulge** to stick out in a rounded shape **public library** the New York Public Library on Fifth Avenue between 40th and 42nd Streets; it is a leading research library **stuffiness** quality of not having enough fresh air **in earnest** in fact, actually **fold** Falte **crevice** narrow crack usually in a rock **garment** piece of clothing **noxious** [ˈnɑːk.ʃəs] here: so bad as to seem poisonous **odor** [ˈoʊ.dər] smell **stench** awful smell **to invade** to enter by force **nostril** one of the openings of the nose through which you breathe **to thumb through** to look through quickly **Enyclopaedia Britannica** the largest encyclopedia in the English language, now published in the U.S.A. **to come to naught** to prove to be unsucessful

from me looked up from his newspaper and started to sniff, then looked disgustedly in my direction. For a moment I was tempted to jump to my feet and scold him for his rudeness, but I realized that I didn't have the energy for it. Before he had a chance to say anything, I stood up from my chair and left.

Outside, the weather was gloomy: a raw and sullen kind of day, all mist and hopelessness. I could feel myself gradually running out of ideas. A strange weakness had crept into my bones, and it was all I could do to keep from stumbling. I bought a sandwich at a deli not far from the Colisseum, but then had trouble maintaining interest in it. After several bites, I wrapped it up again and stored it in my knapsack for later. My throat was hurting, and I had broken out in a sweat. Crossing the street at Columbus Circle, I went back into the park and started looking for a place to lie down. I had never slept during the day before, and all my old hiding places suddenly seemed precarious, exposed, useless without the protection of night. I kept walking north, hoping I would find something before I collapsed. The fever was mounting inside me, and a stuporous exhaustion seemed to be eating up portions of my brain. There was almost no one in the park. Just as I was about to ask myself why, it started to drizzle. If my throat hadn't been hurting so much, I probably would have laughed. Then, very abruptly and violently, I began to throw up. Bits of vegetable soup and sandwich came bursting out of my mouth, splattering on the ground before me. I gripped my knees and stared down at the grass, waiting for the spasm to end. This is human loneliness, I said to myself. This is what it means to have no one. I was not angry anymore, however, and I thought those words with a kind of brutal candor, an absolute objectivity. Within two or three minutes, the whole episode felt like something that had taken place months before. I kept on walking,

**to sniff** to breathe in air in order to smell s.th. **disgustedly** in a way that shows s.o. feels sick about seeing s.th. unpleasant **to be tempted to do s.th.** to want to do s.th. that one really shouldn't do **to scold** to criticize s.o. severely for having done s.th. wrong **rudeness** impolite behavior **raw** cold and wet **sullen** gloomy **mist** light fog **deli** delicatessen—a shop that sells various kinds of food, especially food that is unusual or imported and already cooked or prepared **Colisseum** Coliseum—a large building on Columbus Circle built in the 60s for exhibitions and has since been remodeled **precarious** dangerous **exposed** unprotected **to mount** to increase **stuporous** being in a state of shock, not being able to speak or think clearly **to drizzle** to rain slightly **to throw up** to vomit (sich erbrechen) **to splatter** to fall (a liquid) in many drops **to grip** to take hold firmly **spasm** here: the times when one has to suddenly vomit **candor** honesty and truthfulness

not willing to give up my search. If someone had appeared just then, I probably would have asked him to take me to a hospital. But no one appeared. I don't know how long it took me to get there, but at a certain point I found a cluster of large rocks surrounded by overgrown foliage and trees. The rocks formed a natural cave, and without stopping to consider the matter any further, I crawled into this shallow indentation, pulled some loose branches in with me to block up the opening, and promptly fell asleep.

I don't know how much time I spent in there. Two or three days, I would think, but it hardly matters now. When Zimmer and Kitty asked me about it, I told them three, but that was only because three is a literary number, the same number of days that Jonah spent in the belly of the whale. Most of the time I was barely conscious and even when I seemed to be awake, I was so bound up in the tribulations of my body that I lost all sense of where I was. I remember long bouts of vomiting, frenzied moments when my body wouldn't stop shaking, periods when the only sound I heard was the chattering of my teeth. The fever must have been quite high, and it brought ferocious dreams with it—endless, mutating visions that seemed to grow directly out of my burning skin. Nothing could hold its shape in me. Once, I remember, I saw the Moon Palace sign in front of me, more vivid than it had ever been in life. The pink and blue neon letters were so large that the whole sky was filled with their brightness. Then, suddenly, the letters disappeared, and only the two *o*s from the word *Moon* were left. I saw myself dangling from one of them, struggling to hang on like an acrobat who had botched a dangerous stunt. Then I was slithering around it like a tiny worm, and then I wasn't there anymore. The two *o*s had turned into eyes, gigantic human eyes that were looking down at me with scorn and impatience. They kept on

**cluster** a group of things close together **overgrown** grown more than the usual size **foliage** leaves **shallow** not deep **indentation** here: how far the cave goes to the back **literary** having to do with literature **Jonah** a Hebrew prophet in the Old Testament who was swallowed by a large fish and then vomited out onto dry land **belly** stomach **whale** Wal **to be bound up in s.th.** to be concerned with only one thing **tribulation** serious problem or trouble **bout** short period of time when you suffer from an illness **frenzied** being extremely excited or anxious **chattering** clicking together **ferocious** violent, frightening **to mutate** to change **to dangle** to hang loosely **to botch** to ruin s.th. or do s.th. badly because of being incompetent **to slither** to slide along twisting from side to side like a snake **two os** cf. the eyes on the billboard in *The Great Gatsby* by F. Scott Fitzgerald **scorn** contempt, feeling no respect for s.o. **impatience** Ungeduld

staring at me, and after a while I became convinced that they were the eyes of God.

The sun appeared on the last day. I don't remember doing it, but at some point I must have crawled from the cave and stretched myself out on the grass. My mind was in such a muddle that I imagined the warmth of the sun could evaporate my fever, literally suck the illness out of my bones. I remember pronouncing the words *Indian summer* over and over to myself, saying them so many times that they eventually lost their meaning. The sky above me was immense, a dazzling clarity that had no end to it. If I went on staring at it, I felt, I would dissolve in the light. Then, without any sense of falling asleep, I suddenly began to dream of Indians. It was 350 years ago, and I saw myself following a group of half-naked men through the forests of Manhattan. It was a strangely vibrant dream, relentless and exact, filled with bodies darting among the light-dappled leaves and branches. A soft wind poured through the foliage, muffling the footsteps of the men, and I went on following them in silence, moving as nimbly as they did, with each step feeling that I was closer to understanding the spirit of the forest. I remember these images so well, perhaps, because it was precisely then that Zimmer and Kitty found me: lying there on the grass with that odd and pleasant dream circulating in my head. Kitty was the one I saw first, but I didn't recognize her, even though I sensed that she was familiar to me. She was wearing her Navaho headband, and my initial response was to take her for an afterimage, a shadow-woman incubated in the darkness of my dream. Later on, she told me that I smiled at her, and when she bent down to look at me more closely, I called her Pocahontas. I remember that I had trouble seeing her because of the sunlight, but I have a distinct recollection that there were tears in her eyes when she bent down, although she would never admit that afterward. A moment later, Zimmer entered the

**muddle** state of confusion **to evaporate** to cause a liquid to change to gas so that it slowly disappears **Indian summer** a period of warm weather in fall **to dazzle** to shine very brightly so as to hurt one's eyes **clarity** clearness **to dissolve** to disappear in liquid **vibrant** exciting and full of energy **relentless** continuing without stopping even though painful **light-dappled** marked by spots of light **to muffle** to cause a sound to become softer **nimbly** quickly and lightly **to circulate** to move around **initial** first **afterimage** a picture in the mind that one still have after one can't see the picture any more **to incubate** to develop the embryo in an egg by giving it heat **Pocahontas** (1595-1617) daughter of an Indian chief in the English colony Virginia, who prevented Captain John Smith from be executed by her father **distinct** clear **recollection** the act of remembering s.th.

picture as well, and then I heard his voice. "You dumb bastard," he said. There was a brief pause, and then, not wanting to confuse me with too long a speech, he said the same thing again: "You dumb bastard. You poor dumb bastard."

**dumb bastard** (slang) fool, idiot

# 3

I stayed in Zimmer's apartment for more than a month. The fever broke on the second or third day, but for a long time after that I had no strength, could barely even stand up without losing my balance. In the beginning, Kitty came to visit about twice a week, but she never said very much, and more often than not she would leave after twenty or thirty minutes. Had I been more alert to what was going on, I might have wondered about this, especially after Zimmer told me the story of how I had been rescued. It was somewhat strange, after all, that a person who had spent three weeks turning the world upside-down to find me should suddenly act with such reserve the moment I was found. But that was the way it was, and I did not question it. I was too weak to question anything just then, and I accepted her comings and goings for what they were. They were natural events, and they carried the same force and inevitability as the weather, the motions of the planets, or the light that came filtering through the window at three o'clock every afternoon.

Zimmer was the one who took care of me during my convalescence. His new apartment was on the second floor of an ancient West Village tenement building, a dingy hogan of a place crowded with books and

**to break** here: to start to go down **alert** able to think quickly and clearly **to turn the world upside-down** to search in every possible place **reserve** quality of being silent about one's feelings and emotions **inevitability** the certainty that s.th. will happen and cannot be avoided **to filter** to partially shine through s.th. **convalescence** time one spends getting well again **ancient** very old **West Village** western part of Greenwich Village in the southern part of Manhattan that still contains buildings from the 19th century **tenement building** building with many flats of poor quality **dingy** dark and dirty **hogan** (fig) a wooden dwelling covered with earth, typical of the Navaho Indians of North America

records: two small rooms with no door between them, a rudimentary kitchen, a windowless bathroom. I understood what a sacrifice it was for him to put me up there, but every time I tried to thank him for it, Zimmer would wave me off, pretending it didn't matter. He fed me out of his own pocket, allowed me to sleep in his bed, asked for nothing in return. At the same time, he was furious with me, and he made no bones about telling me how disgusted he was. Not only had I acted like an imbecile, but I had nearly killed myself in the process. It was inexcusable for a person of my intelligence to act like that, he said. It was grotesque, it was asinine, it was unhinged. If I was in trouble, why hadn't I turned to him for help? Didn't I know that he would have been willing to do anything for me? I said very little in response to these attacks. I understood that Zimmer's feelings had been hurt, and I was ashamed of myself for having done that to him. As time went on, it became increasingly difficult for me to make sense of the disaster I had created. I had thought I was acting with courage, but it turned out that I was merely demonstrating the most abject form of cowardice: rejoicing in my contempt for the world, refusing to look things squarely in the face. I felt nothing but remorse now, a crippling sense of my own stupidity. The days went by in Zimmer's apartment, and as I slowly put myself back together, I realized that I would have to start my life all over again. I wanted to atone for my errors, to make amends to the people who still cared about me. I was tired of myself, tired of my thoughts, tired of brooding about my fate. More than anything else, I felt a need to purify myself, to repent for all my excesses of self-involvement. From total selfishness, I resolved to achieve a state of total selflessness. I would think of others before I thought of

**rudimentary** very basic, primitive **sacrifice** Opfer **to put s.o. up** to provide s.o. with a place to sleep and eat **to wave s.o. off** to give s.o. a sign that one refuses to consider the other person's idea **to make no bones about s.th.** (coll) to be direct about s.th. **disgusted** feeling very disappointed and annoyed about s.th. **imbecile** [ˈɪm.bə.sɪl] s.o. who behaves very stupidly **in the process** while doing s.th. **asinine** [ˈæs.ɪ.naɪn] extremely stupid and silly **unhinged** like s.o. who is crazy **abject** miserable **cowardice** lack of courage **to rejoice** to feel very happy about s.th. **to look things squarely in the face** to deal with s.th. honestly and directly **remorse** feeling sorry for what you have done **crippling** here: lessening the ability to live or think properly **to atone** to do s.th. to show that you are sorry for having done s.th. wrong **to make amends** to say you are sorry for the harm you have caused and try to make things better **to brood** to keep thinking about s.th. that makes you upset **to repent** to be sorry for what one has done, especially in a religious sense **excesses** harmful or immoral actions **self-involvement** only being concerned about oneself

myself, consciously striving to undo the damage I had done, and in that way perhaps I would begin to accomplish something in the world. It was an impossible program, of course, but I stuck to it with almost religious fanaticism. I wanted to turn myself into a saint, a godless saint who would wander through the world performing good works. No matter how absurd it sounds to me now, I believe that was precisely what I wanted. I was desperate for a certainty, and I was prepared to do anything to find it.

There was one more obstacle in my way, however. Luck got me around it in the end, but only by the smallest hair's breadth of a margin. A day or two after my temperature returned to normal, I happened to get out of bed to go to the toilet. It was evening, I think, and Zimmer was working at his desk in the other room. As I shuffled back to bed after I was done, I noticed Uncle Victor's clarinet case lying on the floor. I had not thought of it since my rescue, and I was suddenly horrified to see what poor condition it was in. The black leather covering was half gone, and much of what remained had bubbled and cracked apart. The storm in Central Park had been too much for it, and I wondered if the water had seeped through and damaged the instrument as well. I picked up the case and carried it into bed with me, fully prepared for the worst. I unsnapped the locks and opened it, but before I had a chance to examine the clarinet, a white envelope fluttered to the floor, and I realized that my troubles were only just beginning. It was the letter from the draft board. Not only had I forgotten the date of my physical, I had forgotten that the letter had been sent to me. In that one instant, everything closed in on me again. I was probably a fugitive from justice, I thought. If I had missed the physical, then the government would already have issued a warrant for my arrest—and that meant there would be hell to pay, consequences I could not even imagine. I tore open the envelope and found the date that had

**consciously** purposely, intentionally **to strive** to do s.th. with great effort **saint** Heilige(r) **breadth** how wide s.th. is **margin** here: Spielraum **to bubble** Blasen bilden **to crack apart** to break apart so lines appear on the surface **to seep** to flow through small holes or spaces **to flutter** to move gently in the air **draft board** a board (Einberufungsausschuss) of local citizens that selected young men in their community between 18 and 26 to serve in the U.S. Armed Forces. At that time there was compulsory service (allgemeine Wehrpflicht) for young men. **physical** physical examination (Musterung) **fugitive** s.o. hiding from the police so as not to be caught **justice** the courts and police **to issue a warrant** einen Haftbefehl ausstellen **hell to pay** very serious consequences

been typed into the blank on the form letter: September 16. This meant nothing to me, since I no longer knew what day it was. I had lost the habit of looking at clocks and calendars, and I couldn't even make a guess.

"One small question," I said to Zimmer, who was still bent over his work. "Do you happen to know what day it is?"

"It's Monday," he said, without looking up.

"I mean the date. The month and the number. You don't have to give me the year. I'm fairly certain of that."

"September fifteenth," he said, still not bothering to look up.

"September fifteenth?" I said. "Are you sure of that?"

"Of course I'm sure. Beyond a shadow of a doubt."

I sank back onto the pillow and closed my eyes. "It's extraordinary," I muttered. "It's absolutely extraordinary."

Zimmer turned from his desk at last and gave me a puzzled look. "Why on earth should it be extraordinary?"

"Because it means I'm not a criminal."

"What?"

"Because it means I'm not a criminal."

"I heard you the first time. Saying it again doesn't make it any clearer."

I held up the letter and waved it in the air. "Once you look at this," I said, "you'll understand what I mean."

I was due to report at Whitehall Street the next morning. Zimmer had already been through his physical in July (he had been given a deferment because of asthma), and we spent the next two or three hours discussing what was in store for me. It was essentially the same conversation that millions of young men in America had during those years. Unlike the vast majority of them, however, I had done nothing to prepare myself for the moment of truth. I did not have a note from a doctor, I had not gorged myself on drugs to distort my motor responses, I had not staged a series of mental breakdowns to establish a history of psychological disturbance. I had always known that I would never join the army, but once

**blank** empty space **due** expected **Whitehall Street** street near the southern tip of Manhattan where indeed physical examinations by the American Armed Forces were carried out **deferment** here: a formal notice by the draft board that one is not qualified to serve in the armed forces because of mental or physical problems—however, service could be possible in the future **in store** s.th. that is about to happen **to gorge yourself on s.th.** to eat so much that your stomach is quickly filled **to distort** to alter or change so that s.th. seems different or strange **motor responses** normal reactions of the body **to stage** to plan or organize

I reached that conclusion, I had not given the subject much thought. As with so many other things, inertia had got the better of me, and I had steadfastly shut the problem out of my mind. Zimmer was appalled, but even he was forced to admit that it was too late to do anything about it now. I would either pass the physical or flunk it, and if I passed, there were only two options available to me: I could leave the country or go to prison. Zimmer told a number of stories about people who had gone abroad, to Canada, to France, to Sweden, but I wasn't terribly interested. I had no money, I said, and I wasn't in the mood to travel.

"So you'll turn out to be a criminal anyway," he said.

"A prisoner," I corrected him. "A prisoner of conscience. There's a difference."

I was still in the first stages of recovery, and when I stood up the next morning to get dressed—in Zimmer's clothes, which were several sizes too small for me—I realized that I was in no shape to be going anywhere. I was utterly depleted, and just trying to walk across the room demanded all my energy and concentration. Until then, I hadn't been out of bed for more than a minute or two at a time, groping my way feebly to the toilet and back. If Zimmer hadn't been there to hold me up, I doubt that I would have made it out the door. He literally kept me on my feet, walking me down the stairs with both arms around my body and then letting me lean on him as we staggered along to the subway. It was a sad and gruesome spectacle, I'm afraid. Zimmer took me to the front door of the building on Whitehall Street and then pointed to a restaurant directly opposite, where he said I could find him after I was done. He squeezed my arm for encouragement. "Don't worry," he said. "You'll make a hell of a soldier, Fogg. It's written all over you." "You're fucking right," I answered. "Best fucking soldier in the whole goddamned Army. Any

**inertia** [ɪ'nɜːrʃə] lack of energy and a feeling that you do not want to do anything **to get the better of s.o.** to make s.o. behave in a way that one would not normally behave **appalled** very shocked **to flunk** (AE coll) to fail a test **prisoner of conscience** a person in prison only for his/her political or religious beliefs **recovery** process of getting better after an illness, etc. **in no shape** in no condition **utterly** completely **depleted** here: with no strength left **to grope** to find your way with your hands **feebly** weakly **literally** actually, really **to stagger** to walk with difficulty as if about to fall **gruesome** shocking and unpleasant **spectacle** unusual scene **to squeeze** to press firmly **encouragement** saying or doing s.th. to give s.o. more courage or confidence to do s.th.

fool can see that." I gave Zimmer a mock salute and then tottered into the building clinging to the walls for support.

Much of what followed is lost to me now. Bits and pieces remain, but nothing that adds up to a full-fledged memory, nothing that I can talk about with any conviction. This inability to see what happened proves how wretchedly frail I must have been. It took all my strength just to stand there, trying not to fall down, and I did not pay attention as I should have. I think, in fact, that my eyes were mostly shut during those hours, and when I did manage to open them, it was seldom long enough for the world to get in. There were fifty or a hundred of us who marched through the process together. I remember sitting at a desk in a large room and listening to a sergeant talk to me, but I can't remember what he said, am unable to bring back a single word of it. They gave us forms to fill out, and then there was a written test of some kind, although it's possible that the test came first and the forms second. I remember checking off the organizations I had belonged to and taking some time with that: SDS from college, SANE and SNCC from high school, and then having to explain the circumstances of my arrest the year before. I was the last one in the room to finish, and by the end the sergeant was standing over my shoulder, muttering something about Uncle Ho and the American flag.

After that, there is a break of several minutes, perhaps half an hour. I see corridors, fluorescent lights, clusters of young men standing around in their underpants. I can remember the intense vulnerability I felt then, but numerous other details have vanished. Where we changed out of our

**mock** as if the real thing, but to make fun of s.th. **to totter** to walk with difficulty from side to side as if about to fall **full-fledged** completely developed **conviction** the feeling of being sure about s.th. and having no doubts **wretchedly** horribly, extremely **frail** thin and weak **to check off** (AE) to make a mark next to a list (BE to tick off) **SDS** Students for a Democratic Society, a student organization in the 1960s that became increasingly radical and was opposed to the Vietnam war **SANE** The National Committee for Sane Nuclear Policy, founded in 1957 to stop nuclear testing and prevent a nuclear war **SNCC** Student Nonviolent Coordination Committee—founded in the late 50s and continuing into the 60s. A black civil rights movement often active in the South, it became increasingly radical. **circumstances** time, place, etc., that accompanies or influences an event or condition **to mutter** to speak in a low voice that is difficult to understand **Uncle Ho** so named by Vietnam protestors, the leader of the North Vietnam Communist government Ho Chi Minh (1890-1969) **American flag** Vietnam protestors often burned the American flag. **fluorescent light** Leuchtstofflampe **intense** very strong **vulnerability** state of being capable of being physically or emotionally wounded or hurt

clothes, for example, and what we said to each other as we waited in line. More specifically, I have been unable to conjure up any images concerning our feet. Above the knees we had nothing on but our jockey shorts, but everything below them remains a mystery to me. Were we allowed to wear our shoes and/or our socks, or did they make us walk through those halls barefooted? I draw nothing but blanks on this subject, cannot detect even the faintest glimmer.

Eventually, I was told to enter a room. A doctor thumped me on the chest and back, looked into my ears, grabbed hold of my balls and asked me to cough. These things required little effort, but then it was time for him to take a blood sample, and suddenly the examination became more eventful. I was so anemic and emaciated that the doctor couldn't find a vein in my arm. He poked a needle into me two or three times, jabbing and bruising my skin, but no blood flowed into the tube. I must have looked awful by then—all pale and queasy, like someone on the verge of blacking out—and after a while he gave up and told me to sit down on a bench. He was rather kind about it, I believe, or at least indifferent. "If you feel dizzy again," he said, "just sit on the floor and wait until it passes. We don't want you falling down and hitting your head, do we?"

I distinctly remember sitting on the bench, but after that I see myself lying on a table in another room. It is impossible to know how much time elapsed between these two events. I don't think I fainted, but when they tried to get blood from me again, they probably didn't want to take any chances. A rubber cord was secured around my bicep to make the vein stand out, and when the doctor finally got the needle in—I can't remember if it was the same doctor or another one—he said something about how thin I was and asked if I had eaten breakfast that morning. In

**in line (AE)** in a queue (BE) **to conjure up** to make s.th. reappear especially in a magic trick **jockey shorts** Jockey (trademark) underwear for men **to draw nothing but a blank** to be unsuccessful in attempting to find an answer or information **to detect** to notice or discover something difficult to find **faint** very small, hardly noticeable **glimmer** normally: a very weak light; here: any kind of sign **to thump** to hit very hard with your fist **balls** (slang) testicles (Hoden) **anemic** [əˈniː.mɪk] with the blood having too few red blood cells **emaciated** extremely thin because of too little food or illness **vein** Vene **to poke** to stick into **to jab** to poke or thrust sharply **to bruise** [uː] to injure so that a brown or purple mark appears on the skin **queasy** felling as if you have to vomit **on the verge of** about to **to black out** to faint, to become unconscious **dizzy** schwindlig **distinctly** clearly **to elapse** to pass **to secure** to tie or fasten on s.th. firmly **bicep** [ˈbaɪ.sep] i.e. biceps

what was surely my most lucid moment of the day, I turned to him and gave the simplest, most heartfelt answer I could think of. “Doctor,” I said, “do I look like someone who can go without eating breakfast?”

There was more, there must have been a lot more, but I can’t pin down much of it. They gave us lunch somewhere (in the building? in a restaurant outside the building?), but the only thing I remember about the meal is that no one wanted to sit next to me. In the afternoon, back in the corridors upstairs, they finally got around to measuring and weighing us. I tipped the scales at some ridiculously low figure—112 pounds, I think it was, or perhaps 115. From that point on I was separated from the rest of the group. They sent me in to see a psychiatrist, a pudgy man with squat, truncated fingers, and I remember thinking that he looked more like a wrestler than a doctor. There was no question of telling him lies. I had already entered my new period of potential sainthood, and the last thing I wanted was to do something I would regret later. The psychiatrist sighed once or twice during our conversation, but other than that he seemed unperturbed by my remarks or my appearance. I imagined that he was an old hand at these interviews by now, and there wasn’t much that could upset him anymore. For my part, I was rather surprised by the vagueness of his questions. He asked me if I took drugs, and when I told him no, he raised his eyebrows and asked me again, but I gave him the same answer the second time and he didn’t pursue it. Standard questions followed after that: what my bowel movements looked like, whether or not I had nocturnal emissions, how often did I think of suicide. I answered as simply as I could, without embellishment or commentary. As I spoke, he checked off little boxes on a sheet of paper and did not look up at me. There was something that comforted me about discussing such intimate matters in this way—as though I were talking to an accountant or a garage mechanic. When he reached the bottom of the page, how-

**lucid** [u:] being able to think clearly **heartfelt** very strongly felt and sincere **to pin down** to be able to describe clearly **to tip the scales** to weigh (usually before a boxing or wrestling match) **ridiculously** absurdly **112 pounds** 51 kg (1 kg = 2.2 pounds) **pudgy** rather fat **squat** short and broad **truncated** shorter than usual as if having been cut off **wrestler** Ringer **potential** what may happen in the future, possible **sainthood** Heiligkeit **unperturbed** not worried or upset because s.th. has happened **old hand** s.o. with a lot of experience **to pursue** to continue to ask about s.th. **bowel movement** Stuhlgang **nocturnal emission** release of semen (Samen) during sleep **suicide** the act of killing yourself **embellishment** addition of unnecessary details **commentary** explanatory comments **accountant** Buchhalter

ever, the doctor raised his eyes again and fixed them on me for a good four or five seconds.

"You're in pretty sorry shape, son," he finally said.

"I know that," I said. "I haven't been very well. But I think I'm getting better now."

"Do you want to talk about it?"

"If you like."

"You can start by telling me about your weight."

"I've had the flu. I caught one of those stomach things a couple of weeks ago and haven't been able to eat."

"How much weight have you lost?"

"I don't know. Forty or fifty pounds, I think."

"In two weeks?"

"No, it's taken about two years. But most of it came off this summer."

"Why was that?"

"Money, for one thing. I haven't had enough money to buy food."

"You don't have a job?"

"No."

"Have you been looking for one?"

"No."

"You'll have to explain that to me, son."

"It's a fairly complicated business. I don't know if you'll be able to understand."

"Let me be the judge of that. Just tell me what happened and don't worry about how it sounds. We're not in any rush."

For some reason, I felt an overpowering urge to pour out my story to this stranger. Nothing could have been more inappropriate, but before I had a chance to stop myself, words were coming out of my mouth. I could feel my lips moving, but at the same time it was as though I was listening to someone else. I heard my voice rattling on about my mother, about Uncle Victor, about Central Park and Kitty Wu. The doctor nodded politely, but it was obvious that he had no idea what I was talking about. As I continued to explain the life I had lived for the past two years, I could see that he was actually becoming uncomfortable. This frustrated me, and the more his incomprehension showed, the more desperately I

**sorry shape** very bad physical condition **let me be the judge of that** let me form my own opinion **overpowering** strong, intense **inappropriate** not suitable, not correct **to rattle on** to talk quickly for a long time, about things that are not interesting **incomprehension** inability to understand s.th.

tried to make things clear to him. I felt that my humanity was somehow at stake. It didn't matter that he was an army doctor; he was also a human being, and nothing was more important than getting through to him. "Our lives are determined by manifold contingencies," I said, trying to be as succinct as possible, "and every day we struggle against these shocks and accidents in order to keep our balance. Two years ago, for reasons both personal and philosophical, I decided to give up the struggle. It wasn't because I wanted to kill myself—you mustn't think that—but because I thought that by abandoning myself to the chaos of the world, the world might ultimately reveal some secret harmony to me, some form or pattern that would help me to penetrate myself. The point was to accept things as they were, to drift along with the flow of the universe. I'm not saying that I managed to do this very well. I failed miserably, in fact. But failure doesn't vitiate the sincerity of the attempt. If I came close to dying, I nevertheless believe that I'm a better person for it."

It was a horrible botch. My language became increasingly awkward and abstract, and eventually I could see that the doctor had stopped listening. He was staring at some invisible point above my head, his eyes clouded over in a mixture of confusion and pity. I don't know how many minutes my monologue went on, but it lasted long enough for him to determine that I was a hopeless case—an authentically hopeless case, and not one of the spurious madmen he had been trained to detect. "That will do, son," he finally said, cutting me off in midsentence. "I think I'm beginning to get the picture." For the next minute or two I sat silently in my chair, shaking and sweating as he scribbled a note on a piece of official stationery. He folded it in half and then handed it to me across the desk. "Take this to the commanding officer down the hall," he said, "and tell the next person to come in on your way out."

I remember walking down the hall with the note in my hand, struggling against the temptation to look at it. It was impossible not to feel that I was being watched, that there were people in the building who could

**humanity** Menschlichkeit **at stake** at risk **manifold** a great many **contingency** an event or situation that might happen in the future, especially that might cause problems **succinct** clearly expressed in a few words **to abandon oneself to s.th.** to no longer act and allow yourself to be controlled by s.th. **ultimately** finally **to reveal** to show s.th. that was hidden before **to penetrate** here: to understand **to vitiate** to reduce the effect **sincerity** honest motives **botch** failure **awkward** clumsy, poorly done **to cloud over** to seem to become troubled **spurious** not genuine or real **to scribble** to write very quickly **stationary** paper for writing letters on **temptation** a strong desire to have or do something even though you know you should not

read my thoughts. The commanding officer was a large man in full uniform with a jigsaw puzzle of medals and decorations on his chest. He looked up from a pile of papers on his desk and casually waved me in. I handed him the psychiatrist's note. As soon as he glanced at it, he broke into a big toothy grin. "Thank goodness," he said. "You just saved me a couple of days' work." Without any further explanation, he started tearing up the papers on his desk and throwing them into the trash basket. He seemed enormously satisfied. "I'm glad you flunked, Fogg," he said. "We were going to have to do a full-scale investigation on you, but now that you're unfit, we won't have to bother."

"Investigation?" I said.

"All those organizations you belonged to," he said, almost merrily. "We can't have pinko subversives and agitators in the army, can we? It's not good for morale."

I don't remember the precise sequence of events after that, but a short time later I found myself sitting in a room along with the other misfits and rejects. There must have been a dozen of us in there, and I don't think I've ever seen a more pathetic bunch of people gathered in one place. One boy, with hideous acne all over his face and back, sat trembling in a corner talking to himself. Another had a withered arm. Another, who weighed no less than three hundred pounds, stood against a wall making farting noises with his lips, laughing after each outburst like a troublesome seven-year-old. These were the simpletons, the grotesques, the young men who did not belong anywhere. I was almost unconscious with fatigue by then and did not talk to any of them. I settled into a chair by the door and closed my eyes. The next time I opened them, an officer was shaking my arm and telling me to wake up. You can go home now, he said, it's all over.

I walked across the street in the late-afternoon sun. Zimmer was waiting for me in the restaurant, just as he had promised.

**commanding officer** the officer in charge of a unit **jigsaw puzzle** Puzzlespiel **casually** in a way not seeming to care **to glance** to look at s.th. once **full-scale** to the fullest amount **pinko** (AE slang) leftist **subversive** s.o. who secretly supports action against the government **misfit** s.o. who doesn't fit into society because of being so different **reject** s.o. who has not been accepted because of being below standards **pathetic** causing you to feel sorry or sympathy **bunch** group **hideous** horrible, ugly **withered** thin and weak, not properly developed **outburst** sudden activity **troublesome** causing a lot of trouble **simpleton** s.o. with very little intelligence **unconscious** bewusstlos **to settle into** to sit down so as to make oneself comfortable settle

I gained weight rapidly after that. Within the next ten days or so, I believe I put on eighteen or twenty pounds, and by the end of the month I was beginning to resemble the person I had once been. Zimmer fed me conscientiously, stocking the refrigerator with all kinds of food, and when I seemed steady enough to venture out of the apartment again, he began taking me to a local bar every night, a dark and quiet place without much traffic, where we would drink beer and watch the ball games on TV. The grass was always blue on that TV, the bats were a fuzzy orange, and the players looked like clowns, but it was pleasant to be huddled there in our little booth, talking for hours on end about the things that lay before us. It was an exquisitely tranquil period in both our lives: a brief moment of standing still before moving on again.

It was during those talks that I began to learn something more about Kitty Wu. Zimmer found her remarkable, and it was hard not to hear the admiration in his voice when he spoke of her. Once, he even went so far as to say that if he hadn't already been in love with someone else, he would have fallen head over heels for her. She was as close to perfection as any girl he had ever met, he said, and when it came right down to it, the only thing that puzzled him about her was how she could have been attracted to such a dreary specimen as me.

"I don't think she's attracted to me," I said. "She just has a good heart, that's all. She took pity on me and did something about it—in the same way other people take pity on wounded dogs."

"I saw her every day, M. S. Every day for almost three weeks. She couldn't stop talking about you."

"That's absurd."

"Believe me, I know what I'm talking about. The girl is madly in love with you."

"Then why doesn't she come to see me?"

"She's busy. Her classes have started at Juilliard, and she has a part-time job as well."

"I didn't know that."

**conscientiously** with a lot of care and attention **to stock** to provide a supply of s.th. that has been bought **to venture out** to risk going out where there might be danger **without much traffic** here: without many customers coming in and out **bat** Schläger (in baseball) **fuzzy** not clear **to huddle** to gather close together **booth** (AE) a partly enclosed place in a restaurant with a table between two long seats **tranquil** peaceful **head over heels** suddenly and passionately **to come right down to it** to consider the most important aspect of s.th. **dreary** sad, dull **specimen** here: individual **M.S.** Marco Stanley, cf. beginning of novel

"Of course not. That's because you don't know anything. You lie around in bed all day, you visit the refrigerator, you read my books. Every once in a while, you take a stab at doing the dishes. How could you possibly know anything?"

"I'm gaining strength. In a few more days I'll be back to normal."

"Physically. But your mind still has a long way to go."

"What does that mean?"

"It means you've got to look under the surface, M. S. You've got to use your imagination."

"I always thought I did too much of that. I'm trying to be more realistic now, more down to earth."

"With yourself, yes, but you can't do that with other people. Why do you think Kitty's backed off? Why do you think she doesn't come around to see you anymore?"

"Because she's busy. You just told me that."

"That's only part of it."

"You're going around in circles, David."

"I'm just trying to show you that there's more to it than you think."

"All right, then, what's the other part?"

"Discretion."

"That's the last word I'd use to describe Kitty. She's probably the most open and spontaneous person I've ever met."

"That's true. But underneath all that, there's a tremendous reserve, a real delicacy of feeling."

"She kissed me the first time I saw her, did you know that? Just as I was about to leave, she cut me off at the door, flung her arms around me, and planted a big kiss on my lips. That's hardly what I would call delicate or reserved."

"Was it a good kiss?"

"As a matter of fact, it was an extraordinary kiss. It was one of the best kisses I've ever had the pleasure to experience."

"You see? That proves my point exactly."

"It doesn't prove anything. It was just one of those things that happens on the spur of the moment."

**to take a stab at s.th.** (coll) to try to do s.th. **to back off** to stay away, to withdraw **tremendous** great **delicacy** sensitivity **to cut s.o. off** to stop s.o. from going farther **to fling/flung/flung** to throw **to plant** to put on s.th. firmly **delicate** fine, with great care **on the spur of the moment** done suddenly without thinking

"No, Kitty knew what she was doing. She's someone who follows her impulses, but those impulses are also a form of knowledge."

"You sound awfully sure of yourself."

"Put yourself in her position. She falls in love with you, she kisses you on the lips, she drops everything to go out and find you. But what have you done for her? Not a thing. Not even the shadow of a thing. What separates Kitty from other people is that she's willing to accept that. Just imagine it, Fogg. She saves your life, and yet you don't owe her anything. She doesn't expect gratitude from you. She doesn't even expect friendship. She might wish for those things, but she'll never ask for them. She has too much respect for other people to force them into doing things against their will. She's open and spontaneous, but at the same time she'd rather die than have you feel she's throwing herself at you. That's where discretion comes into it. She's gone far enough, and at this point she has no choice but to hold her ground and wait."

"What are you trying to say?"

"That it's up to you, Fogg. You're the one who has to make the next move."

According to what Kitty had told Zimmer, her father had been a Kuomintang general in pre-Revolutionary China. Back in the thirties, he had held the position of mayor or military governor of Peking. Although he was a member of Chiang Kai-shek's inner circle, he had once saved Chou En-lai's life by offering him a safe conduct out of the city after Chiang had entrapped him there on the pretext of arranging a meeting between

**shadow of a thing** even the slightest thing **to owe s.o. s.th.** to feel you have to do or give s.th. to s.o. because this person has helped you **gratitude** the feeling of being grateful **to hold one's ground** to take no further action and wait and see what happens **according to** laut, nach **Kuomintang** [ˌkwoʊ.mɪnˈtæŋ] Nationalist Party (Guomindang) that ruled China from 1928 to 1949 under the leadership of general Chiang Kai-shek (1887-1975). Becoming increasingly corrupt and conservative the party was forced to move to the island off China, Taiwan when the Communists—in a civil war—took over China in 1949-1950. **pre-Revolutionary China** i.e. before the Communists took over 1949-1950 **mayor** Oberbürgermeister **Chou En-lai** [ˌtʃoʊ.enˈlaɪ] Zhou Enlai (1898-1976) a pragmatic western educated Chinese Communist leader, who originally worked with Chiang Kaishek. There was an attempt on Zhou Enlai's life near Shanghai in 1927 that was planned by Chiang Kaishek. One of the many theories about why he could escape was because of a sympathetic Kuomintang general. He was foreign minister of China from 1949 to 1958. **safe conduct** official protection for s.o. when he/she is passing through a dangerous area **to entrap** to put into a trap (Falle) by using tricks **on the pretext** for a false reason

the Kuomintang and the Communists. Still, the general remained loyal to the Nationalist cause, and after the Revolution he made the move to Taiwan along with the rest of Chiang's followers. The Wu household was enormous, consisting of an official wife, two concubines, five or six children, and a full staff of domestic servants. Kitty was born to the second concubine in February 1950, and sixteen months later, when General Wu was appointed ambassador to Japan, the family moved to Tokyo. This was undoubtedly a clever move on Chiang's part: to honor the fractious, outspoken general with such an important post, and at the same time to remove him from the center of power in Taipei. General Wu was in his late sixties by then, and his days as a man of influence were apparently over.

Kitty spent her childhood in Tokyo, was sent to American schools, which accounted for her flawless English, and was given every advantage her privileged circumstances could offer: ballet lessons, American Christmas, chauffeur-driven cars. For all that, it was a lonely childhood. She was ten years younger than her nearest half-sister, and one of her brothers, a banker who lived in Switzerland, was a full thirty years older than she was. Worse than that, her mother's position as second concubine left her with scarcely more power in the family hierarchy than one of the servants. The sixty-four-year-old wife and the fifty-two-year-old first concubine were jealous of Kitty's young and attractive mother and did everything they could to weaken her status in the household. As Kitty explained it to Zimmer, it was a little like living in an imperial Chinese court, with all its attendant rivalries and factions, its secret machinations, its silent plots and false smiles. The general himself was rarely to be seen. When not occupied with his official duties, he spent most of his time cultivating the affections of various young women of less than reputable character. Tokyo was a city rich in temptation, and the opportunities for

**to appoint** to choose someone for a position or a job **move** s.th. you decide to do, an action taken **fractious** easily irritated **outspoken** expressing one's opinion even if unpopular **to account for** to be the reason for **flawless** with no mistakes **for all that** in spite of all that **imperial** kaiserlich **court** Hof **attendant** accompanying, taking place as a result **faction** small group within a larger group that disagrees with the larger group **machinations** secret and clever plans **plot** a secret plan to doing s.th. harmful or illegal **to cultivate** to try to make friends with s.o. because you want s.th. from him/her **affection** a feeling of fondness or tenderness for a person or thing

such dalliances were inexhaustible. Eventually, he took on a mistress, set her up in a fashionable apartment, and spent lavish sums in order to keep her happy: shelling out for clothes, for jewelry, and finally a sports car. In the long run, however, these things were not enough, and not even a painful and expensive potency cure could reverse the tide. The mistress's attentions began to wander, and one night, when the general walked in on her unannounced, he found her in the arms of a younger man. The battle that ensued was horrific: shrieking voices, sharp fingernails, a torn and bloody shirt. It was the last illusion of a foolish old man. The general went home, hung up his tattered shirt in the middle of his room, and attached a sheet of paper to it with the date of the incident: October 14, 1959. He kept it there for the rest of his life, relishing it as a monument to his destroyed vanity.

At some point, Kitty's mother died, although Zimmer was unclear as to the causes or circumstances. The general was past eighty then and in failing health, but in a last flurry of concern for his youngest daughter, he arranged to have her sent to boarding school in America. Kitty was just fourteen when she arrived in Massachusetts to enter the freshman class of the Fielding Academy. Given who she was, it did not take her long to fit in and find a place for herself. She acted and danced, she made friends, she studied hard enough to get decent grades. By the time her four years there had ended, she knew that she would not be going back to Japan. Nor to Taiwan for that matter, or anywhere else. America had become her country, and by juggling the small inheritance she received after her

**dalliance** flirtation **inexhaustible** endless **to take on** to hire or employ **mistress** a woman who has a sexual relationship with a man who is married **to set s.o. up** to make the necessary arrangements for s.o. **lavish** large and generous **to shell out** (coll) to pay a lot of money for s.th. **potency cure** [ˈpoʊ.tənt.sɪ kjʊr] any method or medicine that increases a man's ability to have sex **to reverse the tide** reverse = to change s.th. so that it returns to an earlier and better state, tide = Gezeiten, i.e. to become younger again **to ensue** [enˈsuː] to follow **to shriek** to scream or shout loudly with a high voice **tattered** torn **to relish** to enjoy **vanity** quality of having too much pride **failing** becoming increasingly worse **flurry** a period of sudden quick action **boarding school** school where students can also live **freshman** (AE) first year at a college or university **Fielding Academy** does not exist; cf. the English writer Henry Fielding (1707-1754) and his picaresque novel *Tom Jones* **given** considering **to fit in** to be accepted by other people in a group **decent** good, acceptable **to juggle** here: to carefully spend **inheritance** money or property you receive from s.o. who has died—Auster received an inheritance from his father when he died that permitted him to start his career as a writer.

father's death, she had managed to cover the tuition costs at Juilliard and move to New York. She had been in the city for more than a year now and was just starting her second full year of classes.

"It sounds familiar, doesn't it?" Zimmer asked.

"Familiar?" I said. "It's one of the most exotic stories I've ever heard."

"Only on the surface. Scratch away some of the local color, and it boils down to almost the same story of someone else I know. Give or take a few details, of course."

"Mmm, yes, I see what you mean. Orphans in the storm, that kind of thing."

"Exactly."

I paused for a moment to consider what Zimmer had said. "I suppose there are certain resemblances," I finally added. "But do you think she's telling the truth?"

"I have no way of knowing for sure. But based on what I've seen of her so far, I'd be pretty shocked if she wasn't."

I took another sip of beer and nodded. Much later, when I got to know her better, I learned that Kitty never lied about anything.

The longer I stayed with Zimmer, the more uncomfortable I began to feel. He footed the bill for my recovery, and while he never complained about it, I knew his finances were not so solid that he could go on doing it much longer. Zimmer received a little help from his family in New Jersey, but basically he had to fend for himself. Around the twentieth of the month, he began graduate school at Columbia in comparative literature. The university had lured him into the program with a fellowship—free tuition plus a two-thousand-dollar stipend—but even if that was a nice sum back in those days, it was hardly enough to live on for a year. Still, he went on taking care of me, dipping into his meager savings without

**tuition costs** (AE) money that has to be paid to a school or university to be a student there **local color** the details of a setting that often seem unusual or exotic **it boils down to** it is essentially **orphans in a storm** a common scene in the sentimental novels of the 18th and 19th centuries, cf. Charles Dickens (orphan = child without parents) **sip** a very small amount of drink **to foot the bill** to pay for s.th. **to fend for oneself** to look after oneself without outside help **graduate school** (AE) part of a university after the first four years where one can earn a master of arts or get a doctorate **fellowship** (AE) money given to a student to study in graduate school **stipend** [aɪ] money paid to a student to live on—Auster was offered a stipend at Columbia, but he turned it down. **to dip into** to use some of the money you have **meager** very small

compunction. Generous as Zimmer was, there must have been more to it than pure altruism. Going back to our first year together as roommates, I had always felt that he was somewhat intimidated by me, overwhelmed, so to speak, by the sheer intensity of my follies. Now that I had fallen on hard times, perhaps he saw it as an opportunity to gain the upper hand, to right the internal balance of our friendship. I doubt that Zimmer himself was even aware of it, but a certain edgy superiority had crept into his voice when he spoke to me now, and it was hard not to sense the pleasure he got from teasing me. I bore with it, however, and did not take offense. My estimation of myself had sunk so low by then that I secretly welcomed his badgering as a form of justice, as a richly deserved punishment for my sins.

Zimmer was a small, wiry person with curly black hair and a contained, upright posture. He wore the metal-rimmed glasses that were common among students back then and was in the early stages of growing a beard, which made him look something like a young rabbi. Of all the undergraduates I had known at Columbia, he was the most brilliant and conscientious, and there was no doubt that he had it in him to become a fine scholar if he stuck with it. We shared the same passion for obscure and forgotten books (Lycophron's *Cassandra*, Giordano Bruno's philosophical dialogues, the notebooks of Joseph Joubert, to mention just some of the things we discovered together), but whereas I tended to

**compunction** without a feeling of shame or guilt **altruism** the principle or practice of unselfish concern for the welfare of others **to be intimidated** to be made scared or timid **sheer** absolute **folly** stupid action **to fall on hard times** to have problems because of no longer having enough money **to gain the upper hand** to have more power than someone else, so that you are able to control a situation **to right** to correct **edgy** nervous, worried **to tease** to make fun of s.o., (necken, hänseln) **to bear/bore/born with s.th.** to continue with s.th. that is unpleasant **to take offense** to feel insulted because of what s.o. has said **estimation** opinion of the value of s.th. or s.o. **badgering** annoying s.o. repeatedly, especially by asking him/her to do something **wiry** ['waɪə.ri] slender and strong **contained** restrained, under control **posture** the way one holds one's body when standing or sitting **metal-rimmed** with a thin metal frame (Gestell) **conscientious** careful and hard-working **scholar** an expert in a non-scientific field such as literature **obscure** not well known **Lycophron** ['likə.frɑ:n] 3rd century BC Greek poet and scholar whose only surviving work is *Cassandra* or *Alexandra* **Giordano Bruno** (1558-1600) Italian philosopher and astronomer who was burned at the stake for believing the earth went round the sun **Joseph Joubert** 1754-1824) French essayist—all three men are mentioned in Auster's *The Book of Memory*

be crazily enthusiastic and scattered about these works, Zimmer was thorough and systematic, penetrating to a degree that often astonished me. For all that, he did not take any special pride in his critical talents, dismissing them as something of secondary importance. Zimmer's chief concern in life was writing poetry, and he spent long, hard hours at it, laboring over each word as if the fate of the world hung in the balance—which is surely the only sensible way to go about it. In many respects, Zimmer's poems resembled his body: compact, tightly sprung, inhibited. His ideas were so densely woven together that it was often difficult to make sense of them. Still, I admired the strangeness of the poems and the flintlike quality of their language. Zimmer trusted my opinions, and I was always as honest as possible when he asked for them, encouraging him as best I could, but at the same time refusing to mince words when something felt wrong to me. I had no literary ambitions of my own, and that probably made it easier. If I criticized his work, he knew it was not because of some unspoken competition between us.

He had been in love with the same person for the past two or three years, a girl by the name of Anna Bloom or Blume, I was never sure of the spelling. She had grown up across the street from Zimmer in the New Jersey suburbs and had been in the same class as his sister, which meant that she was a couple of years younger than he was. I had met her only once or twice, a diminutive, dark-haired girl with a pretty face and a bristling, animated personality, and had suspected that she was probably a bit too much for Zimmer's studious nature to handle. Earlier in the summer, she had suddenly taken off to join her older brother, William, who worked as a journalist in some foreign country, and since then Zimmer had not received a word from her—not a letter, not a postcard, nothing. As the weeks went by, he grew more and more desperate over this silence. Every day began with the same ritual of going downstairs to check the

**scattered** disorganized, chaotic **to penetrate** to carefully research **to dismiss** to refuse to consider seriously **to labor** work hard on s.th. **to hang in the balance** to be a serious situation where the result could easily be dangerous **tightly sprung** straff gefedert **inhibited** not relaxed enough to show one's emotions **densely** in closely set way **weave/wove/woven** weben, flechten **flintlike** flint-like: hard like a flint (a stone made of quartz) **to refuse to mince words** to openly express your opinion even if it offends s.o. **Ann Bloom/Blume** Anna Blume is mentioned in several poems by the German Dadaist Kurt Schwitters (1887-1948); Anna Blume is also the altruistic heroine in the dystopian novel *The Country of Last Things* **diminutive** small or short **bristling** aggressive **animated** lively **studious** [u:] serious, thoughtful, hard-working

mailbox, and each time he went in or out of the building there would be another obsessive opening and closing of the empty box. This could happen at any hour, even as late as two or three in the morning, when there was no earthly chance that anything new could have arrived. But Zimmer was powerless to resist the temptation. Many times, returning home from the White Horse Tavern around the corner, the two of us half drunk on beer, I would have to witness the painful sight of my friend fumbling for his mailbox key and then blindly reaching out his hand for something that was not there, for something that would never be there. Perhaps that was why Zimmer endured my presence in his apartment for so long. If nothing else, I was someone to talk to and to distract him from his troubles, an odd and unpredictable form of comic relief.

Still, I was a drain on his funds, and the longer he did not say anything about it, the worse I felt. My plan was to go out looking for a job as soon as I was strong enough (any job, it didn't matter what it was) and start paying back the money he had spent on me. That didn't solve the problem of finding another place to live, but at least I persuaded Zimmer to let me spend the nights on the floor so he could go back to sleeping in his own bed. A couple of days after we switched rooms, he started his classes at Columbia. One night during the first week, he came home with a large bundle of papers and grimly announced that a friend of his in the French department had been hired to do a rush translation which she now realized she didn't have time to do. Zimmer had asked if she would be willing to farm it out to him, and she had agreed. That was how the manuscript entered the house, a tedious document of about a hundred pages concerning the structural reorganization of the French consulate in New York. The moment Zimmer started telling me about it, I understood that I had found a chance to make myself useful. My French was as good as his, I explained, and since I wasn't terribly pressed with respon-

**no earthly chance** no chance at all **White Horse Tavern** old-fashioned bar (pub) on West 11th Street made famous by the Welsh writer Dylan Thomas **to witness** to see, to be present at **to fumble for** to try to find s.th. without using one's hands properly **to distract s.o.** here: to draw s.o.'s attention away from s.th. unpleasant **comic relief** a comic episode to reduce the tension in a serious play as is typical of many of Shakespeare's tragedies, e.g. *Macbeth*, *Hamlet*, etc. **to switch** to exchange **bundle** a number of things or a quantity of material gathered or loosely bound together **grimly** worriedly, unhappily because of s.th. unpleasant **to farm s.th. out to s.o.** to give s.o work instead of doing it oneself **tedious** boring **pressed** under pressure because of not having much time

sibilities at the moment, why didn't he hand the translation over to me and let me take care of it? Zimmer objected, but I was expecting that, and little by little I wore down his resistance. I wanted to square our account, I said, and doing this job was the quickest, most practical way to go about it. I would turn the money over to him, two or three hundred dollars, and at that point we would be even again. This last argument was the one that finally convinced him. Zimmer enjoyed playing the role of martyr, but once he understood that my own well-being was at stake, he relented.

"Well," he said, "I suppose we could split the money if it's so important."

"No," I said, "you still don't understand. All the money goes to you. It wouldn't make sense any other way. Every penny goes to you."

I got what I wanted, and for the first time in months I began to feel there was a purpose to my life again. Zimmer would wake up early to go uptown to Columbia, and for the rest of the day I was left to my own devices, free to plant myself at his desk and work without interruption. The text was abominable, filled with all kinds of bureaucratic gibberish, but the more trouble it gave me, the more defiantly I stuck to the task, refusing to let go of it until some semblance of meaning began to shine through the clumsy, garbled sentences. The difficulty of the job was what encouraged me. If the translation had been easier, I would not have felt that I was performing an adequate penance for my past mistakes. In some sense, then, the utter uselessness of the project was what gave it its value. I felt like someone who had been sentenced to a term of hard labor on a chain gang. My job was to take a hammer and smash stones into smaller

**to object** to protest **to wear/wore/worn down** to make s.o. less determined **to square our account** to pay back the money you gave me so I owe you nothing any more **martyr** [ˈmɑːr.tər] normally: someone who is killed or punished because of their religious or political beliefs; here s.o. who must suffer terribly **at stake** at risk **to split** to divide up **to be left to one's own devices** to leave s.o. alone so that this person can do what he/she wishes **to plant oneself** (coll) to place oneself somewhere **abominable** awful, terrible **gibberish** nonsense—Auster himself is quite fluent in French and translated similar texts as a student and later French poets **semblance** resemblance **clumsy** poorly constructed **garbled** confusing **penance** the act of willingly making yourself suffer, especially for religious reasons, to show you are sorry for having done s.th. wrong **utter** complete **to sentence s.o.** to give s.o. a punishment (by a judge) after having been found guilty in court **term** a period of time s.o. must spend in prison **hard labor** a punishment with hard physical work **chain gang** a group of prisoners chained together to work outside of prison **to smash** to break into small pieces stones, and once those stones had been smashed, to smash them into even smaller stones. There was no purpose to this labor. But the fact was that I wasn't interested in results. The labor was an end in itself, and I threw myself into it with all the determination of a model prisoner.

On days when the weather was good, I would sometimes go out for a brief stroll around the neighborhood to clear my head. It was October now, the best month of the year in New York, and I took pleasure in studying the early fall light, watching how it seemed to take on a new clarity as it slanted against the brick buildings. It was no longer summer, but winter still felt a long way off, and I savored this balance between hot and cold. Everywhere I went during those days, the streets were filled with talk of the Mets. It was one of those rare moments of unanimity when everyone was thinking about the same thing. People walked around with transistor radios tuned to the game, large crowds gathered in front of appliance store windows to watch the action on silent televisions, sudden cheers would erupt from corner bars, from apartment windows, from invisible rooftops. First it was Atlanta in the playoffs, and then it was Baltimore in the Series. Out of eight October games, the Mets lost only once, and when the adventure was over, New York held another ticker-tape parade, this one even surpassing the extravaganza that had been thrown for the astronauts two months earlier. More than five hundred tons of paper fell into the streets that day, a record that has not been matched since.

**brief** short **stroll** a leisurely walk **to take on** to begin to have the appearance of **clarity** clearness **to slant** to move at an angle (auf etwas schräg fallen) **brick** Backstein **to savor** to enjoy **unanimity** complete agreement—as opposed to the deep divisions in America because of the Vietnam war **tuned to** set to a certain station (on the radio) **appliance store** a store that sells electrical equipment such as refrigerators, washing machines, TVs, etc **to erupt** to suddenly start **Atlanta** the Atlanta Braves, which lost to the Mets **playoffs** games that decide which team in the National League and which team in the American League will play in the World Series **Baltimore** the Baltimore Orioles **Series** World Series that ended with the victory of the Mets in the last game of the Series on October 16, 1969 **lost only once** That was one game in the World Series. **parade** There actually was a ticker-tape parade for the Mets on October 20, 1969. **to surpass** to be greater than **extravaganza** any large and expensive entertainment **to throw for** (coll) to organize **astronauts** The astronauts who landed on the moon, but it was four months earlier.

I took to eating my lunches in Abingdon Square, a little park about a block and a half east of Zimmer's apartment. There was a rudimentary playground for children in there, and I enjoyed the contrast between the dead language of the report I was translating and the furious, hell-bent energy of the toddlers who stormed and squealed around me. I found that it helped to focus my concentration, and on several occasions I even took my work out there and translated while sitting in the midst of that bedlam. As it turned out, it was on one of those afternoons in mid-October that I finally saw Kitty Wu again. I was battling my way through a sticky passage, and I did not notice her until she had already sat down on the bench beside me. This was the first time I had seen her since Zimmer's lecture in the bar, and the suddenness of the encounter caught me with my guard down. I had spent the past few weeks imagining all the brilliant things I would say when I saw her again, but now that she was there in the flesh, I could barely get a word out of my mouth.

"Hello there, Mr. Writer," she said. "It's good to see you up and about again."

She was wearing sunglasses this time, and her lips were painted a bright shade of red. Because her eyes were invisible behind the dark lenses, it was all I could do not to stare directly at her mouth.

"I'm not really writing," I said. "It's a translation. Something I'm doing to earn a little money."

"I know. I ran into David yesterday, and he told me about it."

Bit by bit, I found myself relaxing into the conversation. Kitty had a natural talent for drawing people out of themselves, and it was easy to fall in with her, to feel comfortable in her presence. As Uncle Victor had once told me long ago, a conversation is like having a catch with someone. A good partner tosses the ball directly into your glove, making it almost impossible for you to miss it; when he is on the receiving end, he catches

**to take to doing s.th.** to start to do s.th. regularly **Abingdon Square** small triangular park near Bank Street in the West Village (where Zimmer had his apartment) **block** (AE) the distance along a city street from where one street crosses it to the next **rudimentary** very poorly equipped **hell-bent** wild **toddler** child who has just learned to walk **to squeal** to make high loud sounds **bedlam** a wild noisy place **sticky** difficult **passage** section **lecture** Vortrag **encounter** a meeting that was not planned **with one's guard down** unprepared **shade of red** a certain kind of red **lenses** the glass part of glasses you see through **to fall in with s.o.** to accept what a person does or says, to associate with s.o., to be in harmony with **catch** (baseball) throwing a baseball back and forth between two people just for fun or practice **to toss** to throw

everything sent his way, even the most errant and incompetent throws. That's what Kitty did. She kept lobbing the ball straight into the pocket of my glove, and when I threw the ball back to her, she hauled in everything that was even remotely in her area: jumping up to spear balls that soared above her head, diving nimbly to her left or right, charging in to make tumbling, shoestring catches. More than that, her skill was such that she always made me feel that I had made those bad throws on purpose, as if my only object had been to make the game more amusing. She made me seem better than I was, and that strengthened my confidence, which in turn helped to make my throws less difficult for her to handle. In other words, I started talking to her rather than to myself, and the pleasure of it was greater than anything I had experienced in a long time.

As we went on talking there in the October sunlight, I began trying to think of ways to prolong the conversation. I was too excited and happy to want it to end, and the fact that Kitty was carrying a large shoulder bag with bits of dance paraphernalia sticking out from the top—a leotard sleeve, a sweatshirt collar, the corner of a towel—made me worry that she was about to get up and rush off to another appointment. There was a hint of chill in the air, and after twenty minutes of talking on the bench, I noticed her shiver ever so slightly. Plucking up my courage, I made some remark about how it was getting cold, and perhaps we should go back to Zimmer's apartment where I could make us some hot coffee. Miraculously, Kitty nodded and said she thought that was a good idea.

I set about making the coffee. The living room was separated from the kitchen by the bedroom, and instead of waiting for me in the living room, Kitty sat down on the bed so that we could go on talking. The shift to the indoors had changed the tone of the conversation, and both of us became

**errant** away from a direct course **to lob** to throw high up **pocket** center of the glove where it is best to catch a baseball **to haul in** here: to catch s.th. that is even far away **even remotely** even a bit or slightly **to spear** (baseball) to catch with a sudden thrust of the arm **to soar** [sɔːr] to fly high in the sky **to dive** to suddenly bend down to catch **nimbly** quickly and lightly **to charge in** to move suddenly forward **to tumble** to fall suddenly **shoestring** (Schnürsenkel) **catch** (baseball) a catch close to or near the feet **in turn** seinerseits **to prolong** here: to try to make s.th. take place for a longer time **paraphernalia** different kinds of articles or equipment **leotard** [ˈliː.ə.tɑːrd] tight-fitting clothing worn over the whole body from the arms to the feet by dancers when practising **sleeve** Ärmel **chill** a feeling of coldness **to shiver** to shake slightly **to pluck up one's courage** to find the courage to do s.th. **miraculously** completely unexpectedly **shift** change **tone** quality, character

more quiet and tentative, as if searching for a way to interpret our new lines. There was an eerie sense of anticipation in the air, and I was glad to have the job of making coffee to mask the confusion that had suddenly taken hold of me. Something was about to happen, but I was too afraid to dwell on it, feeling that if I allowed myself to hope, the thing could be destroyed before it ever took shape. Then Kitty became very silent, said nothing for twenty or thirty seconds. I continued puttering around the kitchen, opening and closing the refrigerator, taking out cups and spoons, pouring milk into a pitcher, and so on. For a brief moment, my back was turned to Kitty, and before I was fully aware of it, she had left her seat on the bed and come into the kitchen. Without saying a word, she slid up behind me, put her arms around my waist, and leaned her head against my back.

"Who's that?" I said, pretending I didn't know.

"It's the Dragon Lady," Kitty said. "She's coming to get you."

I took hold of her hands, trying not to tremble as I felt the smoothness of her skin. "I think she's got me already," I said.

There was a slight pause, and then Kitty tightened her grip around my waist. "You do like me a little bit, don't you?"

"More than a little bit. You know that. A lot more than a little bit."

"I don't know anything. I've been waiting too long to know anything."

The whole scene had an imaginary quality to it. I knew that it was real, but at the same time it was better than reality, more nearly a projection of what I wanted from reality than anything I had experienced before. My desires were very strong, overpowering in fact, but it was only because of Kitty that they were given a chance to express themselves. Everything hinged on her responses, the subtle promptings and knowledge of her gestures, her lack of hesitation. Kitty was not afraid of herself, and she lived inside her body without embarrassment or second thoughts. Per-

**tentative** hesitant, uncertain, cautious **lines** here: any part of the text of a character in a play that an actor/actress must read or play on the stage **eerie** strange, weird, ghostly **to dwell on s.th.** to spend too much time thinking or talking about s.th. **to putter around** (AE) to busy yourself doing things that are not important **pitcher** (AE) large container with a handle to hold a liquid (Krug) **Dragon Lady** evil woman who appeared in a cartoon series in the 1940s, 50s, and 60s *Terry and the Pirates* **smoothness** flat and soft surface **to hinge on** to depend on **subtle** ['sʌt.l] cleverly done so that the real purpose is not immediately noticeable **prompting** hint, suggestion to say or do s.th. **second thoughts** doubts

haps it had something to do with her being a dancer, but more than likely it was the other way around. Because she took pleasure in her body, it was possible for her to dance.

We made love for several hours in the fading afternoon light of Zimmer's apartment. Without question, it was one of the most memorable things that had ever happened to me, and in the end I believe I was fundamentally altered by it. I am not just talking about sex or the permutations of desire, but some dramatic crumbling of inner walls, an earthquake in the heart of my solitude. I had become so accustomed to being alone that I did not think such a thing could ever happen. I had resigned myself to a certain kind of life, and then, for reasons that were totally obscure, this beautiful Chinese girl had dropped down in front of me, descending like an angel from another world. It would have been impossible not to fall in love with her, impossible not to be swept away by the simple fact that she was there.

After that, the days became more crowded for me. I worked on the translation in the morning and afternoon, and in the evening I would go off to meet Kitty, usually in the Columbia-Juilliard neighborhood uptown. If there was any difficulty, it was only because we didn't have much chance to be by ourselves. Kitty lived in a dormitory room that she shared with another student, and there was no door in Zimmer's apartment to shut off the bedroom from the living room. Even if there had been a door, it would have been unthinkable to take Kitty back there with me. Given the circumstances of Zimmer's love life at the moment, I wouldn't have had the heart to do it: inflicting the sounds of our lovemaking on him, forcing him to listen to our groans and sighs as he sat there in the next room. Once or twice, the Juilliard roommate went out for the evening, and we took advantage of her absence to stake out a claim to Kitty's narrow bed. On a number of other occasions, we had trysts in

**to fade** to slowly lose color and brightness **memorable** enjoyable, worth remembering **permutation** alteration, change **to crumble** to break into small pieces **to resign oneself to s.th.** to accept s.th. that you can't change **obscure** difficult to understand **to be swept away by s.th.** to become so interested in s.th. that one cannot think of anything else **Columbia-Julliard neighborhood** by the end of 1969, however, Julliard would move further downtown **uptown** area north of 59th Street in Manhattan **dormitory** (AE) building on campus where students can live **to inflict s.th. on s.o.** to make s.o. suffer because of s.th. **groan** Stöhnen **roommate** s.o. who shares a room with you **to stake out a claim** to publicly state that you have a right to s.th. (sich ein Anrecht auf etwas sichern) **tryst** [trɪst] an arrangement between lovers to meet at a secret place

empty apartments. Kitty was the one who worked out the details of these meetings, contacting friends and the friends of friends to ask them for the use of a bedroom for several hours. There was something frustrating about all this, but at the same time it was thrilling, a source of excitation that added an element of danger and uncertainty to our passion. We took chances with each other that strike me as impossible now, outrageous risks that easily could have led to the most embarrassing kind of trouble. Once, for example, we stopped an elevator between floors, and as the angry tenants of the building yelled and pounded because of the delay, I pulled down Kitty's jeans and panties and brought her to an orgasm with my tongue. Another time, we did it on the bathroom floor at a party, locking the door behind us and paying no attention to the people who were lined up in the hall, waiting their turn to use the john. It was erotic mysticism, a secret religion restricted to just two members. All through that early period of our affair, we had only to look at each other to become aroused. The moment Kitty came near me, I would start to think about sex. I found it impossible to keep my hands off her, and the more familiar her body became to me, the more I wanted to touch it. Once, we even went so far as to make love after one of Kitty's dance rehearsals, right in the dressing room after the others had left. She was scheduled to be in a performance the following month, and I tried to go to the evening rehearsals whenever I could. Watching Kitty dance was the next best thing to holding her, and I would follow her body around the stage with a kind of delirious concentration. I loved it, but at the same time I did not understand it. Dancing was utterly foreign to me, a thing that stood beyond the grasp of words, and I was left with no choice but to sit there in silence, abandoning myself to the spectacle of pure motion.

**thrilling** very exciting or stimulating **to strike s.o. as** to appear, to seem **tenant** s.o. who lives in a house or apartment and pays rent **to yell** to shout **to pound** to hit s.th. several times and make a lot of noise **delay** a situation in which s.o. has to wait **panties** women's underpants **the john** (AE) bathroom, toilet **mysticism** a belief that there is a reality beyond normal human understanding or experience that explains everything in the real world **to restrict** to limit **to become aroused** to become sexually excited **rehearsal** Probe **dressing room** room in a theater where actors or dancers get dressed for a performance **to be scheduled to do s.th.** here: to be expected to perform at a certain place and time according to a schedule **delirious** wildly excited, especially with joy or enthusiasm **beyond the grasp of words** to difficult to be expressed in words **to abandon yourself to s.th.** to allow strong feelings because of s.th. to take control **spectacle** a very unusual scene or show

I finished the translation at the end of October. Zimmer collected the money from his friend a few days later, and that night Kitty and I joined him for a meal at the Moon Palace. I was the one who chose the restaurant, more for its symbolic value than the quality of its food, but we ate well in spite of that, since Kitty spoke Mandarin to the waiters and was able to order dishes that were not on the menu. Zimmer was in good form that night, rattling on about Trotsky, Mao, and the theory of permanent revolution, and I remember how at a certain point Kitty put her head on my shoulder, smiling a languorous and beautiful smile, and how the two of us then leaned back against the cushions of the booth and let David run on with his monologue, nodding in agreement as he resolved the dilemmas of human existence. It was a superb moment for me, a moment of astonishing joy and equilibrium, as though my friends had gathered there to celebrate my return to the land of the living. Once the dishes had been cleared away, we all opened our fortune cookies and analyzed them with mock solemnity. Oddly enough, I can remember mine as though I were still holding it in my hands. It read: "The sun is the past, the earth is the present, the moon is the future." As it turned out, I was to encounter this enigmatic phrase again, which in retrospect made it seem that my chance discovery of it in the Moon Palace had been fraught with a weird and premonitory truth. For reasons I did not examine at the time, I stuck the little slip of paper into my wallet and carried it around with me for the next nine months, holding onto it long after I had forgotten it was there.

**Mandarin** official language of China spoken by a majority of educated Chinese **Trotsky** (1879-1940) Russian revolutionary and Communist theorist, assassinated by a Stalinist agent in Mexico **Mao** Mao Zedong (1893-1976) founder of the Chinese Communist party and head of the Chinese government after 1949 **permanent revolution** Mao Zedong's theory that there constantly has to be revolutions to prevent a bourgeois society from forming **languorous** [ˈlæŋ.gərəs] characterized by a pleasant feeling of tiredness **cushion** soft pillow to sit on **to resolve** to find a way to deal with s.th., to find a solution **equilibrium** a calm balance of feelings **fortune cookie** a small Chinese cookie containing a piece of paper that says what will happen to you in the future often served with dessert in a Chinese restaurant **mock** not real, pretended **solemnity** seriousness **oddly enough** it seems strange **"The sun…future."** a quote from Nikola Tesla (1856-1943) Serbian-born poet, eccentric, and physicist **enigmatic** mysterious **in retrospect** seen from the present **fraught** filled **premonitory** giving a warning that s.th. unpleasant will happen **slip** piece **wallet** small leather case for money you put in your pocket

In the morning, I started looking for a job. Nothing came of it that day, and the next day drew a similar blank. Realizing that the newspapers were not going to get me anywhere, I decided to go uptown to Columbia and try my luck at the student employment office. As an alumnus of the university, I was entitled to use this service, and since there were no fees to pay if they found you a job, it seemed like a sensible place to begin. Within ten minutes of entering Dodge Hall, I saw the answer to my problems typed out on an index card fastened to the lower left-hand corner of the bulletin board. The job description read as follows: "Elderly gentleman in wheelchair requires young man to serve as live-in companion. Daily walks, light secretarial duties. $50 per week plus room and board." This last detail was what clinched it for me. Not only could I start earning some money for myself, but I would be able to leave Zimmer's apartment at last. Even better, I would be moving to West End Avenue and Eighty-fourth Street, which meant that I would be much closer to Kitty. It seemed perfect. The job itself was not much to write home about, but the fact was that I had no home to write to anyway.

I called for an interview on the spot, afraid that someone else would beat me out for the position. Within two hours, I was sitting with my prospective employer in his living room, and by eight o'clock that night he called me at Zimmer's to tell me I had the job. He made it sound as though it had been a difficult decision for him and that I had been chosen over several other worthy candidates. In the long run, I doubt that it would have changed anything, but if I had known that he was lying then, I might have had a better idea of what I was getting into. For the truth was that there were no other candidates. I was the only person who had applied for the job.

**to draw a blank** to be unsuccessful **alumnus** [əˈlʌm.nəs] (AE) a former student of a school, college, or university **to be entitled to do s.th.** to be given the right to so s.th. **Dodge Hall** a building on the campus of Columbia University **index card** Karteikarte **bulletin board** (AE) noticeboard (BE) **room and board** (AE) a room to sleep in and meals **clinched it** (coll) made me finally decide to do it **West End Avenue** a quiet middle class street not far from the Hudson River **not much to write home about** a set expression, i.e. nothing very important **on the spot** immediately **prospective** likely

# 4

The first time I set eyes on Thomas Effing, he struck me as the frailest person I had ever seen. All bones and trembling flesh, he sat in his wheelchair covered in plaid blankets, his body slumped to one side like some minuscule broken bird. He was eighty-six years old, but he looked older than that, a hundred or more, if that is possible, an age beyond counting. Everything about him was walled off, remote, sphinxlike in its impenetrability. Two gnarled, liver-spotted hands gripped the armrests of the chair and occasionally fluttered into movement, but that was the only sign of conscious life. You could not even make visual contact with him, for Effing was blind, or at least he pretended to be blind, and on the day I went to his house for the interview, he was wearing two black patches over his eyes. As I look back on this beginning now, it seems appropriate that it should have taken place on November first. November first: the Day of the Dead, the day when unknown saints and martyrs are remembered.

**frail** thin and weak **plaid** with a pattern of squares that originally came from Scotland (tartan pattern) **slumped** collapsed, sunk **minuscule** [ˈmɪn.ə.skjuːl] extremely small **remote** distant in manner **sphinxlike** puzzling and mysterious like a sphinx **impenetrability** the "quality" or "characteristic" of being incapable of being understood **gnarled** [nɑːrld] twisted and rough **liver-spotted** mit Leberflecken **armrest** a support for the arms on a sofa or chair **conscious** alert and awake, aware of the surroundings **patch** a piece of material **appropriate** suitable for the occasion **November first** in the Roman Catholic Church All Saints' Day, when all the saints and martyrs are remembered **the Day of the Dead** Auster probably means November 2nd—in the Roman Catholic Church All Souls' Day, when people visit the family graves and remember the dead

It was a woman who answered the door to the apartment. She was a dowdy, heavyset person of indeterminate middle age, dressed in a billowy house frock decorated with pink and green flowers. Once she was quite certain that I was the Mr. Fogg who had called for an appointment at one o'clock, she extended her hand to me and announced that she was Rita Hume, Mr. Effing's nurse and housekeeper of the past nine years. As she did so, she looked me over thoroughly, studying me with the unabashed curiosity of a woman meeting her mail-order husband for the first time. There was something so forthright and amiable about these stares, however, that I did not take offense. It would have been hard to dislike Mrs. Hume, with her broad and doughy face, her powerful shoulders, and her two gigantic breasts, breasts so large that they seemed to be made of cement. She hauled around this cargo with an expansive, waddling sort of stride, and as she led me down the hallway toward the living room, I could hear her breath whistling in and out of her nostrils.

It was one of those enormous West Side apartment with long corridors, sliding oak partitions between rooms, and ornate moldings on the walls. There was a dense, Victorian clutter about the place, and I found it difficult to absorb the sudden plenitude of objects around me: the books and pictures and little tables, the jumble of carpets, the hodgepodge of woody dimness. Halfway down the hall, Mrs. Hume took hold of my

**dowdy** ['daʊ.di] unfashionable **heavyset** large and broad **indeterminate** impossible to know exactly **billowy** massive **frock** dress **appointment** Termin **to extend** to draw out, stretch **Hume** [hju:m] (1711-1776) Scottish philosopher and historian, for whom the only reality was what is perceived. Cause and effect can only be inferred (folgern) on the basis of perceived probability. **unabashed** not ashamed or embarrassed **mail-order** having to do with a business that sells goods and services by mail **forthright** not hesitating to speak the truth **amiable** pleasant and friendly **stare** the act of looking at s.th./s.o. fixedly **to take offense** to feel offended (beleidigt) **doughy** ['dəʊ.i] soft and pale **cement** Beton **to haul** to pull or carry s.th. heavy **cargo** (Fracht), i.e. her body **expansive** grand, open **to waddle** to walk with short steps, swinging from one side to another **stride** way of walking **nostrils** the holes in the nose one breathes through **West Side** area to the west of Central Park **oak** Eiche **partition** a door or screen that divides a room into two parts **ornate** elaborately decorated **molding** a thin decorative line of stone or wood around the edge of a wall **dense** many things closely packed together **Victorian** highly ornamented and massive as at the time of Queen Victoria **clutter** a disorderly mass of objects **to absorb** to understand a sudden large amount of information **plenitude** a large amount of s.th. **jumble** a disordered mass **hodgepodge** a large amount of things without any sensible order **dimness** gloominess, darkness

arm and whispered into my ear. "Don't be put off if he acts a little strange," she said. "He often gets carried away, but it doesn't really mean anything. He's had a rough time of it these past few weeks. The man who took care of him for thirty years died in September, and it's been hard for him to adjust."

I felt I had an ally in this woman, and that served as a kind of protection against whatever strange thing was about to happen. The living room was inordinately large, with windows that looked out onto the Hudson and the New Jersey Palisades beyond. Effing was sitting in his wheelchair in the middle of the room, positioned across from a sofa with a low table in between. Perhaps my initial impression of him was caused by the fact that he did not respond to us when we entered the room. Mrs. Hume announced that I had arrived, that "Mr. M. S. Fogg is here for the interview," but he did not say a word to her, did not even stir a muscle. It was a supernatural inertness, and my first reaction was to think he was dead. Mrs. Hume merely smiled at me, however, and gestured for me to take a seat on the sofa. Then she was gone, and I found myself alone with Effing, waiting for him to break the silence.

It took a long time, but when it finally came, his voiced filled the room with surprising force. It did not seem possible that his body could emit such sounds. The words crackled out of his windpipe with a furious, rasping kind of energy, and all of a sudden it was as if some radio had been switched on, tuned to one of those distant stations you sometimes capture in the middle of the night. It was totally unexpected. A chance synapse of electrons was carrying this voice to me from a thousand miles away, and the clarity of it stunned my ears. For a moment or

**to be put off** to be discouraged **to get carried away** to get so enthusiastic about s.th. that one doesn't know when to stop **a rough time of it** difficulties, unpleasant experiences **to adjust** to get used to a new situation **ally** s.o. who supports you in a difficult situation **Hudson** Hudson River between Manhattan and New Jersey **New Jersey Palisades** high cliffs on the west bank of the Hudson to the north of Manhattan **initial** first **to respond** to react **to stir** to move slightly **supernatural** impossible to explain by natural causes **inertness** inactivity **to gesture** to motion with the hands **to emit** to give or send forth **to crackle** to make a short sharp sound **windpipe** tube between the lungs and mouth through which winds passes **furious** extremely angry **to rasp** to make an unpleasant sound like that of two surfaces rubbing together **chance** happening by chance **synapse** ['sɪn.æps] a connection through which nerve impulses pass **to stun** to surprise or shock

two, I actually wondered if a ventriloquist wasn't hiding somewhere in the room.

"Emmett Fogg," the old man said, spitting out the words with contempt. "What kind of sissy name is that?"

"M. S. Fogg," I replied. "The M stands for Marco, the S is for Stanley."

"That's no better. If anything, it's worse. What are you going to do about it, boy?"

"I'm not going to do anything about it. My name and I have been through a lot together, and I've grown rather fond of it over the years."

Effing snorted at this, an ornery kind of laugh that seemed to dismiss the subject once and for all. Immediately after that he straightened himself up in his chair. It was remarkable how quickly this transformed his appearance. He was no longer a comatose semi-corpse lost in a twilight reverie; he had become all sinew and attention, a seething little mass of resurrected strength. As I eventually learned, this was the real Effing, if real is a word that can be used in talking about him. So much of his character was built on falsehood and deception, it was nearly impossible to know when he was telling the truth. He loved to trick the world with his sudden experiments and inspirations, and of all the stunts he pulled, the one he liked best was playing dead.

He leaned forward in his chair, as if to tell me the interview was about to begin in earnest. In spite of the black patches over his eyes, his gaze was directed straight at me. "Answer me, Mr. Fogg," he said. "Are you a man of vision?"

"I used to think I was, but I'm not so sure anymore."

"When you see a thing before your eyes, are you able to identify it?"

**ventriloquist** [ven'trɪl.ə.kwɪst] a person who can speak without moving his/her lips so as to make it appear the voice is coming from somewhere else **sissy** (coll) not manly **to grow fond of s.th./s.o.** to start to like s.th./s.o. very much **to snort** to express impatience or amusement by breathing air noisily through one's nose **ornery** stubborn, bad-tempered **to dismiss** to no longer consider **once and for all** completely **to straighten oneself up** to sit up **comatose** in the state of a coma **semi-corpse** half dead person **twilight** (fig) a time when the days just changes to night **reverie** ['revə.ri] daydreaming **sinew** ['sɪn.juː] muscle **to seethe** to be in a state of great activity **to resurrect** to return to life **falsehood** being dishonest and lying **deception** doing tricks **inspiration** being sudden stimulated to do s.th. creative **to pull a stunt** (coll) to suddenly do. s.th. to attract people's attention **in earnest** properly, as planned **gaze** a long steady look **man of vision** 1. a person who especially uses the sense of sight 2. a person who has great plans for the future

"More often than not, yes. But there are times when it becomes rather difficult."

"For example."

"For example, I sometimes have trouble distinguishing men from women in the street. So many people have long hair now, a quick glance doesn't always tell you enough. Especially when you find yourself looking at a feminine man or a masculine woman. The signals can get quite confused."

"And when you find yourself looking at me, what words come to you then?"

"I say that I'm looking at a man in a wheelchair."

"An old man?"

"Yes, an old man."

"A very old man?"

"Yes, a very old man."

"Have you noticed anything in particular about me, boy?"

"The patches over your eyes, I suppose. And the fact that your legs seem paralyzed."

"Yes, yes, my infirmities. They fairly jump out at you, don't they?"

"In a manner of speaking, yes."

"Have you drawn any conclusions about the patches?"

"Nothing definite. My first thought was that you were blind, but that doesn't really follow from the evidence. If a person can't see, why would he bother to make sure that he can't see? That wouldn't make sense. New possibilities therefore occur to me. Perhaps the patches cover something worse than blindness. A hideous deformity, for example. Or perhaps you've just had an operation and have to wear the patches for medical reasons. On the other hand, it could be that you're partially blind and that strong light irritates your eyes. Or it could be that you enjoy wearing patches for their own sake, because you think they're attractive. There are any number of possible answers to your question. At this point, I don't have enough information to say what that answer is. When it comes right down to it, the only thing I know for certain is that you're wearing

**to distinguish** to recognize the difference between two things **paralyzed** unable to move or feel a part of the body **infirmity** physical weakness **evidence** data that proves that s.th. is true or false **hideous** [ˈhɪd.i.əs] awful, extremely ugly **deformity** the condition when a part of the body does not have its normal shape **partially** not completely **for their own sake** just for the purpose of wearing patches **when it comes right down to it** in the final analysis, after everything has been considered

black patches over your eyes. I can state that they are there, but I don't know why they are there."

"In other words, you won't take anything for granted."

"That can be dangerous. It often happens that things are other than what they seem, and you can get yourself into trouble by jumping to conclusions."

"And my legs?"

"That question strikes me as somewhat simpler. From the looks of them under the blanket, they seem to have withered and atrophied, which would indicate that they haven't been used in many years. If that's the case, then it would be reasonable to assume that you aren't able to walk. Perhaps you've never been able to walk."

"An old man who can't see and can't walk. What do you think of that, boy?"

"I would think that such a man is more dependent on others than he would like to be."

Effing grunted, leaned back in his chair, and then tilted his head toward the ceiling. For the next ten or fifteen seconds, neither one of us spoke.

"What kind of voice do you have, boy?" he said at last.

"I don't know. I can't really hear it when I talk. The few times I've heard it played back to me on a tape recorder, I thought it sounded awful. But apparently everyone thinks that."

"Can it go the distance?"

"The distance?"

"Can it work over the long haul. Can you talk for two or three hours without growing hoarse. Can you sit there reading to me for an entire afternoon and still get the words out of your mouth. That's what I mean by going the distance."

"I think I can do that, yes."

"As you yourself observed, I've lost the power of sight. My relationship with you will be composed of words, and if your voice can't go the distance, you won't be worth a goddamned thing to me."

**to take s.th. for granted** to assume s.th. is true without making sure **to jump to conclusions** to come to a conclusion too quickly before checking all the facts **withered** thin and weak **atrophied** wasted away because of a disease or insufficient growth **to indicate** to show **to assume** to think s.th. is true, although you have no proof of it **to grunt** grunzen **to tilt** to move upwards **to go the distance** to be able to complete a task **over the long haul** over a lengthy period of time **hoarse** [hɔːrs] having a low rough voice because of illness or using it too much

"I understand."

Effing leaned forward again, then paused briefly for dramatic effect. "Are you afraid of me, boy?"

"No, I don't think so."

"You should be. If I make up my mind to hire you, you'll learn what fear is, I guarantee it. I might not be able to see or walk, but I have other powers, powers that few men have ever mastered."

"What kinds of powers?"

"Mental powers. A force of will that can bend the physical world into any shape I want."

"Telekinesis."

"Yes, if you wish. Telekinesis. Do you remember the blackout of a few years ago?"

"The fall of 1965."

"Precisely. I was the one who caused it. I had recently lost my sight, and one day I found myself sitting alone in this room, cursing what fate had done to me. At approximately five o'clock, I said to myself: I wish the whole world had to live in the same darkness I do. In less than an hour, all the lights in the city went out."

"It could have been a coincidence."

"There are no coincidences. That word is used only by ignorant people. Everything in the world is made up of electricity, animate and inanimate things alike. Even thoughts give off an electrical charge. If they're strong enough, a man's thoughts can change the world around him. Don't forget that, boy."

"I won't forget it."

"And you, Marco Stanley Fogg, what powers do you have?"

"None that I'm aware of. I have the normal human powers, I suppose, but nothing beyond that. I can eat and sleep. I can walk from one place to another. I can feel pain. Occasionally, I can even think."

"A rabble-rouser. Is that what you are, boy?"

**to master** to become thoroughly good at s.th. **mental** having to do with the mind **telekinesis** the ability to move things just with thoughts **blackout** On November 9, 1965 by 5.40 p.m. local time there was a power failure (Stromausfall) that effected most of the northeastern United States, especially New York City. **precisely** exactly **sight** ability to see **to curse** verfluchen **fate** das Schicksal **coincidence** a chance occurrence of events that is remarkable either for being at the same time or for apparently being connected **animate** living **inanimate** not living **charge** Ladung **rabble-rouser** s.o. who manipulates a crowd for political purposes so that the people become angry and violent

"Hardly. I doubt that I could persuade anyone to do anything."

"A victim, then. It's either one or the other. You either do or get done to."

"We're all victims of something, Mr. Effing. If only of the fact that we're alive."

"Are you sure you're alive, boy? Maybe you just imagine you are."

"Anything is possible. It could be that you and I are figments, that we're not really here. Yes, I'm willing to accept that as a possibility."

"Do you know how to hold your tongue?"

"If it's called for, I suppose I'm as good at being silent as the next man."

"And what man would that be, boy?"

"Any man. It's a form of expression. I can talk or be silent, depending on the nature of the situation."

"If I take you on, Fogg, you'll probably grow to hate me. Just remember that it's all for your own good. There's a hidden purpose to everything I do, and it's not for you to judge."

"I'll try to keep that in mind."

"Good. Now come over here and let me feel your muscles. I can't have some weakling pushing me around the streets, can I? If your muscles can't do the job, you won't be worth a goddamned thing to me."

* * *

I said my good-byes to Zimmer that night, and the next morning I put the few things I owned into my knapsack and traveled uptown to Effing's apartment. As chance would have it, I did not see Zimmer again for thirteen years. Circumstances pulled us apart, and when I finally ran into him by accident in the spring of 1982 at the junction of Varick Street and West Broadway in lower Manhattan, he had changed so much that at first I did not recognize him. He was twenty or thirty pounds heavier, and as he walked along with his wife and two little boys, I actually took note of his utterly conventional appearance: the paunch and thinning hair of early middle age, the placid, bemused look of a seasoned family man. We were

**figment** ['fɪg.mənt] s.th. that is imagined or invented or not real **to hold one's tongue** to stop speaking **if it's called for** if necessary **to take s.o. on** to hire s.o. **junction** a place where one road joins another **Varick Street and West Broadway** streets in Greenwich Village—for a while Auster lived on Varick Street, in the 1960s many artists lived on West Broadway where there were many art galleries **conventional** middle-class, conforming to normal standards **paunch** (humorous) large noticeable stomach **placid** calm and peaceful **bemused** lost in thought **seasoned** made fit by experience

walking in opposite directions and passed each other by. Then, very suddenly, I heard him call out my name. It is a common occurrence, I suppose, to bump into someone from your past, but seeing Zimmer like that stirred up an entire world of forgotten things for me. It almost didn't matter what had become of him, that he was teaching at a university somewhere in California, that he had published a four-hundred-page study of French film, that he had not written a poem in more than ten years. The important thing, quite simply, was that I had seen him. We stood there on the corner talking about the old days for fifteen or twenty minutes, and then he and his family scampered off to wherever it was they were going. I have not seen or heard from him since, but I suspect that the idea to write this book first came to me after that meeting four years ago, at the precise moment when Zimmer vanished down the street and I lost sight of him again.

After I arrived at Effing's apartment, Mrs. Hume sat me down in the kitchen for a cup of coffee. Mr. Effing was taking his morning nap, she said, and he wouldn't be up until ten o'clock. In the meantime, she told me what my duties in the house would be, when we would be eating our meals, how many hours I would be spending with Effing every day, and so on. She was the one who took care of the "body work," as she put it, dressing and washing him, taking him in and out of bed, shaving him, getting him on and off the toilet, whereas my job was somewhat more complex and loosely defined. I was not exactly being hired to be his friend, but it was something very close to that: a sympathetic companion, a person to break the monotony of his loneliness. "Lord knows the man doesn't have much time left," she said. "The least we can do is see to it that his last days aren't too miserable." I said that I understood.

"It will improve his spirits to have a young person around," she continued. "Not to speak of my spirits."

"I'm just glad to have the job," I said.

"He enjoyed your conversation yesterday. He said you gave him good answers."

"I didn't know what to say, really. He can be hard to follow sometimes."

**to bump into s.o.** to meet by chance **to stir up** here: to cause to become remembered again **to scamper off** to run with quick short steps like a small animal **to take a nap** to sleep for a short time, especially during the day **sympathetic** showing understanding **companion** here: s.o. paid to live and travel with an older person **spirits** how one feels at the moment **Not to speak of my spirits.** The same is true of my spirits.

"Don't I know it. But there's always something cooking in that brain of his. He's a bit loony, but I wouldn't call him senile."

"No, he's a sharp customer. I suspect he'll be keeping me on my toes."

"He told me you had a pleasant voice. That's a promising start, anyway."

"I can't imagine him using the word *pleasant*."

"That might not have been the exact word, but that's what he meant. He said your voice reminded him of someone he used to know."

"I hope it was someone he liked."

"He didn't tell me. That's one thing you'll learn about Mr. Thomas. He never tells you anything he doesn't want to."

My room was at the end of a long hall. It was a spare little place with a single window that looked out onto the back alley, a rudimentary enclosure no larger than a monk's cell. This was familiar territory to me, and it didn't take me long to feel at home among the minimal furnishings: an old-fashioned iron bedstead with vertical bars at either end, a chest of drawers, and a bookcase along one wall, filled mostly with French and Russian books. There was only one picture in the room, a large etching in a black varnished frame that depicted a mythological scene crowded with human figures and a plethora of architectural details. Later on, I learned that it was a black-and-white rendering of one of the panels from a series of paintings by Thomas Cole entitled *The Course of Empire*, a visionary saga of the rise and fall of the New World. I unpacked my clothes and saw that everything I owned fit comfortably into the top drawer of the

**Don't I know it.** I certainly know that, too. **to cook** (coll) to be planned, developed **loony** crazy (from the Latin luna = moon) **sharp customer** (coll) a person who is mentally fit **to keep s.o. on his/her toes** to make sure that someone is ready for anything that might happen **spare** with not much in it **back alley** narrow street behind houses in a city **enclosure** area surrounded by a wall or fence **monk's cell** small room of a monk (Mönch) **bedstead** frame of a bed **bar** Pfosten **chest of drawers** (AE) a piece of furniture with drawers, bureau (BE) **bookcase** a set of shelves for keeping books on **etching** Kupferstich **varnished** painted with a clear liquid that gives the wood a hard shiny surface **to depict** to clearly show **plethora** great amount **rendering** copy, version **panel** thin board with a painting on it **Thomas Cole** (1801-1848) British-born American landscape painter, who founded the Hudson River School that would influence American painters for the rest of the century. He admired the untouched beauty of the American landscape that, he thought, had a moral lesson to teach. *The Course of Empire* was in fact more general and not just about the New World. Cf. the many internet sites **visionary** with a clear idea of what the future will be like **saga** a long and complicated story

bureau. I had only one book with me, a paperback copy of Pascal's *Pensées* that Zimmer had given to me as a going-away present. I placed it on top of the pillow for the time being and then stepped back to study my new room. It wasn't much, but it was mine. After so many months of uncertainty, it comforted me just to be able to stand inside those four walls, to know there was a place in the world I could now call my own.

It rained steadily for the first two days I was there. With no chance to go out for an afternoon walk, we spent the whole time in the living room. Effing was less combative than he had been during the interview, and for the most part he sat there in silence, listening to the books I read to him. It was difficult for me to judge the nature of this silence, whether he was using it to test me in a way I did not understand, or whether it was simply a reflection of his mood. As with so much of Effing's behavior during the time I stayed with him, I was torn between reading a dark purpose into his actions and dismissing them as the products of random impulse. The things he said to me, the books he chose for me to read, the strange errands he sent me on—were these part of an elaborate and obscure plan, or did it only come to look that way in retrospect? At times I felt that he was trying to pass on some mysterious and arcane knowledge to me, acting as a self-appointed mentor to my inner progress, but without letting me know it, forcing me to play a game without telling me the rules. This was Effing as crackpot spiritual guide, as an eccentric master struggling to initiate me into the secrets of the world. At other times, however, when his selfishness and arrogance thundered out of control, he struck me as nothing more than a vicious old man, a burnt-out maniac living in the borderland between madness and death. All in all, he heaped a considerable amount of abuse on me, and it wasn't long before I grew wary of him, even as my fascination for him increased. Several times, when I was on the verge of giving up, Kitty talked me into staying, but in the long run I believe I wanted to stay, even when it felt impossible to last

**Pascal** (1623-1662) French scientist and philosopher, who believed that reason was not enough to understand the world—mystic faith was needed for a true understanding of the universe *Pensées* were religious writings. **steadily** continuously **combative** willing to fight **reflection** indication, sign **to dismiss** to consider unimportant, to reject **random** happening without any plan **errand** a short trip to undertake a task **elaborate** complicated **obscure** difficult to understand **in retrospect** looking to the past from the present **arcane** strange, mysterious **self-appointed** named by oneself **crackpot** bizarre, crazy **vicious** cruel, wanting to hurt others **maniac** a crazy person who behaves in a dangerous way **to heap abuse on s.o.** to say a lot of rude and insulting things to s.o. **wary** ['wer.i] watchful, cautious **on the verge** just about to

another minute. Whole weeks went by when I could barely stand to turn my eyes in his direction, when I had to gird myself merely to sit in the same room with him. But I stuck it out, I held on until the bitter end.

Even in his most placid humors, Effing took pleasure in pulling little surprises. On that first morning, for example, he wheeled himself into the room wearing a pair of dark blind-man's glasses. The black eyepatches, which had caused so much discussion during the interview, were nowhere to be seen. Effing made no comment about this switch. Taking my lead from him, I gathered that this was one of those instances when I was supposed to hold my tongue, and therefore I said nothing about it either. The next morning, he had on a pair of normal prescription glasses with metal frames and preposterously thick lenses. They magnified and distorted the shape of his eyes, making them look as large as bird's eggs, bulging blue spheres that seemed about to spring from his head. It was hard for me to tell if those eyes could see or not. There were moments when I was convinced that it was all a bluff and that he could see as sharply as I did; at other moments, I became just as convinced that he was totally blind. That was how Effing wanted it, of course. He would cast out intentionally ambiguous signals and then revel in the uncertainty they caused, adamantly refusing to divulge the facts. On some days, he left his eyes uncovered, wearing neither patches nor glasses. On still other days, he would come in with a black blindfold tied around his head, which made him look like a prisoner about to be shot by a firing squad. It was impossible for me to know what these various costumes meant. He never said a word about them, and I never had the courage to ask. The important thing, I decided, was not to let his antics get under my skin. He could do what he pleased, but as long as I did not fall into his trap, none

**barely** hardly **to gird oneself to do s.th.** to prepare oneself for an action **to stick/stuck/stuck s.th. out** to continue to do s.th. even if it is difficult, painful, or boring **placid humors** here: peaceful moods **to pull** to prepare and carry out **switch** change **taking my lead from him** reacting appropriately to Effing's new course of action **to gather** to conclude, to assume **prescription glasses** glasses that have been prescribed (verschrieben) by a doctor **preposterously** absurdly, ridiculously **to magnify** to make larger **to distort** to change the shape of s.th. so that it seems unnatural **to bulge** to stick out in a round shape **to cast out** here: to make use of **ambiguous** [æmˈbɪg.ju.əs] with a meaning that is unclear **to revel** to enjoy s.th. that others don't expect you to enjoy **adamantly** stubbornly, refusing to change your mind **to divulge** to make known **blindfold** a piece of cloth to cover the eyes **firing squad** a group of soldiers whose duty it is to execute s.o. by shooting **antic** absurd action **to get under s.o.'s skin** (coll) to annoy

of it could affect me. That was what I told myself in any case. In spite of my resolve, it was sometimes hard to resist him. Especially on the days when he left his eyes uncovered, I would often find myself staring straight into them, unable not to look, defenseless against their power to lure me in. It was as though I was trying to discover some truth in them, some opening that would lead me directly into the darkness of his skull. I never got anywhere with it, however. For all the hundreds of hours I spent gazing into them, Effing's eyes never told me a thing.

He had selected all the books in advance, and he knew exactly what he wanted to hear. These readings were not a form of recreation so much as a line of pursuit, a dogged investigation of certain precise and narrow subjects. That did not make his motives any more apparent to me, but at least there was a kind of subterranean logic to the enterprise. The initial sequence of books dealt with the question of travel, most often travel into the unknown and the discovery of new worlds. We began with the journeys of Saint Brendan and Sir John de Mandeville, then moved on to Columbus, Cabeza de Vaca, and Thomas Harriot. We read excerpts from Doughty's *Travels in Arabia Deserta*, plodded through the whole of John Wesley Powell's book about his mapping expedition down the Colorado River, and ended up by reading a number of eighteenth- and nineteenth-century captivity stories, firsthand accounts written by white settlers who had been abducted by Indians. I found these books uniformly inter-

**resolve** determination **to resist** to prevent yourself from doing s.th. (widerstehen) **to lure s.o. in** to attract s.o. with the promise of a reward or pleasure **skull** Schädel **recreation** an activity you do for pleasure or amusement **a line of pursuit** a field of study that should be investigated further **dogged** very determined **apparent** easy to understand, obvious **subterranean** hidden **Saint Brendan** (484 AD-578 AD) Irish monk who was said to have sailed across the Atlantic and land in what is today Newfoundland **Sir John de Mandeville** 14th century author of tales about his travels **Columbus** (1451-1506) Christopher Columbus, explorer whose rediscovery of America marked the beginning of the European settlement of the New World **Cabeza de Vaca** (1490-1560) Spanish explorer of what is now Texas and the Gulf region—He claimed there were cities full of riches. **Thomas Harriot** (1560-1621) English mathematician and scientist—sent by Sir Walter Raleigh to investigate a settlement in Virginia **Doughty** (1843-1926) Charles Doughty—English traveler in Arabia; his *Travels in Arabia Deserta* was published in 1888. **to plod through** to work one's way through slowly **John Wesley Powell** (1834-1902) American geologist and Indian ethnologist. He lost his right arm in the Civil War and showed a great deal of interest and understanding for the situation of the Native American. **firsthand account** a story that is written by the person who experienced all the adventures **to abduct** to kidnap **uniformly** all

esting, and once my voice became accustomed to working for long stretches at a time, I believe I developed an adequate reading style. It all hinged on clarity of enunciation, which in turn depended on modulations of tone, subtle pauses, and a steadfast attentiveness to the words on the page. Effing rarely made any comments while I read, but I knew that he was listening from the occasional noises that escaped from him whenever we reached a particularly knotty or exciting passage. These reading sessions were probably when I felt in greatest harmony with him, but I soon learned not to confuse his silent concentration with good will. After the third or fourth book on travel, I made a casual suggestion that he might find it amusing to listen to parts of Cyrano's journey to the moon. This got no more than a snarl from him. "Keep your ideas to yourself, boy," he said. "If I wanted your opinion, I'd ask for it."

The far wall of the living room was fitted with a bookcase that spanned from the floor to the ceiling. I don't know how many books were on those shelves, but there must have been at least five or six hundred, perhaps a thousand. Effing seemed to know where all of them were, and when the time came for us to start a new book, he would tell me exactly where to go. "Second shelf," he would say, "twelve or fifteen spaces from the left. Lewis and Clark. A red book with cloth binding." He never made a mistake, and as the evidence of his powers of recall mounted, I could not help being impressed. I once asked him if he was familiar with the memory systems of Cicero and Raymond Lull, but he dismissed my question with a wave of the hand. "You can't study those things," he said. "It's a talent you're born with, a natural gift." He paused for a moment, then continued in a sly, mocking voice. "But how can you be sure that I know where the books are? Stop and think about it. Maybe I creep out here at night and rearrange them while you're asleep. Or

**stretch** a continuous period of time **enunciation** careful pronunciation **modulation of tone** change of sound quality **steadfast** constant **attentiveness** paying attention carefully **knotty** ['nɑː.ti] extremely difficult or complicated **snarl** an angry sound **to span** to stretch from one place to another **Lewis and Clark** Meriwether Lewis (1774-1809) and William Clark (1770-1838)—two explorers who were sent by the American government to find an overland route to the Pacific, strengthen American claims to the west, and find information about the Indians and the Far West. **Cicero** [sɪs.ər.ə] a major Roman orator, politician, and man of letters (106-43 BC), whose *de oratore* suggested ways of being a successful public speaker, including systems of memorizing. **Raymond Lull** Catalanian philosopher and theologian (1232-1316) He developed a system of memory that was supposed to enable a person to have a better knowledge of God. **sly** schlau, verschlagen **to creep** to move on your hands and knees

maybe I move the books by telepathy when your back is turned. Isn't that so, young man?" I took this to be a rhetorical question and didn't say anything to contradict him. "Just remember, Fogg," he continued, "never take anything for granted. Especially when you're dealing with a person like me."

We spent those first two days in the living room as the hard November rain beat against the windows outside. It was very still in Effing's house, and there were times when I paused for a breath in my reading and the loudest sound I heard was the ticking of the clock on the mantel. Occasionally, Mrs. Hume would make some noise or other in the kitchen, and down below there was the muffled noise of traffic, the whoosh of tires as they moved along the rainy streets. It felt both odd and pleasant to be sitting indoors as the world went about its business, and this sense of detachment was probably enhanced by the books themselves. Everything in them was faraway, shadowy, fraught with marvels: an Irish monk who sailed across the Atlantic in the year 500 and found an island he thought was Paradise; the mythical kingdom of Prester John; a one-armed American scientist smoking a peace pipe with the Zuni Indians in New Mexico. Hours went by, and neither one of us budged from our spots, Effing in his wheelchair, I on the sofa across from him, and there were times when I became so engrossed in what I was reading that I hardly knew where I was anymore, that I felt I was no longer sitting in my own skin.

We ate lunch and dinner in the dining room at noon and six o'clock every day. Effing was very precise about sticking to this schedule, and whenever Mrs. Hume poked her head into the doorway to announce that a meal was ready, he would abruptly turn his attention away from the book. It didn't matter where we were in the story. Even if we were only

**to take** here: to assume **to contradict** to deny that what s.o. has said is correct **mantel** the shelf over a fireplace **muffled** not quite so loud because of being far away or covered or wrapped by s.th. **whoosh** sound of s.th. rushing by **detachment** feeling of being separated or disconnected **to enhance** to intensify, to increase **marvel** s.th. that causes wonder **Irish monk** Auster probably means Saint Brendan, who searched for the "Land Promised to the Saints." The island could have been any island in the Atlantic. **Prester John** legendary king and priest in the middle-ages, who was thought to have a mythical kingdom in Africa or Asia **one-armed American scientist** i.e. John Wesley Powell **Zuni Indians** ['zu:.ni] Pueblo Indians in New Mexico, whose original seven villages where thought to be the mythical Seven Cities of the Cibola **to budge** to move, however slightly **spot** place, position **engrossed** so interested that you don't notice anything else **to stick to s.th.** to continue with s.th. without changing **to poke** to push through an opening

a page or two from the end, Effing would cut me off in mid-sentence and tell me to stop. “Time to eat,” he would say, “we’ll pick this up again later.” It was not that he was particularly hungry—he in fact ate very little—but the compulsion to order his days in a strict and rational manner was too strong to be ignored. Once or twice he seemed genuinely sorry that we had to interrupt our reading, but never to such an extent that he was willing to deviate from the schedule. “Too bad,” he would say. “Just when it was getting interesting.” The first time this happened, I offered to continue reading for a while longer. “Impossible,” he said. “We can’t disrupt the world for the sake of momentary pleasures. There’ll be time enough for this tomorrow.”

Effing didn’t eat much, but the little he did eat was consumed in a mad free-for-all of slobbering grunts and spills. It disgusted me to watch this spectacle, but I had no choice but to endure it. Whenever Effing sensed that I was staring at him, he would immediately bring out an even more repulsive battery of tricks: letting the food dribble out of his mouth and down his chin, burping, feigning nausea and heart attacks, removing his false teeth and putting them on the table. He was especially fond of soups, and all during the winter we began every meal with a different one. Mrs. Hume made these soups herself, delicious pots of vegetable soup and watercress soup and leek-and-potato soup, but I quickly came to dread the moment when I would have to sit down and watch Effing suck it into his mouth. It was not that he slurped; he positively vacuumed it up, piercing the air with all the clamor and commotion of a defective Hoover. This noise was so unnerving, so distinctive, that I began hearing

**compulsion** a strong and unreasonable desire that is difficult to control **genuinely** really **extent** degree **to deviate** to start to do s.th. different from what has been done before **to disrupt** to interrupt the progress of s.th. **free-for-all** a disorderly fight, here: completely chaotic activities **to slobber** to allow food or saliva (Speichel) to fall or drip out of the mouth **spill** causing a liquid to fall, usually unintentionally **to disgust** to sicken **to endure** to deal with s.th. unpleasant, to bear **to sense** to become aware of **repulsive** disgusting, distasteful **battery** number **to dribble** to let saliva come out of one’s mouth and run down one’s chin **to burp** aufstoßen **to feign** to pretend to have s.th. **nausea** a feeling that you are about to vomit **watercress** Brunnenkresse **leek** Lauch **to dread** to feel anxious or worried about something that might happen in the future **to slurp** to drink a liquid making a sucking noise **positively** really, truly **to vacuum up** to suck up like a vacuum cleaner **to pierce** to sound sharply **clamor** loud noise **commotion** sudden noisy activity **Hoover** (BE) vacuum cleaner (trademark) **unnerving** upsetting **distinctive** so different that it is easy to recognize

it all the time, even when we were not sitting at the table. Even now, if I manage to concentrate hard enough, I can bring it back in many of its most subtle characteristics: the shock of the first moment when Effing's lips met the spoon, shattering the quiet with a monumental intake of breath; the prolonged, high-pitched ruckus that followed, a blistering uproar that seemed to turn the liquid into a concoction of gravel and broken glass as it traveled down his throat; the swallow, the short pause that came next, the clank of the spoon as it hit the bowl, and then the heave and shudder of an outward breath. He would smack his lips at that point, perhaps even grimace with pleasure, and then begin the process all over again, filling the spoon and lifting it to his mouth (always with his head hunched forward—to shorten the journey between bowl and mouth—but nonetheless with a shaking hand, which would send small streams of soup splattering back into the bowl as the spoon neared his lips), and then there would be a new explosion, a new splitting of the ears as the suction was turned on again. Mercifully, he rarely finished an entire bowl of the stuff. Three or four of these cacophonous spoonfuls were generally enough to exhaust him, after which he would shove the bowl aside and calmly ask Mrs. Hume what she had prepared for the main course. I don't know how many times I heard this noise, but often enough to know that it will never leave me, that I will be carrying it around in my head for the rest of my life.

Mrs. Hume showed remarkable patience during these exhibitions. She never registered alarm or disgust, acting as though Effing's behavior was part of the natural order of things. Like someone who lived next to railroad tracks or an airport, she had grown accustomed to periodic eruptions of deafening noise, and whenever Effing would begin one of his

**to shatter** (fig) to break into small pieces **high-pitched** with a very high and loud sound **ruckus** [ˈrʌk.əs] (AE) loud argument, confused situation **blistering** here: exploding **concoction** combination of unusual things **gravel** small stones used for the surface of a road, etc. **swallow** the act of allowing food to go down one's throat **clank** sound that metal makes when it is hit **heave** a strong rising or falling movement **shudder** uncontrollable, violent shaking **to smack one's lips** to open and close the lips loudly to show pleasure **to hunch** to bend or draw a part of the body up or together **to splatter** to allow small drops of liquid to fall in many different directions **splitting** a very loud sound that hurts the ears **suction** the act or process of sucking **mercifully** luckily **cacophonous** having an unpleasant mixture of sounds **main course** the main part of a meal **exhibition** example of foolish behavior **to register** to show, to express

bouts of slurping or slobbering, she would simply stop talking and wait for the disturbance to pass. The bullet train to Chicago would speed through the night, rattling the windows and shaking the foundations of the house, and then, just as quickly as it had come, it would be gone. Every once in a while, when Effing was in particularly obnoxious form, Mrs. Hume would look over in my direction and give me a wink, as if to say: don't let him bother you; the old man is out of his mind, and there's nothing we can do about it. Thinking back on it now, I realize how important she was to keeping a measure of stability in the household. A more volatile person would have been tempted to respond to Effing's outrages, and that would have made things even worse, for once he was challenged, the old man became ferocious. Mrs. Hume's phlegmatic temperament was well suited for fending off incipient dramas and unpleasant scenes. She had a large soul to go along with her large body, and it could absorb a great deal without any noticeable effect. In the beginning, it would sometimes upset me to watch her take so much abuse from him, but I came to understand that it was the only reasonable strategy for handling his eccentricities. Smile, shrug it off, humor him. She was the one who taught me how to act with Effing, and without her example to follow, I doubt that I would have lasted in the job very long.

She always came to the table armed with a fresh towel and a bib. The bib would be tied around Effing's neck before the meal began, and the towel would be used for wiping his face in sudden emergencies. In that regard, it was something like sitting down to eat with a small child. Mrs. Hume took on the role of attentive mother with great assurance. Having raised three children of her own, she once told me, she didn't have to think twice about it. Seeing to these physical obligations was one thing, but there was also the responsibility of talking to Effing in such a way that he was kept under verbal control. When it came to that, she conducted herself with all the skill of an experienced prostitute manipulating

**bout** moment, episode **bullet train** high-speed passenger train **to rattle** to make s.th. shake violently **in obnoxious form** [əbˈnɑːkʃəs] behaving disgustingly **to give s.o. a wink** to give s.o. a sign by opening and closing an eye that not everything should be taken seriously **volatile** easily becoming angry or violent **to be tempted to do s.th.** to want to do s.th. even though one knows it's wrong **outrage** example of shocking behavior **ferocious** extremely savage or cruel **to fend off** to defend oneself against s.th. **incipient** just beginning **eccentricity** example of strange behavior **to shrug s.th. off** to not take s.th. so seriously **bib** a small piece of cloth or plastic tied under a baby's chin to protect its clothes when eating **assurance** confidence because of having a lot of experience **to see to s.th.** here: to take care of **obligation** task, duty

a difficult client. No request was too absurd to be denied, no suggestion could shock her, no comment was too outlandish not to be taken seriously. Once or twice a week, Effing would begin to accuse her of plotting against him—of poisoning his food, for example (as he contemptuously spat out half-chewed bits of carrots and chopped meat onto his plate), or of scheming to rob him of his money. Rather than take offense, she would calmly tell him that all three of us would soon be dead, since we were all eating the same thing. Or else, if he kept insisting she would change tactics and confess to the deed. "It's true," she would say. "I put six tablespoons of arsenic in the mashed potatoes. It should start working in about fifteen minutes, and then all my troubles will be over. I'll be a rich woman, Mr. Thomas"—she always called him Mr. Thomas—"and you'll be rotting in your grave at last." This kind of talk never failed to amuse Effing. "Ha!" he would blurt out. "Ha, ha! You're after my millions, you greedy bitch. I knew it all along. Next it will be furs and diamonds, won't it? Well, it won't do you any good, fatso. You'll still look like a blubbery washerwoman, no matter what clothes you wear." And then, paying no heed to the contradiction, he would zestfully begin shoveling more of the poisoned food into his mouth.

Effing put her through her paces, but at bottom I believe that Mrs. Hume was devoted to him. Unlike most people who take care of the very old, she did not treat him as if he were a retarded child or a block of wood. She gave him the liberty to rant and carry on, but when the situation called for it, she was also capable of dealing with him quite firmly. She had devised any number of epithets and names for him, and she did

**outlandish** strange **to plot against s.o.** to make a secret plan to harm s.o. **contemptuously** in a way showing that one feels s.o. is not important and deserves no respect **to spit/spat/spat** to force a small amount of saliva out of one's mouth **to scheme** to make secret plans to achieve s.th. that is immoral or harmful **to take offense** to feel insulted **to confess to the deed** to admit that one did s.th. harmful or against the law **arsenic** Arsen **mashed potatoes** Kartoffelbrei **to rot** verrotten **to blurt out** to say suddenly without thinking **greedy** always wanting money **bitch** (slang) miserable woman **fur** Pelzkleidung **fatso** (slang) insulting way of addressing s.o. who is fat **blubbery** (coll) excessively fat **washerwoman** woman who washes other people's clothes **to pay no heed to s.th.** to pay no attention to s.th. **to put s.o. through his/her paces** to make s.o. work hard to see how well this person can do s.th. **at bottom** actually, basically **to be devoted to s.o.** to show great love and loyalty to s.o. **to rant** to talk in a loud and confused way **to carry on** to behave improperly **when the situation called for it** when it was necessary **to devise** to work out, to plan **any number** quite a number of **epithet** descriptive word or phrase

not hesitate to use them when provoked: old coot, rapscallion, jackdaw, humbug, an inexhaustible supply. I don't know where Mrs. Hume found these words, but they flew off her tongue in bunches, always managing to combine a tone of insult with one of rugged affection. She had been with Effing for nine years, and since she was not someone who seemed to enjoy suffering for its own sake, she must have found a measure of satisfaction in the job somewhere. From my point of view, the fact of those nine years was overwhelming. When you stopped to consider that she took off only one day every month, it became almost inconceivable. At least I had the nights to myself, and after a certain hour I could come and go as I wished. I had Kitty, and I also had the consolation of knowing that my job with Effing was not the central purpose of my life, that sooner or later I would be moving on to something else. Mrs. Hume had no such escape. She was on duty all the time, and her only chance to leave the house was when she went out to do the marketing for an hour or two every afternoon. It was hardly what you could call a real life. She had her *Reader's Digest* and *Redbook* magazines, she had an occasional paperback mystery novel, she had the small black-and-white television that she would watch in her room after Effing had been put to bed, always with the sound turned on very low. Her husband had died of cancer thirteen years before, and her three grown-up children lived far away: a daughter in California, another daughter in Kansas, a son stationed with the army in Germany. She wrote letters to all of them, and her greatest pleasure was in receiving photographs of her grandchildren, which she would stick into the corners of her dressing-table mirror. On her days off, she would go to visit her brother Charlie at the V.A. Hospital in the Bronx. He had been a bomber pilot during the Second World War, and from the little she told me about him, I gathered he was not right in the head. She would faithfully trudge off to see him every month, always remembering to carry along a little bag of chocolates and a pile of sports magazines, and

**old coot** (AE coll) unpleasant old man **rapscallion** person who behaves badly, but one still likes **jackdaw** a black bird, here: thief **humbug** [ˈhʌm.bʌg] a person who pretends be s.o. he/she is not **bunch** large group **rugged** rough, not polite **inconceivable** unthinkable **consolation** s.th. that makes you feel better when you are sad or disappointed **on duty** working **Reader's Digest** collection of short stories and articles from various magazines **Redbook** magazine often sold in supermarkets **V.A. Hospital** Veterans Administration Hospital—government hospital for people who are or were in the armed forces **the Bronx** a borough (Stadtteil) of New York City to the north of Manhattan **to trudge off** to walk slowly to somewhere because of being tired

in all the time I knew her, I never heard her complain about having to go. Mrs. Hume was a rock. When it comes right down to it, no one has ever taught me as much as she did.

Effing was a difficult case, but it would be wrong to define him in terms of difficulty alone. If he had been nothing but nastiness and foul temper, there would have been a predictability to his moods that would have made it simpler to deal with him. One would have known what to expect from him; it would have been possible to know where one stood. The old man was too elusive for that, however. If he was difficult, it was largely because he was not difficult all the time, and for that reason he managed to keep one in a constant state of disequilibrium. Entire days would go by when nothing but bitterness and sarcasm poured from his mouth, but just when I was persuaded there was not a particle of kindness or human sympathy left in him, he would come out with a remark of such devastating compassion, a phrase that revealed such a deep understanding and knowledge of others, that I would be forced to admit that I had misjudged him, that he was finally not as bad as I had thought. Little by little, I began to perceive another side to Effing. I would not go so far as to call it a sentimental side, but there were times when it came very close to that. At first, I wanted to dismiss it as a charade, as a trick to keep me off balance, but that would have implied that Effing had calculated these softenings of heart in advance, whereas in fact they always seemed to occur spontaneously, emerging from some haphazard detail of a particular event or conversation. If this good side of Effing was genuine, however, then why didn't he allow it to come out more often? Was it merely an aberration of his true self, or was it in fact the essence of who he really was? I never reached any definite conclusions about this, except perhaps that it was impossible to exclude either alternative. Effing was both things at once. He was a monster, but at the same time he had it in him to be a good man, a man I could even bring myself to admire. This prevented me from hating him as thoroughly as I would have liked.

**in terms of** in connection with, with the expression **nastiness** being unkind, unpleasant, insulting **foul temper** very bad mood **predictability** certainty that s.th. will happen **elusive** difficult to understand or identify **disequilibrium** [ˌdɪs.iː.kwɪˈlɪb.ri.əm] a state of uncertainty **devastating** here: unbelievable **compassion** a feeling of pity for the suffering or misfortune of others with the desire to help **charade** behavior that is pretended **to emerge** to appear, to happen **haphazard** [ˌhæpˈhæz.əd] not planned, happening by chance **aberration** an action that is different from what usually happens or what someone usually does **essence** the most basic quality

Because I could not dismiss him from my mind on the strength of a single feeling, I wound up thinking about him almost constantly. I began to see him as a tortured soul, as a man haunted by his past, struggling to hide some secret anguish that was devouring him from within.

My first glimpse of this other Effing came during dinner on the second night I was there. Mrs. Hume was asking me questions about my childhood, and I happened to mention how my mother had been run over by a bus in Boston. Effing, who until then had not been paying any attention to the conversation, suddenly laid down his fork and turned his face in my direction. In a voice I had not heard from him before—all tinged with tenderness and warmth—he said, "That's a terrible thing, boy. A truely terrible thing." There was not the slightest suggestion that he did not mean it. "Yes," I said, "the whole business hit me hard. I was only eleven when it happened, and I went on missing my mother for a long time after that. To be perfectly honest, I still miss her now." Mrs. Hume shook her head as I spoke those words, and I could see her eyes glistening over in a rush of sadness. After a slight pause, Effing said, "Cars are a menace. If we don't watch out, they'll get us all. The same thing happened to my Russian friend two months ago. He walked out of the house one fine morning to buy a newspaper, stepped down from the curb to cross Broadway, and got himself run over by a goddamned yellow Ford. The driver sped right on through, didn't even bother to stop. If not for that maniac, Pavel would be sitting in the same chair you're sitting in now, Fogg, eating the same food you're putting into your mouth. Instead, he's lying six feet under the ground in some forgotten corner of Brooklyn."

"Pavel Shum," added Mrs. Hume. "He started working for Mr. Thomas in Paris back in the thirties."

"His name was Shumansky then, but he shortened it when we came to America in thirty-nine."

"That explains all the Russian books in my room," I said.

"The Russian books, the French books, the German books," Effing said. "Pavel was fluent in six or seven languages. He was a man of

**on the strength of** on the basis of **to wind up doing s.th.** (coll) to end up doing s.th. (am Ende etwas tun) **haunted** constantly reminded about s.th. unpleasant **anguish** extreme misery **to devour** to eat, here: to destroy **glimpse** brief view, quick sight **tinged with** showing a small amount of **tenderness** warm and loving feelings **to glisten over** to shine from becoming wet with tears **rush** sudden strong feeling **menace** s.th. dangerous **curb** (AE) kerb (BE) Bordstein **maniac** person who behaves in a crazy way

learning, a genuine scholar. When I met him in thirty-two, he was working as a dishwasher in a restaurant and living in a sixth-floor maid's room without any plumbing or heat. One of the White Russians who came to Paris during the Civil War. They all lost everything they had. I took him in, gave him a place to live, and he helped me out in exchange. This went on for thirty-seven years, Fogg, and the only thing I regret is that I didn't die before he did. The man was the one true friend I ever had."

All of a sudden, Effing's lips began to tremble, as though he were on the point of tears. In spite of everything that had gone before, I could not help feeling sorry for him.

The sun came out again on the third day. Effing took his usual morning nap, but when Mrs. Hume wheeled him out of his bedroom at ten o'clock, he was all set to go on our first walk, bundled up in heavy woolen garments and waving a stick in his right hand. Whatever else could have been said about him, Effing did not take things dispassionately. He looked forward to an excursion through the streets of the neighborhood with all the enthusiasm of an explorer about to begin a journey to the Arctic. There were countless preparations to be attended to: checking the temperature and wind velocity, mapping out a route in advance, making sure that he had on the proper amount of clothing. In cold weather, Effing wore all manner of superfluous outer protection, wrapping himself up in sweaters and scarves, an enormous greatcoat that reached down to his ankles, a blanket, gloves, and a Russian fur hat equipped with earflaps. On especially frigid days (when the temperature dropped below thirty degrees), he also wore a ski mask. All these clothes fairly buried him under their bulkiness, making him seem even punier and more ridiculous than usual, but Effing could not tolerate physical discomfort, and since he was not troubled by the thought of calling atten-

**genuine** real **scholar** well-educated person and an expert in the sciences or humanities (Geisteswissenschaften) **maid** Dienstmädchen **plumbing** pipes in a building used for water **White Russian** anti-Communist **Civil War** war in Russia between the Communists and anti-Communists from 1918 to 1920—The Communists won. **bundled up** dressed warmly **garment** piece of clothing **dispassionately** in a way not influenced by emotions **velocity** speed **all manner of** a kinds of **superfluous** unnecessary **greatcoat** a long heavy coat **earflap** a warm covering for the ears that can be folded down from a hat **30 degrees** 30 degrees Fahrenheit (32°F = 0°C) **fairly** more than a little **bulkiness** quality of being big and heavy **puny** [pju:ni] small, thin, and weak

tion to himself, he played these sartorial extravagances to the hilt. On the day of our first walk, the weather was actually quite nippy, and as we made our preparations to leave, he asked me if I had an overcoat. No, I said, I just had my leather jacket. That wouldn't do, he said, that wouldn't do at all. "I can't have you freezing your ass off in the middle of a walk," he explained. "You need clothing that will take you the distance, Fogg." Mrs. Hume was ordered to fetch the coat that had once belonged to Pavel Shum. It turned out to be a battered tweed relic that fit me rather well: brownish in color with flecks of red and green dispersed throughout the material. In spite of my objections, Effing insisted that I keep it, and there wasn't much I could say after that without provoking a dispute. That was how I came to inherit my predecessor's overcoat. I found it eerie to walk around in it, knowing that it had belonged to a man who was now dead, but I continued to wear it on all our outings for the rest of the winter. To assuage my compunctions, I tried to think of it as a kind of uniform that went with the job, but that didn't do much good. Whenever I put it on, I couldn't help feeling that I was stepping into a dead man's body, that I had been turned into Pavel Shum's ghost.

It didn't take me long to get the hang of the wheelchair. There were a few bumps on the first day, but once I learned how to tilt the chair at the proper angle when we went up and down curbs, things went fairly smoothly. Effing was exceedingly light, and pushing him around caused little strain on my arms. In other respects, however, our excursions were rather difficult for me. As soon as we got outside, Effing would begin jabbing his stick into the air, asking in a loud voice what object he was pointing at. As soon as I told him, he would insist that I describe it for him. Garbage cans, shop windows, doorways: he wanted me to give him a precise account of these things, and if I couldn't muster the phrases

**sartorial** having to do with the quality or kind of the clothes one wears **to play to the hilt** to do s.th. as much as possible **nippy** a bit cold **to freeze your ass off** (AE slang) to feel extremely cold because of extremely low temperatures **battered** damaged by heavy wear **tweed** thick woolen cloth originally made in Scotland **relic** [ˈrel.ɪk] s.th. that has survived from the past **fleck** a small marking **dispersed** scattered, distributed over a wide area **predecessor** person who had the job before **eerie** weird, strange **to assuage** to make an unpleasant feeling less painful **compunction** a deep feeling of shame or guilt **to get the hang of s.th.** (coll) to learn how to use s.th. **bump** a small raised area on a surface **exceedingly** extremely **caused little strain on my arms** did not cause any physical injury to my hands **to jab** to push s.th. into s.th. else with short quick movements **garbage can** (AE) dustbin (BE) **account** description **to muster** to try to find **phrase** expression

swiftly enough to satisfy him, he would explode in anger. "Dammit, boy," he would say, "use the eyes in your head! I can't see a bloody thing, and here you're spouting drivel about 'your average lamppost' and 'perfectly ordinary manhole covers.' No two things are alike, you fool, any bumpkin knows that. I want to see what we're looking at, goddammit, I want you to make things stand out for me!" It was humiliating to be scolded like that in the middle of the street, standing there as the old man lashed out at me, having to take it as people turned their heads to watch the uproar. Once or twice, I was tempted just to walk away and leave him there, but the fact was that Effing was not entirely wrong. I was not doing a very good job. I realized that I had never acquired the habit of looking closely at things, and now that I was being asked to do it, the results were dreadfully inadequate. Until then, I had always had a penchant for generalizing, for seeing the similarities between things rather than their differences. Now I was being plunged into a world of particulars, and the struggle to evoke them in words, to summon up the immediate sensual data, presented a challenge I was ill prepared for. To get what he wanted, Effing should have hired Flaubert to push him around the streets—but even Flaubert worked slowly, sometimes laboring for hours just to get a single sentence right. I not only had to describe things accurately, I had to do it within a matter of seconds. More than anything else, I hated the inevitable comparisons with Pavel Shum. Once, when I was having a particularly rough time of it, Effing went on about his departed friend for several minutes, describing him as a master of the poetic phrase, a peerless inventor of apt and stunning images, a stylist whose words could mirac-

**swiftly** quickly **to spout drivel** to talk nonsense **manhole cover** a hole on the surface of a road covered by a lid, that is used to examine or repair pipes, wires etc **bumpkin** stupid person from the countryside **humiliating** making you feel ashamed or embarrassed, because you have been made to look stupid **to scold** to angrily criticize someone for having done s.th. wrong **to lash out at s.o.** to suddenly speak angrily to s.o. **uproar** loud confusion **dreadfully** extremely **penchant** ['pen.tʃənt] tendency, liking for **to be plunged into s.th.** to be forced into s.th. **to evoke** to form, to produce, to cause to appear **to summon s.th. up** to produce, to cause to appear with great effort **ill** poorly **Flaubert** Gustave Flaubert (1821-1880) French writer especially famous for *Madame Bovary*—He was known for spending a lot of time on just one sentence before considering it good enough. His descriptions in novels were precise and detailed. **to labor on s.th.** to work very hard on s.th. **departed** dead **peerless** with no-one better **apt** just right for the occasion **stunning** very impressive

ulously reveal the palpable truth of objects. "And to think," Effing said, "English wasn't even his first language." That was the only time I ever talked back to him on the subject, but I felt so wounded by his remark that I couldn't resist. "If you want another language," I said, "I'll be happy to oblige you. How about Latin? I'll talk to you in Latin from now on if you like. Better yet, I'll talk to you in Pig Latin. You shouldn't have any trouble understanding that." It was a stupid thing to say, and Effing quickly put me in my place. "Shut up and talk, boy," he said. "Tell me what the clouds look like. Give me every cloud in the western sky, every one as far as you can see."

In order to do what Effing asked, I had to learn how to keep myself separate from him. The essential thing was not to feel burdened by his commands, but to transform them into something I wanted to do for myself. There was nothing inherently wrong with the activity, after all. If regarded in the proper way, the effort to describe things accurately was precisely the kind of discipline that could teach me what I most wanted to learn: humility, patience, rigor. Instead of doing it merely to discharge an obligation, I began to consider it as a spiritual exercise, a process of training myself how to look at the world as if I were discovering it for the first time. What do you see? And if you see, how do you put it into words? The world enters us through our eyes, but we cannot make sense of it until it descends into our mouths. I began to appreciate how great that distance was, to understand how far a thing must travel in order to get from the one place to the other. In actual terms, it was no more than two or three inches, but considering how many accidents and losses could occur along the way, it might just as well have been a journey from the earth to the moon. My first attempts with Effing were dismally vague, mere shadows flitting across a blurred background. I had seen these things before, I told myself, and how could there be any difficulty in describing them? A fire hydrant, a taxi cab, a rush of steam pouring up from the pavement—they were deeply familiar to me, and I felt I knew them by heart. But that did not take into account the mutability of those

**to reveal** to show s.th. that was previously hidden **palpable** here: as if able to be touched or felt **to talk back to s.o.** to talk rudely (unhöflich) to s.o. after being criticized **Pig Latin** a secret language used by children in which any consonants at the beginning of a word are placed at the end, followed by -ay **burdened** put under great stress **inherently** an sich **humility** not being so proud of oneself **rigor** exactness **to discharge** to do properly **in actual terms** in reality **dismally** disastrously, horribly **to flit** to move along rapidly and lightly **blurred** not clear, not sharp **to take into account** to consider **mutability** ability to change

things, the way they changed according to the force and angle of the light, the way their aspect could be altered by what was happening around them: a person walking by, a sudden gust of wind, an odd reflection. Everything was constantly in flux, and though two bricks in a wall might strongly resemble each other, they could never be construed as identical. More to the point, the same brick was never really the same. It was wearing out, imperceptibly crumbling under the effects of the atmosphere, the cold, the heat, the storms that attacked it, and eventually, if one could watch it over the course of centuries, it would no longer be there. All inanimate things were disintegrating, all living things were dying. My head would start to throb whenever I thought of this, imagining the furious and hectic motions of molecules, the unceasing explosions of matter, the collisions, the chaos boiling under the surface of all things. As Effing had warned me at our first meeting: take nothing for granted. From casual indifference, I passed through a stage of intense alarm. My descriptions became overly exact, desperately trying to capture every possible nuance of what I was seeing, jumbling up details in a mad scramble to leave nothing out. The words burst from my mouth like machine-gun bullets, a staccato of rapid-fire assault. Effing constantly had to tell me to slow down, complaining that he couldn't keep up with me. The problem was less in my delivery than in my general approach. I was piling too many words on top of each other, and rather than reveal the thing before us, they were in fact obscuring it, burying it under an avalanche of subtleties and geometric abstractions. The important thing to remember was that Effing was blind. My job was not to exhaust him with lengthy catalogues, but to help him see things for himself. In the end, the words didn't matter. Their task was to enable him to apprehend the objects as quickly as possible, and in order to do that, I had to make them disappear the moment they were pronounced. It took me weeks of

**aspect** appearance, characteristic **gust** a sudden strong movement **odd** occasional, incidental, or happening by chance **flux** continuous change, instability **to construe** to interpret the meaning of s.th., to consider **imperceptibly** hardly noticeably **to crumble** to break apart into little pieces **to disintegrate** to break up into small pieces, to slowly be destroyed **to throb** to pulsate with pain **casual** not seeming to care about anything **nuance** [ˈnjuː.ɑːnts] subtle difference **to jumble up** to mix things up **in a mad scramble** done very quickly without considering the results **staccato** with short abrupt sounds **assault** [əˈsɔːlt] violent attack **delivery** way one gives a speech **approach** method of dealing with s.th. **to obscure** to make unclear, hidden **avalanche** [ˈæv.əlæntʃ] Lawine **subtlety** [ˈsʌt.l.ti] detail that is not immediately noticeable **to apprehend** to perceive, to understand

hard work to simplify my sentences, to learn how to separate the extraneous from the essential. I discovered that the more air I left around a thing, the happier the results, for that allowed Effing to do the crucial work on his own: to construct an image on the basis of a few hints, to feel his own mind traveling toward the thing I was describing for him. Disgusted by my early performances, I took to practicing when I was alone, lying in bed at night, for example, and going around the objects in the room, seeing if I couldn't get any better at it. The harder I worked, the more serious I became about what I was doing. I no longer saw it as an aesthetic activity but as a moral one, and I began to be less irritated by Effing's criticisms, wondering if his impatience and dissatisfaction could not eventually serve some higher purpose. I was a monk seeking illumination, and Effing was my hair shirt, the whip I flayed myself with. I don't think there was any question that I improved, but that does not mean I was ever entirely satisfied with my efforts. The demands of words are too great for that; one meets with failure too often to exult in the occasional success. As time went on, Effing became more tolerant of my descriptions, but I can't say whether that meant they were really any closer to what he wanted. Perhaps he had given up hope, or perhaps he was beginning to lose interest. It was difficult for me to know. In the end, it could be that he was simply getting used to me.

During the winter, we generally confined our walks to the immediate neighborhood. West End Avenue, Broadway, the cross streets in the Seventies and Eighties. Many of the people we passed recognized Effing, and contrary to what I would have thought, they acted as though they were glad to see him. Some even stopped to say hello. Greengrocers, news vendors, old people out on walks of their own. Effing knew them all by the sound of their voices, and he spoke to them in a courteous if somewhat distant manner: a nobleman who had come down from his castle to mingle with the people of the village. He seemed to command their respect, and in the early weeks there was much talk about Pavel Shum, a person they had all apparently known and liked. The story of his death

**extraneous** not essential **illumination** spiritual or intellectual enlightenment, insight or understanding **hair shirt** a shirt made of rough cloth with hair, worn in the past by some religious people to punish themselves **to flay** to whip so the skin comes off in strips **to meet with s.th.** to experience **to exult** to be joyful because of success **to confine** to limit **cross streets** streets that run west to east/east to west **greengrocer** (BE) s.o. who sells fruit and vegetables **news vendor** s.o. who sells newspapers and magazines **courteous** polite **nobleman** Adliger **to mingle with people** to mix with different groups of people

was common knowledge in the neighborhood (some had even witnessed the accident), and Effing endured many earnest handshakes and offers of condolence, taking the attention perfectly in stride. It was remarkable how elegantly he could act when he wanted to, how deeply he seemed to understand the conventions of public behavior. "This is my new man," he would say, gesturing in my direction, "Mr. M. S. Fogg, a recent graduate of Columbia University." All very proper and correct, as though I were some distinguished person who had torn myself away from numerous other commitments to honor him with my presence. The same turnabout also held true in the pastry shop on Seventy-second Street where we sometimes went for a cup of tea before heading home. Not one dribble or slurp, not one noise ever escaped his lips. When strangers were watching him, Effing was an absolute gentleman, an impressive model of decorum.

It was difficult to do much talking when we were out on these excursions. We were both turned in the same direction, and with my head so much higher than his, Effing's words tended to get lost before they ever reached my ears. I would have to lean down to hear what he was saying, and because he didn't like it when we stopped or slackened our pace, he would hold onto his comments until we had come to a corner and were waiting to cross the street. When he wasn't asking me for descriptions, Effing rarely went beyond short statements and questions. What street is this? What time is it? I'm getting cold. There were days when he barely uttered a word from beginning to end, abandoning himself to the motion of the wheelchair as it rolled along the sidewalk, his face turned up to the sun, moaning softly to himself in a trance of physical pleasure. Effing loved to feel the air against his skin, to wallow in the invisible light that came pouring down around him, and on the days when I was able to keep a steady rhythm to our progress, synchronizing my steps to the turning of the wheels, I could feel him gradually subside into the music of it, lolling back like an infant in a stroller.

**to take in stride** to do s.th. without difficulty or effort **commitment** obligation **turnabout** change of attitude **to hold true** to continue to happen **pastry shop** shop that sells pies and other sweet bakery products **model of decorum** perfect example of correct behavior **to slacken one's pace** to walk more slowly **to abandon oneself to s.th.** to let s.th. control you completely because an emotion is so strong **to wallow in s.th.** here: to thoroughly enjoy s.th. **to synchronize** to arrange for two or more actions to happen at exactly the same time **to subside into s.th.** to fall or sink into s.th. **to loll** to lie or sit in a relaxed manner **stroller** (AE) a kind of chair for children with wheels that is pushed

In late March and early April, we began taking longer walks, leaving upper Broadway behind us and branching out into other neighborhoods. In spite of the warmer temperatures, Effing continued to bundle himself up in heavy outergarments, and even on the balmiest days he refused to tackle the outdoors without first putting on his overcoat and wrapping a plaid blanket around his legs. This sensitivity to the weather was so pronounced, it was as if he feared his very insides would be exposed if he didn't take drastic measures to protect them. As long as he was warm, however, he welcomed contact with the air, and there was nothing like a good stiff breeze to brighten his spirits. When the wind blew on him, he would inevitably laugh and start cursing, making a great fuss about it as he shook his stick at the elements. Even in the winter, his preferred haunt was Riverside Park, and he spent many hours sitting there in silence, never dozing off as I expected he would, but just listening, trying to follow the things that were going on around him: the birds and squirrels rustling among the leaves and twigs, the wind fluttering through the branches, the sounds of traffic on the highway below. I began carrying a nature guide with me on these trips to the park so that I could look up the names of shrubs and flowers when he asked me what they were. I learned to identify dozens of plants in this way, examining leaves and bud formations with an interest and curiosity I had never felt for these things before. Once, when Effing was in a particularly receptive mood, I asked him why he didn't live in the country. It was still rather early at that point, I think, late November or the beginning of December, and I hadn't yet grown afraid of asking him questions. The park seemed to give him such pleasure, I said, it was a pity he couldn't be surrounded by nature all the time. He waited a long moment before answering me, so long that I began to think he hadn't heard the question. "I've already done it," he said at last. "I've done it, and now it's all in my head. All alone in the middle of nowhere, living in the wilderness for months, for months and months...an entire lifetime. Once you've done that, boy, you never forget it. I don't need to go anywhere. The moment I start to think about it, I'm

**to branch out** here: to use new roads or streets **balmy** mild and pleasant **to tackle** to deal with s.th. difficult **pronounced** very noticeable **to make a great fuss** to complain about s.th. that is not that important **elements** the weather **haunt** a place one wants to go to often **Riverside Park** park along the Hudson River between 72nd Street and 125th Street **to doze off** to go to sleep when not intended **squirrel** Eichhörnchen **to rustle** to move along quickly **the highway below** the Hendrik Hudson Parkway **bud** Knospe **formation** arrangement, shape **receptive** willing to listen

back. That's where I spend most of my time these days—back in the middle of nowhere."

In mid-December, Effing suddenly lost interest in travel books. We had read close to a dozen by then and were plodding our way through *A Canyon Voyage* by Frederick S. Dellenbaugh (a narrative of Powell's second expedition down the Colorado) when he stopped me in the middle of a sentence and announced: "I think we've had enough, Mr. Fogg. It's getting rather tedious, and we don't have any time to waste. There's work to be done, business to take care of."

I had no idea what business he was referring to, but I gladly put the book back on the shelf and waited for his instructions. They turned out to be something of a disappointment. "Go down to the comer," he said, "and buy a copy of *The New York Times*. Mrs. Hume will give you the money."

"Is that all?"

"That's all. And make it fast. There's no more time for dawdling."

Until then, Effing had not shown the slightest interest in following the news. Mrs. Hume and I would sometimes talk about it at meals, but the old man had never joined in, had never so much as offered a comment. But now that was the only thing he wanted, and for the next two weeks I spent every morning diligently reading articles to him from *The New York Times*. Reports from the Vietnam War dominated, but he asked to hear about any number of things as well: congressional debates, three-alarm fires in Brooklyn, stabbings in the Bronx, stockmarket listings, book reviews, basketball scores, earthquakes. None of this seemed to

**to plod one's way through s.th.** here: to read through s.th. with difficulty **Frederick Samuel Dellenbaugh** [ˈdel.ɪn.bɔː] ( 1853-1935) artist, Indian ethnologist and topographer who accompanied Powell when he was 17 and wrote *A Canyon Voyage* 30 years later **narrative** description of what happened, account, story **tedious** boring, tiring **The New York Times** most respected and prestigious newspaper in America **to dawdle** to waste time **diligently** carefully **to dominate** here: to be the most important subject—among other things Nixon widened the Vietnam war with an invasion of Cambodia (April/May 1970) and a number of students were killed in Kent State (Ohio) (May 4, 1970) during a demonstration against the Vietnam war **three-alarm** needing three fire brigades **Brooklyn** borough (part) of New York City to the southeast of Manhattan on Long Island, largely middle and lower middle class **stabbing** a crime in which a knife is used to kill s.o. **stock market** Börse **book review** an article that criticizes a novel or collections of short stories, etc. **scores** Ergebnisse

tally with the urgent tone he had used in sending me out for the paper the first time. Effing was clearly up to something, but I was hard-pressed to imagine what it was. He was coming to it obliquely, circling around his intentions in a slow game of cat and mouse. No doubt he was trying to confuse me, but at the same time these strategies were so transparent, it was as if he were telling me to be on my guard.

We always ended up our morning news sessions with a thorough scanning of the obituary pages. These seemed to hold Effing's attention more firmly than the other articles, and I was sometimes astonished to see how closely he listened to the colorless prose of these accounts. Captains of industry, politicians, flagpole sitters, inventors, stars of the silent screen: they all engaged his curiosity in equal measure. Days passed, and little by little we began to devote more of each session to the obituaries. He made me read through some of the stories two or three times, and on days when deaths were sparse, he would ask me to read the paid announcements that appeared in fine print at the bottom of the page. George So-and-So, age sixty-nine, beloved husband and father, mourned by his family and friends, will be laid to rest this afternoon at one o'clock in Our Lady of Sorrows Cemetery. Effing never seemed to tire of these dull recitations. Finally, after almost two weeks of saving them for the end, he abandoned the pretense of wanting to hear the news at all and asked me to turn to the obituary page first. I said nothing about this change of order, but once we had studied the deaths and he did not ask me to read anything else, I realized that we had at last come to a turning point.

"We know what they sound like now, don't we, boy?" he said.

**to tally with s.th.** to match, to correspond with s.th. **tone** way one's voice sounds **to be up to s.th.** to have s.th. planned that may be unpleasant for others **I was hard-pressed...** It was very difficult for me... **obliquely** indirectly **transparent** obvious **to be on one's guard** to be careful that nothing bad will happen to you **to scan** to read quickly **obituary page** page with reports about people who have died **captain of industry** s.o. who has founded or runs an important industry **flagpole sitter** It was popular in America to see how long one could sit a top of a flagpole in the 1920s. **silent screen** i.e. the film industry until the end of the 1920s when films began to be made with sound **to engage** to attract s.o. and keep his/her interest **in equal measure** to the same extent **to devote** to spend one's time with s.th. **session** Sitzung **sparse** small in number **fine print** printed in small letters **to mourn** to feel or express sadness for the death or loss of s.o. **lady** i.e. the Virgin Mary **sorrow** sadness, grief **dull** boring **recitation** here: the reading of newspaper articles **to abandon** to stop doing s.th., to give up **pretense** the act of pretending, a false appearance

"I suppose we do," I answered. "We've certainly read enough of them to get the general drift."

"It's depressing, I admit. But I felt a little research was in order before we started on our project."

"Our project?"

"My turn is coming. Any numbskull can see that."

"I don't expect you to live forever, sir. But you've outlived most people already, and there's no reason to think you won't go on doing it for a long time to come."

"Perhaps. But if I'm mistaken, it would be the first time in my life I've ever been wrong."

"You're saying you know."

"That's right, I know. A hundred little signs have told me. I'm running out of time, and we've got to get started before it's too late."

"I still don't understand."

"My obituary. We have to start putting it together now."

"I've never heard of someone writing his own obituary. Other people are supposed to do it for you—after you're dead."

"When they have the facts, yes. But what happens when there's nothing in the file?"

"I see your point. You want to gather together some basic information."

"Exactly."

"But what makes you think they'll want to print it?"

"They printed it fifty-two years ago. I don't see why they won't jump at the chance to do it again."

"I don't follow you."

"I was dead. They don't print obituaries of living people, do they? I was dead, or at least they thought I was dead."

"And you didn't say anything about it?"

"I didn't want to. I liked being dead, and after it got written up in the papers, I was able to stay dead."

"You must have been someone important."

"I was very important."

"Why haven't I ever heard of you, then?"

"I used to have another name. I got rid of it after I died."

**general drift** general meaning **in order** suitable for the circumstances, appropriate **numbskull** ['nʌm.skʌl] (coll) stupid person **in the file** in den Akten **to jump at the chance** to immediately react at an opportunity **to get rid of s.th.** to free yourself of s.th.

"What was it?"

"A sissy name. Julian Barber. I always detested it."

"I never heard of Julian Barber either."

"It was too long ago for anyone to remember. I'm talking about fifty years ago, Fogg. Nineteen sixteen, nineteen seventeen. I slipped into obscurity, as they say, and never came back."

"What did you do when you were Julian Barber?"

"I was a painter. A great American painter. If I'd stuck with it, I'd probably be recognized as the most important artist of my time."

"A modest assessment, I'm sure."

"I'm just giving you the facts. My career was too short, and I didn't do enough work."

"Where are your paintings now?"

"I don't have the slightest idea. All gone, I assume, all vanished into thin air. That doesn't concern me now."

"Then why do you want to write the obituary?"

"Because I'm going to die soon, and then it won't matter if I keep the secret or not. They botched it the first time. Maybe they'll get it right when it really counts."

"I see," I said, not seeing anything at all.

"My legs figure heavily in this, of course," he continued. "You've no doubt wondered about them. Everyone does, it's only natural. My legs. My shriveled, useless legs. I wasn't born a cripple, you know, we might as well clarify that at the start. I was a sprightly lad in my youth, all bounce and mischief, romping around with the rest of them. That was on Long Island, in the big house where we spent the summers. It's all tract houses and parking lots out there now, but then it was paradise, nothing but meadows and seashore, a little heaven on earth. When I moved to Paris in 1920, there was no need to give anyone the facts. It didn't matter what

**to slip into obscurity** to disappear, to become forgotten without people noticing **to stick with s.th.** (coll) to continue doing s.th. **modest assessment** (ironic) reasonable, not exaggerated opinion or judgement **to concern s.o.** to affect, to involve, to be of interest to s.o. **to botch** to ruin or spoil s.th. by doing s.th. badly **figure heavily** play an important role **shriveled** shrunken and wrinkled because of illness or lack of use (zusammengeschrumpft, verkümmert) **cripple** Krüppel **to clarify** to make clearer and easier to understand **sprightly** active and full of energy **lad** boy **bounce** energy **mischief** behavior typical of boys that causes trouble **to romp around** to play or run about wildly, or joyfully **Long Island** island to the east of Manhattan **tract house** one of numerous houses of similar design built on a piece of land—such houses were built on Long Island in the years after World War Two.

they thought anyway. As long as I was convincing, who cared what had really happened? I made up several stories, each one an improvement on the ones that came before it. I'd pull them out according to the circumstances and my mood, always changing them slightly as I went along, embellishing an incident here, perfecting a detail there, toying with them over the years until I got them just right. The best were probably the war stories, I became quite good at those. I'm talking about the Great War, the one that ripped the heart out of things, the war to end all wars. You should have heard me go on about the trenches and the mud. I was eloquent, inspired. I could explain fear like no one else, the guns booming in the night, the dumb-faced doughboys crapping in their puttees. Shrapnel, I would say, over six hundred fragments of it in my two legs—that's how it happened. The French ate it up, they couldn't get enough. I had another story about the Lafayette Escadrille. The vivid, spine-tingling account of how I was shot down by the Boche. That was a good one, believe me, it always left them begging for more. The problem was remembering which story I had told when. I kept it all straight in my head for years, making sure not to give people a different version when I saw them again. That added a certain thrill to it, knowing that I could be caught at any moment, that someone could stand up out of the blue and start calling me a liar. If you're going to lie, you might as well make it dangerous for yourself."

"And in all those years you never told anyone the real story?"

"Not a soul."

**to embellish** to make a story more interesting by adding details that are not true **to toy with s.th.** to play with s.th. **Great War** World War One **ripped the heart out of things** completely destroyed the old order **the war to end all wars** statement made by President Woodow Wilson (1856-1924) during World War One. He believed there would be no future wars with the League of Nations. **to go on about s.th.** to talk about s.th. that may not be true **trench** a long narrow hole dug into the surface of the ground as was common in World War One **mud** Schlamm **inspired** stimulated to great creativity **to boom** to make a deep long sound **doughboy** [doʊ.bɔɪ] (coll) American soldier in World War One **to crap** (slang) scheißen **puttee** [pʌt'iː] a strip of cloth wrapped around the lower part of the leg as a part of the uniform worn in World War One **shrapnel** small pieces of metal from a bomb or bullet **ate it up** (coll) loved to hear it **Lafayette Escadrille** a unit of American pilots who fought for the French before America entered World War One in 1917—it was named for the French hero who helped the Americans in the American Revolution **spine-tingling** causing a sensation of fear—spine = Rückgrat, to tingle = kribbeln **the Boche** [bɔːʃ] (slang, derogatory) the Germans **to beg for s.th.** to ask in an urgent way **thrill** excitement **out of the blue** from anywhere

"Not even Pavel Shum?"

"Least of all Pavel Shum. The man was discretion itself. He never asked me, and I never told him."

"And now you're prepared to tell?"

"In due time, boy, in due time. You have to be patient."

"But why are you going to tell me? We've only known each other for a couple of months."

"Because I have no choice. My Russian friend is dead, and Mrs. Hume isn't cut out for these things. Who else is there, Fogg? Like it or not, you're the only listener I have."

I was expecting him to go right back to it the next morning, to pick up again and start where we had left off. Considering what had happened the day before, that would have been logical, but I should have known better than to expect logic from Effing. Rather than say anything about our previous conversation, he immediately rushed into a tangled and confusing discourse about a man he had apparently once known, rambling crazily from one thing to another, producing a whirlwind of fractured reminiscences that made no sense to me. I did my best to follow him, but it was as though he had already started without me, and by the time I walked in on him, it was too late to catch up.

"A midget," he said. "The poor bugger looked like a midget. Eighty, ninety pounds if he was lucky, and that sunken, far-off look in his eyes, the eyes of a madman, all ecstatic and miserable at once. That was just before they locked him up, the last time I saw him. New Jersey. It was like going to the end of the goddamned earth. Orange, East Orange, fuck the name. Edison was in one of those towns, too. He didn't know Ralph, though, probably never heard of him. Ignorant asshole. Fuck Edison.

**itself** a perfect example of s.th. **in due time** at the right moment **to be cut out for s.th.** to be suited for s.th. **tangled** complicated, chaotic **discourse** talk, speech **to ramble** to talk in a confused way **whirlwind** (fig) an extremely strong wind that moves quickly with a circular movement **fractured** in pieces, broken, confused **reminiscence** story about the past **midget** [mɪdʒ.ɪt] an unusually small person who has not grown properly **bugger** (slang) here: fellow **sunken** eingesunken **East Orange** It was indeed East Orange and not Orange, a town in New Jersey near Manhattan. **Fuck the name.** (slang, vulgar) The name is not important. **Edison** Thomas A. Edison (1847-1931) American inventor, who had one laboratory in West Orange, New Jersey—He invented the lightbulb among other things. **Fuck Edison.** (slang, vulgar) Edison should go to hell. He was a notorious anti-Semite: For a time Auster's father worked for Edison until Edison fired him when he found out that Auster's father was Jewish.

Fuck Edison and his goddamned lightbulb. Ralph tells me he's running out of money. What do you expect with eight brats in the house and a thing like that for a wife? I did what I could. I was rich back then, money was no problem. Here, I say, reaching into my pocket, take this, it doesn't matter to me. I can't remember how much it was. A hundred dollars, two hundred dollars. Ralph was so grateful he started to cry, just like that, standing there in front of me and bawling like a baby. It was pathetic. When I think about it now, it makes me want to puke. One of the greatest men we've ever had, and there he was all broken apart, on the verge of losing his mind. He used to tell me about his travels out West, wandering through the wilderness for weeks on end, never seeing a soul. Three years he was out there. Wyoming, Utah, Nevada, California. It was a savage place back in those days. No lightbulbs or moving pictures then, you can count on that, no goddamned automobiles to run you over. He liked the Indians, he told me. They were good to him and let him stay in their villages when he passed through. That's what happened to him when he finally cracked. He put on an Indian costume some chief had given him twenty years before and started walking through the streets of goddamned New Jersey dressed like that. Feathers sticking out of his head, beads, sashes, long hair, a dagger around his waist, the whole kit and boodle. Poor little bugger. As if that wasn't bad enough, he got it into his head to start making his own money. Hand-painted thousand-dollar bills

**Ralph** Ralph Albert Blakelock (1847-1919) American self-taught landscape painter. For most of his life he was unable to get much money for his paintings. He went mad because he couldn't support his family of ten children and was put in a hospital for the mentally ill from 1899-1916. His paintings were mostly melancholy landscape scenes from the west, where he had traveled earlier. It wasn't until the end of his life that his talent was recognized. Auster himself had written an article about Blakelock for an art magazine. Most of his information seems to come from an article that Lloyd Goodrich wrote for a Blakelock exhibition for the Whitney Museum of Modern Art in New York in 1947. The description of Blakelock on the following pages is usually correct. **brat** badly behaving child **to bawl** to cry noisily **to puke** (coll) to vomit **on the verge of** just about to **on end** without pause or interruption **savage** wild, uncivilized **cracked** (coll) crazy **Indian costume** Some scholars believe Blakelock never walked on the streets of New Jersey as described by Effing. **beads** small balls of wood, glass, etc. held together with a string and worn around the neck **sash** a long piece of ribbon, silk, etc., worn around the waist like a belt or over one shoulder **dagger** a short knife used to stab s.o. **the whole kit and boodle** (coll) everything you can image

with his own picture on them—right in the middle, like the portrait of some founding father. One day he walks into the bank, hands one of those bills to the teller, and asks him to change it. No one thinks it's very funny, especially after he starts to raise a stink. You can't fuck with the almighty dollar and expect to get away with it. So they drag him out of there in that greasy Indian costume, kicking and hollering in protest. It wasn't long before they decided to cart him off for good. Some place in New York State, I think it was. Lived in the nuthouse until the end, but he went on painting, if you can believe it, the son of a bitch didn't know how to stop. He painted on anything he could get his hands on. Paper, cardboard, cigar boxes, even windowshades. And the twist of it was that his old work started to sell then. Big prices, mind you, unheard-of sums for pictures no one would even look at a few years before. Some god-damned senator from Montana shelled out fourteen thousand dollars for *Moonlight*—the highest price ever paid for the work of a living American artist. Not that it did Ralph or his family any good. His wife was living on fifty dollars a year in some shack near Catskill—the same territory that Thomas Cole used to paint—and she couldn't even afford the car-fare to visit her husband in the loony bin. He was a stormy little runt,

**founding father** George Washington, Thomas Jefferson, etc. who helped to write the American Constitution **teller** s.o. whose job it is to receive and pay out money in a bank—Some biographers say there is no evidence that Blakelock made his own money for the purpose of using it as real money. **to raise a stink** to make a lot of trouble, or a commotion **to fuck with s.th.** (slang, vulgar) to play around with s.th., to misuse s.th. **to get away with it** to not get punished **greasy** oily, with fat **to holler** (coll) to shout **to cart him off for good** (coll) to send him away for the rest of his life—for a time Blakelock could leave the hospital after 1916 **some place in New York** Middletown, in southeast New York **nuthouse** (coll) hospital for the insane **cardboard** thick brown paper used for making boxes, etc. **windowshade** (AE) a rolled up covering that can be pulled down over a window **the twist of it was** the irony was **senator** Senator W.A. Clark bought Moonlight for $13,900 in 1913, the highest sum of money ever paid for an American painting up until that time. The painting was originally purchased by an actor, Lew Bloom in the 1890s. **Moonlight** (cf. the front cover of this edition) painted between 1885-1889. Critics didn't think much of it at the time. **shack** a roughly built hut **Catskill** the Catskill Mountains, a part of the Appalachian Mountains in southeast New York—indeed Cole did paint many scenes from the Catskill Mountains **carfare** (AE) the money needed to travel somewhere by bus or train **loony bin** (coll) hospital for the insane **stormy** violent and emotional **runt** (coll, derogatory) an undersized person

I'll grant you that, always in a frenzy, pounding out music on the piano while he painted his pictures. I saw him do it once, dashing back and forth between the piano and the easel, I'll never forget it. God, how it all comes back to me now. Brush, palette knife, pumice stone. Smack it on, flatten it down, rub it off. Again, then again. Smack it on, flatten it down, rub it off. There was never anything like it. Never. Never, never, never." Effing paused for a moment to catch his breath, and then, as if coming out of a trance, he turned his face in my direction for the first time. "What do you think of that, boy?"

"It would help if I knew who Ralph was," I answered politely.

"Blakelock," Effing whispered, as though struggling to hold his feelings in check. "Ralph Albert Blakelock."

"I don't think I've ever heard of him."

"Don't you know anything about painting? I thought you were supposed to be educated. What the hell did they teach you in that fancy college of yours, Mr. Smart Ass?"

"Not much. Nothing about Blakelock in any case."

"It won't do. I can't go on talking to you if you don't know anything."

It seemed pointless to try to defend myself, so I held my tongue and waited. A long time passed—two or three minutes, an eternity when you are waiting for someone to speak. Effing let his head drop down to his chest, as though he couldn't stand it anymore and had decided to take a nap. When he lifted it again, I was fully expecting him to fire me. If he hadn't already felt stuck with me, I'm certain that's precisely what he would have done.

"Go into the kitchen," he said at last, "and ask Mrs. Hume for subway fare. Then put on your coat and gloves and walk out the door. Take the elevator downstairs, go outside, and walk to the nearest subway station. Once you get there, enter the station and buy two tokens. Put one of the

**I'll grant you that** I'll admit that **in a frenzy** wildly excited **to pound out** to play very loudly **to dash** to run somewhere very quickly **pumice stone** Bimssstein **to smack s.th. on** to throw on a surface with force—Effing's description is correct. **fancy** (coll, derogatory) high priced **Mr. Smart Ass** (coll, vulgar) Klugscheißer **It won't do.** It is completely unsatisfactory. **pointless** useless **to take a nap** to sleep for a short time, especially during the day **to feel stuck with s.o.** (coll) to feel you have no choice but to keep s.o. even though you'd rather get rid of this person **subway fare** the amount of money needed to ride the subway (the New York underground system)—at the time 30 cents **nearest subway station** 86th Street and Broadway **token** a special coin for the subway that has to be purchased at a subway station before going onto the platform

tokens in your pocket. Put the other token in the turnstile, walk downstairs, and take the southbound Number One train to Seventy-second Street. Get off at Seventy-second Street, cross the platform, and wait for the downtown express—the number two or three train, it doesn't matter. When the doors open, get on that train and find yourself a seat. The rush hour is over now, so you shouldn't have any trouble. Find a seat and don't say a word to anyone. That's very important. From the moment you leave the house until you return, I don't want you to utter a sound. Not one peep. Pretend you're a deaf-mute if someone talks to you. When you buy your tokens from the vendor, just put up two fingers to indicate how many you want. Once you've settled into your seat on the downtown express, stay on until you reach Grand Army Plaza in Brooklyn. The ride should take you somewhere between thirty and forty minutes. During that time, I want you to keep your eyes shut. Think about as little as you can—nothing, if possible—and if that's too much to ask, then think about your eyes and the extraordinary power you possess to see the world. Imagine what would happen to you if you couldn't see it. Imagine yourself looking at something under the various lights that make the world visible to us: sunlight, moonlight, electric light, candlelight, neon light. Make it a very simple and ordinary something. A stone, for example, or a small block of wood. Think carefully about how the appearance of that object changes when placed under these different lights. Think nothing more than that, assuming you have to think about something. When the subway reaches Grand Army Plaza, open your eyes again. Get off the train and walk upstairs. From there I want you to go to the Brooklyn Museum. It's located on Eastern Parkway, no more than a five-minute walk from the subway exit. Don't ask for directions.

**turnstile** the token has to be put into a slot next to the turnstile (Drehkreuz) that then turns and allows you to go onto the platforms **southbound** travelling towards the south **Number One train** Broadway local (stopping very often) train **number two or three downtown express** 7th Avenue express (not making so many stops) that also goes to Brooklyn **not one peep** not any kind of sound **deaf-mute** a person who can't hear or speak **the vendor** the person who sells the subway token in a small locked room or house at the subway station **Grand Army Plaza** a large square (actually oval) with a triumphal arch honoring the soldiers of the North who fought in the Civil War—built at the end of the 19th century **Brooklyn Museum** the main building was built in 1897 and includes, among other things, exhibits about the Indians of North and South America, oriental art, American painting and sculpture from the 18th to early 20th centuries

Even if you get lost, I don't want you talking to anyone. You'll find it eventually, it shouldn't be hard. The museum is a big stone building designed by McKim, Mead and White, the same firm that designed the buildings at the university you just graduated from. The style should be familiar to you. Stanford White, by the way, was shot and killed by a man named Henry Thaw on the roof of Madison Square Garden. That was in nineteen-o-something, and it happened because White had done things to Mrs. Thaw he probably shouldn't have done. It was big news back in those days, but you needn't concern yourself with that. Just concentrate on finding the museum. When you do, walk up the steps, enter the lobby, and pay your admission fee to the person in the uniform sitting behind the desk. I don't know how much it costs, but no more than a dollar or two. You can get the money from Mrs. Hume when she gives you the subway fare. Remember not to speak when you pay the guard. All these things must happen in silence. Find your way to the floor where they keep the permanent collection of American paintings and enter the gallery. Do your best not to look at anything too closely. In the second or third room, you'll find Blakelock's painting *Moonlight* on one of the walls, and at that point you'll stop. Look at the painting. Look at the painting for no less than an hour, ignoring everything else in the room. Concentrate. Look at it from various distances—from ten feet away, from two feet away, from one inch away. Study it for its overall composition, study it for its details. Don't take any notes. See if you can memorize all the elements of the picture, learning the precise location of the human figures, the natural object, the colors on each and every spot of the canvas. Close your eyes and test yourself. Open them again. See if you can't begin to enter the landscape before you. See if you can't begin to enter the mind of the artist who painted the landscape before you. Imagine that you are Blakelock, painting the picture yourself. After an hour of this, take a short break. Wander around the gallery if you like and

**McKim, Mead, and White** perhaps the most important firm of architects at the end of the 19th century in America—famous for its classical style It designed numerous buildings in New York and throughout the country including a number of buildings for Columbia University. **Stanford White** (1853-1906) one the architects of McKim, Mead, and White—The information Effing gives is correct. Madison Square Garden (the first one) was at the time on 26th Street, and designed by White. **...he probably shouldn't have done...** Stanford White had sex with Mrs. Thaw on a swing (Schaukelstuhl) he built on the roof of Madison Square Garden; cf. E.L. Doctorow's novel *Ragtime* **admission fee** fee you have to pay before entering a museum, cinema, etc. **composition** the way the parts are put together

look at some of the other pictures. Then return to the Blakelock. Spend another fifteen minutes in front of it, giving yourself up to it as though there was nothing else but this painting in the entire world. Then leave. Retrace your steps through the museum, go outside, and walk to the subway. Take the express train back to Manhattan, switch to the local at Seventy-second Street, and come back here. When you're riding on the train, do the same thing you did before: keep your eyes closed, say nothing to anyone. Think about the painting. Try to see it in your mind. Try to remember it, try to hold on to it for as long as you can. Is that understood?"

"I think so," I said. "Is there anything else?"

"Nothing else. But just remember: if you don't do exactly what I say, I'll never talk to you again."

I kept my eyes closed on the train, but it was difficult to think of nothing. I tried fixing my mind on a small stone, but even that was more difficult than it seemed. There was too much noise around me, too many people were talking and jostling against my body. Those were the days before they had loudspeakers on the trains to announce the stops, and I had to keep track of where we were in my head, using my fingers to mark off the number of stops we made: one down, seventeen to go; two down, sixteen to go. Inevitably, I got drawn into listening to the conversations of the passengers who were sitting nearby. Their voices imposed themselves on me, and there was nothing I could do to shut them out. With each new voice I heard, I wanted to open my eyes and see the person it belonged to. This temptation was almost irresistible. As soon as you hear someone speak, you form a mental image of the speaker. In a matter of seconds, you have absorbed all kinds of salient information: sex, approximate age, social class, birthplace, even the color of the person's skin. If you are able to see, your natural impulse is to take a look and find out how closely this mental image matches up with the real thing. More often than not, the correspondences are rather close, but there are also times when you make astonishing blunders: college professors who talk like truck drivers, little girls who turn out to be old women, black people who

**to retrace** to go back the way you have come **to jostle** to bump or push s.o. roughly **to keep track of s.th.** to follow the passage, course, or progress of s.th. **to mark off** here: to use a system (here one's fingers) so that one remembers what has been already done **one down** one thing done **to be drawn into s.th.** to be forced to get involved with s.th. you really don't want to have anything to do with **imposed themselves on me** forced themselves on me **salient** most important **approximate** not exact **blunder** stupid mistake

turn out to be white. I couldn't help thinking about these things as the train rattled through the darkness. Forcing myself to keep my eyes closed, I began to hunger for a glimpse of the world, and in that hunger, I understood that I was thinking about what it meant to be blind, which was precisely what Effing had wanted me to do. I pursued this thought for several minutes. Then, in a sudden panic, I realized that I had lost track of how many stops we had made. If I hadn't heard a woman ask someone if Grand Army Plaza was coming up next, I might have traveled clear to the end of Brooklyn.

It was a weekday morning in winter, and the museum was nearly deserted. After paying my admission at the front desk, I held out five fingers to the elevator man and rode upstairs in silence. The American paintings were on the fifth floor, and except for a drowsing guard in the first room, I was the only person in the entire wing. This fact pleased me, as though it somehow enhanced the solemnity of the occasion. I walked through several empty rooms before I found the Blakelock, doing my best to follow Effing's instructions and ignore the other pictures on the walls. I saw a few flashes of color, registered a few names—Church, Bierstadt, Ryder—but fought against the temptation to have a real look. Then I came to *Moonlight*, the object of my strange and elaborate journey, and in that first, sudden moment, I could not help feeling disappointed. I don't know what I had been expecting—something grandiose, perhaps, some loud and garish display of superficial brilliance—but certainly not the somber little picture I found before me. It measured only twenty-seven by thirty-two inches, and at first glance it seemed almost devoid of color: dark brown, dark green, the smallest touch of red in one corner.

**to rattle** to move along with noise because of shaking **clear** (coll) all the way **deserted** completely empty because everyone has left **drowsing** being almost asleep **guard** person who watches over a museum, etc. **wing** smaller part of a building that sticks out from the main building **to enhance** to increase **solemnity** [sə'lem.nəti] seriousness **Church** Frederick Edwin Church (1826-1900) American landscape artist, who studied for two years with Thomas Cole. His paintings were very detailed and dramatic. He was popular in his day, but today he would be considered slightly kitschy. **Bierstadt** Albert Bierstadt (1830-1902) German-American landscape artist, who painted dramatic scenes of the Far West that do not have much appeal today. He was very successful in his lifetime. **Ryder** Albert Pinkham Ryder (1847-1917) American landscape painter whose painting technique and style were very similar to Blakelock, e.g. his moonlight scenes. He was much admired by Blakelock. **garish** colorful in a vulgar way **brilliance** splendor, magnificence **somber** sad and serious **27 by 32 inches** 68.7 by 81.3 cm **devoid of** completely lacking in

There was no question that it was well executed, but it contained none of the overt drama that I had imagined Effing would be drawn to. Perhaps I was not disappointed in the painting so much as I was disappointed in myself for having misread Effing. This was a deeply contemplative work, a landscape of inwardness and calm, and it confused me to think that it could have said anything to my mad employer.

I tried to put Effing out of my mind, then stepped back a foot or two and began to look at the painting for myself. A perfectly round full moon sat in the middle of the canvas—the precise mathematical center, it seemed to me—and this pale white disc illuminated everything above it and below it: the sky, a lake, a large tree with spidery branches, and the low mountains on the horizon. In the foreground, there were two small areas of land, divided by a brook that flowed between them. On the left bank, there was an Indian teepee and a campfire; a number of figures seemed to be sitting around the fire, but it was hard to make them out, they were only minimal suggestions of human shapes, perhaps five or six of them, glowing red from the embers of the fire; to the right of the large tree, separated from the others, there was a solitary figure on horseback, gazing out over the water—utterly still, as though lost in meditation. The tree behind him was fifteen or twenty times taller than he was, and the contrast made him seem puny, insignificant. He and his horse were no more than silhouettes, black outlines without depth or individual character. On the other bank, things were even murkier, almost entirely drowned in shadow. There were a few small trees with the same spidery branches as the large one, and then, toward the bottom, the tiniest hint of brightness, which looked to me as though it might have been another figure (lying on his back—possibly asleep, possibly dead, possibly staring up into the night) or else the remnant of another fire—I couldn't tell which. I got so involved in studying these obscure details in the lower part of the picture that when I finally looked up to study the sky again, I

**to execute** to produce, to perform **overt** [oʊˈvɜːrt] open, obvious **contemplative** causing one to think for a long time or meditate **inwardness** quality of being directed to the mind **disc** s.th. in the shape of a flat circular plate **spidery** like a spider's web (Spinnennetz), thin, very fine **brook** a small stream **ember** a piece of wood or coal which is no longer burning but still red and hot **solitary** alone **to gaze at s.th.** to look long and fixedly at s.th. **puny** small, weak, and thin **silhouette** [ˌsɪl.uˈet] a dark shadow or shape, seen against a light background **murky** gloomy, dark **drowned** here: as if having disappeared **hint** suggestion, trace **remnant** a small part of s.th. which remains after the rest of it has been used **to get involved in s.th.** here: to become very interested in s.th. **obscure** unclear, difficult to understand

was shocked to see how bright everything was in the upper part. Even taking the full moon into consideration, the sky seemed too visible. The paint beneath the cracked glazes that covered the surface shone through with an unnatural intensity, and the farther back I went toward the horizon, the brighter that glow became—as if it were daylight back there, and the mountains were illumined by the sun. Once I finally noticed this, I began to see other odd things in the painting as well. The sky, for example, had a largely greenish cast. Tinged with the yellow borders of clouds, it swirled around the side of the large tree in a thickening flurry of brushstrokes, taking on a spiralling aspect, a vortex of celestial matter in deep space. How could the sky be green? I asked myself. It was the same color as the lake below it, and that was not possible. Except in the blackness of the blackest night, the sky and the earth are always different. Blakelock was clearly too deft a painter not to have known that. But if he hadn't been trying to represent an actual landscape, what had he been up to? I did my best to imagine it, but the greenness of the sky kept stopping me. A sky the same color as the earth, a night that looks like day, and all human forms dwarfed by the bigness of the scene—illegible shadows, the merest ideograms of life. I did not want to make any wild, symbolic judgments, but based on the evidence of the painting, there seemed to be no other choice. In spite of their smallness in relation to the setting, the Indians betrayed no fears or anxieties. They sat comfortably in their surroundings, at peace with themselves and the world, and the more I thought about it, the more this serenity seemed to dominate the picture. I wondered if Blakelock hadn't painted his sky green in order to emphasize this harmony, to make a point of showing the connection between

**to take into consideration** here: to consider, to direct your attention to s.th. **visible** obvious to the eye, easy to see **cracked** broken with fine lines **glaze** a kind of transparent paint that is used on the surface of a painting to change the colors **glow** a soft steady light **to illumine** to make a light shine on s.th. **cast** trace **to tinge** to give s.th. a small amount of a particular color **border** a band surrounding s.th. **to swirl around s.th.** to spin around s.th. **flurry** sudden burst of activity **brushstroke** a single movement of a brush when painting **taking a spiralling aspect** beginning to look like s.th. winding or twisting upwards or downwards **vortex** a whirling mass or motion of liquid, gas, flame, etc. **celestial** having to do with the sky **matter** substance, material **deft** skilful **to dwarf s.th.** to be so big that other things seem to be very small **illegible** [ɪˌledʒ.əbl] here: not easy to see what s.th. is **the merest** hardly **ideogram** [ˈɪd.i.oʊ.græm] sign, symbol, especially as used for writing Japanese or Chinese **to betray** to show, to indicate **serenity** quality of being calm and peaceful

heaven and earth. If men can live comfortably in their surroundings, he seemed to be saying, if they can learn to feel themselves a part of the things around them, then perhaps life on earth becomes imbued with a feeling of holiness. I was only guessing of course, but it struck me that Blakelock was painting an American idyll, the world the Indians had inhabited before the white men came to destroy it. The plaque on the wall noted that the picture had been painted in 1885. If I remembered correctly, that was almost precisely in the middle of the period between Custer's Last Stand and the massacre at Wounded Knee—in other words, at the very end, when it was too late to hope that any of these things could survive. Perhaps, I thought to myself, this picture was meant to stand for everything we had lost. It was not a landscape, it was a memorial, a death song for a vanished world.

I stayed with the painting for more than an hour. I stood back from it, I moved up close to it, I gradually learned it by heart. I wasn't sure if I had discovered what Effing thought I would, but by the time I left the museum, I felt that I had discovered something, even if I didn't know what it was. I was exhausted, absolutely drained of energy. When I got back on the IRT express and closed my eyes again, it was all I could do not to fall asleep.

It was just past three o'clock when I returned to the apartment. According to Mrs. Hume, Effing was taking a nap. Since the old man never took a nap at that time of day, I interpreted it to mean that he didn't want to talk to me. That was just as well. I was in no mood to talk to him either. I drank a cup of coffee with Mrs. Hume in the kitchen, and then I

**to imbue** here: to fill **holiness** quality of being sacred or holy (heilig) **American idyll** ['aɪ.dəl] a scene in America in which everything is peaceful and there is perfect happiness—this kind of scene was popular with many American landscape artists, cf. Thomas Cole, and the description of Long Island before the Dutch came at the end of *The Great Gatsby* by F. Scott Fitzgerald **plaque** [plæk] a small piece of metal or stone on a wall with writing on it **Custer's Last Stand** the battle at the Little Big Horn in Dakota Territory in which General Custer (1839-1876) and his troops were killed by the Sioux Indians in 1876 because of total incompetence—It was the last attempt by the Indians to stop the movement of whites across the West. **massacre at Wounded Knee** the last major battle of the Indian Wars in southwest South Dakota in which American troops panicked and killed 200 innocent women and children (Dec. 29, 1890) **memorial** s.th. built to remember an event in the past **to drain** here: to empty **IRT express** i.e. the number 2 or 3 train that Fogg used before—IRT (Interborough Transit) is the name still used for a part of the New York subway system from the time it was privately owned

left the apartment again, putting on my coat and taking the bus uptown to Morningside Heights. I was going to be seeing Kitty at eight o'clock, and in the meantime I thought I would do some research at the Columbia art library. It turned out that information on Blakelock was scant: a few articles here and there, a couple of old catalogues, nothing much. By piecing together the bits, however, I learned that Effing had not been lying to me. That was the essential thing I had come for. He had jumbled up certain details and chronologies, but all the important facts were true. Blakelock's life had been a miserable one. He had suffered, he had gone crazy, he had been neglected. Before they locked him up in the asylum, he had indeed painted money with his own picture on it—not thousand-dollar bills, as Effing had said, but million-dollar bills, sums beyond all imagining. He had traveled out West as a young man and lived among the Indians, he had been incredibly small (under five feet, less than ninety pounds), he had been the father of eight children—all of these things were true. I was particularly interested to learn that some of his early work in the 1870s had been set in Central Park. He had painted the shacks that stood there when the park was still new, and as I looked at the reproductions of these rural places in what had once been New York, I could not help thinking about the miserable time I had spent in there myself. I also learned that Blakelock's best years as an artist had been devoted to painting moonlight scenes. There were dozens of pictures similar to the one I had found in the Brooklyn Museum: the same forest, the same moon, the same silence. The moon was always full in these works, and it was always the same: a small, perfectly round circle in the middle of the canvas, glowing with the palest white light. After I had looked at five or six of them, they gradually began to separate themselves from their surroundings, and I was no longer able to see them as moons. They became holes in the canvas, apertures of whiteness looking out onto

**Morningside Heights** higher area of Manhattan between 110th and 125th Street and between the Hudson River to the west and Harlem to the east **scant** very limited **to jumble s.th. up** to mix up **to neglect** to ignore—But Blakelock was recognized towards the end of his life. **asylum** [əˈsaɪ.ləm] mental hospital **million-dollar bills** according to Lloyd Goodrich Blakelock painted only one one million-dollar bill **...Central Park...shacks...** Fogg is correct here. **rural place** place in the country **devoted** here: spent **moonlight scenes** correct—Moonlights scenes were also popular with American landscape artists of the 19th century. **canvas** a heavy cloth on which oil paintings are painted **pale** blass **aperture** [ˈæp.ə.tʃʊr] hole, opening

another world. Blakelock's eye, perhaps. A blank circle suspended in space, gazing down at things that were no longer there.

The next morning, Effing seemed ready to get down to business. Making no mention of Blakelock or the Brooklyn Museum, he told me to go out to Broadway and buy a notebook and a good pen. "This is it," he said, "the moment of truth. We start writing today."

When I returned, I took my seat on the couch again, opened the notebook to the first page, and waited for him to begin. I assumed he would warm up by giving some facts and figures—his birthdate, the names of his parents, the schools he attended—and then move on to more important things afterward. But that wasn't what happened at all. He just started to talk, throwing us right into the middle of the story.

"Ralph gave me the idea," he said, "but it was Moran who got me to do it. Old Thomas Moran, with his white beard and straw hat. He was living out at the end of the Island in those days, painting little watercolors of the sound. Dunes and grass, the waves and the light, all that bucolic claptrap. Lots of painters go out there now, but he was the first, he started the whole thing. That's why I called myself Thomas when I changed my name. In honor of him. The Effing was another matter, it took me a while to think of that. Maybe you can figure it out for yourself. It was a pun.

"I was a young fellow back then. Twenty-five, twenty-six years old, not even married. I had the house on Twelfth Street in New York, but I spent more time out on the Island. I liked it out there, that's where I did my paintings and dreamed my dreams. The house is gone now, but what do you expect? That was a long time ago, and things move on, as they say. Progress. The bungalows and tract houses have taken over, every nitwit drives his own car. Hallelujah.

**suspended** hanging, floating **to get down to business** to begin with the serious work **to warm up** here: to begin with a short introduction before the more important or difficult work begins **Thomas Moran** (1837-1926) English-American landscape artist and illustrator, who also illustrated reports of the expeditions of professor Hayden to the Yellowstone River (1871) and Powell's expedition down the Colorado River in 1873. His two paintings, *The Grand Canyon* and *The Chasm of the Colorado* hang in the Capitol. **Island** Long Island—It was East Hampton on the southern coast of Long Island near its end. **sound** Long Island Sound—the body of water between Connecticut and Long Island that ends in the Atlantic to the east **dune** a small hill of sand at a beach that can drift **bucolic claptrap** here: a silly or sentimental portrait of a scene in the countryside **pun** [ʌ] Wortspiel **nitwit** fool, idiot

"The name of the town was Shoreham. Still is, as far as I know. Are you writing this down? I'm only going to say these things once, and if you don't get it down, they'll be lost forever. Remember that, boy. If you don't do your job, I'll kill you. I'll strangle you with my own two hands.

"The name of the town was Shoreham. As chance would have it, that's where Tesla build his Wardenclyffe Tower. I'm talking about nineteen-o-one, nineteen-o-two, the World Wireless System. You've probably never heard of it. J. P. Morgan was the financial backer, and Stanford White drew up the architectural plans. We talked about him yesterday. He was shot on the roof of Madison Square Garden, and the project fell apart after that. But the remains stood there for another fifteen or sixteen years, two hundred feet high, you could see it from wherever you were. Gigantic. Like some robot sentry looming over the land. I used to think of it as the Tower of Babel: radio broadcasts in every language, the whole fucking world jabbering away at each other, right in the town where I lived. They finally demolished the thing during the First World War. The Germans were using it as a spy station, they said, and so they tore it down. I was gone by then anyway, it didn't matter to me. Not that I would have cried about it if I'd still been there. Let everything tumble down is what I say. Let everything tumble down and vanish, once and for all.

"I first saw Tesla in 1893. I was just a boy then, but I remember the date well. It was the Columbian Exposition in Chicago, and my father took me there on a train, it was the first time I'd ever been away from home. The idea was to celebrate the four hundredth anniversary of

**Shoreham** town on the northern shore of Long Island about 120 km east of Manhattan **to strangle** to kill s.o. by pressing on his/her throat with ones hands, etc. **Wardenclyffe Tower** Tesla wanted to build this tower (1900-1904) as a communication center for the world. Some of the surrounding buildings still exist. Most of the information Effing gives about Tesla is correct. **J.P. Morgan** John Pierpont Morgan (1837-1913) the most important investment banker and industrialist at turn of the last century—Wardenclyffe Tower was not completed because Morgan decided to withdraw his financial support for this project. **sentry** soldier on guard **to loom** to appear in a large shape that seems threatening **Tower of Babel** (in the Bible) the tower built to reach heaven that resulted in God creating different languages so that the tower could not be completed **to jabber away** to talk excitely **...demolished the thing...** It was demolished because it was feared the tower could be used as a landmark for German submarines. **to tumble down** to fall downwards **Columbian Exposition** world's fair in 1893, which the firm of Westinghouse used to introduce the public to new important inventions in electrical engineering

Columbus's discovery of America. Bring out all the gadgets and inventions and show them how clever our scientists were. Twenty-five million people came to see it, it was like going to the circus. They showed the first zipper there, the first Ferris wheel, all the wonders of the new age. Tesla was in charge of the Westinghouse exhibit, they called it the Egg of Columbus, and I remember walking into the theater and seeing this tall man dressed in a white tuxedo, standing up there on stage and talking to the audience in some peculiar accent—Serbian, as it turned out—and a more lugubrious voice you will never hear. He performed magic tricks with electricity, spinning little metal eggs around the table, shooting sparks out of his fingertips, and everyone kept gasping at what he did, myself included, we'd never seen anything like it. Those were the days of the AC-DC wars between Edison and Westinghouse, and Tesla's show had a certain propaganda value. Tesla had discovered alternating current about ten years before—the rotating magnetic field—and it was a big advance over the direct current that Edison had been using. Much more powerful. Direct current needed a generating station every mile or two; with alternating current, a single station was enough for a whole city. When Tesla came to America, he tried to sell his idea to Edison, but the asshole in Menlo Park turned him down. He thought it would make his

**gadget** device that does s.th. useful **zipper** Reißverschluss **Ferris wheel** large wheel that has seats and turns—often seen in fairs—George Ferris built the first such wheel for the Columbian Exposition in 1893 **Westinghouse** Westinghouse Electric Company—founded by the inventor George Westinghouse (1846-1914)—which bought Telsa's patents for devices that generate and transmit high voltage alternating current (Wechselstrom) systems **exhibit** Ausstellung—Westinghouse and Telsa wanted to prove with this exhibit that alternating current was by no means more dangerous than direct current (Gleichstrom) as Thomas Edison, their rival, maintained. **Egg of Columbus** small egglike objects were used in Tesla's demonstrations to the public—according to legend Christopher Columbus claimed he could make an egg remain upright. Nobody believed him until he tapped one end so that the egg did not fall over **tuxedo** [tʌk'si:.doʊ] (AE) for dinner jacket (BE)—suit worn for formal occasions **Serbian** having to do with Serbia in what is today Yugoslavia **lugubrious** [lə'gu:bri.əs] very sad, mournful **to spin** to cause to turn around very quickly **spark** flash of light caused by an electrical charge **to gasp** to breathe in suddenly and quickly with a loud sound because of being surprised or afraid **AC-DC** Alternating Current-Direct Current **rotating magnetic field** in physics: movement in a magnetic field can produce a current—first discovered by the English scientist Michael Faraday (1791-1867) in 1831 **generating station** Elektrizätswerk **asshole** (slang, vulgar) Arschloch **Menlo Park** one of the two laboratories Edison had in New Jersey **to turn s.o. down** to refuse s.o.'s offer

lightbulb obsolete. There you are again, the goddamned lightbulb. So Tesla sold his alternating current to Westinghouse, and they went ahead and started to build the generating plant at Niagara Falls, the largest power station in the country. Edison went on the attack. Alternating current is too dangerous, he said, it will kill you if you get close to it. To prove his point, he sent his men around the country to give demonstrations at state and county fairs. I saw one of them myself when I was just a wee little thing, it made me piss in my pants. They'd bring up animals onto the stage and electrocute them. Dogs, pigs, even cows. They'd kill them right before your eyes. That's how the electric chair got invented. Edison cooked it up to show the dangers of alternating current, and then he sold it to Sing Sing prison, where they're still using it to this day. Lovely, isn't it? If the world weren't such a beautiful place, we might all turn into cynics.

"The Egg of Columbus put an end to all the controversy. Too many people saw Tesla, and they weren't afraid anymore. The man was a lunatic, of course, but at least he wasn't in it for the money. A few years later, Westinghouse was in financial trouble, and Tesla tore up his royalty agreement with him as a gesture of friendship. Millions and millions of dollars. He just tore it up and went on to something else. It goes without saying that he eventually died broke.

"Now that I'd seen him, I began following Tesla in the papers. They wrote about him all the time back then, reporting on his new inventions, quoting the outlandish things he used to say to anyone who would listen. He was good copy. An ageless ghoul who lived alone in the Waldorf: morbidly afraid of germs, paralyzed by every kind of phobia, subject to

**obsolete** no longer useful because s.th. newer and better has been invented—of course, the light bulb could also be adapted to AC current **Niagara Falls** [naɪˈæg.əˈrə]—the generating plant was built in 1896 **wee little** tiny, very small **to electrocute** to kill with an electric shock **to cook s.th. up** to invent s.th. at short notice **Sing Sing** prison in southeastern New York that holds prisoners to be executed on the electric chair **royalty agreement** a contract that payment shall be made to a writer, inventor, etc. depending on how much is sold **…it goes without saying…** …it's so obvious that it's not really necessary to mention it… **outlandish** strange and unusual **to be good copy** to be interesting news **ghoul** [gu:l] evil person interested in disgusting things **Waldorf** the old Waldorf-Astoria hotel at the present site of the Empire State Building—At the end of his life Tesla lived in the New Yorker Hotel. **morbidly** psychologically abnormally **germ** microorganism that causes disease **phobia** abnormal fear of s.th. or a situation **subject to** likely to be affected by s.th.

fits of hypersensitivity that nearly drove him mad. A fly buzzing in the next room sounded like a squadron of planes to him. If he walked under a bridge, he could feel it pressing against his skull, as though it was about to crush him. He had his laboratory in lower Manhattan, West Broadway, I think it was, West Broadway and Grand. God knows what he didn't invent in that place. Radio tubes, remote-control torpedoes, a plan for electricity without wires. That's right, no wires. You'd plant a metal rod in the ground and suck the energy right out of the air. Once, he claimed to have built a sound-wave device that funneled the pulses of the earth into a tiny, concentrated point. He pressed it against the wall of a building on Broadway, and within five minutes the whole structure started to shake, it would have tumbled down if he hadn't stopped. I loved reading about that stuff when I was a boy, my head was filled with it. People made all sorts of speculations about Tesla. He was like some prophet of the future age, and no one could resist him. The total conquest of nature! A world in which every dream was possible! The most outrageous bit of nonsense came from a man named Julian Hawthorne, who happened to be the son of Nathaniel Hawthorne, the great American writer. Julian. That was my name, too, if you'll remember, and so I followed the younger Hawthorne's work with a certain degree of personal interest. He was a popular writer of the day, a genuine hack who wrote as badly as his father wrote well. A wretched human being. Imagine growing up with Melville and

**hypersensitivity** being excessively sensitive **to buzz** to make a low continuous sound like a bee or fly **squadron** unit **skull** Schädel **West Broadway and Grand** streets below Greenwich Village on the western side of Manhattan—at the time West Broadway was called South Fifth Avenue **tube** Röhre **remote-control** controlled from a distance **rod** here: a metal stick or shaft that is used as a ground (Erdung) to release electrons **to funnel** to concentrate or focus—Tesla was experimenting to determine how earthquakes functioned. **Julian Hawthorne** minor writer of mostly supernatural stories (1846-1934)—He was a good friend of Telsa, and wrote a number of articles about him for the leading Philadelphia newspaper. **Nathaniel Hawthorne** (1804-1864) one the most important American novelists and short story writers of the 19th century—He was greatly influenced by the Puritan tradition of his ancestors, cf. *The Scarlet Letter* **degree** amount **hack** a writer of little talent who writes for money **wretched** [ˈretʃɪd] of poor quality, miserable **Melville** Herman Melville (1819-1891) important American novelist and short story writer famous for his novel *Moby Dick*—His greatness as a writer was not recognized until the 1920s.

Emerson around the house and turning out like that. He wrote fifty-some books, hundreds of magazine articles, all of it trash. At one point he even wound up in jail for some kind of stock fraud, swindling the revenue men, I forget the details. At any rate, this Julian Hawthorne was a friend of Tesla's. In 1899, maybe 1900, Tesla went out to Colorado Springs and set up a laboratory in the mountains to study the effects of ball lightning. One night, he was working late and forgot to turn off the receiver. Strange noises started coming through the machine. Static, radio signals, who knows what. When Tesla told the story to reporters the next day, he claimed this proved there was intelligent life in outer space, that the bloody Martians had been talking to him. Believe it or not, no one laughed at what he said. Lord Kelvin himself, drunk in his cups at some banquet, declared it to be one of the major scientific breakthroughs of all time. Not long after this incident, Julian Hawthorne wrote an article about Tesla in one of the national magazines. Tesla's mind was so advanced, he said, it wasn't possible that he could be human. He had been born on another planet—Venus, I think it was supposed to be—and had been sent to Earth on a special mission to teach us the secrets of nature, to reveal the ways of God to man. Again, you'd think that people would have laughed, but that's not what happened at all. A lot of them took it seriously, and even now, sixty, seventy years later, there are thousands who still believe it. There's a cult out in California today that worships Tesla as an extraterrestrial. You don't have to take my word for it. I've got

**Emerson** Ralph Waldo Emerson (1803-1882) American poet, essayist, and philosopher—He was friends with the most important literary figures of his day. He believed that each individual was his own God and that reality was something that each person had the ability to perceive especially when in close contact with nature. **trash** nonsense **to wind up** to get into an unpleasant situation **stock** Aktie **fraud** method of getting money by using tricks **revenue men** the Internal Revenue Service—the government department that collects taxes **Colorado Springs** town in Colorado—Telsa was there in 1899 and 1900 and created man-made lightning—The strange noises he heard were signals form distant stars and not from aliens. **ball lightning** a rare form of lightning in the shape of a red glowing ball **static** noise caused by electricity in the air **bloody** (BE) damn **Lord Kelvin** William Thomas Kelvin (1824-1907) British scientist and mathematician famous for his discoveries about thermodynamics and thermoelectricity—Because of the discovery of what appeared to be canals on Mars Kelvin and many of his contemporaries believed that there was the real possibility of intelligent beings on Mars. **drunk in his cups** (BE) completely drunk **to reveal** to tell about or show s.th. that was unknown or secret before **extraterrestrial** person from another planet—some of the cults are the Heaven's Gate Cult and the Scientologists

some of their literature in the house, and you can see for yourself. Pavel Shum used to read it to me on rainy days. It's riotous stuff. Makes you laugh so hard, you think your belly's going to split in two.

"I mention all this to give you an idea of what it was like for me. Tesla wasn't just anyone, and when he came to build his tower in Shoreham, I couldn't believe my luck. Here was the great man himself, coming to my little town every week. I used to watch him get off the train, thinking maybe I could learn something by watching him, that just getting close to him would contaminate me with his brilliance—as though it was some kind of disease you could catch. I never had the courage to talk to him, but that didn't matter. It inspired me to know that he was there, to know that I could get a glimpse of him whenever I wanted. Once, our eyes met, I remember that well, it was very important, our eyes met and I could feel him looking right through me, as though I didn't exist. It was an incredible moment. I could feel his glance going through my eyes and out the back of my head, sizzling up the brain in my skull and turning it into a pile of ashes. For the first time in my life, I realized that I was nothing, absolutely nothing. No, it didn't upset me in the way you might think. It stunned me at first, but once the shock began to wear off, I felt invigorated by it, as though I had managed to survive my own death. No, that's not it, not exactly. I was only seventeen years old, hardly more than a boy. When Tesla's eyes went through me, I experienced my first taste of death. That's closer to what I mean. I felt the taste of mortality in my mouth, and at that moment I understood that I was not going to live forever. It takes a long time to learn that, but when you finally do, everything changes inside you, you can never be the same again. I was seventeen years old, and all of a sudden, without the slightest flicker of a doubt, I understood that my life was my own, that it belonged to me and no one else.

"I'm talking about freedom, Fogg. A sense of despair that becomes so great, so crushing, so catastrophic, that you have no choice but to be liberated by it. That's the only choice, or else you crawl into a corner and die. Tesla gave me my death, and at that moment I knew that I was going to become a painter. That's what I wanted, but until then I hadn't had the

**riotous** here: unbelievably funny **belly** stomach **to contaminate** here: (iron.) to influence in a bad way **brilliance** intelligence, mental ability **glance** quick look **to sizzle up** to burn up **to stun** to shock so that one can't react immediately **to wear off** to gradually stop **invigorated** feeling stronger and with more energy than you did before **mortality** being human and having to die **flicker** hint, sign **despair** feeling of hopelessness **crushing** severe, great

balls to admit it. My father was all stocks and bonds, a fucking tycoon, he took me for some kind of pansy. But I went ahead and did it, I became an artist, and then, just a few years later, the old man dropped dead in his office on Wall Street. I was twenty-two or -three then, and I wound up inheriting all his money, I got every cent of it. Ha! I was the richest goddamned painter there ever was. A millionaire artist. Just think of it, Fogg. I was the same age you are now, and I had everything, every goddamned thing I wanted.

"I saw Tesla again, but that was later, much later. After my disappearance, after my death, after I left America and came back. Nineteen thirty-nine, nineteen forty. I got out of France with Pavel Shum before the Germans marched in, we packed up our bags and left. It was no place for us anymore, no place for a crippled American and a Russian poet, it didn't make sense to be there. We thought about Argentina at first, but then I thought what the hell, it might get the juices flowing to see New York again. It had been twenty years, after all. The World's Fair had just started when we arrived. Another hymn to progress, but it didn't do much for me this time, not after what I'd seen in Europe. It was all a sham. Progress was going to blow us up, any jackass could tell you that. You should meet Mrs. Hume's brother some time, Charlie Bacon. He was a pilot during the war. They had him out in Utah towards the end, training with that bunch that dropped the A-bomb on Japan. He lost his mind when he found out what was going on. The poor wretch, who can blame him? There's progress for you. A bigger and better mousetrap every month. Pretty soon, we'll be able to kill all the mice at the same time.

**to have the balls** (slang, vulgar) to have the courage **stock** Aktie **bond** festverzinsliches Wertpapier **fucking** (slang, vulgar) miserable **tycoon** very rich person who is successful in business or industry **to take s.o. for** to consider s.o. to be **pansy** a weak and feminine man **to inherit** to receive money or property from s.o. who has died **...the Germans marched in...** between May 13 and June 22, 1940 **crippled** hurt or wounded so that one can't use the arms or legs any more **to get the juices flowing** to become more active, lively, or energetic **The World's Fair** the fair in New York City in 1939/1940 **sham** s.th. that deceives **jackass** here: fool **Bacon** cf. Francis Bacon (1561-1626) English philosopher and essayist who believed the only knowledge of importance to man was what was observed in the natural world (empiricism), the so-called inductive scientific method; mastery over the natural world could then be possible. **Utah** the Great Salt Lake Desert to the west of Salt Lake City was used as a testing ground for pilots **A-bomb** atomic bomb—One of the pilots of the plane that dropped the bomb did indeed become insane afterwards. **wretch** s.o. you feel sorry for **(building a better) mousetrap** finding technically better ways to do things that may not really be a sign of progress

"I was back in New York, and Pavel and I started taking walks around the city. The same as we do now, pushing the wheelchair, pausing to look at things, but much longer, we'd keep going for the whole day. It was the first time Pavel had been in New York, and I showed him the sights, wandering from neighborhood to neighborhood, trying to reacquaint myself with it in the process. One day in the summer of thirty-nine, we visited the Public Library at Forty-second and Fifth, then stopped for a breather in Bryant Park. That's when I saw Tesla again. Pavel was sitting on a bench beside me, and just ten or twelve feet away from us there was this old man feeding the pigeons. He was standing up, and the birds were fluttering all around him, landing on his head and arms, dozens of cooing pigeons, shitting on his clothes and eating out of his hands, and the old man kept talking to them, calling the birds his darlings, his sweethearts, his angels. The moment I heard that voice, I knew it was Tesla, and then he turned his face in my direction, and there he was. An eighty-year-old man. Spectral white, thin, as ugly to look at as I am now. I wanted to laugh when I saw him. The one-time genius from outer space, the hero of my youth. He was nothing but a broken-down old man now, a bum. You're Nikola Tesla, I said to him. Just like that, I didn't stand on formality. You're Nikola Tesla, I said, I used to know you. He smiled at me and made a little bow. I'm busy at the moment, he said, perhaps we can talk some other time. I turned to Pavel and said, Give Mr. Tesla some money, Pavel, he can probably use it to buy more birdseed. Pavel stood up, walked over to Tesla, and held out a ten-dollar bill to him. It was a moment for the ages, Fogg, a moment that can never be equaled. Ha! I'll never forget the confusion in that son of a bitch's eyes. Mr. Tomorrow, the prophet of a new world! Pavel held out the ten-dollar bill to him, and I could see him struggling to ignore it, to tear his eyes away from the money—but he couldn't do it. He just stood there, staring at it like some insane beggar. And then he took the money, just snatched it out of Pavel's

**to reacquaint** to get to know again **Public Library** the New York Public Library, one of the most important research libraries in America **breather** ['bri:.ðər] a short stop to rest **Bryant Park** park directly behind the New York Public Library **to coo** to make a low soft cry as a pigeon **spectral** ['spek.trəl] like a ghost **bum** (AE, coll) s.o. who has no home or job, and asks people for money **to stand on formality** to act in the polite and correct way expected in good society **bow** bending the top part of your body forward to show respect for s.o. **birdseed** mixture of seeds to feed birds **can never be equaled** there can never be anything as good or the same **son of a bitch** (AE, coll) (iron.) worthless person **insane** mad, crazy **beggar** s.o. who lives by asking people for food and money **to snatch** to grab, to take with force

hand and shoved it into his pocket. That's very kind of you, he said to me, very kind. The little darlings need every morsel they can get. Then he turned his back to us and muttered something to the birds. Pavel wheeled me away at that point, and that was the end of it. I never saw him again."

Effing paused for several moments, savoring the memory of his cruelty. Then, in a more subdued tone, he started in again. "I'm getting on with it, boy," he said. "Don't worry about that. Just keep the pen moving, and we'll be all right. In the end, everything will get said, everything will come out. I was talking about Long Island, wasn't I? About Thomas Moran and how the business got started. You see, I haven't forgotten. Just keep writing down the words. There won't be any obituary unless you write down the words.

"Moran was the one who talked me into it. He'd been out West in the seventies, he'd seen the whole place from top to bottom. He didn't travel alone the way Ralph did, of course, wandering through the wilderness like some benighted pilgrim, he wasn't, how shall I say, he wasn't on the same kind of quest. Moran did it in style. He was the official artist for the Hayden expedition in seventy-one, and then he went back out there with Powell in seventy-three. We read Powell's book a couple of months ago, all the illustrations in it were by Moran. Remember the picture of Powell dangling over the edge of the cliff, hanging on for dear life with his one arm? Good stuff, you have to admit, the old man knew how to draw. Moran got famous for what he did out there, he was the one who showed Americans what the West looked like. The first painting of the Grand Canyon was by Moran, it's hanging in the Capitol building in Washington; the first painting of Yellowstone, the first painting of the Great Salt Desert, the first paintings of the canyon country in southern Utah—they were all done by Moran. Manifest Destiny! They mapped it out,

**to shove** to put s.th. hurriedly into s.th. **to savour** to enjoy **subdued** more quiet, less excited **tone** way of speaking **I'm getting on with it.** I'm managing, I'm able to cope with it. **benighted** ignorant **pilgrim** person who travels to a place for religious reasons (Pilger) **quest** the act or an instance of looking for or seeking, during the Middle Ages the search for the Holy Grail **to dangle** to hang **for dear life** with the greatest effort to avoid harm **stuff** (coll) here: subject for a painting **Grand Canyon** "The Grand Canyon of Yellowstone" **Yellowstone** "Hot Springs of Yellowstone" 1872 **Great Salt Desert** large desert to the west of Salt Lake City **canyon country in southern Utah** Bryce Canyon, Glen Canyon, White Canyon, Cataract Canyon, etc. **Manifest Destiny** 19th century slogan that the U.S. should rule all of the North American continent, first used by John L. O'Sullivan in 1845 when there was opposition to annexing Texas

they made pictures of it, they digested it into the great American profit machine. Those were the last bits of the continent, the blank spaces no one had explored. Now here it was, all laid out on a pretty piece of canvas for everyone to see. The golden spike, driven right through our hearts!

"I wasn't a painter like Moran, you shouldn't get that idea. I was part of the new generation, and I didn't hold with any of that romantic bullshit. I'd been to Paris back in o-six and o-seven, and I knew what was going on. The Fauves, the Cubists, I got wind of that stuff when I was young, and once you get a taste of the future, there's no turning back. I knew the crowd over at Stieglitz's gallery on Fifth Avenue, we used to go out drinking together and talk about art. They liked my work, they touted me as one of the new hotshots. Marin, Dove, Demuth, Man Ray, there wasn't anyone I didn't know. I was a cunning little devil back then, my head was full of smart ideas. Everyone talks about the Armory Show now, but that was old news for me by the time it happened. Still, I was different from most of the others. The line didn't interest me. Mechanical abstraction, the canvas as the world, intellectual art—I saw it as a dead end. I was

**to digest** here: to make suitable **American profit machine** Moran made prints and paintings for the railroad companies to encourage people to settle in the West and buy land from them and use the railroad for the transport of goods **blank** empty, not filled out **spike** thin small object with a sharp point—an allusion to the golden spike that was hammered into the track of the first transcontinental railroad completed on May 10, 1869 in Utah **bullshit** (AE, vulgar) nonsense **Fauves** [foʊvs] French art movement at the beginning of the 20th century that included Matisse and Braque. It used unusual colors and forms and had a revolutionary impact on the development of modern art. **Cubists** art movement begun in 1907 that included Braque, Cézanne, and Picasso—They tried to subjectively show objects from several sides at the same time. **Stieglitz** Alfred Stieglitz (1864-1946) American photographer and art exhibitor—He had a famous gallery founded in 1905 on Fifth Avenue that exhibited photos and modern French and American paintings. **to tout** to praise **hotshot** (AE, slang) a very talented or successful person **Marin** ['me.rɪn] John Marin (1870-1953) American abstract landscape artist **Dove** Arthur Dove (1880-1946) American abstract painter **Demuth** ['deɪ.mu:θ] Charles Demuth (1883-1935) American watercolor painter whose paintings were influenced by the geometric shape of machines **Man Ray** (1890-1976) surrealist American photographer, painter, and sculptor **the Armory Show** (1913 in New York) one of the most important exhibitions of art ever held in the United States: it was a sensational introduction of modern art from Europe thus changing the direction of painting in America **the line** a sharp boundary between two objects in a picture or painting **mechanical abstraction** geometric forms based on machines or technology **dead end** (fig) a road with one end blocked

a colorist, and my subject was space, pure space and light: the force of light when it hits the eye. I still worked from nature, and that's the reason why I enjoyed talking to someone like Moran. He was the old guard, but he'd been influenced by Turner, and we had that in common, along with a passion for landscape, a passion for the real world. Moran kept talking to me about the West. If you don't go out there, he said, you'll never understand what space is. Your work will stop growing if you don't make the trip. You've got to experience that sky, it will change your life. On and on, always the same thing. He kept at it every time I saw him, and after a while I finally said to myself, why not, it won't hurt me to go out there and see it.

"It was 1916. I was thirty-three years old and had been married for about four years. Of all the things I've ever done, that marriage ranks as my worst mistake. Elizabeth Wheeler was her name. She was from a rich family, so she didn't marry me for my money, but she might just as well have, considering the way things were between us. It didn't take me long to find out the truth. She wept like a schoolgirl on our wedding night, and after that the gates slammed shut. Oh, I stormed the castle every now and then, but more from anger than anything else. Just to let her know she couldn't get away with it all the time. Even now, I wonder what possessed me to marry her. Perhaps her face was too pretty, perhaps her body was too round and plump, I don't know. They were all virgins when they got married in those days, I thought she would learn to like it. But it never got any better, the whole thing was tears and struggle, fits of screaming, disgust. She took me for a beast, an agent of the devil. A pox on that frigid bitch! She should have lived in a convent. I showed her the darkness and uncleanliness that keep the world going, and she never forgave me for it. Homo erectus, it was nothing but horror to her: the mys-

**colorist** an artist who tries to achieve special effects with colors **the old guard** the established artists **Turner** Joseph Mallord William (1775-1851), English painter and watercolourist; major figure in English landscape painting; especially noted for his use of the effects of light **to rank** einstufen **gates slammed shut** i.e. she refused to have any more sex **...stormed the castle...** forced her to allow me to have sex with her **to get away with s.th.** to not be caught or punished for s.th. you have done wrong **to possess s.o.** to cause s.o. to do s.th. stupid **plump** well filled or round **disgust** very strong feeling of dislike that makes you sick **a pox on...** damn... **bitch** (slang) miserable woman **convent** a building or set of buildings where nuns live **homo erectus** (upright man) species of modern man that lived between 1.6 years and 200,000 years ago, also a reference to a sexually excited male

tery of male flesh. Once she finally saw what happens to it, she fell apart. I won't go on about this. It's an old story, I'm sure you've heard it before. I found my pleasures elsewhere. There was no lack of opportunity, I assure you, my cock never suffered from neglect. I was a dapper young gentleman, money was no object, my groin was constantly ablaze. Ha! I wish we had time to talk about some of that. The pulsing quims I've inhabited, the adventures of my middle leg. The other two might be defunct, but their baby brother has kept up a life of his own. Even now, Fogg, if you can believe it. The little man has never quit.

"All right, all right, enough. It's not important. I'm just giving you the background, trying to set the scene. If you need an explanation for what happened, my marriage to Elizabeth will help. I'm not saying it was the sole cause, but it was certainly a factor. When the situation presented itself to me, I had no regrets about vanishing. I saw my chance to be dead, and I took it.

"I didn't plan it that way. Three or four months, I thought, and then I'd come back. The New York crowd thought I was crazy to go out there, they couldn't see the point. Go to Europe, they said to me, there's nothing to learn in America. I explained my reasons to them, and just talking about it got me more and more excited. I threw myself into the preparations, I couldn't wait to be off. Early on, I decided to take someone along with me, a young fellow by the name of Edward Byrne—Teddy, as his parents called him. His father was a friend of mine, and he talked me into including the lad. I had no serious objections. I thought I would welcome the companionship, and Byrne was a spirited boy, I'd been out sailing with him a couple of times, and I knew that he had a good head on his shoulders. Steadfast, quick to learn, a strong and athletic young man of eighteen or nineteen. His dream was to become a topographer, he wanted

**male flesh** i.e. penis **to fall apart** to break down, to collapse **cock** (slang, vulgar) penis **dapper** nicely dressed **no object** no problem **groin** where the top of the legs join together **ablaze** here: full of sexual desire **pulsing** here: sexually excited **quim** (slang, vulgar) vagina **to inhabit** here: to penetrate **middle leg** (slang, vulgar) penis **defunct** no longer useful **baby brother** (slang) penis **little man** (slang) penis **to quit** here: to stop functioning **to set the scene** to describe the situation before a story begins **sole** only **crowd** here: the people one knows from the same social class **to talk s.o. into doing s.th.** to persuade s.o. to do s.th. **lad** young man **spirited** full of energy **steadfast** loyal and reliable **topographer** a person who prepares a map with a detailed description of the surface features of a region

to catch on with the U.S. Geological Survey and spend his life tramping around the great outdoors. It was that kind of age, Fogg. Teddy Roosevelt, handlebar mustaches, all that manly bluster. Byrne's father bought him a mess of equipment—sextant, compass, theodolite, the whole works—and I got myself enough art supplies to last me a couple of years. Pencils, charcoals, pastels, paints, brushes, rolls of canvas, paper—I was counting on getting a lot of work done. Moran's talk had sunk in by then, and I was expecting great things from the trip. I was going to do my best work out there, and I didn't want to get caught short of materials.

"For all her stoniness in bed, Elizabeth began to have qualms about my going away. As the time approached for me to leave, she grew more and more unhappy about it: bursting into tears, imploring me to call off the trip. I still don't understand it. You'd think she would have been glad to get rid of me. An unpredictable woman she was, always doing the opposite of what you'd expect. On the last night before I left, she even went so far as to make the supreme sacrifice. I think she got herself a little tipsy first—you know, to buck up her courage and then she actually went ahead and offered herself to me. Arms open, eyes closed, as if she were some bloody martyr. I'll never forget it. Oh, Julian, she kept saying, oh, my darling husband. Like most crazy people, she probably knew what was going to happen in advance, she probably sensed that things were

**to catch on with s.th.** to work for s.th./s.o. that has become popular **U.S. Geological Survey** Federal government agency that was helped to be founded by John Powell in 1879. This agency prepares topographic maps and other maps of interest to geologists for all of the United States. **to tramp** to walk long and far, to hike **Teddy Roosevelt** Theodore Roosevelt (1858-1919) 26th president of the U.S.A. He was enthusiastic about the outdoors, traveling and hunting in the West, South America and Africa. One of the most popular presidents, he started an adventurous foreign policy that included sending the American fleet around the world and building the Panama Canal and in domestic politics broke up the industrial monopolies and reformed the food and drug industries. **handlebar mustache** [ˈmʌs.tæʃ] a long thick moustache that curves upwards at both ends **bluster** aggressive way of talking **a mess** (coll) a large amount of different kinds of things **theodolite** [θiˈɑː.dəlaɪt] an optical instrument used for measuring angles when surveying (vermessen) **the whole works** (coll) everything you can think of **charcoal** a black substance made from burning wood that can be used for drawing **pastel** a colored stick made from chalk **to sink in** to be fully understood **for all the stoniness in bed** in spite of her lack of interest in sex **qualm** feeling, doubt or worry about what you are doing is right **to implore s.o. to do s.th.** to ask s.o. to do s.th. in an anxious way, to beg **unpredictable** not knowing what to expect **supreme** greatest **sacrifice** Opfer **tipsy** slightly drunk **to buck up** here: to increase **bloody** (BE) damn

about to change for good. I did it to her that night—it was my duty, after all—but I didn't let it stop me from leaving the next day. As it happened, it was the last time I ever saw her. So be it. I'm just giving you the facts, you can make of them what you will. There were consequences from that night, I'd be remiss if I didn't mention them, but a long time passed before I knew what they were. Thirty years, in fact, a whole lifetime into the future. Consequences. That's the way it is, boy. There are always consequences, whether you like it or not.

"Byrne and I went by train. Chicago, Denver, all the way to Salt Lake City. It was an endless trip back in those days, and when we finally got out there, I felt that I'd been traveling for a year. It was April 1916. In Salt Lake, we found a man to serve as our guide, but later that same afternoon, if you can believe it, he burned his leg in a blacksmith's shop, and we had to hire someone else. It was a bad omen, but you never think of those things at the time, you just go ahead and do what you have to do. The man we got was named Jack Scoresby. He was a former cavalry soldier, forty-eight, fifty years old, an old-timer in those parts, but people said he knew the territory well, he knew it as well as anyone else we could find. I had to take them at their word. The people I talked to were strangers, and they could have told me anything they wanted, it made no difference to them. I was just a greenhorn, a rich greenhorn from back East, and why should they give a good goddamn about me? That was how it happened, Fogg. There was no choice but to plunge in blindly and hope for the best.

"I had my doubts about Scoresby from the start, but we were too eager to be off on our trek to waste any more time. He was a dirty little man with a snickering laugh, all whiskers and buffalo grease, but he talked a good game, I'll grant him that. He promised to take us places where few men had ever been, that's how he put it, he'd show us things that only God and Injuns had ever set eyes on before. You knew he was full of shit, but it was hard not to get excited anyway. We spread out a map on a table in the hotel and planned the route we'd be following.

**I did it to her** (coll) I had sex with her. **remiss** lacking in care, negligent **blacksmith** person who makes horseshoes and other metal equipment for horses **to hire** (AE) to employ s.o. **to give a good goddam about s.o.** (coll) to care about the welfare of s.o. **to plunge in** to start doing s.th. quickly without worrying **trek** long and difficult journey **to snicker** (AE) to laugh in an unkind way especially when s.o. else makes mistakes **grease** Fett **to talk a good game** (coll) to convince people that you are competent **I'll grant him that** I'll have to admit in his case **Injun** ['ɪn.dʒən] (slang) Indian **to be full of shit** (slang, vulgar) to say things that are untrue

Scoresby seemed to know what he was talking about, and he kept making incidental comments and asides to show off his knowledge: how many horses and donkeys would be necessary, how to behave with Mormons, how to deal with the scarcity of water in the south. It was obvious that he thought we were fools. The idea of going out to gawk at scenery made no sense to him, and when I told him I was a painter, it was all he could do not to laugh. Still, we struck what seemed like a fair bargain, and the three of us shook hands on it. I figured that things would fall into place once we got to know each other.

"The night before we left, Byrne and I sat up talking. He showed me his surveying equipment, and I remember being in one of those excited moods when everything suddenly seems to fit together in a new way. Byrne told me that you can't fix your exact position on the earth without referring to some point in the sky. Something to do with triangulation, the technique of measurement, I forget the details. The crux was compelling to me though, it's never left me since. A man can't know where he is on the earth except in relation to the moon or a star. Astronomy comes first; land maps follow because of it. Just the opposite of what you'd expect. If you think about it long enough, it will turn your brain inside-out. A here exists only in relation to a there, not the other way around. There's this only because there's that; if we don't look up, we'll never know what's down. Think of it, boy. We find ourselves only by looking to what we're not. You can't put your feet on the ground until you've touched the sky.

"I did some good work in the beginning. We headed due west from the city, camped out by the lake for a day or two, and then moved on into the Great Salt Desert. It was like nothing I had ever seen before. The flattest, most desolate spot on the planet, a boneyard of oblivion. You travel along day after day, and you don't see a goddamned thing. Not a tree, not a

**incidental** seemingly by chance **aside** an unimportant remark **donkey** Esel **Mormons** religious sect founded by Joseph Smith in 1830 that eventually settled in Salt Lake City in 1847 **scarcity** an inadequate supply **to gawk at s.th.** to look at s.th. for a long time, in a way that looks stupid **to strike a fair bargain** to reach a fair agreement **to fall into place** to happen as had been hoped **surveying** Vermessung **triangulation** [traɪˌæŋ.gjəˈleɪ.ʃən] method of finding distance and position using triangles (Dreieck) **crux** the essential part **compelling** extremely exciting and interesting **to leave s.o.** here: to forget **to turn inside-out** to change so the inside faces outwards **due west** directly west **the lake** the Great Salt Lake **desolate** empty and gloomy **oblivion** state of being completely forgotten

shrub, not a single blade of grass. Nothing but whiteness, cracked earth stretching into the distance on all sides. The ground tastes of salt, and way out at the edge, the horizon is ringed with mountains, a huge ring of mountains oscillating in the light. It makes you think you're nearing water, surrounded by all that shimmer and glare, but it's only an illusion. It's a dead world, and the only thing you ever get closer to is more of the same nothing. God knows how many pioneers bogged down and gave up the ghost in that desert, you'd see their white bones jutting straight out of the ground. That's what did in the Donner party, everyone knows about them. They got stuck in the salt, and by the time they reached the Sierra Mountains in California, the winter snows blocked their way, and they fell to eating each other to stay alive. Everyone knows that, it's American folklore, but a true fact nevertheless, a true and unimpeachable fact. Wagon wheels, skullbones, empty bullet shells—I saw all those things out there, even as late as 1916. A giant cemetery was what it was, a blank page of death.

"For the first couple of weeks, I drew like a fiend. Odd stuff, I'd never done work like that before. I hadn't thought the scale would make a difference, but it did, there was no other way to wrestle with the size of things. The marks on the page became smaller and smaller, small to the point of vanishing. It was as if my hand had a life of its own. Just get it down, I kept saying to myself, just get it down, and don't worry, you can think about it later. We stopped off in Wendover for a little while and got cleaned up, then crossed into Nevada and went south, traveling along the edge of the Confusion Range. Again, it all jumped out at me in ways I wasn't prepared for. The mountains, the snow on top of the mountains,

**blade** long flat leaf **cracked** here: with deep lines in the surface because of being so dry **ringed with mountains** there were mountains all over the horizon **to oscillate** to move or swing from side to side regularly **shimmer** a soft shaking light **glare** bright unpleasant light **to bog down** to get stuck so that one can't move on **to jut** to stick **Donner party** group of emigrants to California that got stuck in the snow in the winter of 1846/1847 **Sierra Mountains** Sierra Nevada Mountains in eastern California that rise to 4,418 meters **to fall to doing s.th.** to start doing s.th. that's difficult to do **folklore** stories and legends that have to do with a country **unimpeachable** so definite that it cannot be doubted **shell** Patrone **like a fiend** [fi:nd] at great speed without thinking of anything else **scale** size, dimension **to wrestle with s.th.** to deal with a difficult problem **just get it down** just draw the pictures **Wendover** small town west of the Great Salt Lake Dessert near the border with Nevada **the Confusion Range** range of dry rocky mountains in west central Utah 40 km east of the Nevada border

the clouds hovering around the snow. After a while, they began to merge together and I couldn't tell them apart. Whiteness, and then more whiteness. How can you draw something if you don't know it's there? You see what I'm talking about, don't you? It didn't feel human anymore. The wind would blow so hard that you couldn't hear yourself think, and then it would suddenly stop, and the air would be so still, you'd stand there wondering if you hadn't gone deaf. Unearthly silence, Fogg. The only thing you could hear was your heart beating in your chest, the sound of blood rushing through your brain.

"Scoresby didn't make life any easier. He did his job, I suppose, leading us along, building fires, hunting our food, but his scorn for us never let up, bad will poured out of him and tainted the atmosphere. He sulked and spat, muttered under his breath, mocked us with his sullenness. After a while, Byrne got so wary of him that he wouldn't talk when Scoresby was around. Scoresby would go off hunting while we did our work—young Teddy scrambling among the rocks and taking his measurements, I parked on some ledge or other with my paints and charcoals—but in the evenings the three of us would cook our dinner together in front of the campfire. Once, hoping to turn things around a little, I offered to play cards with Scoresby. He seemed to like the idea, but like most stupid men, he had an inflated notion of his own intelligence. He figured he was going to beat me and win a lot of money. Not only beat me at cards, but beat me in every way, really show me who was boss. We played blackjack, and all the cards came to me, he lost six or seven hands in a row. It shook his confidence, and then he started playing badly, making outrageous bets, trying to bluff me, doing everything wrong. I must have won fifty or sixty dollars from him that night, a fortune to a simpleton like that. When I saw how upset he was, I tried to

**to hover** to remain in the air **to merge** to combine **to go deaf** to become unable to hear any more **scorn** the feeling that s.o. is stupid or not as good as other people (Verachtung) **to let up** to become less **to sulk** to have an unhappy look on your face because you are angry or annoyed by s.th. **to spit/spat/spat** to force saliva out of your mouth **to mutter** to speak in a low voice when annoyed **sullenness** silently showing anger or a bad mood **wary** ['wer.i] watchful because of possible danger **to scramble** to climb over s.th. with difficulty **ledge** a narrow flat surface of rock **inflated notion** unreasonably positive opinion or idea **to figure** (AE) to suppose, to think **...all the cards came to me.** I got the winning cards. **hand** set of cards given to a player **in a row** one after the other **to shake one's confidence** to cause one to doubt one's own ability **outrageous** extraordinary, shocking **simpleton** s.o. with very little intelligence

undo the damage and called off the debt. What did I care about the money? Don't worry about it, I said to him, I just got lucky, I'm willing to forget it, no hard feelings, something along those lines. It was probably the worst thing I could have said. Scoresby thought I was patronizing him, he thought I was trying to humiliate him, and his pride was hurt, hurt twice over. From then on, there was bad blood between us, and it was beyond me to set it right. I was a stubborn son of a bitch myself, you've probably noticed that. I gave up trying to appease him. If he wanted to act like an ass, let him bray till kingdom come. There we were out in that enormous country, with nothing around us, nothing but empty space for miles around, and for all that it was like being locked in prison—like sharing a cell with a man who won't stop looking at you, who just sits there waiting for you to turn around so he can stick a knife in your back.

"That was the trouble. The land is too big out there, and after a while it starts to swallow you up. I reached a point when I couldn't take it in anymore. All that bloody silence and emptiness. You try to find your bearings in it, but it's too big, the dimensions are too monstrous, and eventually, I don't know how else to put it, eventually it just stops being there. There's no world, no land, no nothing. It comes down to that, Fogg, in the end it's all a figment. The only place you exist is in your head.

"We worked our way across the center of the state, then angled down into the canyon country in the southeast, what they call the Four Corners, where Utah, Arizona, Colorado, and New Mexico come together. That was the strangest place of all, a dream world, all red earth and contorted rocks, tremendous structures rising out of the ground, they stood there like the ruins of some lost city built by giants. Obelisks, minarets, palaces: everything was at once recognizable and alien, you couldn't help

**to call off** to decide that a planned event will not take place **no hard feelings** not feeling anger towards s.o. any more **along those lines** s.th. like that **to patronize s.o.** to treat s.o. as if this person were stupid, but in fact is not **to humiliate s.o.** to hurt the dignity or pride of s.o. **beyond me** too difficult for me **stubborn** refusing to change one's opinion, to agree or give in **to appease** to make s.o. less angry by doing what this person wants **ass** (Esel) here: foolish person **to bray** to make a noise like a donkey or ass **till kingdom come** for ever **to swallow up** verschlucken **to take it in** aufnehmen **to find one's bearings** to determine where one is **it comes down to that** that is the final conclusion, the essence **figment** [ˈfɪg.mənt] s.th. not real, just imagined **angled down to** here: hiked at an angle sharply southeast to **canyon country** i.e. Glen Canyon **contorted** twisted into a strange shape **obelisk** a tall pointed stone as found in Egypt **alien** strange, out of place

seeing familiar shapes when you looked at them, even though you knew it was all chance, the petrified sputum of glaciers and erosion, a million years of wind and weather. Thumbs, eye sockets, penises, mushrooms, human beings, hats. It was like making pictures out of clouds. Everyone knows what those places look like now, you've seen them a hundred times yourself. Glen Canyon, Monument Valley, the Valley of the Gods. That's where they shoot all those cowboy-and-Indian movies, the god-damned Marlboro man gallops through there on television every night. But pictures don't tell you anything about it, Fogg. It's all too massive to be painted or drawn; even photographs can't get the feel of it. Everything is so distorted, it's like trying to reproduce the distances in outer space: the more you see, the less your pencil can do. To see it is to make it vanish.

"We wandered around in those canyons for several weeks. Sometimes we spent the night in ancient Indian ruins, the cliff dwellings of the Anasazi. Those were the tribes who disappeared a thousand years ago, no one knows what happened to them. They left behind their stone cities, their pictographs, their shards of pottery, but the people themselves just melted away. It was late July or early August by then, and Scoresby's hostility had grown, it was only a matter of time before something snapped, you could feel it in the air. The country was barren and dry, sagebrush everywhere, not a tree to be seen. The temperatures were atrociously hot, and we had to ration our water supply, which put everyone in a foul temper. One day we had to destroy a donkey, which put an extra burden

**petrified** changed into stone after a long time **sputum** liquid coughed up from the mouth and lungs **glacier** [ˈgleɪ.ʃər] Gletscher **eye socket** the hollow part of the skull into which the eye fits **Glen Canyon** canyon to the west of Monument Valley through which the Colorado River flows **Monument Valley** area in southeast Utah with bizarre rock formations **Valley of the Gods** near Monument Valley but with smaller rock formations **cowboy-and-Indian movies** The director John Ford made a number of classical westerns in Monument Valley beginning with *Stagecoach* in 1939. Nature represented purity while civilization represented corruption. **distorted** changed in appearance or shape so that it seems strange **Anasazi** [ˌæn.əˈsæzi:] group of Native Americans that inhabited southern Colorado and Utah, and northern New Mexico and Arizona from about 100 AD **pictograph** a picture or symbol standing for a word or group of words **shard** broken piece **pottery** pots, plates, etc. made of baked clay (Ton) **to melt away** to gradually disappear **hostility** feeling of strong dislike **to snap** here: to suddenly happen because of great tension **barren** unproductive, unable to support the growth of plants **sagebrush** a shrub of dry areas in southwestern America **atrociously** shockingly **foul temper** (BE) very bad mood

on the two others. The horses were beginning to wilt. We were five or six days from the town of Bluff, and I thought we should try to get ourselves there as quickly as possible to regroup. Scoresby mentioned a shortcut that would knock off a day or two from the journey, and so we set out in that direction, traveling over rugged ground with the sun in our faces. It was difficult going, rougher than anything we had tried before, and after a while it dawned on me that Scoresby was leading us into a trap. Byrne and I weren't the riders he was, and we could barely negotiate the terrain. Scoresby was in front, Byrne was second, and I was in the rear. We inched up several steep cliffs, then started riding along a ridge at the top. It was very narrow, all strewn with rocks and pebbles, and the light was bouncing off the rocks as if to blind us. We couldn't turn back at that point, but I didn't see how we could go on much further. All of a sudden, Byrne's horse lost its footing. He wasn't more than ten feet in front of me, and I remember the frantic clattering of stones, the whinnying of the horse as it scrambled to gain a purchase with its hooves. But the ground kept giving way, and before I had a chance to react, Byrne let out a scream, and then he was tumbling over the edge, horse and all, the two of them crashing down the side of the cliff. It was a long fucking way, it must have been two or three hundred feet, and nothing but jagged rocks from top to bottom. I jumped off the horse and fetched the medical box, then rushed down the escarpment to see what I could do. At first I thought Byrne was dead, but then I managed to find his pulse. Other than that, there was precious little to feel encouraged about. His face was covered with blood, and his left leg and left arm were both fractured, I could see that just by looking at them. Then I rolled him onto his back and saw a large gash just below his ribs—an ugly, pulsing wound at least six or seven inches across. It was awful, the boy was all torn to pieces. I

**to wilt** to lose strength **Bluff** small town in southeast Utah **to regroup** to reorganize so as to begin again **to knock off a day** (coll) to reduce the time to do s.th. by one day **rugged** ['rʌg.ɪd] rough and uneven **rough** difficult **to dawn on s.o.** to realize for the first time **trap** Falle **to negotiate** here: to succeed in getting over a difficult area of land **terrain** a particular type of land **ridge** a long area of high land, especially at the top of a mountain **strewn** lying about over a surface **frantic** frightened and excited **clattering** a rattling sound **to whinny** to make a high sound as a horse **to scramble** to climb up or down with difficulty **to gain a purchase** to get a firm hold with the legs so to be able to walk properly again **to give way** to break away because of too much weight **jagged** with a rough uneven and sharp surface **escarpment** a steep slope or cliff **precious** very **gash** a large deep wound from a cut

was about to open the medicine box when I heard a shot ring out behind me. I turned around and saw Scoresby standing over Byrne's fallen horse, a smoking pistol in his right hand. Broken leg, he said curtly, nothing else to be done. I told him that Byrne was in a bad way and needed our immediate attention, but when Scoresby came over for a look, he sneered and said, We shouldn't waste our time on this one. The only cure for him is a dose of the same medicine I just gave the horse. Scoresby raised his pistol and pointed it at Byrne's head, but I knocked his arm to the side. I don't know if he was planning to pull the trigger, but I couldn't take the risk. Scoresby gave me an evil look when I hit his arm and warned me to keep my hands to myself. I'll do that when you stop pointing guns at helpless people, I said. Then Scoresby turned and pointed the gun at me. I'll point it at anyone I like, he said, and suddenly he broke out into a smile, a huge idiot's grin, relishing the power he held over me. Helpless, he repeated. That's just what you are, Mr. Painter, a helpless bag of bones. I thought he was going to shoot me then. As I stood there waiting for him to pull the trigger, I wondered how long it would take me to die after the bullet entered my heart. I thought: this is the last thought I will ever have. It seemed to go on forever, the two of us staring into each other's eyes, waiting for him to go ahead with it. Then Scoresby started to laugh. He was utterly pleased with himself, as if he had just won an enormous victory. He put the gun back in his holster and spat on the ground. It was as though he had already killed me, as though I was already dead.

"He walked back over to the horse and started removing the saddle and saddlebags. I was still shaken by the gun business, but I crouched down beside Byrne and went to work, doing what I could to wash and bandage his wounds. A couple of minutes later, Scoresby returned and announced that he was ready to leave. Leave? I said, what are you talking about? We can't take the boy with us, he's in no condition to be moved. Leave him behind, then, Scoresby said. He's finished anyway, and I'll be damned if I'm going to sit around this asshole of a canyon waiting for God knows how long just for him to stop breathing. It's not worth it. Do what you like, I said, but I'm not going to leave Byrne while he's still alive. Scoresby grunted. You talk like a hero in a goddamned book, he

**to ring out** to make a ringing sound **curtly** abruptly and impolitely **cure** medicine that can heal a wound **trigger** Abzug **to relish** [ˈrel.ɪʃ] to enjoy **to go ahead with s.th.** to start to do s.th. **holster** a leather case for holding a pistol **gun business** i.e. the incident with the pistol **to crouch** to lower your body close to the ground **to grunt** to make a short low sound in your throat to show you are irritated

said. You could be stuck down here for a week before he finally croaks, and what's the point of that? He's my responsibility, I said. That's all there is to it. He's my responsibility, and I'm not going to leave him.

"Before Scoresby left, I tore out a page from my sketch pad and wrote a letter to my wife. I don't remember what I said. Something melodramatic, I'm fairly sure of it. This will probably be the last time you ever hear from me, I think I actually wrote that. The idea was that Scoresby would post the letter when he got to town. That was our agreement, in any case, but I knew that he had no intention of keeping his promise. It would implicate him in my disappearance, and why should he want to run the risk of being questioned by anyone? Much better for him just to ride off and forget the whole thing. As it turned out, that's exactly what happened. At least I assume it was. Much later, when I read the articles and obituaries, there was never any mention of Scoresby—even though I made a point of putting his name in the letter.

"He also talked about organizing a search party if I didn't show up within a week, but I knew he wasn't going to do that either. I told him so to his face, but instead of denying it, he gave me another one of his insolent smirks. Last chance, Mr. Painter, he said, are you coming with me or not? I just shook my head, too angry to speak anymore. Scoresby tipped his hat to me in farewell, and then he started climbing back up the cliff to retrieve his horse and be on his way. Just like that, without another word. It took him a few minutes to get to the top, and I kept my eyes on him the whole time. I didn't want to take any chances. I figured he would try to kill me before he left, it seemed almost inevitable. Eliminate the evidence, make sure that I couldn't tell anyone what he'd done—leaving a young boy to die like that in the middle of nowhere. But Scoresby never turned around. It wasn't out of kindness, I assure you. The only possible explanation was that he felt it wasn't necessary. He didn't have to kill me, because he didn't think I could make it back on my own.

"Scoresby rode off. Within an hour, I began to feel that he had never existed. I can't tell you how odd that sensation was. It wasn't as though I had decided not to think about him, I could barely remember him when

**to croak** (slang) to die **sketch pad** several sheets of paper bound together for drawing on **to post** (BE) to mail (AE) **to implicate** to show that s.o. is involved in s.th. wrong or a crime **to make a point of doing s.th.** to do s.th. on purpose so that people notice **insolent** rude, not showing any respect **smirk** an unpleasant smile to show you are happy about s.o.'s else's difficulties **to tip one's hat** to raise one's hat when greeting s.o. or when departing **to retrieve** to get back **inevitable** certain to happen

I did. The way he looked, the sound of his voice, none of it came back to me anymore. That's what the silence does to you, Fogg, it obliterates everything. Scoresby was erased from my mind, and whenever I tried to think of him after that, it was like trying to remember someone from a dream, like looking for someone who had never been there.

"It took three or four days for Byrne to die. For my sake, it was probably a good thing it took so long. It kept me busy, and because of that, I didn't have time to be afraid. The fear didn't come until later, until after I had buried him and was alone. On the first day, I must have climbed the mountain ten times, unpacking food and equipment from the donkey and hauling it down below. I broke up my easel and used the wood to make splints so I could set Byrne's arm and leg. I built a small lean-to with a blanket and a tripod to protect his face from the sun. I took care of the horse and the donkey. I changed the bandages with strips of clothing. I built a fire, I cooked food, I did whatever had to be done. Guilt kept me going, it was impossible not to blame myself for what had happened, but even guilt was a comfort. It was a human feeling, a sign that I was still attached to the same world that other men lived in. Once Byrne was gone, there would be nothing to think about anymore, and I was afraid of that emptiness, it scared me half to death.

"I knew it was hopeless, I knew it from the first moment, but I kept deluding myself into thinking he would pull through. He never regained consciousness, but every now and then he would start to babble, the way people do when they talk in their sleep. It was a delirium of incomprehensible words, sounds that never quite became words, but each time it happened, I thought he might be on the verge of coming out of it. He seemed to be separated from me by a thin veil, an invisible membrane that

**to obliterate** to completely destroy **to erase** to remove completely **to haul** to drag or pull s.th. heavy **easel** a wooden frame one puts a painting on while painting **splint** a flat piece of wood, metal, etc. placed around a broken bone to keep it in position while healing **to set** here: to put the broken bones into the proper position for healing **lean-to** a primitive building with a sloping roof built against a larger building or wall **tripod** ['traɪ.pɑːd] here: a support with three legs with a small telescope used for surveying (Stativ) **to delude oneself** to make oneself believe something that is not true, to deceive onself **to pull through** to become healthy again after a serious illness or accident **to regain consciousness** to be able to use your mental powers and sense again (das Bewusstsein wieder erlangen) **to babble** to speak quickly in a way difficult to understand **incomprehensible** impossible to understand **on the verge of doing s.th.** just about to do s.th. **veil** a thin transparent material as worn over the face of a woman (Schleier)

kept him on the other side of this world. I tried to encourage him with the sound of my voice, I talked to him constantly, I sang songs to him, praying that something would finally get through to him and wake him up. It didn't do the slightest bit of good. His condition kept getting worse. I couldn't get any food into him, the best I could manage was to dab his lips with a water soaked cloth, but that wasn't enough, it gave him no nourishment. Bit by bit, I could see the strength ebb out of him. The stomach wound had stopped bleeding, but it wasn't mending properly. It had turned yellow-green, it was oozing pus, ants kept crawling over the bandage. There was no way anyone could survive that.

"I buried him right there at the foot of the mountain. I'll spare you the details. Digging the grave, dragging his body to the edge, feeling it fall away from me when I pushed it in. I was already going crazy by then, I think. I almost couldn't bring myself to fill in the hole. Covering him up, flinging dirt onto his dead face, it was all too much for me. I did it with my eyes closed, that's how I finally solved the problem, I shoveled the dirt back in there without looking. Afterward, I didn't make a cross or say any prayers. Fuck God, I said to myself, fuck God, I won't give him the satisfaction. I planted a stick in the ground and attached a piece of paper to it. Edward Byrne, I wrote, 1898-dash-1916. Buried by his friend, Julian Barber. Then I started to scream. That's how it happened, Fogg. You're the first person I've ever told this to. I started to scream, and after that I just let myself be crazy."

**to dab** to touch lightly **water-soaked** completely wet **nourishment** substances in food that are necessary to grow and stay healthy **to ebb out** (fig) to flow out **to mend** to heal **it was oozing pus** [pʌs] pus (yellow liquid produced in an infected area) was slowly flowing out **ant** Ameise **to spare s.o. the details** to not tell s.o. the details because it's too unpleasant or embarrassing (Auster has said that Bryne's death scene is based on his own experience of seeing a boy killed by lightning in summer camp.) **to fling** to throw quickly with force

# 5

That was as far as we got that day. As soon as he had uttered the last sentence, Effing paused to catch his breath, and before he was able to go on with his story, Mrs. Hume walked in and announced that it was time for lunch. After the terrible things he had recounted, I thought it would be difficult for him to regain his composure, but the interruption hardly seemed to affect him. "Good," he said, clapping his hands together. "Time for lunch. I'm famished." It bewildered me how he could shift so rapidly from one mood to another. Just moments before, his voice had been shaking with emotion. I had thought he was on the brink of collapse, and now, all of a sudden, he was brimming with enthusiasm and good cheer. "We're getting on with it now, boy," he said to me as I wheeled him into the dining room. "That was just the beginning, what you might call the preface. Wait till I get warmed up. You haven't heard anything yet."

Once we sat down at the table, there was no more mention of the obituary. The lunch proceeded as normal, with the usual accompaniment of slurps and outrages, neither more nor less than on any other day. It was as though Effing had already forgotten that he had spent the past three hours spilling his guts to me in the other room. We made our usual small

**to recount** to describe to s.o. a series of events **to regain one's composure** to become calm again after having been excited **famished** (coll) extremely hungry **to bewilder** to confuse **on the brink of** just about to **to brim with s.th.** to be very full of s.th. **to get warmed up** here: to get to the important part, which will really be exciting to hear **with the accompaniment of slurps** with slurps (making a loud noise while drinking s.th.) happening at the same time **outrage** example of shocking behavior **to spill one's guts** (AE, coll) to tell s.o. everything you know about something, especially because you are upset

talk, and toward the end of the meal we went through the daily weather briefing in preparation for our afternoon excursion. That was how it went for the next three or four weeks. Mornings, we worked on the obituary; afternoons, we went out for walks. I filled more than a dozen notebooks with Effing's stories, generally at a clip of twenty or thirty new pages a day. I had to write at great speed to keep up with him, and there were times when my transcriptions were barely legible. At one point I asked him if we could switch to a tape recorder, but Effing refused. No electricity, he said, no machines. "I hate the noise of those infernal things. All whirr and whoosh, it's enough to make you sick. The only sound I want to hear is your pen moving across the paper." I explained to him that I wasn't a professional secretary. "I don't know shorthand," I said, "and it's not always easy for me to read what I've written." "Then type it up when I'm not around," he said. "I'll give you Pavel's typewriter. It's a beautiful old contraption, I bought it for him when we came to America in thirty-nine. An Underwood. They don't make them like that anymore. It must weigh three and a half tons." That same night, I dug it out from the back of the closet in my room and set it up on a small end table. From then on, I spent several hours every evening transcribing the pages from our morning session. It was tedious work, but Effing's words were still fresh in my mind, and I did not lose very many of them.

After Byrne died, he said, he gave up hope. He made a halfhearted attempt to extricate himself from the canyon, but he soon got lost in a maze of obstacles: cliffs, gorges, unclimbable buttes. His horse collapsed on the second day, but with no firewood to be found, the butchered meat was almost useless. Sagebrush would not ignite. It smoked and sputtered, but it would not produce a fire. To quell his hunger, Effing shaved off slivers of meat from the carcass and singed them with matches. This was enough for one meal, but after the matches ran out, he left the animal

**at a clip of** at a rate of, at a speed of **transcription** writing down exactly what was said **legible** clear enough to read **infernal** here: awful **whirr** (AE) whir—buzzing or vibrating sound **whoosh** sound of moving air or water **contraption** (iron.) machine or device considered to be strange or unlikely to work **Underwood** American company that produced typewriters **to transcribe** here: to type **tedious** boring and tiring **to extricate oneself from s.th.** to escape from a difficult situation **maze** a complicated and confusing arrangement **gorge** a deep narrow valley with steep sides **butte** [bju:t] (AE) a land formation with steep sides and a flat top **to ignite** [ɪgˈnaɪt] to catch fire, to start burning **to sputter** here: to make a series of soft explosive sounds and then go out **to quell** to reduce **sliver** a thin piece **carcass** body of a dead animal **to singe** to burn lightly

behind, unwilling to eat the flesh without cooking it. At that point, Effing was convinced his life was over. He continued blundering among the rocks, leading along the last surviving donkey, but with each step he took, he was tormented by the thought that he was drifting farther and farther from the possibility of rescue. His art supplies were still intact, and he had enough food and water for another two days. It didn't seem to matter anymore. Even if he managed to live through it, he realized that everything was finished for him. Byrne's death had seen to that, and there was no way he could ever bring himself to go home. The shame of it would be too much for him: the questions, the recriminations, the loss of face. Much better that they should think he had died, too, for at least his honor would be preserved, and no one would have to know how weak and irresponsible he had been. That was the moment when Julian Barber was obliterated: out there in the desert, hemmed in by rocks and blistering light, he simply canceled himself out. At the time, it did not seem like such a drastic decision to him. There was no question that he was going to die, and even if he didn't, he would be as good as dead anyway. No one would know the first thing about what had happened to him.

Effing told me that he went crazy, but I wasn't sure how literally I was supposed to take that word. After Byrne's death, he said, he howled almost constantly for three days, smearing his face with the blood that came trickling out of his hands—which had been lacerated by the rocks—but given the circumstances, this behavior did not strike me as unusual. I had done my fair share of screaming during the storm in Central Park, and my situation had been far less desperate than his. When a man feels he has come to the end of his rope, it is perfectly natural that he should want to scream. The air bunches in his lungs, and he cannot breathe unless he pushes it out of him, unless he howls it forth with all his

**to blunder** to walk unsteadily **to torment** to make s.o. suffer, to torture **to drift** to move without any plan **recrimination** angry statement accusing s.o. of having done s.th. wrong **to preserve** to keep safe from harm **to hem in** to surround s.o. closely in such a way that prevents this person from moving **blistering** here: extremely intense **to cancel out** to remove, to eliminate **to not know the first thing about s.th.** to not know anything about s.th. **to howl** to make a long loud cry when in pain or angry **to smear** to spread an oily or smooth substance on a surface **to trickle** to flow slowly in a thin stream **to lacerate** to cut the skin with s.th. sharp **end of his rope** (AE) no longer able to deal with a difficult situation **to bunch** to press into a small space

strength. Otherwise, he will choke on his own breath, the very sky will smother him.

On the morning of the fourth day, with his food gone and his canteen holding less than a cup of water, Effing spotted what looked like a cave at the top of a nearby cliff. It would be a good place to die in, he thought. Out of the sun and inaccessible to vultures, a place so hidden that no one would ever find him. Mustering his courage, he began the laborious trek upward. It took him almost two hours to get there, and when he arrived, he was at the end of his strength, barely able to stand. The cave was a good deal larger than it had appeared from below, and Effing was surprised to discover that he did not have to crouch to enter it. He pulled away the branches and twigs that blocked the opening and went in. Against all his expectations, the cave was not empty. Stretching a good twenty feet into the interior of the cliff, it contained several pieces of furniture: a table, four chairs, a cupboard, a dilapidated potbelly stove. For all intents and purposes, it was a house. The objects looked well cared-for, and everything in the room was neatly arranged, sitting comfortably in a kind of rough domestic order. Effing lit the candle that was on the table and took it with him to the back of the room, exploring the dark corners where the sunlight did not penetrate. Along the left wall he found a bed, and in the bed there was a man. Effing assumed the man was asleep, but when he cleared his throat to announce his presence and got no response, he bent down and held the candle over the stranger's face. It was then that he saw he was dead. Not just dead, but murdered. In the place where the man's right eye should have been, there was a large bullet hole. The left eye stared blankly into the darkness, and the pillow under the head was splattered with blood.

Turning away from the corpse, Effing walked back to the cupboard and found it filled with food. Canned goods, salted meats, flour and

**to choke** to be unable to breathe because the passage to the lungs is blocked **the very sky** even the sky **to smother** to cover the face so that one can't breathe **canteen** a small container for holding water **to spot** to see suddenly **inaccessible** difficult to reach **vulture** large bird that eats dead animals **to muster** to try to find as much as possible in order to do s.th. **laborious** taking a lot of time and effort **a good deal** much **twig** very thin branch that grows from a larger branch **dilapidated** [dɪˈlæp.ɪ.deɪ.tɪd] old and in a very bad condition **potbelly stove** a short rounded stove in which wood or coal is burned **for all intents and purposes** for all practical purposes, virtually **domestic order** everything in the right place as in a well-run home **to penetrate** to enter **blankly** in a way showing no expression **to splatter** to fall in drops **corpse** dead body **flour** Mehl

cooking supplies—there was enough packed onto the shelves to last someone a year. He promptly prepared himself a meal, consuming half a loaf of bread and two cans of beans. Once he had satisfied his hunger, he set about disposing of the dead man's body. He had already worked out a plan; it was simply a matter of putting it into effect. The dead man must have been a hermit, Effing reasoned, living alone like this up in the mountains, and if that were the case, then not many people would have known he was there. From all that he could gather (the flesh still undecomposed, the absence of any overpowering smell, the bread not yet stale), the murder must have been committed quite recently, perhaps as recently as several hours ago—which meant that the only person who knew the hermit was dead was the man who had murdered him. There would be nothing to prevent him from taking the hermit's place, Effing thought. They were more or less the same age, they were more or less the same size, they both had the same light brown hair. It would not be very difficult to grow a beard and start wearing the dead man's clothes. He would take on the hermit's life and continue to live it for him, acting as though the soul of this man had now passed into his possession. If anyone came up there to pay him a visit, he would simply pretend to be someone he was not—and see if he could get away with it. He had a rifle for self-defense if something went wrong, but he figured the odds were with him in any case, since it did not seem likely that a hermit would have many visitors.

After removing the stranger's clothes, he dragged the body out of the cave and took it around to the back side of the cliff. There he discovered the most remarkable thing of all: a small oasis thirty or forty feet below the level of the cave, a lush area with two towering cottonwood trees, an active brook, and innumerable shrubs whose names were unfamiliar to him. It was a miniature pocket of life in the midst of overpowering barrenness. As he buried the hermit in the soft earth beside the brook, he

**to consume** to eat **to set about doing s.th.** to start doing s.th. **to dispose of s.th.** to get rid of s.th. **hermit** a person living alone away from civilization **to gather** to conclude, to assume **undecomposed** still fresh, not rotten or decayed **overpowering** intense, very strong **stale** no longer fresh or good to eat **to commit** to do, to carry out **to get away with s.th.** to not be caught or punished for s.th. one has done wrong **the odds were with him** the chances of success were quite good **lush** with a lot of healthy plants **towering** very tall **cottonwood tree** a North American poplar (Pappel) **active brook** a small stream not dried out, with water running through it **innumerable** a great number of **in the midst** in the middle **barrenness** condition of not being able to support the growth of plants

realized that everything would be possible for him in this place. He had food and water; he had a house; he had found a new identity for himself, a new and utterly unexpected life. The reversal was almost too much for him to comprehend. Just one hour before, he had been ready to die. Now, he was trembling with happiness, unable to stop himself from laughing as he flung one shovelful of dirt after another onto the dead man's face.

Months passed. In the beginning, Effing was too stunned by his good fortune to pay much attention to the things around him. He ate and slept, and when the sun was not too strong, he would sit on the rocks outside his cave and watch the bright, multicolored lizards that went flitting about his feet. The view from the cliff was immense, encompassing untold miles of terrain, but he did not look out at it very often, choosing instead to confine his thoughts to the immediate vicinity: his trips to the stream with the water bucket, the gathering of firewood, the inside of his cave. He had had his fill of scenery, and for now he was content to ignore it. Then, very suddenly, this sense of calm abandoned him, and he entered a period of almost unbearable loneliness. The horror of the past months engulfed him, and for the next week or two he came dangerously close to killing himself. His mind swarmed with delusions and fears, and more than once he imagined that he was already dead, that he had died the moment he entered the cave and was now the prisoner of some demonic afterlife. One day, in a fit of madness, he took out the hermit's rifle and shot his donkey, thinking that it had been turned into the hermit himself, a spectre of wrath who had come back to haunt him with his insidious braying. The donkey knew the truth about him, and he had no choice but to eliminate this witness to his fraud. After that, he became obsessed with

**utterly** completely **reversal** a change that is the opposite of what happened before **to fling/flung/flung** to throw quickly with force **stunned** so surprised that one cannot react immediately **lizard** small reptile that has four legs and a long tail **to flit** to continuously move about quickly **encompassing** including **untold** so much that it can't be measured **to confine** to limit, to restrict **vicinity** the area around a certain place **to have one's fill of s.th.** to have more than enough of s.th. unpleasant **to be content** to be happy and satisfied **to abandon** (fig) to leave behind **to engulf** here: to affect very strongly **to swarm** to be full of **delusion** false ideas about oneself or one's situation **demonic** having to do with an evil spirit or hell **spectre** ghost **wrath** [ræθ] extreme anger **to haunt** to visit or appear (said of a ghost) frequently **insidious** causing harm in a way that is not immediately noticed **fraud** crime of deceiving **to become obsessed with s.th.** to completely fill one's mind with s.th. so that one can't think of anything else

trying to uncover the identity of the dead man, systematically ransacking the interior of the cave for clues, looking for a diary, a packet of letters, the flyleaf of a book, anything that might reveal the hermit's name. But nothing turned up, he never found the slightest particle of information.

After two weeks, he slowly began to return to himself, eventually subsiding into something that resembled peace of mind. It couldn't go on forever, he told himself, and that alone was a comfort, a thought that gave him the courage to continue. At some point, the food supplies were going to run out, and then he would have to go somewhere else. He gave himself approximately a year, a bit more than that if he was careful. By then, people would have given up hoping that he and Byrne would be coming back. He doubted that Scoresby would ever mail his letter, but even if he did, the results would be essentially the same. A search party would be sent out, financed by Elizabeth and Byrne's father. They would wander around the desert for several weeks, hunting assiduously for the missing men—there was sure to be a reward offered as well—but they would never find a thing. At most, they might discover Byrne's grave, but that was not very likely. Even if they did, it would not get them any closer to him. Julian Barber was gone, and no one was ever going to track him down. It was all a matter of holding out until they had stopped looking for him. The obituaries would be published in the New York papers, a memorial service would be held, and that would be the end of it. Once that happened, he could go wherever he liked; he could become whoever he wanted to be.

Still, he knew that it would not be to his advantage to rush things. The longer he kept himself hidden, the safer it would be when he finally left. He therefore set about organizing his life in the strictest possible way, doing everything he could to stretch out the time he would spend there: limiting himself to one meal a day, laying in an ample supply of firewood for the winter, keeping his body fit. He made charts and schedules for

**to ransack** to search a place thoroughly so that everything becomes untidy **clue** any piece of information that helps to solve a mystery **flyleaf** empty page at the beginning or end of a book **to reveal** to make s.th. known that was previously secret or unknown **to subside** to return to a normal level **to resemble** to be similar to **peace of mind** in state of not worrying **approximately** about **search party** a group of people organized to look for s.o. lost **assiduously** with great care and a lot of work **to track s.o. down** to find s.o. by following the marks, signs, or information left behind **memorial service** a service held as a remembrance of s.o. who has died **to lay in** to collect and store for future use **ample** more than enough

himself, and each night before going to bed he wrote down meticulous accounts of the resources he had used during the day, pushing himself to maintain the most rigorous discipline. In the beginning, he found it hard to achieve the goals he had set, often succumbing to the temptation of another slice of bread or another plate of canned stew, but the effort in itself seemed worthwhile, and it helped to keep him alert. It was a way of testing himself against his own weaknesses, and as the actual and the ideal gradually came closer together, he could not help thinking of it as a personal triumph. He knew that it was no more than a game, but a fanatical devotion was required to play it, and that very excess of concentration was what allowed him to keep from slipping into despondency.

After two or three weeks of this new, disciplined life, he began to feel the urge to paint again. One night, sitting with a pencil in his hand and writing up his brief report of the day's activities, he suddenly started to sketch out a little drawing of a mountain on the opposite page. Before he even realized what he was doing the sketch was finished. It took no more than half a minute, but in that abrupt, unconscious gesture, he found a strength that had never been present in any of his other work. That same night, he unpacked his art supplies, and from then until his colors finally ran out, he continued to paint, leaving the cave every morning at dawn and spending the entire day outside. It lasted for two and a half months, and in that time he managed to finish nearly forty canvases. Without any question, he told me, it was the happiest period of his life.

He was working under the demands of a double restriction, and each one wound up helping him in a different way. First, there was the fact that no one would ever see these paintings. That was a foregone conclusion, but rather than torment Effing with a sense of futility, it actually

**meticulous** very careful about the details, correct **account** description **to succumb to s.th.** to not be able to resist s.th. **temptation** Versuchung **worthwhile** worth the effort and time **alert** able to think quickly, quick to notice things **devotion** a great deal of concentration, time and energy (Hingabe) **excess** larger amount than is necessary **to slip into s.th.** to slowly fall into a state of s.th. **despondency** feeling of despair **urge** sudden strong need or wish **to sketch out** to quickly draw the basic details **unconscious** not done on purpose, without realizing what one has done **gesture** movement made with the hands, i.e. here: the act of drawing **to wind/wound/wound up** to arrive at a certain situation in the end, to end up **foregone** certain, inevitable **to torment** to cause pain or suffering, to tortue **futility** uselessness because there's no chance of success

seemed to liberate him. He was working for himself now, no longer burdened by the threat of other people's opinions, and that alone was enough to produce a fundamental change in how he approached his art. For the first time in his life, he stopped worrying about results, and as a consequence the terms "success" and "failure" had suddenly lost their meaning for him. The true purpose of art was not to create beautiful objects, he discovered. It was a method of understanding, a way of penetrating the world and finding one's place in it, and whatever aesthetic qualities an individual canvas might have were almost an incidental by-product of the effort to engage oneself in this struggle, to enter into the thick of things. He untaught himself the rules he had learned, trusting in the landscape as an equal partner, voluntarily abandoning his intentions to the assaults of chance, of spontaneity, the onrush of brute particulars. He was no longer afraid of the emptiness around him. The act of trying to put it on canvas had somehow internalized it for him, and now he was able to feel its indifference as something that belonged to him, as much as he belonged to the silent power of those gigantic spaces himself. The pictures he produced were raw, he said, filled with violent colors and strange, unpremeditated surges of energy, a whirl of forms and light. He had no idea if they were ugly or beautiful, but that was probably beside the point. They were his, and they didn't look like any other paintings he had seen before. Fifty years later, he said, he was still able to remember each one of them.

The second constraint was more subtle, but it nevertheless exerted an even stronger influence on him: eventually, his materials were going to run out. There were only so many tubes of paint and so many canvases, after all, and as long as he continued to work, they were bound to be used

**to liberate** to free **burdened** worried about, under stress because of **to approach** to begin to deal with s.th. in a certain way **term** expression **to penetrate** here: to understand the inner meaning of s.th. **incidental** happening at the same time as s.th. more important **by-product** an unplanned additional result of s.th. that has been done **to engage oneself** to actively take part in, participate in **the thick of things** the most active part of s.th. **voluntarily** done willingly **to abandon s.th. to** here: to no longer follow s.th., following s.th. new instead **the assaults of chance, of spontaneity** here: the steady and forceful influence of chance and spontaneity (the quality of happening on impulse or voluntarily) that happen repeatedly **onrush** (fig) a strong fast movement forward **brute** entirely physical, instinctive, savage **particulars** specific details **to internalize** to make s.th. a part of your beliefs, the way you think or behave, a part of your personality **raw** very direct, not refined **unpremeditated** not planned in advance **surge** sudden increase **whirl** a rapid spinning or turning **beside the point** not important **constraint** restriction **bound** sure, certain

up. From the very first moment, therefore, the end was already in sight. Even as he painted his pictures, it was as though he could feel the landscape vanishing before his eyes. This gave a particular poignancy in everything he did during those months. Each time he completed another canvas, the dimensions of the future shrank for him, steadily drawing him closer to the moment when there would be no future at all. After a month and a half of constant work, he finally came to the last canvas. More than a dozen tubes of paint were still left, however. Scarcely breaking stride, Effing turned the pictures around and began a new series on the backs of the canvases. It was an extraordinary reprieve, he said, and for the next three weeks he felt as though he had been reborn. He worked on this second cycle of landscapes with even greater intensity than the first, and when all the backs were finally covered, he began painting on the furniture inside his cave, frantically inscribing his brushstrokes onto the cupboard, the table, and the wooden chairs, and when all these surfaces were covered as well, he squeezed out the last bits of color from the shriveled tubes and began work on the southern wall, sketching the outlines of a panoramic cave painting. It would have been his masterpiece, Effing said, but the colors ran dry when it was only half-finished.

Then it was winter. He still had several notebooks and a box of pencils, but rather than switch from painting to drawing, he hunkered down during the cold months and spent his time writing. In one notebook he recorded his thoughts and observations, attempting to do in words what he had previously been doing in images, and in another he continued with the log of his daily routine, maintaining an exact account of his expenditures: how much food he had eaten, how much food was left, how many candles he had burned, how many candles were still intact. In January, it snowed every day for a week, and he took pleasure in seeing the whiteness fall on the red rocks, transforming the landscape that had become so familiar to him. In the afternoon, the sun would come out and melt the snow in irregular patches, creating a beautiful dappled effect, and

**poignancy** ['pɔɪ.njənt.si] quality of being moving, causing sad feelings **to shrink/shrank/shrunk** to become smaller **to break stride** to stop what one's doing, to slow down **reprieve** a delay before s.th. bad happens **to inscribe** to mark, to draw **brushstroke** single movement of a brush when painting **shriveled** here: completely flat and shrunken because of having all the paint pressed out **to hunker down** (AE, coll) to settle in, to stay somewhere for a long period of time before becoming active again **log** a report of daily events, especially when on a journey on a ship or plane **expenditures** money spent **intact** not damaged **patch** small area that is different from the surrounding area **dappled** marked with spots of color, light, or shade

when the wind picked up, it would blow the white, dusty particles into the air, swirling them around in brief, tempestuous dances. Effing would stand and watch these things for hours on end, never seeming to tire of them. His life had slowed down to such an extent that the smallest changes were now visible to him. After his paints ran out, he had gone through an anguished period of withdrawal, but then he had found that writing could serve as an adequate substitute for making pictures. By mid-February, however, he had filled all his notebooks, and there were no pages left to write on anymore. Contrary to what he had been expecting, this did not dampen his spirits. He had descended so deeply into his solitude by then that he no longer needed any distractions. He found it almost unimaginable, but little by little the world had become enough for him.

In late March, he finally had his first visitor. As luck would have it, Effing was sitting on the roof of his cave when the stranger made his appearance at the bottom of the cliff, and this allowed him to follow the man's progress up the rocks, watching for the better part of an hour as the small figure clambered toward him. By the time the man reached the top, Effing was waiting for him with the rifle in his hands. He had played out this scene for himself a hundred times before, but now that it was happening, he was shocked to discover how scared he was. It wouldn't take more than thirty seconds for the situation to clarify itself: whether or not the man knew the hermit, and if he did, whether the disguise could fool him into thinking that Effing was the person he was pretending to be. If the man happened to be the hermit's killer, then the question of the disguise would be irrelevant. Likewise if he was a member of the search party, a last benighted soul still dreaming of the reward. Everything would be settled within a few moments, but until it was, Effing had no

**to pick up** to begin to get stronger **to swirl** to make s.th. twist around or turn quickly **tempestuous** stormy **for hours on end** for a great number of hours without a break **anguished** characterized by suffering caused by extreme pain or worry **withdrawal** the act of no longer taking part in an activity **to dampen s.o.'s spirits** to make s.o. feel less happy or enthusiastic **to descend** to move from a higher to a lower position **solitude** state of being alone, often considered pleasant **distraction** s.th. which makes you stop paying attention to what you are doing **to clamber** to climb with difficulty, especially by using both hands and feet **to play out** to imagine an action, to act out an action in the mind **to clarify itself** to become clear **disguise** a change made in one's appearance so that nobody can recognize you **likewise** similarly **benighted** ignorant, without understanding **to settle** here: to decide, to determine

choice but to expect the worst. He realized that on top of all his other sins, there was a good chance that he was about to become a murderer.

The first thing he noticed about the man was that he was big, and immediately after that he noticed how oddly he was dressed. The man's clothing had apparently been put together from a random assortment of patches—a square of bright red material here, a rectangle of blue and white checks there, a piece of wool in one place, a piece of denim in another—and this costume gave him a weirdly clownish aspect, as though he had just wandered off from some traveling circus. Instead of a wide-brimmed Western hat, he wore a battered derby with a white feather protruding from the band. His straight black hair hung all the way down to his shoulders, and as he continued to approach, Effing saw that the left side of his face was deformed, creased with a broad, jagged scar that ran from his cheek to his lower lip. Effing assumed the man was an Indian, but at that point it hardly mattered what he was. He was an apparition, a nightmare buffoon who had materialized out of the rocks. The man grunted with exhaustion as he hoisted himself onto the top ledge, and then he stood up and smiled at Effing. He was only ten or twelve feet away. Effing raised his rifle and pointed it at him, but the man seemed more puzzled than afraid.

"Hey, Tom," he said, speaking in a slow, halfwit's voice. "Don't you remember who I am? It's your old pal, George. You don't have to play no tricks with me."

Effing hesitated for a moment, then lowered the rifle, still keeping his finger on the trigger as a precaution. "George," he muttered, speaking almost inaudibly so his voice would not betray him.

"I been locked up all winter," the big man said. "That's why I didn't come to see you." He continued walking toward Effing and did not stop

**random** chosen without any plan **assortment** a collection of various kinds **rectangle** Rechteck **checks** a pattern of squares on cloth **denim** cotton cloth used for making jeans **weirdly** [wɪrdli] unusually, bizarrely **aspect** appearance **wide-brimmed** mit einer breiten Krempe **battered** old and in bad condition **derby** (AE) a black round hat, (BE) bowler **to protrude** to stick out **deformed** not in the normal shape **creased** with lines made by pressing or folding **jagged** not straight but with rough pointed edges **scar** Narbe **apparition** ghostlike appearance **buffoon** [bəˈfuːn] silly person **to materialize** to appear in an unexpected and strange way **to hoist oneself** to raise or lift oneself **halfwit** person with a weak mind **pal** (coll) close friend **precaution** an action taken to avoid a dangerous event **inaudibly** in a way too quiet to be heard **to betray** to show feelings one is trying to hide **locked up** i.e. in jail

until he was close enough to shake hands. Effing transferred the rifle to his left hand and extended his right in greeting. The Indian looked searchingly into his eyes for a moment, but then the danger suddenly passed. "You're looking good, Tom," he said. "Real good."

"Thanks," Effing said. "You look good, too."

The big man burst out laughing, seized by a kind of oafish delight, and from that moment on, Effing knew he was going to get away with it. It was as though he had just told the funniest joke of the century, and if so little could produce so much, it wouldn't be hard to keep up the deception. It was astonishing, in fact, how smoothly everything went. Effing's resemblance to the hermit was only approximate, but it seemed that the power of suggestion was strong enough to transform the physical evidence into something it was not. The Indian had come to the cave expecting to find Tom the hermit, and because it was inconceivable to him that a man who answered to the name of Tom could be anyone other than the Tom he was looking for, he had hastily altered the facts to match his expectations, justifying any discrepancies between the two Toms as a product of his own faulty memory. It didn't hurt, of course, that the man was a simpleton. Perhaps he knew all along that Effing wasn't the real Tom. He had climbed up to the cave looking for a few hours' companionship, and since he got what he was looking for, he wasn't about to question who had given it to him. In the end, it was probably a matter of complete indifference to him whether he had been with the real Tom or not.

They spent the afternoon together, sitting in the cave and smoking cigarettes. George had brought along a pouch of tobacco, his usual gift to the hermit, and Effing smoked one after the other in a trance of pleasure. He found it odd to be with someone after so many months of isolation, and for the first hour or so he had trouble getting any words out of his mouth. He had lost the habit of speech, and his tongue no longer worked as it once had. It felt clumsy to him, a lunging, thrashing serpent that no

**to transfer** to move from one place to another **to be seized** to be suddenly affected by an extremely strong feeling **oafish** stupid **delight** joy, extreme pleasure **deception** the act of deliberately making s.o. believe s.th. which is not true **approximate** almost the same **power of suggestion** the ability to put s.th. in a person's mind **inconceivable** too unusual to be thought possible **hastily** hurriedly **faulty** not working properly **companionship** here: being able to enjoy each other's friendship **pouch** [paʊtʃ] a small leather bag **trance** here: in a sleeplike state because of great pleasure **clumsy** not easily managed **to lunge** to make a sudden movement towards s.th. **to thrash** to move violently from side to side **serpent** large snake

longer obeyed his commands. Fortunately, the original Tom had not been much of a talker, and the Indian did not seem to expect more than an occasional response from him. George was evidently enjoying himself to the utmost, and after every three or four sentences, he would throw back his head and laugh. Each time he laughed, he would forget his train of thought and start in on another topic, which made it difficult for Effing to follow what he was saying. A story about the Navaho reservation would suddenly turn into a story about a drunken brawl in a saloon, which would then turn into an excited account of a train robbery. From all that Effing could gather, his companion went by the name of George Ugly Mouth. That was what people called him, in any case, but the big man didn't seem to mind. On the contrary, he gave the impression of being rather pleased that the world had given him a name that belonged to him and no one else, as though it were a badge of distinction. Effing had never met anyone who combined such sweetness and imbecility, and he did his best to listen carefully to him, to nod in all the right places. Once or twice, he was tempted to ask George if he had heard anything about a search party, but each time he managed to fight back the impulse.

As the afternoon wore on, Effing was gradually able to piece together some facts about the original Tom. George Ugly Mouth's rambling, half-formed narratives began to loop back among themselves with a certain frequency, intersecting at enough points to take on the structure of a larger, more unified story. Incidents were repeated, crucial passages were left out, events from the beginning were not told until the end, but enough was finally given for Effing to conclude that the hermit had been involved in criminal activities of some sort with a band of outlaws known as the Gresham brothers. He couldn't be sure if the hermit had been an active participant or if he had simply let the gang use the cave as a hideout,

**evidently** apparently **to the utmost** to the greatest degree **train of thought** logically connected series of thoughts **brawl** noisy fight **on the contrary** quite the opposite was true **badge of distinction** here: s.th. that shows s.o. has a special quality **imbecility** stupidity **to nod** nicken **to be tempted to do s.th.** to have the desire to do s.th. although one knows it's wrong **to wear on** to continue seemingly too slowly **to ramble** to talk in a confused way **to loop back** to move back in a curve or circle to the original position **to intersect** to meet **crucial** [ˈkruː.ʃəl] very important **Gresham brothers** There were many groups of train robbers after 1870, for whom it was profitable to steal shipments of gold and money sent to towns in the West. **participant** s.o. who takes part in an event **hideout** a place to go where no-one can find you—according the park rangers of Glen Canyon there are no caves in the area but one way or another, it seemed to account for the murder that had been committed, not to speak of the abundant food supply he had found there on the first day. Afraid to reveal his ignorance, Effing didn't press George for details, but from what the Indian said, it seemed likely that the Greshams would be returning before too long, perhaps by the end of spring. George was too distracted to remember where the gang was now, however, and he kept bouncing up from his chair to walk around the room and study the paintings, shaking his head in admiration. He hadn't known that Tom could paint, he said, repeating the remark several dozen times over the course of the afternoon. They were the beautifulest things he'd ever seen, the beautifulest things in the whole world. If he behaved himself, he said, maybe one day Tom could teach him how to do it, and Effing looked him in the eyes and said yes, maybe one day he would. Effing was sorry that anyone had seen the paintings, but at the same time he was glad to get such an enthusiastic response, realizing that it was probably the only response these works would ever get.

After George Ugly Mouth's visit, things were no longer the same for Effing. He had worked steadily for the past seven months at being alone, struggling to build his solitude into something substantial, an absolute stronghold to delimit the boundaries of his life, but now that someone had been with him in the cave, he understood how artificial his situation was. People knew where to find him, and now that it had happened, there was no reason to think it wouldn't happen again. He had to be on his guard, to be constantly on the alert for intruders, and the demands of this vigilance took their toll, eating away at him until the harmony of his world was destroyed. There was nothing he could do about is. He had to spend his days watching and waiting, he had to prepare himself for the things that were going to happen. At first, he kept expecting George to come back, but as the weeks went by and the big man did not show up, he began to turn his attention to the Gresham brothers. It would have

**to account for s.th.** to be the reason why s.th. has happened **abundant** more than enough **distracted** not able to think clearly **to bounce up** to continuously move up and down **in admiration** having a very high opinion **over the course** during **substantial** solid and strong—cf. Auster's *The Book of Memory* where he seeks solitude in his little room in New York in 1979. **stronghold** here: s.th. that is so strong it cannot be destroyed **to delimit** to determine the limit **on the alert** ready to deal with a dangerous situation **intruder** s.o. who enters an area illegally or without being invited **vigilance** being watchful, especially when s.th. dangerous might happen **took their toll** had a damaging effect on him

been logical to call it quits at that point, to gather up his things and leave the cave for good, but something in him resisted giving in so easily to the threat. He knew it was madness not to leave, a meaningless gesture that was almost certain to get him killed, but the cave was the only thing he had to fight for now, and he couldn't bring himself to run away from it.

The crucial thing was not to let them catch him by surprise. If they walked in on him while he was asleep, then he wouldn't have a chance, they'd kill him before he got out of bed. They had already done that once, and it would be nothing for them to do it again. On the other hand, if he rigged up some kind of alarm that would warn him when they were approaching, it probably wouldn't give him more than a few moments' advantage. Enough time to wake up and grab the rifle, perhaps, but if all three brothers came at once, the odds would still be against him. He could buy more time if he barricaded himself inside the cave, blocking up the entrance with stones and branches, but then he would be giving away the one thing he had over his attackers: the fact that they did not know he was there. As soon as they saw the barricade, they would realize that someone was living in the cave and would respond accordingly. Effing spent nearly all his waking hours thinking about these problems, contemplating the various strategies that were available to him, trying to come up with a plan that would not be suicidal. In the end, he stopped sleeping in the cave altogether, setting up his blankets and pillow on a ledge halfway down the other side of the cliff. George Ugly Mouth had talked about the Gresham brothers' fondness for whiskey, and Effing figured it would be only natural for such men to start drinking once they settled into the cave. They would be bored out there in the desert, and if they ever went so far as to get drunk, the alcohol would become his staunchest ally. He did his best to eliminate all obvious traces of himself from the cave, setting his paintings and notebooks in the darkness at the back and discontinuing his use of the stove. There was nothing to be done about the pictures on the furniture and the wall, but at least if the stove was not warm when they walked in, the Greshams might assume that the person who had made the pictures was gone. It was by no means certain they would think that, but Effing couldn't see any other way around the

**to call it quits** to give up doing s.th., to stop doing s.th. **to gather up one's things** to get one's things together and pack them for transport **for good** permanently **to rig s.th. up** to set s.th. up, to prepare s.th. from things lying around **accordingly** as would be suitable for the situation **to contemplate** to think about, to consider **suicidal** [ˌsuː.əˈsaɪ.dəl] likely to lead to one's own death **fondness** liking **staunch** loyal, dependable

impasse. He needed them to know that someone else had been there, for if the cave looked as though it had been empty since their previous visit in the summer, there would be nothing to account for the fact that the hermit's body was missing. The Greshams would wonder about that, but once they realized that another person had been living in the cave, perhaps they would stop wondering. At least that was Effing's hope. Given the myriad imponderables of the situation, he didn't allow himself to hope very much.

He went through another month of hell, and then they finally came. It was the middle of May, a little more than a year since he had set out from New York with Byrne. The Greshams came riding up at dusk, announcing their presence with a burst of noise that echoed among the rocks: loud voices, laughter, a snatch of raucous singing. Effing had ample time to prepare for them, but that did not stop his pulse from pounding out of control. In spite of the warnings he had given himself about staying calm, he realized that he would have to put an end to the business that night. It wasn't going to be possible to hold out any longer.

He crouched on the narrow ledge behind the cave, waiting for his moment as the darkness gathered around him. He heard the Greshams approach, listened to a few scattered remarks about things he didn't understand, and then heard one of them say, "I guess we'll have to air out the place after we dump old Tom." The other two laughed, and immediately after that the voices stopped. That meant they had gone inside the cave. Half an hour later, smoke started coming out of the tin pipe that jutted from the roof, and then he began to detect the smells of cooking meat. For the next two hours, nothing happened. He listened to the horses clear their throats and stamp their hooves on a patch of ground below the cave, and bit by bit the dark blue evening turned black. There was no moon that night, and the sky was brilliant with stars. Every once in a while, he could hear the muffled remnant of a laugh, but that was the extent of it. Then, periodically, the Greshams started coming out of the cave one by one to piss against the rocks. Effing hoped that meant they were in there playing cards and getting drunk, but it was impossible to be sure of anything. He decided to wait until the last one had emptied his bladder, and then he would give it another hour or hour and a half. By then they would probably be asleep, and no one would hear him enter the cave. In the meantime, he wondered how he was going to use the rifle

**impasse** a difficult situation for which no progress seems possible **myriad** [ˈmɪr.i.əd] great number of **imponderables** (usually plural) unpredictable factors

with only one hand. If the lights were out in the cave, he would have to carry a candle in order to see his targets, and he had never practiced shooting with just one hand. It was a Winchester repeating rifle that had to be recocked after every shot, and he had always done that with his left hand. He could stick the candle in his mouth, of course, but it would be dangerous to have the fire so close to his eyes, not to speak of what would happen if the flame ever touched his beard. He would have to hold the candle as if it were a cigar, he decided, wedging it between the forefinger and middle finger of his left hand, hoping that the other three fingers would somehow be able to grip the barrel at the same time. If he jammed the butt of the rifle against his stomach rather than his shoulder, perhaps he would be able to recock quickly enough with his right hand after pulling the trigger. Again, he couldn't be sure of anything. These were desperate, last-minute calculations, and as he sat there waiting in the darkness, he cursed himself for his negligence, marveling at the depth of his stupidity.

As it turned out, the light was not an issue. When he crept out from his hiding place and crawled around to the front of the cave, he discovered that a candle was still burning within. He paused at the side of the entrance and held his breath, listening for sounds, ready to rush back to his ledge if the Greshams were not asleep. After a few moments, he heard what sounded like a snore, but this was immediately followed by a number of sounds that seemed to be coming from the vicinity of the table: a sigh, a silence, and then a small thud, as though a glass had just been set down on the surface. At least one of them was still awake, he thought, but how could he be sure it was only one? Then he heard a deck

**Winchester** trademark for a lever (Hebel) action rifle that became very popular in the West after the Civil War **repeating rifle** rifle that can be fired several times without reloading **to recock** to reset the hammer (Hahn) of a weapon into position so that a pull of the trigger (Abzug) will fire the weapon **not to speak of** it was also important to think of **to wedge** to squeeze into a narrow space **forefinger** the finger next to the thumb **to grip** to hold tightly **barrel** Lauf **to jam** to push with force **butt** the end of the wooden part of a rifle **calculations** thoughts about how to carefully plan an outcome **to curse oneself** sich selbst beschimpfen **negligence** the quality of not being careful enough about s.th.that one is responsible for **to marvel at s.th.** to be full of surprise or wonder about s.th. **to crawl** to move along on one's hands and knees with the body close to the ground **snore** the loud sound one makes while sleeping when air passes through the nose **in the vicinity of** near **sigh** Seufzer **thud** a sound that a heavy object makes when it falls on s.th. **deck** a set of 52 cards

of cards being shuffled, the sound of seven short bumps on the table, and then a brief pause. Then six bumps and another pause. Then five bumps. Then four, then three, then two, then one. Solitaire, Effing thought, solitaire beyond any shadow of a doubt. One of them was sitting up, and the other two were asleep. It had to be that, or else the card player would be talking to one of the others. But he wasn't talking, and that could only mean there was no one for him to talk to.

Effing swung the rifle into firing position and strode to the entrance of the cave. It wasn't difficult to hold the candle in his left hand, he discovered; his panic had been for nothing. The man at the table jerked his head up sharply when Effing appeared, then stared at him in horror. "Jesus fucking Christ," the man whispered. "You're supposed to be dead."

"I'm afraid you've got it the wrong way around," Effing replied. "You're the one who's dead, not me."

He pulled the trigger, and an instant later the man went flying back in his chair, screaming as the bullet hit him in the chest, and then, suddenly, there was no sound from him at all. Effing recocked the rifle and pointed it at the second brother, who was hastily trying to scramble out of his bedroll on the floor. Effing killed him with one shot as well, hitting him square in the face with a bullet that tore out the back of his head, carrying it across the room in a spurting mess of brains and bone. Things did not go so easily with the third Gresham, however. That one was lying on the bed at the back of the cave, and by the time Effing had finished with the first two, number three had grabbed his gun and was getting ready to fire it. A bullet shot past Effing's head and ricocheted off the iron stove behind him. He recocked his rifle and jumped for cover behind the table to his left, accidentally extinguishing both candles in the process. The cave went pitch dark, and the man at the back suddenly began to sob

**to shuffle** to mix **bump** the sound of s.th. hitting a hard surface **solitaire** (AE) a game of cards for one person (BE) patience **beyond a shadow of a doubt** without any doubt **to stride/strode/stridden** to walk quickly with long steps **to jerk** to move in a short quick movement **fucking** (slang, vulgar) used for emphasis **to scramble out of s.th.** to get out of s.th. with difficulty **bedroll** (AE) a number of blankets rolled together or sleeping bag used to sleep outdoors **square** directly, in the middle of **to spurt** to pour out suddenly **to ricochet** [ˈrɪk.ə.ʃeɪ] to go off in another direction after hitting a hard surface at an angle **for cover** for protection behind s.th. **to extinguish** to put out a fire **in the process** while doing s.th. **pitch dark** completely dark **to sob** to cry noisily taking sudden breaths

hysterically, blubbering a stream of nonsense about the dead hermit and firing his gun wildly in Effing's direction. Effing knew the contours of the cave by heart, and even in the blackness he could tell exactly where the man was standing. He counted six shots, realizing that the raving third brother would find it impossible to reload his gun without any light, and then stood up and walked toward the bed. He pulled the trigger of the rifle, heard the man shriek as the bullet entered his body, then recocked the rifle and fired again. Everything went silent in the cave. Effing breathed in the smell of gun powder that floated through the air, and suddenly he began to feel his body shake. He staggered outside as best he could and fell to his knees, then promptly threw up on the ground.

He slept right there at the mouth of the cave. When he woke the next morning, he immediately set about disposing of the bodies. He was surprised to discover that he felt no remorse, that he could look at the men he had killed without feeling the slightest twinge of conscience. One by one, he dragged them out of the room and down the backside of the cliff, burying them next to the hermit under the cottonwood tree. It was early afternoon by the time he finished with the last corpse. Exhausted by his efforts, he returned to the cave to eat some lunch, and it was then, just as he sat down at the table and began to pour himself a glass of the Gresham brothers' whiskey, that he saw the saddlebags lying under the bed. As Effing put it to me, it was precisely at that moment that everything changed for him again, that his life suddenly veered in a new direction. There were six large saddlebags in all, and as he dumped the contents of the first one onto the table, he knew that his time in the cave had come to an end—just like that, with the speed and force of a book slamming shut. There was money on the table, and each time he emptied another saddlebag, the pile continued to grow. When he finally counted it up, the cash alone came to more than twenty thousand dollars. Mixed in among

**to blubber** to speak while sobbing **contour** outline, the shape of the outer edges **six shots** i.e. a Colt revolver which could fire six times before reloading **raving** behaving in a crazy way **to float** to move very slowly in the air **to stagger** to walk unsteadily, almost falling **promptly** immediately **to throw up** to vomit (Notice the parallels in action and vocabulary with the scene in Central Park!) **remorse** sense of guilt **twinge** slight feeling **conscience** the sense of right and wrong that directs a person's thoughts and actions **to veer** to change direction suddenly **to dump** to drop, fall, or let fall heavily **to slam** to close noisily

the currency, he found a number of watches, bracelets, and necklaces, and in the last bag there were three tightly bound fascicles of bearer bonds, representing another ten thousand dollars' worth of investments in such things as a Colorado silver mine, the Westinghouse utility company, and Ford Motors. It was an incredible sum back in those days, Effing said, an absolute fortune. If handled correctly, it would be enough money to last him the rest of his life.

There was never any question of returning the stolen money, he said, never any question of going to the authorities and reporting what had happened. It wasn't that he was afraid of being found out when he told his story, it was simply that he wanted the money for himself. This urge was so strong that he never bothered to examine what he did. He took the money because it was there, because in some sense he felt that it already belonged to him, and that was that. The question of right and wrong never entered into it. He had killed three men in cold blood, and now he had taken himself beyond the niceties of such considerations. In any case, he doubted that many people would mourn the loss of the Gresham brothers. They had disappeared, and it wouldn't be long before the world got used to the fact that they weren't there anymore. The world would get used to it, in the same way it was used to living without Julian Barber.

He spent the whole of the next day preparing to leave. He straightened the furniture, washed off blood stains wherever he found them, and stored his notebooks in the cupboard. He regretted having to say good-bye to his paintings, but there was nothing else to be done, and so he stacked them neatly at the foot of the bed and turned them against the wall. It took him no more than a couple of hours to do this, but for the rest of the morning and all through the afternoon, he stood out in the hot sun collecting stones and branches to block up the mouth of his cave. He

**currency** metal and paper money **bracelet** a band worn around the wrist as an ornament **necklace** a chain or string of jewels worn around the neck **fascicle** ['fæs.ɪ.kl] bundle, number of things held loosely together **bearer bond** a financial document with interest (Zinsen) sold by a firm to the public to raise money—It does not have the name of the owner in it, so it's easy to sell if stolen. (Inhaberschuldverschreibung) **Westinghouse** the same company Tesla worked for **utility company** a company that produces electricity **authorities** the local government, the police force **urge** strong desire **to bother** to make the effort to do s.th. **to enter into s.th.** to be s.th. that should be considered **niceties** small details or points of difference **consideration** a fact to be taken into account when making a judgment or decision **to mourn** to feel or express sadness for the death of s.o. **to straighten** to make tidy **stain** spot or mark **to store** to keep somewhere for future use **to stack** to put one on top of the other

doubted that he would ever be coming back, but he nevertheless wanted to keep the place hidden. It was his private monument, the tomb in which he had buried his past, and whenever he thought about it in the future, he wanted to know that it was still there, exactly as it had been. In that way it would continue to serve as a mental refuge for him, even if he never set foot in it again.

He slept out in the open that night, and the following morning he prepared himself for his journey. He packed the saddlebags, he gathered up food and water, he strapped everything onto the three horses the Greshams had left behind. Then he rode off, trying to imagine what he would do next.

It took us more than two weeks to get that far. Christmas had long since come and gone, and a week after that the decade had ended. Effing paid little attention to these milestones, however. His thoughts were fixed on an earlier time, and he burrowed through his story with inexhaustible care, leaving nothing out, backtracking to fill in minor details, dwelling on the smallest nuances in an effort to recapture his past. After a while, I stopped wondering whether he was telling me the truth or not. His narrative had taken on a phantasmagoric quality by then, and there were times when he did not seem to be remembering the outward facts of his life so much as inventing a parable to explain its inner meanings. The hermit's cave, the saddlebags of money, the Wild West shootout—it was all so farfetched, and yet the very outrageousness of the story was probably its most convincing element. It did not seem possible that anyone could have made it up, and Effing told it so well, with such palpable sincerity, that I simply let myself go along with it, refusing to question whether these things had happened or not. I listened, I recorded what he said, I did not interrupt him. In spite of the revulsion he sometimes inspired in me, I could not help thinking of him as a kindred spirit. Per-

**tomb** [tuːm] a grave, especially above the ground **mental** only in the mind **refuge** a place that provides protection or shelter from danger **to strap** to tie with a long strip of leather **decade** here: New Year 1969/1970 **to burrow** (fig) to dig through **to backtrack** (fig) to return by the same route by which one has come **to dwell on s.th.** to spend a lot of time talking about s.th. **to take on** to acquire **phantasmagoric** [ˌfæn.tæz.məˈgɔːr.ɪk] like a series of strange scenes in a dream **shootout** a fight that is concluded with the use of guns **farfetched** improbable **outrageousness** quality of being shocking and unusual **palpable** easy to notice **sincerity** quality of being honest **revulsion** feeling of strong dislike **kindred spirit** [ˈkɪn.drəd] a person with the same thoughts and feelings

haps it started when we got to the episode about the cave. I had my own memories of living in a cave, after all, and when he described the loneliness he had felt then, it struck me that he was somehow describing the same things I had felt. My own story was just as preposterous as Effing's, but I knew that if I ever chose to tell it to him, he would have believed every word I said.

As the days went by, the atmosphere in the house became more and more claustrophobic. The weather was ferocious outside—freezing rain, ice-covered streets, winds that blew right through you—and for the time being we had to suspend our afternoon walks. Effing began doubling up on the obituary sessions, withdrawing to his room for a short nap after lunch and then storming out again at two-thirty or three, ready to go on talking for several more hours. I don't know where he found the energy to continue at such a pace, but other than having to pause between sentences a bit more than usual, his voice never seemed to let him down. I began to live inside that voice as though it were a room, a windowless room that grew smaller and smaller with each passing day. Effing wore the black patches over his eyes almost constantly now, and there was no chance to deceive myself into thinking there was some connection between us. He was alone with the story in his head, and I was alone with the words that poured from his mouth. Those words filled every inch of the air around me, and in the end there was nothing else for me to breathe. If not for Kitty, I probably would have been smothered. After my work with Effing was done, I usually managed to see her for several hours, spending as much of the night with her as possible. On more than one occasion, I did not return until early the next morning. Mrs. Hume knew what I was up to, but if Effing had any idea of my comings and goings, he never said a word. The only thing that mattered was that I appear at the breakfast table every morning at eight o'clock, and I never failed to be there on time.

Once he left the cave, Effing said, he traveled through the desert for several days before coming to the town of Bluff. From then on, things became easier for him. He worked his way north, slowly moving from town to town, and made it back to Salt Lake City by the end of June,

**preposterous** absurd **ferocious** violent, causing fear **to suspend** to stop for a short time **to double up** to do twice as much as before **to storm out** to go somewhere in a noisy way **pace** speed **to let s.o. down** to disappoint, here: to no longer function **to smother** [ˈsmʌð.ər] to cause to die because of not being able to breathe **to be up to** to being doing s.th., especially s.th. bad **to work one's way** to go somewhere steadily with great effort

where he linked up with the railroad and bought a ticket for San Francisco. It was in California that he invented his new name, turning himself into Thomas Effing when he signed the hotel register on the first night. He wanted the Thomas to refer to Moran, he said, and it wasn't until he put down the pen that he realized that Tom had also been the hermit's name, the name that had secretly belonged to him for more than a year. He took the coincidence as a good omen, as though it had strengthened his choice into something inevitable. As for his surname, he said, it would not be necessary for him to provide me with a gloss. He had already told me that Effing was a pun, and unless I had misread him in some crucial way, I felt I knew where it had come from. In writing out the word *Thomas*, he had probably been reminded of the phrase *doubting Thomas*. The gerund had then given way to another: *fucking Thomas*, which for convention's sake had been further modified into *f-ing*. Thus, he was Thomas Effing, the man who had fucked his life. Given his taste for cruel jokes, I imagined how pleased he must have been with himself.

Almost from the very start, I kept expecting him to tell me about his legs. The rocks of Utah struck me as a likely place for such an accident, but each day his narrative advanced a little farther, and still he made no mention of what had crippled him. The trek with Scoresby and Byrne, the encounter with George Ugly Mouth, the shootout with the Greshams: one by one, he had come through these events unscathed. Then he was in San Francisco, and I began to have my doubts that he would ever get to it. He spent more than a week describing what he had done with the money, enumerating the investments he had made, the financial deals he had pulled off, the frantic risks he had taken on the stockmarket. Within nine months he was rich again, almost as rich as he had been before: he owned a house on Russian Hill with a staff of servants, he had women whenever he wanted them, he traveled among the most elegant circles of society. He might have settled permanently into this kind of life

**to link up with s.th.** to make a connection with s.th. **hotel register** a book in a hotel that lists the people who are staying at the hotel **coincidence** two things happening by chance at the same time **inevitable** impossible to avoid **surname** last name **gloss** a short explanation **doubting Thomas** a person who doesn't accept anything unless there is proof—from the Bible: Thomas did not believe that Christ was alive again after having been crucified on the cross. **fucking** (slang, vulgar) damn **for convention's sake** to be more acceptable in society **unscathed** [ʌnˈskeɪðd] not harmed **to enumerate** to name the things in a list **to pull off** (coll) to succeed in doing **frantic** done in a hurried and unplanned way **stockmarket** Börse **Russian Hill** area in San Francisco where the very rich live

(which in fact was the same life he had known since boyhood), if not for an incident that took place about a year after his arrival. Invited to a dinner party with about twenty other guests, he was suddenly confronted with a figure from his past, a man who had worked as a colleague of his father's in New York for more than ten years. Alonzo Riddle was an old man by then, but when he was introduced to Effing and shook his hand, there was no question that he recognized him. Overcome by astonishment, Riddle even went so far as to blurt out that Effing was the spitting image of someone he had once known. Effing made light of the coincidence, joking pleasantly about how every man is supposed to have an exact double somewhere, but Riddle was too stunned to let go of it, and he began to tell the story of Julian Barber's disappearance to Effing and the other guests. It was a horrible moment for Effing, and he squirmed through the rest of the evening in a state of panic, unable to free himself from Riddle's wondering and suspicious eyes.

After that, he understood how precarious his situation was. Sooner or later, he was bound to run into another person from his past, and there was nothing to guarantee that he would be as lucky as he had been with Riddle. The next person would be surer of himself, more belligerent in his accusations, and before Effing knew it, the whole thing could blow up in his face. As a precautionary measure, he abruptly stopped giving parties and accepting invitations, but he knew that these things were not going to help him in the long run. Eventually, people would notice that he had withdrawn from them, and that would arouse their curiosity, which in turn would give way to gossip, which could only lead to trouble. It was November 1918. The Armistice had just been signed, and Effing knew that his days in America were numbered. In spite of that certainty, he found himself incapable of doing anything about it. He lapsed

**incident** unusual event **Riddle** Rätsel **overcome** strongly affected, overwhelmed **to blurt out** to say s.th. suddenly without thinking **spitting image** looking exactly like s.o. else **to make light of s.th.** to treat s.th. important as s.th. not very serious **to squirm** here: to feel embarrassed **suspicious** thinking that s.th. is wrong **precarious** dangerous **bound** likely **belligerent** unpleasant, aggressive **accusation** a statement that s.o. is guilty **to blow up in his face** to have disastrous consequences **precautionary measure** s.th. done to prevent s.th. unpleasant from happening **to arouse** to stimulate, to cause to start **to give way to** to allow s.th. else to happen **gossip** information about a person's private life that is often false **the Armistice** November 11, 1918, the day Germany formally agreed to stop fighting to end World War One

into inertia, could not make plans or think about the possibilities that were open to him. Overwhelmed by guilt, by the terrible thing he had done to his life, he indulged in reckless fantasies of returning to Long Island with some colossal lie to account for what had happened. That was out of the question, but he clung to it as a dream of redemption, tenaciously conjuring one false exit after another, and could not bring himself to act. For several months, he shut himself off from the world, sleeping in his darkened room by day and venturing out to Chinatown at night. It was always Chinatown. He never wanted to go there, but he could never find the courage not to go. Against his will, he began haunting the brothels and opium dens and gambling parlors that were hidden in the labyrinth of its narrow streets. He was looking for oblivion, he said, trying to drown in a degradation that would equal the loathing he felt for himself. His nights became a miasma of clattering roulette wheels and smoke, of Chinese women with pockmarked faces and missing teeth, of airless rooms and nausea. His losses were so extravagant that by August he had squandered close to a third of his fortune on these debaucheries. It would have gone on until the end, he said, until he had either killed himself or run out of money, if fate had not caught up with him and broken him in two. What happened could not have been more violent or sudden, but for all the misery it unleashed, the fact was that nothing less than a disaster could have saved him.

**to lapse into inertia** [ˌɪnˈɜːrʃə] to go into a state of inactivity because of a lack of energy and desire **to indulge in s.th.** to let yourself do what you enjoy even though it may be bad for you **reckless** not caring about the dangerous results of doing s.th. **to account for s.th.** to explain the reason for s.th. **to cling/clung/clung** (fig) to hold tightly to s.th. **redemption** state of being saved from sin or the power of evil **tenaciously** [təˈneɪ.ʃəs.lɪ] in a way unwilling to stop trying even when the situation becomes difficult, stubbornly **to conjure** [ˈkʌn.dʒər] here: to invent in the mind **false exit** senseless solution **to venture out** to go out even if it might be unpleasant or dangerous **Chinatown** largest Chinese community outside China **to haunt** to visit frequently **brothel** [ˈbrɑːθəl] a house or place where prostitutes work **opium den** a secret place where opium can be smoked **parlor** special room equipped for a special activity **oblivion** state of total forgetfulness **degradation** situation in which one has lost all self-respect and respect from others **to loathe** [loʊð] to hate very much **miasma** [maɪˈæz.mə] a thick unhealthy atmosphere **to clatter** to make a rattling noise **pockmarked** pockennarbig **nausea** [nɑː.zi.ə] feeling like you want to vomit **to squander** to spend wastefully **debauchery** [dɪˈbɑː.tʃər.i] any kind of immoral behavior **fate** Schicksal **misery** great suffering **to unleash** to suddenly let a strong force have its effect

It was raining that night, Effing said. He had just spent several hours in Chinatown and was walking home, all wobbly with the dope in his system, barely conscious of where he was. It was three or four o'clock in the morning, and he had begun climbing the steep hill that led to his neighborhood, pausing at nearly every lamppost to hang on for a moment and catch his breath. Somewhere at the beginning of the walk he had lost his umbrella, and he was soaked to the skin by the time he reached the last hill. With the rain pounding on the sidewalk and his head swimming in its opium stupor, he didn't hear the stranger come up from behind him. One moment he was trudging along the street, and the next moment it was as though a building had fallen on top of him. He had no idea what it was—a club, a brick, the butt of a revolver, it could have been anything. All he felt was the force of the blow, a tremendous thud at the base of his skull, and then he went down, immediately collapsing onto the pavement. He must have been unconscious for only a few seconds, for the next thing he remembered was opening his eyes and feeling a spray of water against his face. He was sliding down the hill, shooting down the slippery street at a speed he could not control: head first, on his belly, arms and legs flailing as he struggled to grab hold of something to stop his wild descent. No matter how hard he tried, he couldn't stop, couldn't get up, couldn't do anything but roll about like some wounded insect. At a certain point, he must have twisted his body in such a way that his trajectory began to carry him down the sidewalk at a slight angle, and suddenly he saw that he was about to vault off the curb and go flying into the street. He braced himself for the jolt, but just as he came to the edge, he spun out another eighty or ninety degrees and went straight into a lamppost, his spine smashing into the ironwork at full force. At the

**wobbly** unsteady **conscious** noticing, aware **lamppost** a tall pole with a lamp at the top, streetlight **soaked to the skin** with the clothes completely wet **stupor** state in which one cannot think or speak properly because of too much alcohol or the use of drugs **to trudge along** to walk along with slow heavy steps because of being tired **club** a thick heavy stick used for hitting people **brick** Backstein **blow** hitting s.o. hard **tremendous** very powerful **thud** sound of a heavy object falling on s.th. **base** near the neck **skull** Schädel **pavement** (AE) hard surface of the street **unconscious** bewusstlos **belly** stomach **to flail** to move your arms or legs around in an uncontrolled way **descent** the process of going down **trajectory** the path of an object moving in space **slight** small **angle** Winkel **to vault off** here: to be thrown off **to brace oneself for s.th.** to prepare yourself for s.th. unpleasant **jolt** [dʒoʊlt] a sudden blow **to spin/spun/spun out** to turn suddenly **spine** Rückgrat **to smash** to hit s.th. violently **ironwork** the iron pole

same instant, he heard something snap, and then he felt a pain that resembled nothing he had ever felt before, a pain so grotesque and powerful that he thought his body had literally exploded.

He never gave me the precise medical details of his injury. The prognosis was the thing that counted, and it wasn't long before the doctors had reached a unanimous verdict. His legs had died on him, and no matter how much therapy he subjected himself to, he would never walk again. Strangely enough, he said, this news came almost as a relief. He had been punished, and because the punishment was a terrible one, he was no longer obligated to punish himself. His crime had been paid for, and suddenly he was empty again: no more guilt, no more fears of being caught, no more dread. If the nature of the accident had been different, it might not have had the same effect on him, but because he had not seen his attacker, because he never understood why he had been attacked in the first place, he could not help interpreting it as a form of cosmic retribution. The purest kind of justice had been meted out; a harsh and anonymous blow had descended from the sky, and he had been crushed, arbitrarily and without mercy. There had been no time to defend himself or plead his case. Before he knew it had begun, the trial was over, the sentence had been handed down, and the judge had disappeared from the courtroom.

It took him nine months to recover (to the extent that he was able to recover), and then he began making preparations to leave the country. He sold his house, transferred his assets into a numbered Swiss bank account, and bought a false passport under the name of Thomas Effing from a man

**to snap** to break with a sudden sharp noise **literally** really **prognosis** medical opinion about how a disease will develop **unanimous** with everyone agreeing **verdict** the final decision or opinion **to subject oneself to s.th.** to force oneself to go through s.th. or experience s.th. **relief** a feeling of cheerfulness that follows a time of anxiety, pain, or distress **to be obligated to do s.th.** to have to do s.th., to have the duty to do s.th. **dread** fear about what might happen in the future **cosmic** having to do with the universe **retribution** punishment **justice** here: fair punishment **to mete out** to give **arbitrarily** happening by chance, without being planned **mercy** Gnade **to plead** [pli:d] to argue in support of s.th. **trial** Prozess **sentence** punishment determined by a judge **to hand down** to formally announce **assets** money or anything that can be turned into money

with anarcho-syndicalist affiliations. The Palmer raids were in full swing by then, Wobblies were being lynched, Sacco and Vanzetti had been arrested, and most members of radical groups had gone into hiding. The passport forger was a Hungarian immigrant who worked out of a cluttered basement room in the Mission, and Effing remembered paying dearly for the document. The man was on the verge of nervous collapse, he said, and because he suspected Effing of being an undercover agent who would arrest him the moment the work was done, he delayed the job for several weeks, offering farfetched excuses each time another deadline passed. The price kept going up as well, but because the money was the least of Effing's concerns at that point, he finally broke the deadlock by telling the man that he would double his highest asking price if he could have the passport ready promptly at nine o'clock the next morning. It was too tempting for the Hungarian not to risk it—the sum was now more than eight hundred dollars and when Effing handed him the cash the next morning and did not arrest him, the anarchist broke down and wept, hysterically kissing Effing's hand in gratitude. That was the last encounter he had with anyone in America for twenty years, and the memory of that shattered man never left him. The whole country had gone to hell, he thought, and he managed to say good-bye to it without any regrets.

**anarcho-syndicalist affiliations** with connections with anarchists and syndicalists (who believed industry and government should be in the hands of the workers.) There was a hysterical fear (the so-called Red Scare) of anarchists, syndicalists, and communists in America after World War One. Many were jailed, killed, or deported. **Palmer raids** raid = Razzia, as U.S. Attorney General (Generalbundesanwalt), 1919-1921, Alexander Palmer was responsible for rounding up 3,000 foreigners for deportation because they supposedly wanted to overthrow the American government. Only a few hundred were actually deported. **in full swing** at the height of activity **Wobblies** another name for a group of syndicalists known as the Industrial Workers of the World **Sacco and Vanzetti** two Italian anarchists, who were found to be guilty of murder in a clearly unfair trial in 1921—They were executed in 1927 even after world-wide protest. **forger** person who makes false copies of official documents **cluttered** filled with many things so that it looks untidy **Mission** the Mission district in San Francisco—at the time a blue-collar area with many Irish immigrants **undercover agent** s.o. secretly working for the police **to delay** to wait for a while before continuing with s.th. **farfetched** difficult to believe **deadline** time when s.th. should be completed **to break the deadlock** to end a situation in which no agreement seems possible **promptly** exactly, in time **tempting** so good that even if there's a risk you're willing to do it **to weep/wept/wept** to cry **gratitude** the feeling of being thankful **shattered** ruined **regrets** any sense of loss

In September of 1920, he boarded the S.S. *Descartes* and sailed to France by way of the Panama Canal. There was no particular reason for going to France, but neither was there any reason not to go. For a time he had considered moving to some colonial backwater—to Central America, perhaps, or to an island in the Pacific—but the thought of spending the rest of his life in a jungle, even as a petty king among innocent and doting natives, did not whet his imagination. He was not looking for paradise, he merely wanted a country where he would not be bored. England was out of the question (he found the English despicable), and while the French were not much better, he had fond memories of the year he had spent in Paris as a young man. Italy also tempted him, but the fact that French was the one foreign language he could speak with any fluency tipped the balance to France. At least he would eat well there and have good wines to drink. It was true that Paris was the city where he would be most likely to run into former artist friends from New York, but the prospect of those encounters no longer frightened him. The accident had changed all that. Julian Barber was dead. He wasn't an artist anymore, he wasn't anyone. He was Thomas Effing, a crippled expatriate confined to a wheelchair, and if anyone challenged him about his identity, he would tell him to go to hell. It was that simple. He no longer cared what anyone thought, and if it meant that he was going to have to lie about himself now and then, so be it, he would lie. The whole business was a sham anyway, and it made no difference what he did.

He continued with the story for another two or three weeks, but it no longer gripped me in the same way. The essentials had already been covered; there were no more secrets to be told, no more dark truths to be wrenched out of him. The major turning points in Effing's life had all taken place in America, in the years between his departure for Utah and the accident in San Francisco, and once he arrived in Europe, the story became just another story, a chronology of facts and events, a tale of time passing. Effing was aware of this, I felt, and although he didn't come out

**S.S. Descartes** steamship Descartes (French philosopher 1596-1650) **backwater** an isolated backward area **petty** unimportant **to dote** to love foolishly **to whet** to stimulate, to make more desirable **despicable** awful, extremely unpleasant **to tip the balance** to finally influence the result of a decision **to run into s.o.** to meet s.o. by chance **prospect** probability **expatriate** a person living in a foreign country **to be confined to s.th.** to be only allowed to do s.th., restricted to s.th. **to challenge** to question because of doubts **business** matter **sham** s.th. to deceive people **to grip** to hold s.o.'s interest **essentials** the basic information **to wrench out of s.o.** [rentʃ] (fig) to forcefully pull out of s.o. **to come out** to say publicly or openly

and say it directly, the manner of his telling began to change, to lose the precision and earnestness of the earlier episodes. He digressed more freely now, seemed to forget his train of thought more often, and even fell into a number of outright contradictions. One day, for example, he would claim that he had spent those years in idleness—reading books, playing chess, sitting in corner bistros—and the next day he would turn around and tell me of complicated business ventures, of pictures he had painted and then destroyed, of owning a bookstore, of working as an espionage agent, of raising money for the republican army in Spain. There was no question that he was lying, but it struck me that he was doing it more from habit than from any intention to deceive me. Toward the end, he spoke movingly about his friendship with Pavel Shum, told me in great detail how he had continued to have sex in spite of his condition, and launched into several lengthy harangues on his theories of the universe: the electricity of thoughts, the connectedness of matter, the transmigration of souls. On the last day, he told how he and Pavel managed to escape from Paris before the Germans marched in, went through the story of meeting Tesla in Bryant Park again, and then, without any warning, stopped dead in his tracks.

"That's enough," he said. "We'll leave it there."

"But we still have an hour to go before lunch," I said, looking at the clock on the mantelpiece. "There's plenty of time to start in on the next episode."

"Don't contradict me, boy. When I say we're done, that means we're done."

"But we're only up to 1939. We still have thirty years to account for."

"They're not important. You can dispose of them in one or two sen-

**earnestness** seriousness **to digress** [daɪ'gres] to move away from the main topic or subject **outright** obvious **contradiction** two statements of which one cannot be true at the same time as the other—Widerspruch **to claim** to state s.th. even though it may not be true **idleness** just wasting time, not working **venture** risky business or activity **espionage agent** ['es.pi.ə.nɑːʒ] s.o. who tries to find out the secrets of a company or another country **republican army in Spain** the army fighting against the fascists in the Spanish Civil War (1936-1939) **from habit** because of already being done regularly **movingly** causing one to feel strong emotions **to launch into s.th.** to start with s.th. **harangue** [hə'ræŋ] a loud, forceful, or angry speech that criticizes or blames people for s.th. **transmigration** the passing from one body to another at the time of death **to stop dead in one's tracks** to stop suddenly **mantelpiece** the top part of a fireplace that can be used as a shelf **to dispose of s.th.** to deal with

tences. 'After leaving Europe at the beginning of World War II, Mr. Effing returned to New York, where he spent the last thirty years of his life.' Something like that. It shouldn't be difficult."

"You're not just talking about today, then. You mean the whole story. You're saying that we've come to the end, is that it?"

"I thought I had made that clear."

"It doesn't matter, I understand now. It still doesn't make any sense to me, but I understand."

"We're running out of time, you fool, that's why. If we don't start writing the damned obituary now, it will never get done."

For the next twenty days, I spent every morning in my room, typing out different versions of Effing's life on the old Underwood. There was a short version to be sent out to the newspapers, five hundred deadpan words that touched on only the most superficial facts; there was a fuller version entitled "The Mysterious Life of Julian Barber," which turned out to be a rather sensational account of some three thousand words that Effing wanted me to submit to an art magazine after he died; and finally, there was an edited version of the complete transcript, Effing's story as told by himself. It came to more than a hundred pages, and that was the one I worked hardest on, carefully eliminating repetitions and vulgar turns of phrase, sharpening sentences, struggling to put spoken words into writing without diminishing their force. It was a difficult and tricky process, I learned, and in many instances I had to reconstruct passages almost entirely in order to remain faithful to their original meaning. I didn't know what use Effing was intending to make of this autobiography (in the strictest sense, it was no longer an obituary), but he was obviously keen on having it come out just right, and he pushed me hard on the revisions, scolding and shouting whenever I read him a sentence he did not like. We battled our way through these editorial sessions every afternoon, ranting at each other over the smallest stylistic points. It was a draining experience for both of us (two stubborn souls locked in mortal combat),

**deadpan** without showing any emotion **entitled** with the title **to edit** to prepare a text for publication **turn of phrase** a particular way of saying s.th. **to diminish** to decrease **faithful** here: as close as possible **revision** the act of changing a text so as to improve it **to scold** to angrily criticize **session** meeting for a certain purpose **to rant** to talk or complain in a loud, excited angry way **draining** exhausting **stubborn** unreasonably refusing to change one's mind **to be locked in mortal combat** to fight until one of the participants is killed

but one by one we eventually agreed on the different articles, and by the beginning of March the job was done.

The next day, I found three books lying on my bed. They were all written by a man named Solomon Barber, and while Effing did not mention them when I saw him at breakfast, I assumed that he was the one who had put them there. It was a typical Effing gesture—devious, obscure, apparently without motive—but I knew him well enough by then to understand that this was his way of telling me to read the books. Given the author's name, it seemed fairly certain that it was not a casual request. Several months earlier, the old man had used the word "consequences," and I wondered if he wasn't getting ready to talk about them.

The books were about American history, and each one had been published by a different university press: *Bishop Berkeley and the Indians* (1947), *The Lost Colony of Roanoke* (1955), and *The American Wilderness* (1963). The biographical notes on the dust jackets were scanty, but by piecing together the various bits of information, I learned that Solomon Barber had received a Ph.D. in history in 1944, had contributed numerous articles to scholarly journals, and had taught at several colleges in the Midwest. The reference to 1944 was crucial. If Effing had impregnated his wife just prior to his departure in 1916, then his son would have been born the following year, which meant that he would have been twenty-seven in 1944—a logical age for someone to earn a doctoral degree. Everything seemed to fit, but I knew better than to jump to any conclusions. I had to wait another three days before Effing approached the subject, and it was only then that I learned my suspicions had been correct.

"I don't suppose you've glanced at the books I left in your room on Tuesday," he said, speaking as calmly as someone who had just requested another lump of sugar for his tea.

"I've glanced at them," I said. "I've even gone so far as to read them."

**Solomon** the wise king, son of David in the Old Testament, sol (Latin) = sun, the Roman god personifying the sun **devious** suggesting dishonest behavior or intentions **casual** not seeming to care very much **Berkeley** George Berkeley (1685-1753) British philosopher and bishop, who believed reality was only what one perceived—He wanted to start a missionary for Indians in Bermuda. **Colony of Roanoke** ['roʊə.noʊk] colony in Virginia (1584-1591) sponsored by Sir Walter Raleigh that completely failed **Ph.D.** doctor of philosophy **reference** the mentioning of s.th. **to impregnate** to make a women pregnant **prior to** before **to jump to a conclusion** to decide s.th., or form an opinion too quickly without the proper information **to approach** to deal with **suspicion** a feeling that s.th. is wrong without having the facts **lump** a small solid piece

"You surprise me, boy. Considering your age, I'm beginning to think there might be some hope for you."

"There's hope for everyone, sir. That's what makes the world go round."

"Spare me the aphorisms, Fogg. What did you think of the books?"

"I found them admirable. Well written, tightly argued, and filled with information that was entirely new to me."

"For example."

"For example, I had never known of Berkeley's plan to educate the Indians in Bermuda, and I had never known about the years he spent in Rhode Island. All this came as a surprise to me, but the best part of the book is the way Barber connects Berkeley's experiences with his philosophical works on perception. I found that very deft and original, very profound."

"What about the other books?"

"The same thing. I hadn't known much about Roanoke either. Barber makes a good case for solving the mystery, I thought, and I tend to agree with him that the lost settlers survived by joining forces with the Croatan Indians. I also liked the background material on Raleigh and Thomas Harriot. Did you know that Harriot was the first man to look at the moon through a telescope? I had always thought it was Galileo, but Harriot beat him to it by several months."

"Yes, boy, I knew that. You don't have to lecture me."

"I'm just answering your question. You asked me what I'd learned, and so I told you."

"Don't talk back. I'm the one who asks the questions around here. Is that understood?"

"Understood. You can ask me any questions you want, Mr. Effing, but there's no need for you to go wandering in circles."

"What does that mean?"

**to spare s.o. s.th.** to avoid doing s.th. to s.o. (verschonen) **aphorism** a short saying expressing some kind of truth **admirable** worthy of being respected and admired **tightly argued** using good arguments that are precise and well written **perception** the act of noticing things with your senses **deft** skilful **Thomas Harriot** cf. page 132 **moon** Thomas Harriot was the first to make sketches of the moon after looking through a telescope on July 26, 1609. Galilleo (1564-1642), the famous mathematician and astronomer, did so on November 30, 1609. **to lecture** to criticize s.o. angrily in such a way that the other person thinks it's unfair or unnecessary

"It means that we don't have to waste any more time. You put those books in my room because you wanted to tell me something, and I don't see why you don't just come out and say it."

"My, my, we are being clever today, aren't we?"

"It's not so hard to figure out."

"No, I don't suppose it is. I've more or less told you already, haven't I?"

"Solomon Barber is your son."

Effing paused for a long moment, as if still reluctant to acknowledge where the conversation had taken us. He stared off into space, removed his dark glasses and polished the lenses with a handkerchief—a useless, implausible gesture for a blind man—and then snorted from somewhere deep inside his throat. "Solomon," he said. "A truly awful name. But I had nothing to do with it, of course. You can't give someone a name if you don't know he exists, can you?"

"Have you ever met him?"

"I've never met him, and he's never met me. As far as he knows, his father died in Utah in 1916."

"When did you first hear about him?"

"In 1947. Pavel Shum was responsible for it, he was the one who opened the door. One day, he turned up with a copy of that book about Bishop Berkeley. He was a great reader, Pavel was, I must have told you that, and when he started talking about this young historian named Barber, I naturally pricked up my ears. Pavel knew nothing about my former life, so I had to pretend to be interested in the book in order to find out more about the person who had written it. Nothing was certain at that point. Barber isn't such an uncommon name, after all, and there was no reason for me to think this Solomon was connected to me in any way. Still, I had a hunch about it, and if there's one thing I've learned in my long and stupid career as a man, it's the importance of listening to my hunches. I cooked up a yarn for Pavel, although that probably wasn't necessary. He would have done anything for me. If I had asked him to go to the North Pole, he would have rushed off on the spot. I only needed a

**reluctant** not eager, unwilling **to acknowledge** to admit the truth of s.th. **implausible** not reasonable, not likely to be true **to snort** to make a loud sound by forcing air through the nose to show you are angry or amused **to prick up one's ears** to listen attentively when one hears s.th. interesting **to pretend** to behave in a way that's not really true **hunch** a feeling that s.th. might be true **to cook up** (coll) to invent **yarn** a long story that's probably not true **on the spot** immediately

little information, but I felt it might be too risky to tackle it head on, so I told him that I was thinking about setting up a foundation that would give an annual award to a deserving young writer. This Barber fellow seems promising, I said, why don't we look into him and see if he can use some extra money? Pavel was enthusiastic. As far as he was concerned, there was no greater good in the world than promoting the life of the mind."

"But what about your wife? Didn't you ever find out what happened to her? It wouldn't have been very difficult to find out if she'd had a son or not. There must be a hundred different ways of getting that kind of information."

"Undoubtedley. But I'd promised myself not to make any inquiries about Elizabeth. I was curious—it would have been impossible not to be curious—but at the same time I didn't want to open that old can of worms again. The past was the past, and it was all closed shut for me. Whether she was alive or dead, whether she had remarried or not—what good would it have done to know those things? I forced myself to remain in the dark. There was a powerful tension in that approach, and it helped to remind me who I was, to keep me alert to the fact that I was someone else now. No turning back—that was the important thing. No regrets, no pity, no weak-minded sentiments. By refusing to find out about Elizabeth, I kept myself strong."

"But you wanted to find out about your son."

"That was different. If I had been responsible for bringing another person into the world, it was my right to know about it. I just wanted to get the facts straight, nothing more than that."

"Did it take Pavel long to get the information?"

"Not long. He tracked down Solomon Barber and discovered that he was teaching in some podunk college out in the Midwest—Iowa, Nebraska, I forget where it was. Pavel wrote him a letter about his book, a fan letter, so to speak. There wasn't any trouble after that. Barber sent a gracious response, and then Pavel wrote back to say that he was going to

**to tackle s.th.** to deal with a difficult situation **head on** directly **foundation** organization that gives money for research or help people in difficulty (Stiftung) **to promote** to help, to develop, to support **inquiry** question asked to get information **to open an old can of worms** to deal with an unpleasant problem from the past **tension** stress (Spannung) **approach** way of dealing with s.th. **weak-minded** not having a strong character **straight** accurate **to track down** to seek and find **podunk college** (coll) small and unimportant college **gracious** polite and kind

be passing through Iowa or Nebraska and wondered if they could meet. Just by coincidence, of course. Ha! As if there's any such thing as a coincidence. Barber said that he would be delighted to meet him, and that was how it happened. Pavel took the train to Iowa or Nebraska, they spent an evening together, and then Pavel came back with everything I needed to know."

"Which was?"

"Which was: that Solomon Barber had been born in Shoreham, Long Island, in 1917. Which was: that his father had been a painter who had died in Utah a long time ago. Which was: that his mother had been dead since 1939."

"The same year you returned to America."

"Apparently so."

"And then?"

"And then what?"

"What happened next?"

"Nothing. I told Pavel that I'd changed my mind about the foundation, and that was the end of it."

"And you never had any desire to see him. It's hard to believe you could drop it just like that."

"I had my reasons, boy. Don't think it wasn't hard, but I stuck to it. I stuck to it through thick and thin."

"That was noble of you."

"Yes, very noble. I'm a thoroughgoing prince."

"And now?"

"In spite of everything, I've managed to keep track of his whereabouts. Pavel continued corresponding with him, he kept me abreast of Barber's doings over the years. That's why I'm telling you this now. There's something I want you to do for me after I'm dead. The lawyers could handle it, but I'd rather it was you. You'll do a better job of it than they would."

"What are you planning?"

"I'm going to leave him my money. There'll be something for Mrs. Hume, of course, but the rest of it will go to my son. The poor sap's made

**delighted** very pleased and happy **apparently so** so it appears **to stick to s.th.** to continue doing s.th. without changing **noble** (iron.) morally right/having to do with the nobility (edel/adlig) **thoroughgoing** absolute, complete **to keep track of s.o.** to constantly pay attention to what s.o. is doing **whereabouts** where s.o. is **sap** (coll. AE) foolish person **make a hash of s.th.** to mess up, to destroy

such a hash of his life, maybe it will do him some good. He's a fat, childless, unmarried, broken-down wreck, a walking dirigible disaster. For all his brains and talents, his career has been one long fuck-up. He got bounced out of his first job back in the mid-forties for some kind of scandal—buggering male students for all I know—and then, just when he was getting back on his feet, he got hit with that McCarthy business and sank right to the bottom again. He's spent his life in the most dismal backwaters imaginable, teaching at colleges no one's ever heard of."

"It sounds pathetic."

"That's just what it is. Pathetic. One hundred percent pathetic."

"But how do I fit into this? You leave him the money in your will, and the lawyers give it to him. It all seems rather straightforward."

"I want you to send him my self-portrait. Why do you think we worked so hard on it? It wasn't just to pass the time of day, boy, there was a purpose behind it. There's always a purpose to what I do, remember that. Once I'm dead, I want you to send it to him along with a cover letter explaining how it came to be written. Is that clear?"

"Not really. After keeping your distance from him since 1947, I don't see why you're suddenly so eager to be in touch with him now. It doesn't make any sense."

"Everyone has a right to know about his own past. I can't do much for him, but at least I can do that."

"Even if he'd rather not know?"

"That's right, even if he'd rather not know."

"It doesn't seem fair."

"Who's talking about fair? It has nothing to do with that. I kept myself away from him while I was alive, but now that I'm dead, it's time for the story to come out."

**dirigible** airship **fuck-up** (slang, vulgar) disaster **to get bounced out of s.th.** to get thrown out of s.th. **to bugger** to have anal sex **to get hit with s.o.** (coll) to get involved with s.th. unpleasant **McCarthy business** Senator Joseph McCarthy (1908-1957), the chairman of a U.S. Senate committee (1950-1954), misused the public's fear of Communism during the Cold War. He accused people in the foreign service, education, in the entertainment business, and the army of being communists without sufficient evidence **dismal** gloomy, depressing **backwater** an isolated, backward place **to fit in s.th.** to play a role in s.th. **will** document that states who gets the money and property after s.o. dies **straightforward** simple **self-portrait** here: autobiography **to pass the time of day** to spend one's time doing s.th. without any special purpose **cover letter** (AE) a letter of explanation sent with a document **how it came to be written** how it happened to be written

"You don't look dead to me."

"It's coming, I promise you. It's coming very soon."

"You've been saying that for months, but you're just as healthy as you've ever been."

"What's the date today?"

"March twelfth."

"That means I have two months left. I'm going to die on May twelfth, exactly two months from today."

"You can't possibly know that. No one can."

"But I do, Fogg. Mark my words. Two months from today, I'm going to be dead."

After that strange conversation, we slipped back into our original routine. I would read to him in the morning, and in the afternoon we would go out for our walks. It was the same schedule, but it no longer felt the same to me. Earlier on, Effing had had a program with the books, but now his selections struck me as haphazard, utterly lacking in coherence. One day he would ask me to read him stories from *The Decameron* or *The Thousand and One Nights*, the next day it would be *The Comedy of Errors*, and the day after that he would dispense with books altogether and have me read the spring training news from the baseball camps in Florida. Or perhaps it was that he had decided to choose things randomly from now on, to skim lightly over a multitude of works in order to say good-bye to them, as if that were a way of saying good-bye to the world. For three or four days in a row he had me read him pornographic novels (which were stashed away in a cabinet below the bookcase), but even

**Mark my words.** (old-fashioned) Pay close attention to my words. **haphazard** without any plan **coherence** [koʊˈhɪr.ənts] logical connection of ideas **The Decameron** a collection of tales that has become a classic by the Italian writer Giovanni Boccaccio (1313-1375) written between 1351-1353 **The Thousand and One Nights** a collection of ancient Persian-Indian-Arabian tales (first appearing in its present form in 1450) **The Comedy of Errors** comedy play by Shakespeare (1594) about twins who seek their parents and the resulting confusion of identities **to dispense with s.th.** to no longer use s.th. because it seems to no longer to be useful **baseball camps in Florida** many professional baseball teams have camps in Florida so that their old and new players can practice in the winter and spring months **randomly** done without any chosen plan **to skim** to read s.th. quickly to get the main ideas **multitude** a large number **to stash away** to store in a secret place **cabinet** a piece of furniture with doors and shelves or drawers

those books failed to excite him to say to any noticeable degree. He cackled once or twice with amusement, but he also managed to fall asleep midway through one of the steamiest passages. I kept on reading while he napped, and when he woke up half an hour later, he told me that he had been practicing how to be dead. "I want to die with sex on my brain," he muttered. "There's no better way to go out than that." I had never read any pornography before, and I found the books both absurd and arousing. One day, I memorized several of the best paragraphs and quoted them to Kitty when I saw her that night. They seemed to have the same effect on her. They made her laugh, but at the same time they made her want to take off her clothes and climb into bed.

The walks, too, became different from what they had been. Effing no longer showed much enthusiasm for them, and instead of badgering me to describe the things we encountered along the way, he would sit there in silence, pensive and withdrawn. By force of habit, I kept up my running commentaries, but he barely seemed to be listening, and without Effing's nasty remarks and criticisms to respond to, I could feel my spirits begin to flag as well. For the first time since I had known him, Effing seemed absent, disengaged from the things around him, almost tranquil. I spoke to Mrs. Hume about these changes in him, and she confessed that they had begun to worry her, too. Physically, however, neither one of us could detect any major transformations. He ate as much or as little as he had always eaten; his bowel movements were normal; he did not complain of any new aches or discomforts. This odd period of lethargy lasted for approximately three weeks. Then, just as I was beginning to think that Effing was seriously in decline, he arrived at the breakfast table one morning completely himself again, bursting with good cheer and looking as happy as I had ever seen him.

**to cackle** to laugh in a loud unpleasant way **steamy** sexually exciting, shocking **sex on my brain** thinking about sex **to arouse** to sexually excite **to badger** to constantly ask s.o. to do s.th. in an annoying way **pensive** in deep thought **withdrawn** extremely quiet, not wanting to talk to anyone **by force of habit** because of doing s.th. so often in the past **running** continuous, without interruption **nasty** extremely unpleasant (fies) **my spirits began to flag** I began to become less cheerful and enthusiastic **disengaged** not longer connected **tranquil** ['træŋ.kwɪl] calm, peaceful **to confess** to admit **bowel movement** Stuhlgang **ache** continuous pain **discomfort** a slight pain that makes you uncomfortable **in decline** gradually becoming worse **to burst with good cheer** to suddenly be in a good mood

"It's decided!" he announced, pounding his fist on the table. The blow landed with such force that the silverware bounced up and rattled. "Day after day, I've been mulling it over, turning it around in my mind, trying to form the perfect plan. After much mental labor, I'm happy to report that it's settled. Settled! It's the best idea I've ever had, by God. It's a masterpiece, an absolute masterpiece. Are you ready for some fun, boy?"

"Of course," I said, thinking it best to humor him along. "I'm always ready for fun."

"Splendid, that's the spirit," he said, rubbing his hands together. "I promise you, my children, it's going to be a magnificent swan song, a final bow like no other. What kind of conditions do we have out there today?"

"It's clear and crisp," said Mrs. Hume. "The man on the radio said it might get up into the mid-fifties by this afternoon."

"Clear and crisp," he said, "the mid-fifties. It couldn't be better. And the date, Fogg, where do we find ourselves on the calendar?"

"It's April first, the beginning of a new month."

"April first! The day of pranks and practical jokes. In France they used to call it the day of fish. Well, we'll give them some fish to sniff at, won't we, Fogg? We'll give them a whole basketful!"

"You bet," I said. "We'll give them the works."

Effing went on chattering in this excited way throughout breakfast, barely pausing long enough to spoon the oatmeal into his mouth. Mrs. Hume looked worried, but in spite of everything I felt rather encouraged

**to pound** to hit heavily with a loud noise **silverware** (AE) knives, forks, and spoons **to bounce up** to move up suddenly or violently **to mull s.th. over** to think carefully about a plan **labor** work **settled** decided, arranged **to humor s.o. along** to agree with what a person is saying so as to keep this person in a good mood **splendid** great, wonderful **spirit** the way to feel, attitude **magnificent** impressive **swan song** last performance of a musician or actor, final action or work (from the legend that a swan sings a beautiful song before it dies) **final bow** [baʊ] literally: the last time one bows (to bend the top of the body down and forward) on the stage **crisp** cold and dry **mid-fifties** i.e. about 12° celsius **prank** a trick played on s.o. as a joke **practical joke** a trick that should give s.o. a surprise or shock and make other people laugh **day of fish** As a joke, on April 1st French children place a paper or cloth fish on the back of other people without their knowing it. Often a comment about that person is written on the fish. A practice still common today. **to sniff at s.th.** to smell s.th. **You bet!** (coll) You're right! **to give s.o. the works** (coll) to give s.o. everything that is possible **to chatter** to talk quickly about unimportant matters **oatmeal** Hafermehl

by this rush of manic energy. Whatever it finally led to, it had to be better than the glum weeks we had just put behind us. Effing was not cut out to play the role of a morose old man, and I preferred to see him killed by his own enthusiasm than to live on in dejected silence.

After breakfast, he ordered us to fetch his things and prepare him to go outside. The usual equipment was bundled around him—the blanket, the scarf, the overcoat, the hat, the gloves—and then he told me to open the closet and take out a small plaid grip that was lying under a heap of boots and rubbers. "What do you think, Fogg?" he said. "Do you think it's big enough?"

"It all depends on what you're planning to use it for."

"We're going to use it for the money. Twenty thousand dollars in cash money."

Before I could say anything in response, Mrs. Hume interrupted. "You'll do nothing of the kind, Mr. Thomas," she said. "I won't stand for it. A blind man wandering the streets with twenty thousand dollars in cash. Just put that nonsense out of your head right now."

"Shut up, bitch," Effing snapped. "Shut up, or I'll smack you down. It's my money, and I'll do whatever I want with it. I've got my trusted bodyguard to protect me, and nothing's going to happen. And even if it did, it's none of your business. Do you understand that, you fat cow? One more peep out of you, and I'll send you packing."

"She's only doing her job," I said, trying to defend Mrs. Hume from this crazy assault. "There's nothing to get excited about."

"That goes for you, too, squirt," he shouted at me. "Do what you're told, or say good-bye to your job. One, two, three, and that's the end of you. Just try it if you don't believe me."

"A pox on you," said Mrs. Hume. "You're nothing but an asinine old fart, Thomas Effing. I hope you lose every dollar of that money. I hope it flies out of the satchel and you never see it again."

**rush** sudden activity **manic** showing great excitement, especially when mentally ill **glum** gloomy **to be cut out to do s.th.** to have the qualities to do s.th. **morose** bad-tempered, unhappy and silent **dejected** miserable **to bundle** to dress warmly **closet** (AE) small room with a door built into a larger room to store clothing, shoes, etc. **plaid** kariert **grip** (archaic) bag for traveling **bitch** miserable woman (Miststück) **to snap** to say angrily **to smack** to hit with the open hand **trusted** reliable, loyal, faithful **peep** sound, word **assault** violent attack **that goes for you** that applies to you (das gilt für dich) **squirt** word used for an unimportant young person who is annoying **a pox on you** May s.th. horrible happen to you! **asinine** [ˈæs.ɪ.naɪn] stupid, silly, foolish **fart** Furz **satchel** a small bag carried over the shoulder

"Ha!" Effing said. "Ha, ha, ha! And what do you think I'm planning to do with it, horseface? Spend it? Do you think Thomas Effing would ever stoop to such banalities? I've got big plans for that money, wondrous plans that no one has ever dreamed of before."

"Fiddle faddle," said Mrs. Hume. "You can go out and spend a million dollars for all I care. It won't mean anything to me. I wash my hands of you—of you and all your shenanigans."

"Now, now," Effing said, suddenly exuding an unctuous sort of charm. "There's no need to pout, little ducky." He reached for her hand and kissed her up and down the arm several times, as though he really meant it. "Fogg will take care of me. He's a sturdy lad, and no harm will come to us. Trust me, I've worked out the whole operation to the smallest detail."

"You can't con me," she said, withdrawing her hand in annoyance. "You're up to something stupid, I know it. Just remember that I told you so. I won't have you come crying to me with your apologies. It's too late for that. Once a fool, always a fool. That's what my mother used to tell me, and she was right."

"I'd explain it to you now if I could," Effing said, "but we don't have time. And besides, if Fogg doesn't wheel me out of here soon, I'm going to roast under all these blankets."

"Be gone with you, then," said Mrs. Hume. "See if I care."

Effing grinned, then straightened himself up and turned in my direction. "Are you ready, boy?" he said, barking at me like a sea captain.

"Ready whenever you are," I answered.

"Good. Then let's be off."

Our first stop was the Chase Manhattan Bank on Broadway, where Effing withdrew the twenty thousand dollars. Because of the large sum involved, it took close to an hour to complete the transaction. A bank

**to stoop to s.th.** to do s.th. even though it's morally wrong **fiddle faddle** Nonsense! **to wash your hands of s.o.** to refuse to accept responsibility for s.o. (from the New Testament where Pontius Pilate refused to accept responsibility for Christ's crucifiction.) **shenanigans** (coll) bad but not serious behavior, mischief **to exude** [ɪgˈzuːd] to demonstrate in great quantity **unctuous** exaggerated, a bit too friendly to be sincere **to pout** to push out the lips to show displeasure **little ducky** mein kleines Entchen **sturdy** robust, strong and healthy **to con s.o.** (coll) to swindle, to deceive **to be up to s.o.** to plan s.th., especially s.th. not good **apology** saying your sorry for s.th. you did wrong **to roast** to feel uncomfortably hot **Chase Manhattan Bank** one of the largest commercial banks in New York City **to withdraw** to take money out of a bank account **involved** that was being considered

officer had to give his approval, and then it took some additional time before the tellers managed to rustle up the requisite number of fifty-dollar bills, which was the only denomination that Effing would accept. He was a customer of long standing at that bank, "an important customer," as he reminded the manager more than once, and the manager, sensing the possibility of an unpleasant scene, made every effort to accommodate him. Effing continued to play it close to the vest. He refused to let me help him, and when he removed his passbook from his pocket, he made a point of keeping it hidden from me, as though he were afraid that I would see how much money he had in his account. I was long past feeling offended by this kind of behavior from him, but the fact was that I had not the slightest interest in knowing what the figure was. When the money was finally ready, a teller counted it out twice, and then Effing had me do it once again for good measure. I had never seen so much money in one place before, but by the time I finished counting it, the magic had worn off, and the money was reduced to the thing it really was: four hundred pieces of green paper. Effing smiled with satisfaction when I told him it was all there, and then he told me to pack the bundles into the satchel, which turned out to be ample enough for the entire haul. I zipped up the bag, placed it carefully on Effing's lap, and then wheeled him out of the bank. He made a ruckus the whole way to the door, brandishing his stick and hooting as if there was no tomorrow.

Once we were outside, he had me steer him to one of the traffic islands in the middle of Broadway. It was a noisy spot, with cars and trucks lumbering along on either side of us, but Effing seemed oblivious to the commotion. He asked me if anyone was sitting on the bench, and when I

**officer** a person who holds a position of authority **to give one's approval** to say that s.th. is correct or good **to rustle up** (AE, coll) to find **requisite** required **denomination** value of a bill (AE), Banknote (BE) **of long standing** known for one's good reputation for a long time **to accommodate** to try to do what s.o. wants **to play it close to the vest** to not show anyone what one really plans to do **passbook** (AE) bank book **to make a point of s.th.** to do s.th. on purpose **account** Konto **offended** insulted **for good measure** to be extra careful **to wear off** to slowly lose strength **ample** large **haul** large amount of goods, usually stolen **to zip** to close with a zipper (AE, Reißverschluss) **to make a ruckus** ['rʌkəs] to argue noisily **to brandish** to wave about in a threatening way **to hoot** to laugh loudly because you don't think much of the others **as if there was no tomorrow** as if he were soon to die **traffic island** strip of grass with trees between the dual lanes of Broadway between 59th and 125th Street **to lumber along** to move along in a heavy slow way **oblivious** unaware, not noticing **commotion** noisy activity

assured him there was not he told me to take a seat. He was wearing his dark glasses that day, and with his two arms wrapped around the bag and clutching it to his chest, he looked even less human than he usually did, as though he were an overgrown hummingbird who had just arrived from outer space.

"I want to go over my plan with you before we get started," he said. "The bank was no place to talk, and I didn't want that meddlesome woman eavesdropping on us in the apartment. You've probably been asking yourself a lot of questions, and since you're going to be my cohort in this, it's time to spill the beans."

"I figured you'd get around to it sooner or later."

"It's like this, young man. My time is almost up, and because of that I've spent these past few months taking care of business. I've made out my will, I've written my obituary, I've tied up loose ends. There's only one thing that still bothers me—an outstanding debt, you might call it—and now that I've had a couple of weeks to think about it, I've finally hit on a solution. Fifty-two years ago you will remember, I found a bag of money. I took that money and used it to make more money, money that's kept me alive ever since. Now that I've come to the end, I don't need that bag of money anymore. So what am I supposed to do with it? The only thing that makes any sense is to give it back."

"Give it back? But who are you going to give it to? The Greshams are dead, and it wasn't even theirs in the first place. They stole the money from people you never knew, from anonymous strangers. Even if you managed to find out who they were, they're probably all dead now anyway."

"Precisely. The people are all dead now, and it wouldn't be possible to track down their heirs, would it?"

"That's what I just said."

"You also said that those people were anonymous strangers. Stop and think about that for a moment. If there's one thing this godforsaken city

**to wrap** to fold around so as to cover s.th. **to clutch** to hold tightly **hummingbird** Kolibri **meddlesome** getting involved in the affairs of other people **to eavesdrop** to listen secretly to what other people are saying **cohort** (AE) associate, follower **to spill the beans** (coll) to tell s.o. a secret **to figure** (AE) to think, to conclude **to make out** to prepare or have prepared **to tie up loose ends** to do the things that are necessary in order to finish s.th. **outstanding** here: not yet paid **debt** money that one still owes **to hit on s.th.** (coll) to find, to think of s.th. **anonymous** [əˈnɑː.nəməs] **heir** [eər] person who has the right to receive money or property from another person who has died **godforsaken** depressing and ugly

has in abundance, it's anonymous strangers. The streets are filled with them. Everywhere you turn, there's another anonymous stranger. There are millions of them all around us."

"You can't be serious."

"Of course I'm serious. I'm always serious. You should know that by now."

"You mean to say that we're going to walk around the streets handing out fifty-dollar bills to strangers? It will cause a riot. People will go crazy, they'll tear us apart."

"Not if we handle it correctly. It's all a matter of having the right plan, and that's what we've got. Trust me, Fogg. It will be the greatest thing I've ever done, the crowning achievement of my life!"

His plan was very simple. Rather than march down the street in broad daylight and hand out money to everyone who passed by (which was bound to draw a large, unruly crowd), we would perform a series of swift guerilla attacks in a number of carefully selected areas. The whole operation would be stretched out over a period of ten days; no more than forty people would receive money on any given outing, and that would drastically reduce the possibilities of misadventure. I would carry the money in my pockets, and if anyone tried to rob us, the most he would get was two thousand dollars. Meanwhile, the rest of the money would be sitting in the satchel at home, well out of harm's way. We would range far and wide over the city, Effing said, never going to adjoining neighborhoods on consecutive days. Uptown one day, downtown the next; the East Side on Monday, the West Side on Tuesday. We would never stay anywhere long enough for people to catch on to what we were doing. As for our own neighborhood, we would avoid that until the end. That would make the project look like a once-in-a-lifetime event, and the whole business would be over before anyone could make a move on us.

I immediately understood that there was nothing I could do to stop him. His mind was made up, and rather than try to talk him out of it, I

**in abundance** more than enough of **...handing out...** As a student Auster knew an old man by the name of Humes, who handed out money to people on the street. **riot** violent behavior of people in a public place **crowning** perfect, complete **broad daylight** in the middle of the day when everything is clear to see **bound** likely **unruly** difficult to control **swift** quick **given** particular **outing** short trip **misadventure** unlucky event, accident **out of harm's way** in a safe place **to range** to move around **adjoining** next to each other **East Side** area of Manhattan east of Central Park to the East River **to catch on** to begin to realize s.th. **to make a move on s.o.** to move towards s.o. because you want to attack this person

did what I could to make his plan as safe as possible. It was a decent plan, I said, but it all depended on the time of day we chose for our outings. The afternoons, for example, wouldn't be very good. There were too many people in the streets then, and the crucial thing was to give the money to each recipient without anyone else being able to notice what was happening. In that way, disturbances would be kept to a minimum.

"Hmm," said Effing, following my words with great concentration. "What time do you propose, then, boy?"

"The evening. After the work day is done, but not so late that we could get stranded in some deserted street. Say between the hours of seven-thirty and ten."

"In other words, after we've had our dinner. What you might call a postprandial excursion."

"Exactly."

"Consider it done, Fogg. We'll do our roving after twilight, a pair of Robin Hoods on the prowl, ready to bestow our munificence on the lucky souls who cross our path."

"You should also give some thought to transportation. It's a big city, and some of the places we go to will be miles away from here. If we did everything on foot, we'd be out awfully late on some nights. If we ever had to make a quick escape, we might run into trouble."

"That's sissy talk, Fogg. Nothing's going to happen to us. If your legs get tired, we'll hail a cab. If you feel up to walking, we'll walk."

"I wasn't thinking about myself. I just want to make sure you know what you're doing. Have you thought about hiring a car? We'd be able to get back at a moment's notice then. All we'd have to do is climb in and the chauffeur would drive us off."

"A chauffeur! That's a preposterous idea. It would defeat the whole purpose."

"I don't see why. The point is to give away the money, but that doesn't mean you have to go traipsing around the city in the cold spring air to do it. It would be stupid to get sick just because you were trying to be generous."

**recipient** person who gets/receives s.th. **postprandial** (formal) happening just after dinner **to rove** to travel from one place to another **on the prowl** moving around quietly looking for s.o./s.th. **to bestow** (formal) to give s.o. s.th. of great importance **munificence** (formal) generosity **to hail a cab** (AE) to wave at a taxi driving along the street to indicate you want a ride **preposterous** absurd **to go traipsing** to walk heavily or tiredly

"I want to be able to roam around, to feel out the situations as they come up. You can't do that sitting in a car. You've got to be out there in the streets, breathing the same air as everyone else."

"It was just a suggestion."

"Well, keep your suggestions to yourself. I'm not afraid of anything, Fogg, I'm too old for that, and the less you worry about me the better. If you're in with me, fine. But once you're in, that means you have to shut up. We're going to do this thing my way, come hell or high water."

For the first eight days, everything went smoothly. We both agreed that there should be a hierarchy of worthiness, and that gave me a free hand to act as I saw fit. The idea wasn't to hand out money to anyone who happened to pass by, but to look conscientiously for the most deserving people, to zero in on those whose want was greatest. The poor automatically deserved consideration over the rich, the handicapped were to be favored over the well, the mad were to take precedence over the sane. We established those rules at the outset, and given the nature of New York's streets, it was not very difficult to follow them.

Some people broke down and cried when I gave them the money; others burst out laughing; still others said nothing at all. It was impossible to predict their responses, and I soon learned to stop expecting people to do what I thought they would do. There were the suspicious ones who felt we were trying to trick them—one man even went so far as to tear up the money, and several others accused us of being counterfeiters; there were the greedy ones who didn't think fifty dollars was enough; there were the friendless ones who latched on to us and wouldn't let go; there were the jolly ones who wanted to buy us a drink, the sad ones who wanted to tell us their life stories, the artistic ones who danced and sang songs to show their gratitude. To my astonishment, not one of them tried to rob us. That was probably due to simple good luck,

**to roam around** to walk around at no great haste without any destination in mind **come hell or high water** even if the worst may happen **smoothly** without any problems **hierarchy of worthiness** a list of people from the most deserving to the least deserving **conscientiously** with great care **to zero in on s.o.** to direct all your attention towards s.o. **to take precedence over s.th.** to be considered more important than s.th. **sane** normal in the mind, not crazy **at the outset** from the beginning **counterfeiter** a person who makes a copy of s.th. to deceive people **greedy** wanting more money, food, etc. than really needed **to latch on to s.o.** to keep staying with s.o. although the other person would rather have you go

although it must also be said that we moved quickly, never lingering in one spot for very long. Most of the time, I handed out the money in the streets, but there were several forays into low-life bars and coffee shops—Blarney Stones, Bickfords, Chock Full o' Nuts—where I slapped down a fifty-dollar bill in front of each person sitting at the counter. "Spread a little sunshine!" I would shout, peeling off the money as fast as I could, and before the dazed customers could absorb what was happening to them, I would be racing back out to the street. I gave money to bag ladies and hookers, to winos and bums, to hippies and runaway children, to beggars and cripples—all the riffraff who clutter the boulevards after sundown. There were forty gifts to be given every night, and it never took us more than an hour and a half to finish the job.

On the ninth night it rained, and Mrs. Hume and I managed to persuade Effing to stay in. It rained the following night as well, but there was nothing we could do to hold him back anymore. He didn't care if he caught pneumonia, he said, there was work to be done and by God he was going to do it. What if I went without him? I asked. I would give him a full report when I returned, and that would almost be like having been there himself. No, that was impossible, he had to be there in the flesh. And besides, how could he be sure I wouldn't put the money in my pocket? I could walk around for a while and then make up some story for him when I got back. He wouldn't have any way to know if I was telling the truth.

"If that's what you think," I said, suddenly beside myself with anger, "then you can take your money and shove it up your ass. I quit."

**to linger** to remain at a place a bit longer because you don't really want to leave **foray** (ironic) short sudden attack **Blarney Stone** a chain of low priced restaurants in downtown New York—still exists—also: a stone in Ireland said to give you the ability to persuade people when you kiss it **Bickfords** a chain of low priced cafeterias that no longer exists—Auster was probably thinking of the one on 95th Street and Broadway **Chock Full 'o Nuts** a chain of sandwich and coffee shops that was relatively clean—no longer exists **to slap down** to put s.th. flat down with the open hand **to peel off** to remove from the top of a pile **dazed** shocked **to absorb** to begin to understand **bag lady** homeless woman who carries everything in a shopping bag **hooker** (slang) prostitute **wino** (slang) a drunk who drinks wine **bum** a person who has no home or job and asks people for money **riffraff** people of the lowest class **to clutter** here: to fill in too great numbers **boulevard** ['bʊl.ə.vɑːrd] **in the flesh** in person, actually there **beside myself with anger** so angry that I almost couldn't control myself **to shove** to push in a rough way **to quit** to leave a job because you don't like it

For the first time in the six months I had known him, Effing actually broke down and apologized. It was a dramatic moment, and as he sat there pouring out his regret and contrition, I almost began to feel some sympathy for him. His body trembled, saliva clung to his lips, it seemed as if his whole being was about to disintegrate. He knew that I had meant what I said, and the threat of my walking out was too much for him. He begged my forgiveness, told me I was a good lad, that I was the best lad he had ever known, and he would never say another unkind word to me as long as he lived. "I'll make it up to you," he said, "I promise I'll make it up to you." Then, reaching desperately into the bag, he pulled out a fistful of fifty-dollar bills and held them up in the air. "Here," he said, "these are for you, Fogg. I want you to have something extra. Christ knows you deserve it."

"You don't have to bribe me, Mr. Effing. I'm adequately paid already."

"No, please, I want you to have it. Think of it as a bonus. A reward for outstanding service."

"Put the money back in the bag, Mr. Effing. It's all right. I'd rather give it to people who really need it."

"But you'll stay?"

"Yes, I'll stay. I accept your apology. Just don't ever pull another trick like that again."

For obvious reasons, we didn't go out that night. The next night was clear, and at eight o'clock we went down to Times Square, where we finished our work in a record-breaking twenty-five or thirty minutes. Because it was still early, and because we were closer to home than usual, Effing insisted that we return on foot. In itself, this is a trivial point, and I wouldn't bother to mention it except for a curious thing that happened along the way. Just south of Columbus Circle, I saw a young black man of about my age walking parallel to us on the opposite side of the street. As far as I could tell, there was nothing unusual about him. His clothes were decent, he did nothing to suggest that he was either drunk or crazy.

**contrition** the feeling of guilt for s.th. bad that you have done **whole being** complete body **to disintegrate** to break up, to be destroyed **to make s.th. up to s.o.** to do s.th. for a person because you have caused this person to suffer **to bribe** to pay s.o. money to do s.th. illegal (bestechen) **outstanding** extremely good **to pull a trick** (coll) to play a trick on s.o. **Times Square** 42nd Street where Broadway and Seventh Avenue meet near the New York Public Library—in the middle of the theater and movie center **in itself** considered alone without any other facts **trivial** unimportant **Columbus Circle** traffic circle at the southeast corner of Central Park, 59th Street and 8th Avenue

But there he was on a cloudless spring night, walking along with an open umbrella over his head. That was incongruous enough, but then I saw that the umbrella was also broken: the protective cloth had been stripped off the armature, and with the naked spokes spread out uselessly in the air, it looked as though he was carrying some huge and improbable steel flower. I couldn't help laughing at the sight. When I described it to Effing, he let out a laugh as well. His laugh was louder than mine, and it caught the attention of the man across the street. With a big smile on his face, he gestured for us to join him under the umbrella. "What do you want to be standing out in the rain for?" he said merrily. "Come on over here so you don't get wet." There was something so whimsical and open-hearted about his offer that it would have been rude to turn him down. We crossed over to the other side of the street, and for the next thirty blocks we walked up Broadway under the broken umbrella. It pleased me to see how naturally Effing fell in with the spirit of the joke. He played along without asking any questions, intuitively understanding that nonsense of this sort could continue only if we all pretended to believe in it. Our host's name was Orlando, and he was a gifted comedian tiptoeing nimbly around imaginary puddles, warding off raindrops by tilting the umbrella at different angles, and chattering on the whole way in a rapid-fire monologue of ridiculous associations and puns. This was imagination in its purest form: the act of bringing nonexistent things to life, of persuading others to accept a world that was not really there. Coming as it did on that particular night, it somehow seemed to match the impulse behind what Effing and I had just been doing down at Forty-

**incongruous** strange, unsuitable in a certain situation **to strip** to remove **armature** the metal framework of the umbrella covered by the cloth—In *Robinson Crusoe* (1719/1720) by Daniel Defoe the hero also carries around an umbrella, not his dark colored servant Friday. Like Effing Crusoe lives in a cave, surviving on the stores of civilization, but here from a shipwreck. **spoke** thin metal bars found in the wheel of a bike or an umbrella, etc.(Speiche) **whimsical** unusual or strange in an amusing way **rude** not polite **to fall in with the spirit of the joke** to accept the idea of the joke **Orlando** a main character in Shakespeare's comedy about the confusion of identities "As You Like It"—name and hero of a fantastic novel by Virginia Woolf (1882-1941) about a young Elizabethan nobleman, who ends up as a woman poet 300 years later—The Orlando here as a symbol of death or "angel of death" is an allusion to the Dance of Death of the Middle Ages. **to tiptoe** to walk carefully on your toes **puddle** small pool of water **to ward off** to guard or protect yourself from s.th. **to tilt** to move s.th. sideways from an upright position **to chatter** to talk quickly in a friendly way **rapid-fire** quickly one after the other

second Street. A lunatic spirit had taken hold of the city. Fifty-dollar bills were walking around in strangers' pockets, it was raining and yet not raining, and the cloudburst pouring through our broken umbrella did not hit us with a single drop.

We said our good-byes to Orlando at the corner of Broadway and Eighty-fourth Street, the three of us shaking hands all around and swearing to remain friends for life. As a small coda to our promenade, Orlando stuck out his palm to test the weather conditions, thought for a moment, and then declared that the rain had stopped. Without further ado, he closed up the umbrella and presented it to me as a souvenir. "Here, man," he said, "I think you'd better have it. You never know when it might start raining again, and I wouldn't want you guys to get wet. That's the thing about the weather: it changes all the time. If you're not ready for everything, you're not ready for anything."

"It's like money in the bank," said Effing.

"You got it, Tom," said Orlando. "Just stick it under your mattress and save it for a rainy day."

He held up a black power fist to us in farewell and then sauntered off, disappearing into the crowd by the time he reached the end of the block.

It was an odd little episode, but such things happen in New York more often than you would think, especially if you are open to them. What made this encounter unusual for me was not so much its lightheartedness, but the mysterious way in which it seemed to exert an influence on subsequent events. It was almost as if our meeting with Orlando had been a premonition of things to come, an augury of Effing's fate. A new set of images had been imposed on us, and we were henceforth cast under its spell. In particular, I am thinking about rainstorms and umbrellas, but more than that, I am also thinking about change—and how everything can change at any moment, suddenly and forever.

**to take hold of s.th.** to begin to get complete control of s.th. **cloudburst** sudden heavy fall of rain **to swear** schwören—What more or less happens at the end of "As You Like It." **coda** the concluding section of a piece of music or literature **palm** the open part of the hand (Handfläche) **without further ado** without wasting time **...you got it...** you understood everything properly **black power fist** fist held up high used as a sign of black power by radical Afro-Americans such as the Black Panthers in the 60s and early 70s **to saunter** to walk in an unhurried manner **lightheartedness** cheerfulness **to exert** ausüben **subsequent** following **premonition** a feeling that s.th. unpleasant will soon happen **augury** sign, omen **to impose on s.o.** to force on s.o. (sich aufdrängen) **henceforth** (formal) from this time on **to cast s.o. under a spell** to change or influence s.o. after magic words have been spoken (jdn in seinen Bann ziehen)

The following night was to be the last one. Effing spent the day in an even more restless state than normal, refusing to take his nap, refusing to be read to, refusing every distraction I tried to invent for him. We spent some time in the park in the early afternoon, but the air was misty and threatening, and I prevailed on him to return home sooner than we had been planning to. By evening, a dense fog had settled over the city. The world had turned gray, and the lights of the buildings shone through the moisture as though wrapped in bandages. These were less than promising conditions, but since no rain was actually falling, there seemed to be no point in trying to talk Effing out of our final expedition. I figured that I could dispose of our business in short order and then hustle the old man back to the house, working quickly enough to prevent any serious harm from being done. Mrs. Hume didn't like it, but she gave in after I assured her that Effing would carry along an umbrella. Effing readily agreed to this stipulation, and when I pushed him out the front door at eight o'clock, I felt that things were fairly well under control.

What I did not know, however, was that Effing had replaced his umbrella with the one Orlando had given us the night before. By the time I discovered this, we had already traveled five or six blocks from the house. Snickering to himself with some obscure, infantile pleasure, Effing whisked the broken umbrella out from under his blanket and opened it. Since the handle was identical to the one on the umbrella he had left at home, I assumed this was a mistake, but when I told him what he had done, he boomed back at me to mind my own business.

"Don't be a clod," he said. "I took this one on purpose. It's a magic umbrella, any fool can see that. Once you open it, you become invincible."

I was about to say something in response, but then I thought better of it. The fact was that it wasn't raining, and I didn't want to embroil myself

**distraction** any activity that takes you away from your thoughts **misty** with small drops of water that make it difficult to see **to prevail on s.o. to do s.th.** (formal) to persuade s.o. to do s.th. **dense** thick **moisture** water that is in the air (Feuchtigkeit) **to talk s.o. out of s.th.** to persuade not to do s.th. **to dispose of s.th.** to deal with s.th., to take care of s.th. **in short order** quickly **to hustle s.o.** to move s.o. quickly in a rough way **to give in** to agree to s.th. you were originally opposed to **stipulation** requirement, condition **to snicker** (AE) to laugh in an unpleasant way about s.o. else's problems or mistakes **to whisk** to take s.th. very quickly **to boom** to say in a deep loud voice **clod** a stupid insensitive person **invincible** not able to be defeated **to think the better of s.th.** to not do what you planned to do because you have realized it wasn't such a good idea **to embroil yourself in s.th.** to get involved in s.th.

in a hypothetical argument with Effing. I just wanted to get the job done, and as long as it didn't rain, there was no reason for him not to hold that ridiculous object over his head. I pushed on for another few blocks, handing out fifty-dollar bills to all the likely candidates, and when half the supply was gone, I crossed to the other side of the street and began heading back in the direction of the house. It was then that it started to rain—as if inevitably, as if Effing had willed the drops to fall. They were quite puny at first, almost indistinguishable from the misty air all around us, but by the next block the drizzle had turned into something to be reckoned with. I steered Effing into a doorway, thinking we would stand there and wait out the worst of it, but the moment we stopped, the old man started to complain.

"What are you doing?" he said. "This is no time for a breather. We still have money to hand out. Let's get cracking, boy. Mush, mush, let's go. That's an order!"

"In case you haven't noticed," I said, "it happens to be raining. And I'm not just talking about a spring shower. It's coming down hard. The raindrops are the size of pebbles, and they're bouncing two feet off the pavement."

"Rain?" he said. "What rain? I don't feel any rain." Then, with a sudden forward thrust on the wheels of his chair, Effing broke free of my grasp and glided onto the sidewalk. He took hold of the broken umbrella again, raised it with his two hands high above his head, and shouted into the storm. "There's no rain!" he thundered, as the rain crashed down on him from all sides, drenching his clothes and pelting him in the face. "It might be raining on you, boy, but it's not raining on me! I'm dry as a bone! I've got my trusty umbrella, and all's well with the world. Ha, ha! Blow me down and batter me blue, I don't feel a thing!"

I understood then that Effing wanted to die. He had planned this little farce in order to get himself sick, and he was going about it with a

**hypothetical** [ˌhai.poʊˈθet.ɪkəl] **puny** small and weak **indistinguishable** with such a hardly noticeable difference **drizzle** very light rain **s.th. to be reckoned with** s.th. that must be considered a serious problem **breather** a short time to rest **to get cracking** (coll) to begin work immediately **mush** [mʌʃ] a command used in Canada and Alaska to get a dog team to move faster **pebble** a small smooth stone as found at the bottom of a river **thrust** sudden movement forward **to glide** to move easily along **to thunder** to speak loudly **to drench** to make s.th. thoroughly wet **to pelt** to fall heavily on **trusty** reliable, dependable **blow me down and batter me blue** (used by sailors) Damn! **farce** ridiculous comedy recklessness and joy that fairly stunned me. He waved the umbrella back and forth, urging on the downpour with his laughter, and in spite of the disgust I felt for him at that moment, I couldn't help admiring his courage. He was like some midget Lear resurrected in Gloucester's body. This was to be his last night, and he wanted to go out in a frenzy, to bring his own death down on himself as his final, glorious act. My initial impulse was to haul him back from the sidewalk and get him to a safe spot, but then I took another look at him and realized it was too late. He was already soaked to the skin, and with someone as frail as Effing, that probably meant the damage had been done. He would catch cold, then he would come down with pneumonia, and a short time after that he would die. It all seemed so certain to me, I suddenly stopped struggling against it. I was looking at a corpse, I said to myself, and it didn't matter if I took any action or not. Since then, not a day has gone by when I have not regretted the decision I made that night, but at the time it seemed to make sense, as though it would have been morally wrong to stand in Effing's way. If he was already dead, what right did I have to spoil his fun? The man was hell-bent on destroying himself, and because he had sucked me into the whirlwind of his madness, I didn't lift a finger to stop him. I just stood by and let it happen, a willing accomplice to suicide.

I stepped out from the doorway and took hold of Effing's chair, squinting as the rain gusted against my eyes. "I guess you're right," I said. "The rain doesn't seem to be touching me either." As I spoke, a flash of lightning snaked across the sky, followed by a tremendous clap of thunder. The rain poured down on us without mercy, attacking our

**recklessness** showing no concern about any dangers **fairly** more than a little **to stun** to surprise, to shock **midget** abnormally small person **Lear** [lɪr] King Lear in Shakespeare's tragedy of the same name—In his old age King Lear, king of England, decides to divide his kingdom among his three daughters. Misjudging the real love of his youngest daughter, he gives her part of the kingdom to the other two daughters, who cause him great suffering. **to resurrect** to bring back to life **Gloucester** [ˈglɑːstər] The Earl of Gloucester, a faithful friend of Lear, in a subplot he saves King Lear's life while the latter is raging mad in a storm. One of Lear's daughters finds out about this rescue and plucks out Gloucester's eyes as a punishment. **to go out in a frenzy** here: to die in the middle of great excitement **initial** first **to haul** to carry or pull s.th. heavy **soaked to the skin** with the clothes completely wet **frail** physically weak **to spoil** to ruin, to disrupt **hell-bent** very determined **accomplice** s.o. who helps to commit a crime **to squint** to look at s.th. with the eyes partly closed **to gust** to blow strongly for a moment **to snake** to move with twisted curves like a snake **tremendous** very great

exposed bodies with a barrage of liquid bullets. After the next burst of wind, Effing's glasses were knocked clean off his face, but all he did was laugh, reveling in the violence of the storm.

"It's remarkable, isn't it?" he shouted at me through the noise. "It smells like rain. It sounds like rain. It even tastes like rain. And yet we're perfectly dry. It's mind over matter, Fogg. We've finally done it! We've cracked the secret of the universe!"

It was as though I had crossed some mysterious boundary deep within myself, crawling through a trapdoor that led to the innermost chambers of Effing's heart. It wasn't simply that I had given in to his grotesque ploy, I had made the ultimate gesture of validating his freedom, and in that sense I had proven myself to him at last. The old man was going to die, but for as long as he lived, he would love me.

We careened uptown for another seven or eight blocks, and Effing howled in ecstasy the whole way. "It's a miracle!" he bellowed. "It's a goddamned bloody miracle! Pennies from heaven—get them while they last! Free money! Money for one and all!"

No one heard him, of course, since the streets were entirely empty. We were the only fools who had not scrambled for shelter by then, and in order to get rid of the remaining bills, I made a number of brief visits into bars and coffee shops along the way. I would park Effing by the door as I entered these establishments, listening to his wild laughter as I distributed the money. My ears buzzed with the sound of it: an insane musical accompaniment to our slapstick finale. The whole thing was raging out of control by then. We had turned ourselves into a natural disaster, a

**exposed** not protected by anything **barrage** continuous firing **clean off** with one quick movement **to revel in s.th.** to enjoy s.th.very much **mind over matter** the mind able to win over or ignore the real world **to crack** to discover **trapdoor** a small door in the floor or ceiling (Falltür) **chamber** room **to give in** to decide to accept s.th. although you were opposed to it **ploy** a clever tactic to deceive s.o. **to validate** to confirm (bestätigen) **to careen** (AE) to move forward quickly with sudden sidewards movements **to howl** to cry out loudly like a dog or wolf **to bellow** to shout in a loud deep voice **pennies from heaven** an allusion to the 1936 Hollywood film "Pennies from Heaven" and the song of the same name that became very popular **to scramble for a place** to rush for a place in a disorderly way **establishment** (formal) shop, business, institution, etc. **to buzz** to make a vibrating sound like a *z* **accompaniment** here: music played at the same time as another activity (Begleitung) **to rage out of control** to become so intense or violent that nothing is in control any more

typhoon that swallowed up innocent victims in its path. "Money!" I would shout, laughing and weeping at the same time. "Fifty-dollar bills for everyone!" I was so waterlogged that my boots squirted puddles, I gushed like a human-sized tear, I dripped water on everyone. It was fortunate that we had come to the end. If things had gone on much longer, we probably would have been locked up for reckless endangerment.

The last place we visited was a Child's coffee shop, a squalid, steamy hole in the wall illuminated by glaring fluorescent lights. There were twelve or fifteen customers hunched over the counter, and each one looked more forlorn and miserable than the next. I had only five or six bills left in my pocket, and suddenly I didn't know how to handle the situation. I couldn't think, I couldn't decide anymore. For want of anything better to do, I wadded up the money in my fist and flung it across the room. "Whoever wants it can have it!" I yelled. And then I ran out of there, pushing Effing back into the storm.

He never left the house again after that night. The coughing started early the next day, and by the end of the week the phlegmy rumbling had advanced from his bronchial tubes into his lungs. We called in a doctor, and he confirmed the diagnosis of pneumonia. He wanted Effing to be sent to the hospital immediately, but the old man refused, claiming that he had a right to die in his own bed, and if anyone so much as laid a hand on him with the intention of taking him out of the apartment, he would kill himself. "I'll slit my throat with a razor," he said, "and then you'll have to live with that on your conscience." The doctor had dealt with Effing in the past, and he was clever enough to have come prepared with a list of private nursing services. Mrs. Hume and I made all the necessary arrangements, and for the next week we were up to our elbows in practi-

**typhoon** a violent tropical storm in the Pacific **waterlogged** completely flooded or filled with water **to squirt** to send out a fast and strong thin stream **to gush** to cause to pour out suddenly and in large amounts **to lock up** (coll) to put in jail **reckless** not caring about the dangers **endangerment** putting s.o. or s.th. in danger **Child's coffee shop** a chain of low priced coffee shops that no longer exists **squalid** dirty and unpleasant because of not being properly cared for **to glare** to shine in a bright and unpleasant way **forlorn** miserable, wretched, forsaken **to wad up** (AE) to press s.th. together into a ball or roll **to fling/flung/flung** to throw with violence **phlegmy** [flemi] schleimig **to rumble** to make a series of deep long sounds **bronchial tubes** Bronchien **pneumonia** Lungenentzündung **to slit** to make a long thin cut **razor** Rasiermesser

cal business: lawyers, bank accounts, powers of attorney, and so on. There were endless phone calls to be made, countless papers to be signed, but I doubt that any of that is worth going into now. The important thing was that I eventually made my peace with Mrs. Hume. After I returned to the apartment with Effing on the night of the storm, she was so angry that she didn't utter a word to me for two whole days. She held me responsible for his illness, and because I was basically of the same opinion, I didn't try to defend myself. It made me miserable to be at odds with her. Just when I was beginning to think the rift was permanent, however, the situation suddenly reversed itself. I have no way of knowing how this came about, but I imagine that she must have said something about it to Effing, and that he in time must have persuaded her not to hold it against me. The next time I saw her, she took me in her arms and apologized, fighting back tears of emotion. "His time has come," she stated solemnly. "He's ready to go at any moment now, and there's nothing we can do to stop him."

The nurses worked in eight-hour shifts, and they were the ones who administered the medicines, changed the bedpan, and watched over the I.V. that had been hooked up to Effing's arm. With few exceptions, I found them to be a brusque, coldhearted lot, and it probably goes without saying that Effing wanted as little to do with them as possible. That held true right up to the last days, when he was too weak to notice them anymore. Unless they had some specific task to perform, he insisted that they stay out of his room, which meant that they were generally to be found on the living room sofa, pouting in silent disdain as they flipped through magazines and smoked cigarettes. One or two of them walked out on us, and one or two others had to be fired. Apart from this hard line with the nurses, however, Effing behaved with remarkable gentleness, and from the moment he took to his bed, it was as if his personality had been transformed, purged of its venom by the growing nearness of death.

**power of attorney** the legal authority given to another person to deal with or take care of all legal matters (Vollmacht) **to be at odds with s.o.** to be in conflict with s.o. **rift** break in friendly relations **to reverse itself** to change to the opposite **to apologize** to say you are sorry for causing a problem **to administer** (formal) to give **I.V.** Infusion **to hook up to** to connect to, to place into **brusque** [brʌsk] not using many words, not very polite **lot** (BE) group of people **to hold true** to be valid **to pout** to push out your lips to show you are annoyed **disdain** contempt **to flip through** to turn the pages quickly **to walk out on s.o.** to suddenly leave s.o. **to purge** to get rid of s.th. undesirable **venom** (fig) liquid poison produced by snakes or insects

I don't think he felt much pain, and although there were good days and bad days (at one point, in fact, it seemed as though he had made a complete recovery, but this was followed by a relapse just seventy-two hours later), the progress of his illness was one of gradual diminishment, a slow and ineluctable loss of strength that went on until his heart finally stopped beating.

I spent every day with him in that room, sitting beside his bed because he wanted me to be there. Since the rainstorm, our relationship had changed to such an extent that he now doted on me as if I were his own flesh and blood. He held my hand and told me that I was a comfort to him, muttering how glad he was to have me in the room. At first, I was wary of these sentimental outpourings, but as the evidence of his newfound affection continued to mount, I had no choice but to accept it as genuine. Early on, when he was still strong enough to carry on a conversation, he asked me questions about my life, and I told him stories about my mother and Uncle Victor, about my days in college, about the disastrous period that led to my collapse and how Kitty Wu had saved me. Effing said that he was worried about what would happen to me after he croaked (his word), but I tried to reassure him that I was quite capable of taking care of myself.

"You're a dreamer, boy," he said. "Your mind is on the moon, and from the looks of things, it's never going to be anywhere else. You have no ambitions, you don't give a damn about money, and you're too much of a philosopher to have any feeling for art. What am I going to do with you? You need someone to look after you, to make sure you have food in your belly and a bit of cash in your pocket. Once I'm gone, you'll be right back where you started."

"I've been making plans," I lied, hoping to get him off the subject. "I sent in an application to the library school at Columbia last winter, and they've accepted me. I thought I'd already mentioned it to you. Classes start in the fall."

"And how are you going to pay the tuition?"

"They've given me a full scholarship, plus a stipend to cover living expenses. It's a good deal, a tremendous opportunity. The program lasts for two years, and after that I'll always have a way to make a living."

"It's hard to see you as a librarian, Fogg."

**relapse** here: returning to the original state of bad health **diminishment** here: becoming weaker, getting closer to death **ineluctable** inevitable, inescapable **wary** watchful, careful **outpouring** expression of great emotion **to mount** to increase **to croak** (slang) to die **tremendous** excellent

"I admit it's strange, but I think I might be suited for it. Libraries aren't in the real world, after all. They're places apart, sanctuaries of pure thought. In that way, I can go on living on the moon for the rest of my life."

I knew that Effing didn't believe me, but he played along with my lie for the sake of harmony, not wanting to disrupt the calm that had grown up between us. That was typical of what had become of him during those last weeks. I think he was proud of himself for being able to die in this way, as if the tenderness he had begun to show for me proved that he was still capable of accomplishing anything he wanted to. In spite of his failing strength, he continued to believe that he was in control of his destiny, and this illusion persisted right up to the end: the idea that he had masterminded his own death, that everything was proceeding according to plan. He had announced that May twelfth would be the fatal day, and it seemed now that the only thing that mattered to him was sticking to his word. He had given in to death with open arms, and at the same time he had rejected it, struggling with the last ounce of his energy to subdue it, to ward off the final moment until it came to him on his own terms. Even when he could barely speak anymore, when it required an enormous effort for him to produce the smallest gurgle of sound in his throat, the first thing he wanted to know when I entered the room every morning was what day it was. Because he could no longer keep track of time, he would repeat the question every few hours over the course of the day. On the third or fourth of the month, he suddenly went into dramatic decline, and it seemed unlikely that he would be able to hold on until the twelfth. I began fiddling with the dates in order to reassure him that he was still on schedule, jumping ahead each time he asked the question, and on one particularly rough afternoon I wound up covering three days in the space

**to be suited for s.th.** to have the right qualities to do s.th. **sanctuary** [ˈsæŋk.tʃu.er.i] a peaceful place that is safe and provides protection **for the sake of** for the purpose of **to disrupt** to prevent from continuing **tenderness** kindness, warm affection **failing** decreasing **to persist** to continue in spite of difficulty or opposition **to mastermind** to plan and carry out a complex undertaking **to stick to one's word** to do what you said you would do **to reject** to refuse to accept **with the last ounce of his energy** with every bit of energy **to subdue** to overcome, to bring under control **to ward off** to take steps to prevent s.th. evil, an illness, etc. from harming you **on his own terms** according to his own conditions **to keep track of s.th.** to pay close attention to s.th. **decline** slowly worsening condition **to fiddle with s.th.** to change s.th. with a dishonest purpose in mind, to falsify **rough** difficult, unpleasant **I wound up covering…** the final result was that I covered…

of just a few hours. It's the seventh, I said to him; it's the eighth; it's the ninth, and he was so far gone by then that he failed to notice the discrepancy. When his condition stabilized again later that week, I was still in advance of the calendar, and for the next two days I had no choice but to go on telling him it was the ninth. I felt that was the least I could do for him—to give him the satisfaction of thinking he had won this test of will. No matter how it came out, I was going to make sure his life ended on the twelfth.

The sound of my voice soothed him, he said, and even when he became too weak to say anything, he wanted me to go on talking. He was not concerned with what I said, just so long as he could hear my voice and know that I was there. I rattled on as best I could, shifting from one subject to another as the mood struck me. It was not always easy to sustain this kind of monologue, and whenever I found myself running short on inspiration, I would fall back on one of several devices to get me going again: rehashing the plots of novels and films, reciting poems from memory—Effing was especially fond of Sir Thomas Wyatt and Fulke Greville—or mentioning news items from the morning paper. Strangely enough, I can still remember some of those stories quite well, and whenever I think of them now (the spread of the war to Cambodia, the killings at Kent State), I see myself sitting in that room with Effing, looking down at him as he lay in bed. I see his toothless, gaping mouth; I hear his clogged lungs gasping for air; I see his blind, watery eyes staring up at the ceiling, the spidery hands clutching the blanket, the overwhelming pallor of his wrinkled skin. The association is unavoidable. By some obscure

**to soothe** to make calm or peaceful **to rattle on** to talk quickly and for a long time about unimportant things **to shift** to move from one position to another **as the mood struck me** depending on how I felt at the moment **to sustain** to continue, to keep up **device** trick, special method **to rehash** to rework, or re-use old or already used material **Sir Thomas Wyatt** (1503-1542) English poet and statesman, who introduced the sonnet form from Italy **Fulke Greville** ['grev.ɪl] (1554-1628), English writer who is known for writing poetry in a simple style **Cambodia** President Richard Nixon sent American troops into Cambodia on April 30, 1970 to cut off the supply line of the Vietcong to South Vietnam **Kent State** On May 4, 1970 four students were shot by soldiers at Kent State University in Ohio at a protest rally against Nixon's invasion of Cambodia. **gaping** wide open **clogged** blocked so that hardly any air can come through **to gasp for air** to breathe with difficulty **overwhelming** here: causing a strong emotional reaction **pallor** ['pæl.ər] unhealthy paleness **wrinkled** with lines and folds as a result of age

and involuntary reflex, those events have become situated for me in the contours of Effing's face, and I cannot think of them without seeing him before me again.

There were times when I did nothing more than describe the room we were sitting in. Using the same methods I had developed during our walks, I would pick out an object and begin to talk about it. The pattern on the bedspread, the bureau in the corner, the framed street map of Paris that hung on the wall beside the window. To the extent that Effing could follow what I was saying, these inventories seemed to give him profound pleasure. With so much falling away from him now, the immediate physical presence of things stood at the edge of his consciousness as a kind of paradise, an unobtainable realm of ordinary miracles: the tactile, the visible, the perceptual field that surrounds all life. By putting these things into words for him, I gave Effing the chance to experience them again, as if merely to take one's place in the world of things was a good beyond all others. In some sense, I worked harder for him in that room than I had ever worked before, concentrating on the minutest details and materials—the wools and cottons, the silvers and pewters, the wood grains and plaster swirls—delving into each crevice, enumerating each color and shape, exploring the microscopic geometries of whatever there was to see. The weaker Effing became, the more strenuously I applied myself, doubling my efforts in order to bridge the distance that was steadily growing between us. By the end, I had pushed myself to such lengths of precision that it took me hours to work my way around the room. I advanced by fractions of an inch, refusing to let anything escape me, not

**involuntary** happening without intention or wanting to do s.th. **contour** the outline, the outer edge **bedspread** (AE) an additional decorative cover over the pillow and blanket of a bed **bureau** ['bjʊr.oʊ] (AE) a chest of drawers (BE) **to the extent** in so far as **inventory** list of things in a place **profound** great, intense **consciousness** ability to perceive and understand what is around you, awareness **unobtainable** impossible to get **realm** here: special world **tactile** having to do with the sense of touch **perceptual** having to do with the act of perceiving **beyond all others** more important than all others **minutest** [maɪ'nju:tɪst] smallest **silvers** articles used in the house made of silver **pewter** objects made of pewter (Zinn) **grain** Maserung **plaster** Gips **swirl** decoration with a pattern of circles **to delve into s.th.** to search deeply and intensely **crevice** narrow crack (Riss) **to enumerate** to make a list **strenuously** with great effort and determination **to apply yourself** to work very hard at s.th. **steadily** continuously **by fractions of an inch** fraction = Bruchzahl; inch = 2.54 cm, i.e. very slowly

even the dust motes hovering in the air. I mined the limits of that space until it became inexhaustible, a plenitude of worlds within worlds. At a certain point, I realized that I was probably talking into a void, but I went on talking anyway, hypnotized by the thought that my voice was the one thing that could keep Effing alive. It made no difference, of course. He was slipping away, and for the whole of the last two days I spent with him, I doubt that he heard a word I said.

I wasn't there when he died. After I had sat with him until eight o'clock on the eleventh, Mrs. Hume came in to relieve me and insisted that I take the rest of the night off. "There's nothing we can do for him now," she said. "You've been in here with him since this morning, and it's time you got some air. If he lasts through the night, at least you'll be fresh for tomorrow."

"I don't think there's going to be a tomorrow," I said.

"Maybe not. But that's what we said yesterday, and he's still hanging in there."

I went out to dinner with Kitty at the Moon Palace, and afterward we took in one of the movies on the double bill at the Thalia (I remember it as *Ashes and Diamonds*, but I could be wrong). Normally, I would have taken Kitty back to her dormitory at that point, but I had a bad feeling about Effing, and so after the movie was over, we walked down West End Avenue to check in with Mrs. Hume at the apartment. It was close to one o'clock in the morning when we got there. Rita was in tears when she opened the door, and it wasn't necessary for her to say anything for me to know what had happened. As it turned out, Effing had died less than an hour before our arrival. When I asked the nurse for the exact time, she told me it had been 12:02, two minutes past midnight. So Effing had made it to the twelfth, after all. It seemed so preposterous that I didn't know how to react. There was a strange tingling in my head, and I suddenly felt that the wires in my brain had been crossed. I assumed that I was about

**dust mote** (old-fashioned) very small piece of dust **to mine** here: to search everywhere **plentitude** (formal) a large amount **void** large empty space **to relieve s.o.** to replace s.o. when this person needs rest **to still hang in** (AE, slang) to remain determined in a difficult situation **on the double bill** with two feature films **Thalia** movie theater on 95th Street near Broadway that shows mostly foreign films—still exists **Ashes and Diamonds** 1958 Polish film of high quality about the Resistance in World War Two **to check in with s.o.** to find out from s.o. what the situation is **after all** in spite of what might have been expected **preposterous** absurd **to tingle** to have a feeling of sharp points of slight pain (prickeln) **to cross** to cause to go across one another

to start crying, so I went off into a corner of the room and put my hands over my face. I stood there waiting for the tears to fall, but nothing came. A few more moments went by, and then a spasm of peculiar sounds came rushing from my throat. It took another moment or two before I realized that I was laughing.

According to the instructions he had left behind, Effing's body was to be cremated. There was to be no funeral service or burial, and he specifically requested that no representative of any religion be allowed to participate in the disposal of his remains. The ceremony was to be extremely simple: Mrs. Hume and I were to board the Staten Island ferry, and once we had passed the midway point out from Manhattan (with the Statue of Liberty visible to our right), we were to scatter his ashes over the waters of New York harbor.

I tried to reach Solomon Barber by telephone in Northfield, Minnesota, thinking he should be given an opportunity to attend, but after several calls to his house, where no one answered, I called the history department of Magnus College and was told that Professor Barber was on leave for the spring semester. The secretary seemed reluctant to give me any more information, but after I explained the purpose of my call, she relented somewhat and added that the Professor had gone on a research trip to England. How could I get in touch with him over there? I asked. That would be a problem, she said, since he hadn't given them an address. But what about his mail? I went on, they must be forwarding it to him somewhere. No, she said, as a matter of fact they weren't. He had asked them to hold it for him until he returned. And when would that be? Not until August, she said, apologizing for not being more helpful, and there was something in her voice that made me believe she was telling the truth. Later that same day, I sat down and wrote a long letter to Barber

**spasm** a sudden burst **to cremate** to burn a dead body **funeral service** religious ceremony for s.o. who has died **burial** ceremony of putting a dead person into a grave **specifically** especially **to request** (formal) to ask **disposal** the act of getting rid of s.th. **remains** dead body **Staten Island ferry** a ship that regularly travels between southern Manhattan, past Ellis Island and the Statue of Liberty, to Staten Island **to scatter** to throw over a wide area **Northfield** small town in southeast Minnesota **Magnus** There is no college of this name in or around Northfield. **on leave** not at work for a period of time with permission **reluctant** hesitating **to relent** to change your mind about s.th. decided, to become less determined **to forward a letter** to send a letter to a new address instead of a prior one **to apologize** to say you are sorry for having done s.th. wrong

describing the situation as best I could. It was a difficult letter to compose, and I worked on it for two or three hours. Once it was finished, I typed it up and sent it off in a package along with the revised transcript of Effing's autobiography. As far as I could tell, that ended my responsibility in the matter. I had done what Effing had asked of me, and from then on it would be in the hands of the lawyers, who would be contacting Barber in due course.

Two days later, Mrs. Hume and I collected the ashes from the mortuary. They had been packed into a gray metal urn no larger than a loaf of bread, and it was difficult for me to imagine that Effing was actually in there. So much of him had gone up in smoke, it seemed odd to think there was anything left. Mrs. Hume, who no doubt had a more vivid sense of reality than I did, seemed frightened by the urn, and she held it at arm's length the whole way home, as though it contained poisonous, radioactive materials. Rain or shine, we agreed that we should make our trip on the ferry the next day. It happened to be visiting day for her at the V.A. Hospital, and rather than miss seeing her brother, Mrs. Hume decided that he should go along with us. As she spoke, it occurred to her that perhaps Kitty should go along as well. It didn't seem necessary to me, but when I relayed the message to Kitty, she said that she wanted to go. It was an important event, she said, and she liked Mrs. Hume too much not to be there to lend her moral support. That was how we became four instead of two. I doubt that New York has ever seen a more motley bunch of undertakers.

Mrs. Hume left early the next morning to fetch her brother at the hospital. While she was gone, Kitty arrived at the apartment, dressed in the tiniest of blue miniskirts, her smooth, coppery legs looking splendid in combination with the high heels she had put on for the occasion. I explained to her that Mrs. Hume's brother was supposedly not right in the head, but never having met him myself, I wasn't quite sure what that meant. Charlie Bacon proved to be a large, round-faced man in his early

**to compose** to write **to revise** to change so that there are improvements **lawyer** Rechtsanwalt **in due course** at some appropriate time in the future **mortuary** [ˈmɜːr.tʃu.er.i] (AE) place, especially a funeral home, where a dead body is kept before burial or cremation **vivid** intense **to occur to s.o.** to suddenly come to s.o.'s mind **to relay** to pass a message from one person to another **to lend s.o. moral support** here: to accompany s.o. to show that you support what the other person is doing **motley bunch** a group of people of many different kinds **undertaker** (BE) a person who prepares dead bodies for funerals or burials **coppery** of the color of copper **to prove to be** to be shown to be

fifties with thinning reddish hair and watchful, darting eyes. He showed up with his sister in a somewhat distracted, ebullient state (it was the first time he had left the hospital in over a year), and for the first few minutes he did little more than smile at us and shake our hands. He was wearing a blue windbreaker zipped up to his throat, a freshly ironed pair of khaki pants, and shiny black shoes with white socks. In the pocket of his jacket he carried a small transistor radio with an earplug wire coiling out of it. He kept the plug in his ear at all times, and every minute or two he would stick his hand into his pocket and fiddle with the dials of the radio. Whenever he did this, he would close his eyes and concentrate, as though he were listening to messages from another galaxy. When I asked him which station he liked best, he told me they were all the same. "I don't listen to the radio for fun," he said. "It's my job. If I do it right, I can tell what's going on with the big thumpers under the city."

"The big thumpers?"

"The H-bombs. They've got a dozen of them stored in underground tunnels, and they keep moving them around so the Russians won't know where they are. There must be a hundred different sites—way down at the bottom of the city, deeper than the subway."

"What does that have to do with the radio?"

"They give out the information in code. Whenever there's a live broadcast on one of the stations, that means they're moving the thumpers. Baseball games are one of the best indicators. If the Mets win five to two, that means they're putting the thumpers in position fifty-two. If they lose six to one, that means position sixteen. It's really pretty simple once you get the hang of it."

"What about the Yankees?"

"Whichever team has a game in New York, that's the score you watch. They're never in town on the same day. When the Mets play in New York, the Yankees are on the road, and vice versa."

**to dart** to move suddenly in a certain direction **distracted** unable to think clearly **ebullient** excited and very happy **windbreaker** a warm jacket (trademark) **earplug** small headphone that can be placed in the ear **to coil** to twist in circles **to fiddle with s.th.** here: to adjust or turn without knowing what you're doing **dial** small knob that you turn to listen to a station or adjust the volume **thumper** (ironic) s.th. that makes a low sound when it hits the surface **H-bomb** hydrogen bomb, first exploded in 1952 **to get the hang of s.th.** (coll) to learn how to use or do s.th. **Yankees** New York Yankees, professional football team in New York **score** the number of points each team has won **on the road** playing outside of New York **vice versa** the other way around

"But what good is it going to do us to know where the bombs are?"

"So we can protect ourselves. I don't know about you, but the idea of getting blown up doesn't make me too happy. Somebody's got to keep track of what's going on, and if no one else is going to do it, I guess that somebody is me."

Mrs. Hume was changing her dress while I had this conversation with her brother. Once she was ready, we all left the apartment and caught a cab for the ferry station downtown. It turned out to be a fine day, with clear blue skies and a crisp, windy hum in the air. I remember sitting in the back seat with the urn on my lap, listening to Charlie talk about Effing as the cab tooled down the West Side Highway. They had apparently met several times, and after exhausting the one connection between them (Utah), he proceeded to give a rambling, fragmented account of the days he had spent out there himself. He had done his bomber training at Wendover during the war, he said, way out there in the middle of the desert, destroying miniature cities of salt. He flew thirty or forty missions over Germany, and then, at the end of the war, they sent him back to Utah and put him in the A-bomb program. "We weren't supposed to know what it was," he said, "but I found out. If there's a piece of information to be found, rest assured that Charlie Bacon can find it. First it was Big Boy, the one they dropped on Hiroshima with Colonel Tibbets. I was scheduled to be in the crew of the next plane three days later, the one that went to Nagasaki. There was no way they were going to get me to do that. Destruction on that scale is God's business. Men don't have the right to meddle in it. I fooled them by pretending to be crazy. I just set out one afternoon and started walking into the desert, out into all that heat. I didn't care if they shot me. It was bad enough in Germany, but I

**crisp** cold and dry **hum** low continuous sound **to tool** (coll, AE) to drive **the West Side Highway** highway along the lower westside of Manhattan **apparently** seemingly **to exhaust** here: to discuss thoroughly so that no further interest remains **rambling** disorganized **account** description **Wendover** military base in northwestern Utah that indeed was used during World War Two to train the airplane crew that was to drop the atomic bomb on Japan **rest assured** (formal) you can be very certain **Big Boy** the bomb was called "Little Boy," and was dropped on Hiroshima on August 6, 1945 **Colonel Tibbets** [ˈkɜːr.nəl] Paul W. Tibbets was the pilot of the plane that dropped the first atomic bomb **to be scheduled to do s.th.** to be assigned to do s.th., to be included in a plan to do s.th. **Nagasaki** The second bomb was dropped on Nagasaki on August 9, 1945 because the Japanese still had refused to surrender after August 6, 1945. **on that scale** of that size or extent **to meddle in s.th.** to become involved in s.th. that is not your concern **to set out** to go out

wasn't going to let them turn me into an agent of destruction. No, sir, I'd rather be crazy than have that on my conscience. The way I see it, they wouldn't have done it if those Japs were white. They don't give a damn about yellow people. No offense," he suddenly added, turning to Kitty, "but as far as they're concerned, yellow people are no better than dogs. What do you think we're doing over there in Southeast Asia now? The same stuff, killing yellow people wherever we can find them. It's like slaughtering the Indians all over again. Now we have H-bombs instead of A-bombs. The generals are still making new weapons out in Utah, far away from everything, where no one can see them. Remember those sheep that died last year? Six thousand of them. They shot some new poison gas into the air, and everything died for miles around. No, sir, there's no way I'll put that blood on my hands. Yellow people, white people, what difference does it make? We're all the same, aren't we? No, sir, there's no way you'll get Charlie Bacon to do your dirty work. I'd rather be a crazy man than mess around with those thumpers."

His monologue was broken off by our arrival, and for the rest of the day Charlie withdrew into the arcana of his transistor radio. He enjoyed being out on the boat, however, and in spite of myself, I found that I was in good spirits as well. There was a weirdness to our mission that somehow canceled out the possibility of dark thoughts, and even Mrs. Hume managed to get through the trip without shedding any tears. Most of all, I remember how beautiful Kitty looked in her tiny dress, with the wind blowing through her long black hair and her exquisite little hand in mine. The boat wasn't crowded at that time of day, and there were more seagulls than passengers out on the deck with us. Once we came within sight of the Statue of Liberty, I opened the urn and shook the ashes out into the wind. They were a mixture of white and gray and black, and they disappeared within a matter of seconds. Charlie was standing to my right, and Kitty was on my left with her arm around Mrs. Hume. We all fol-

**Japs** (slang) expression used for the Japanese during World War Two **no offense** I don't want to offend you. **Southeast Asia** i.e. Vietnam **stuff** (coll) action, activity **poison gas** A number of sheep mysteriously died in March 1968 near Dugway, a military base in northwest Utah where experiments were being conducted to test biological and chemical weapons for use in Vietnam—the matter has never really been cleared up. **to mess around with s.th.** (coll) to use s.th. in a careless way **arcana** secrets, mysteries **in good spirits** in a good mood **to cancel out** to offset, to counterbalance, to replace s.th. so that there is the opposite effect **to shed tears** (formal) to cry

lowed the brief, hectic flight of the ashes until there was nothing more to see, and then Charlie turned to his sister and said, "That's what I want you to do for me, Rita. After I die, I want you to burn me up and toss me into the air. It's a glorious sight, dancing out in all directions at once, it's the most glorious sight in the world."

Once the ferry pulled into the dock at Staten Island, we turned around and took the next boat back to the city. Mrs. Hume had prepared a large dinner for us, and less than an hour after returning to the apartment, we sat down at the table and started to eat. Everything was over now. My bag was packed, and as soon as the meal was finished, I would be walking out of Effing's house for the last time. Mrs. Hume was planning to stay on until the estate was settled, and if all went well, she said (referring to the bequest she was supposed to receive), she was going to move to Florida with Charlie and start a new life. For perhaps the fiftieth time, she told me that I was welcome to stay on in the apartment as long as I liked, and for the fiftieth time I told her that I had a place to live with one of Kitty's friends. What were my plans? she wanted to know. What was I going to do with myself? There was no need to lie to her at that point. "I'm not sure," I said. "I have to think about it. But something is bound to turn up before too long."

There were passionate hugs and tears when we said goodbye. We promised to stay in touch with each other, but of course we never did, and that was the last time I ever saw her.

"You're a fine young gentleman," she said to me at the door, "and I'll never forget how good you were to Mr. Thomas. Half the time, he didn't deserve such kindness."

"Everyone deserves kindness," I said. "No matter who they are."

Kitty and I were already out the door and halfway down the hall when Mrs. Hume came trundling after us. "I almost forgot," she said, "there's something I was supposed to give you." We went back into the apartment, where Mrs. Hume opened the hall closet and took down a rumpled brown grocery bag from the top shelf. "Mr. Thomas gave this to me last month," she said. "He wanted me to keep it for you until you left."

**to toss** to throw with a quick gentle movement **to settle an estate** to pay the money or give the property to the people mentioned in a will **bequest** money or property which has been arranged for in s.o.'s will after this person dies **bound** likely **to trundle** to walk heavily **rumpled** zerknittert **grocery bag** large brown paper bag

I was about to tuck the bag under my arm and walk out again, but Kitty stopped me. "Aren't you curious to know what's in it?" she said.

"I thought I'd wait until we got outside," I said. "In case it's a bomb."

Mrs. Hume laughed at that. "I wouldn't put it past the old buzzard," she said.

"Exactly. One last prank from the other side of the grave."

"Well, I'll open the bag if you won't," Kitty said. "Maybe there's something nice in there."

"You see what an optimist she is," I said to Mrs. Hume. "Always hoping for the best."

"Let her open it," said Charlie, eagerly thrusting himself into the conversation. "I'll bet you there's a valuable present inside."

"All right," I said, handing the bag to Kitty. "Since I've been voted down, I'll let you have the honors."

With inimitable delicacy, Kitty parted the bunched-up opening of the bag and peered in. When she looked up at us again, she paused for a moment in confusion, and then her face broke into a broad, triumphant smile. Without saying a word, she turned the bag upside-down and let its contents fall to the floor. Money came fluttering out, an endless shower of old rumpled bills. We watched in silence as the tens and twenties and fifties landed at our feet. All in all, it came to more than seven thousand dollars.

**to tuck** to put s.th. into a small space **I wouldn't put it past...** (coll) I could believe that..., I wouldn't be surprised if... **buzzard** a mean person (buzzard = Bussard) **prank** trick played on s.o. **to thrust oneself into s.th.** to force oneself into s.th. **I'll bet...** I'm quite sure... **to vote s.o. down** here: to reject (especially by a group of people) s.o. else's suggestion or idea **inimitable** so good that it cannot be copied properly **delicacy** careful, graceful style **to part** to pull two sides apart **bunched-up** here: squeezed tightly together **to peer in s.th.** to look into s.th. that is difficult to see

## 6

An extraordinary period followed after that. For the next eight or nine months, I lived in a way that had never been possible for me before, and right up to the end, I believe that I came closer to human paradise than at any other time in the years I have spent on this planet. It was not just the money (although the money cannot be underestimated), but the suddenness with which everything had been reversed. Effing's death had released me from my bondage to him, but at the same time, Effing had released me from my bondage to the world, and because I was young, because I still knew so little about the world, I was unable to understand that this period of happiness could ever end. I had been lost in the desert, and then, out of the blue, I had found my Canaan, my promised land. For the time being, I could only exult, fall to my knees in thanks, and kiss the ground I stood on. It was still too early to think that any of this could be destroyed, too early to imagine the exile that lay ahead.

Kitty's school year ended about a week after I was given the money, and by the middle of June we had found a place to live. For less than three hundred dollars a month, we set up house together in a large, dusty loft on East Broadway, not far from Chatham Square and the Manhattan Bridge. This was the heart of Chinatown, and Kitty was the one who had

**to reverse** to change s.th. so that it is the opposite of what it was before **to release s.o.** to free s.o. from a duty or obligation **bondage to s.o.** here: dependence on s.o. that limits one's freedom **out of the blue** unexpectedly **Canaan** [ˈkeɪ.nən] the promised land of the Israelites **to exult** to be joyful **East Broadway, Chatham Square** area in lower east Manhattan formerly settled by Jewish immigrants, but after 1965 became a part of neighboring Chinatown **Manhattan Bridge** bridge (built 1912) connecting Manhattan with Brooklyn **Chinatown** goes back to the gold rush days; it rapidly expanded after 1965 when restrictions for Asians who wanted to emigrate to America were largely removed

made all the arrangements, using her Chinese connections to bargain the landlord into giving us a five-year lease with partial rent deductions for any structural improvements we happened to make. It was 1970, and beyond a few painters and sculptors who had converted lofts into studios, the idea of living in old commercial buildings was only just beginning to catch on in New York. Kitty wanted the space for her dancing (there were over two thousand square feet), and I myself was charmed by the prospect of inhabiting a former warehouse with exposed pipes and rusted tin ceilings.

We bought a secondhand stove and refrigerator on the Lower East Side, then paid to have a rudimentary shower and hot-water heater installed in the bathroom. After combing the streets for discarded furniture—a table, a bookcase, three or four chairs, a wobbly green bureau—we bought ourselves a foam mattress and a smattering of kitchen supplies. The furniture barely made a dent in the hugeness of the space, but since we both had an aversion to clutter, we found ourselves satisfied with the roughshod minimalism of the decor and made no further additions. Rather than spend excessive amounts on the loft—as it was, I had laid out close to a thousand dollars—I took the two of us on a shopping expedition to buy new clothes. I found everything I needed in less than an hour, and then, for the rest of the day, we went from store to store looking for the perfect dress for Kitty. It wasn't until we returned to Chinatown that we finally found it: a silk *chipao* of lustrous indigo, embellished with red and black embroidery. It was the ideal Dragon Lady's cos-

**to bargain s.o. into doing s.th.** to try to get the best conditions for a business agreement **landlord** a man who owns and leases property **partial** just a bit, not complete **deduction** amount that can be subtracted **beyond** except for **to catch on** to become popular **2,000 square feet** 180 square meters **charmed** delighted, fascinated **to inhabit** to live in **exposed** open to view, not in the wall **tin** Blech **Lower East Side** area north of Chinatown that was settled by Jews from eastern Europe towards the end of the 19th century until the 1920s **rudimentary** very basic, primitive **to comb s.th.** [koʊm] to search through s.th. carefully **to discard** to throw away s.th. no longer needed **wobbly** not stable, unsteady **foam** Schaumgummi **smattering of** a small number of **to make a dent in s.th.** to reduce the size or amount of s.th. **clutter** untidiness **roughshod** here: unattractive, primitive, crude **to lay out** to spend **chipao** [tʃɪp.ˈoʊ] close-fitting Chinese dress that originated 400 years ago **lustrous** shining softly **to embellish** to make more beautiful by adding decorations **embroidery** decoration made by sewing a decoration or pattern on cloth

tume, with a slit down one side and a superb tightness around the hips and breasts. Because of the outrageous price, I remember having to twist Kitty's arm to let me buy it for her, but it was money well spent as far as I was concerned, and I never tired of seeing her wear it. Whenever it had been in the closet too long, I would invent an excuse for us to go to a decent restaurant just for the pleasure of watching her put it on. Kitty was always sensitive to my dirty thoughts, and once she understood the depth of my passion for that dress, she even took to wearing it around the house on certain nights when we stayed in—quietly slipping it over her naked body as a prelude to seduction.

Chinatown was like a foreign country to me, and each time I walked out into the streets, I was overwhelmed by a sense of dislocation and confusion. This was America, but I could not understand what anyone said, could not penetrate the meanings of the things I saw. Even after I got to know some of the shopkeepers in the neighborhood, our contacts consisted of little more than polite smiles and frantic gestures, a sign language bereft of any real content. I could not gain entrance past the mute surfaces of things, and there were times when this exclusion made me feel as though I were living in a dream world, moving through crowds of spectral people who all wore masks on their faces. Contrary to what I might have thought, I did not mind being an outsider. It was a strangely invigorating experience, and in the long run it seemed to enhance the newness of everything that was happening to me. I did not have the feeling that I had moved to another part of town. I had traveled halfway around the world to get where I was, and it stood to reason that nothing should be familiar to me anymore, not even myself.

Once we had settled into the loft, Kitty found herself a job for the rest of the summer. I tried to talk her out of it, preferring just to give her the money and spare her the trouble of going to work, but Kitty refused. She

**slit** a long narrow cut **superb** wonderful, excellent **tightness** quality of fitting closely to the body **to twist s.o.'s arm** (coll) to persuade s.o. to do s.th. he/she doesn't want to do **depth** here: strength **to take to doing s.th.** to start doing s.th. regularly **prelude** s.th. that serves as an introduction to the main event **seduction** the act of persuading s.o. to have sex **dislocation** being in the wrong place **to penetrate** to succeed in understanding s.th. that's difficult to understand **frantic** extremely hurried **bereft** completely without **to gain entrance** to be able to enter **mute** silent **spectral** like a ghost **invigorating** making you healthier and more active **to enhance** to improve, to intensify **it stood to reason** it was reasonable to assume, it was obvious **to spare s.o. s.th.** to save s.o. from having to experience s.th. difficult or unpleasant

wanted things to be even, she said, and she didn't like the idea of having me carry her along. The whole point was to make the money last, to spend it as slowly as we could. Kitty was no doubt wiser in these matters than I was, and I gave in to her superior logic. She signed up with a temporary secretarial agency, and a scant three days later they found her a job in the McGraw-Hill building on Sixth Avenue with one of the trade magazines. We joked about the title of that magazine too often for me not to remember it, and even now I cannot say it without smiling: *Modern Plastics: The Journal of Total Plastics Involvement*. Kitty worked there from nine to five every day, traveling back and forth on the subway with millions of other commuters in the summer heat. It couldn't have been easy for her, but Kitty was not one to complain about such things. She did her dance exercises at home for two or three hours in the evening, and then she was up again bright and early the next day, rushing out for another stint at the office. While she was gone, I took care of the housework and the shopping, and I always made sure there was dinner for her when she came home. This was my first taste of domestic life, and I fell into it naturally, without any second thoughts. Neither one of us talked about the future, but at a certain point, perhaps two or three months after we started living together, I think we both began to suspect that we were heading toward marriage.

I sent Effing's obituary to the *Times*, but I never got an answer from them, not even a rejection note. Perhaps my letter was lost, or perhaps they thought it had been sent by a crank. The longer piece, which I dutifully submitted to *Art World Monthly* as Effing had requested, was turned down, but I don't think their caution was unjustified. As the editor explained it to me in his letter, no one on the staff had heard of Julian Barber, and unless I could provide them with transparencies of his work, it would be too much of a risk for them to run the article. "I don't

**even** divided equally **scant** just **McGraw-Hill building** McGraw-Hill is one of the largest publishers of scholarly and scientific magazines and books; the building, however, was not completed until 1972. **trade magazine** Fachzeitschrift **Modern Plastics** trade magazine actually published by McGraw-Hill **bright and early** very early **stint** day of work **Times** the New York Times **rejection note** a short letter that an offer has been refused **crank** odd person with strange views **piece** piece of writing **dutifully** done because I felt it was the right behavior **to submit** to give to s.o. for consideration **Art World Monthly** does and did not exist; perhaps Auster meant *Artnews*, to which he himself contributed **to turn down** to refuse an offer, to reject **caution** being careful to avoid risks **editor** Redakteur **transparency** a piece of film, plastic, glass that has a picture on it, slide **to run** here: to put in print

know who you are either, Mr. Fogg," the letter went on, "but it sounds to me as though you've created an elaborate hoax. That doesn't mean your story isn't compelling, but I think you might have better luck publishing it if you dropped the charade and submitted it somewhere as a work of fiction."

I felt that I owed it to Effing to make at least some effort on his behalf. The day after I received this letter from *Art World Monthly*, I went to the library and had a photostat made of Julian Barber's 1917 obituary, which I then mailed off to the editor along with a short cover letter. "Barber was a young and admittedly obscure artist at the time of his disappearance," I wrote, "but he did exist. I trust this obituary from *The New York Sun* will prove that the article I sent you was written in good faith." I received an apology in the mail later that week, but it was no more than a preface to another rejection. "I am willing to concede that there was once an American painter by the name of Julian Barber," the editor wrote, "but that doesn't prove that Thomas Effing and Julian Barber were the same man. And even if they were, without any reproductions of Barber's work, it's impossible for us to judge what kind of painter he was. Given his obscurity, it would be logical to assume that we're not talking about a major talent. If so, then it wouldn't make sense for us to devote space to him in our magazine. In my last letter I said that I felt you had the material for a good novel. I take that back now. What you have is a case in abnormal psychology. It might be interesting in itself, but it has nothing to do with art."

I let it go after that. If I had wanted to, I suppose I could have tracked down a reproduction of one of Barber's paintings somewhere, but the fact was that I preferred not knowing what his work looked like. After listening to Effing for so many months, I had gradually begun to imagine his paintings for myself, and I realized now that I was reluctant to let anything disturb the beautiful phantoms I had created. To have published the article would have meant destroying those images, and it did not seem

**elaborate** complicated, complex **hoax** s.th. that should deceive people, practical joke **compelling** fascinating, extremely interesting **to drop the charade** [ʃəˈreɪd] to stop pretending that s.th. is true when it's obvious it's not true anyway **photostat** a photocopy **obscure** not well known **to trust** here: to hope or believe **The New York Sun** mass circulation quality paper that existed until 1950 **in good faith** without intending to deceive anyone **preface** introduction **to concede** to admit **obscurity** being so unknown **to devote space to s.th.** here: to allow space to be used for s.th. **phantom** [ˈfæn.təm] an image in one's imagination

worth it. No matter how great an artist he might have been, Julian Barber's paintings could never match the ones that Thomas Effing had already given to me. I had dreamed them for myself from his words, and as such they were perfect, infinite, more exact in their representation of the real than reality itself. As long as I did not open my eyes, I could go on imagining them forever.

I spent my days in splendid indolence. Beyond the simple chores around the house, there were no responsibilities to speak of. Seven thousand dollars was a substantial sum back in those days, and I was under no immediate pressure to form any plans. I took up smoking again, I read books, I wandered around the streets of lower Manhattan, I kept a journal. These scribblings led to a number of short essays, little bursts of prose that I would generally read to Kitty as soon as they were finished. Ever since our first meeting, when I had impressed her with my harangue on Cyrano, she had been convinced that I would become a writer, and now that I was sitting down with a pen in my hand every day, it was as though her prophecy had been fulfilled. Of all the writers I had read, Montaigne was the greatest inspiration to me. Like him, I tried to use my own experiences as the scaffolding for what I wrote, and even when the material pushed me into rather far-flung and abstract territory, I did not feel that I was saying anything definitive on these subjects so much as writing a subterranean version of my own life story. I can't remember all the pieces I worked on, but at least several of them come back to me when I strain hard enough: a meditation on money, for example, and another one on clothes; an essay on orphans, and a somewhat longer piece on suicide, which was largely a discussion of Jacques Rigaut, a minor French Dadaist who declared at the age of nineteen that he was giving himself ten

**infinite** having no limits **splendid** wonderful **indolence** (formal) laziness **chore** [tʃɔːr] job, task that has to be done regularly **journal** written record of what you do each day **scribblings** hastily written notes **burst** sudden output **harangue on s.o./s.th.** a long angry speech about s.o./s.th. which criticizes or tries to persuade people **Montaigne** Eyquem de Montaigne (1533-1592), French Rennaisance essayist and philsopher—Auster's description is correct **scaffolding** structure with boards used on the outside of a building or for a wall when making repairs or building a new wall or building **far-flung** far away from where one originally started **meditation on s.th.** a serious and deep discussion about s.th. **Jacques Rigaut** (1899-1929) French writer, dandy, gigolo, and drug addict who committed suicide **Dadaist** a follower of Dadaism, movement in art and literature from 1916 to about 1923 marked by nonsense that completely rejected conventional values

more years to live, and then, when he turned twenty-nine, held good to his word and shot himself on the appointed day. I also remember doing some research on Tesla as part of a project to take on the issue of machines versus the natural world. One day, while poking around in a used bookstore on Fourth Avenue, I stumbled onto a copy of Tesla's autobiography, *My Inventions*, which he had originally published in 1919 in a magazine called *The Electrical Engineer.* I took the little volume home with me and started to read it. Several pages into the text, I came across the same sentence that I had found in my fortune cookie at the Moon Palace almost a year before: "The sun is the past, the earth is the present, the moon is the future." I still had the slip of paper in my wallet, and it jolted me to learn that these words had been written by Tesla, the same man who had been so important to Effing. The synchronicity of these events seemed fraught with significance, but it was difficult for me to grasp precisely how. It was as though I could hear my destiny calling out to me, but each time I tried to listen to it, it turned out to be talking in a language I didn't understand. Had some worker in a Chinese fortune cookie factory been reading Tesla's book? It seemed implausible, and yet even if he had, why was I the person at our table who had chosen the cookie with that particular message in it? I couldn't help feeling unsettled by what had happened. It was a node of impenetrability, and it seemed that nothing but some crackpot solution could account for it: strange conspiracies of matter, precognitive signs, premonitions, a view of the world similar to Charlie Bacon's. I dropped my essay on Tesla and began exploring the question of coincidences, but I never got very far with it. It was too difficult a subject for me to handle, and in the end I put it to the

**to hold good to one's word** to keep one's promise **appointed** decided on, chosen **to take s.th. on** to decide to deal with s.th. **to poke around** (coll) to search around **Fourth Avenue** street in the eastern downtown area of Manhattan that was known as Book Row, where a number of used bookstores were located until the 1980s **to stumble onto s.th.** to discover s.th. unexpectedly **The Electrical Engineer** not correct—it was in *The Electrical Experimenter*—"The sun…is the future" is not in *My Inventions.* **volume** (formal) book **slip** small piece **to jolt s.o.** to shock **synchronicity** a seemingly meaningful coincidence in time of two or more similar or identical events for which no cause and effect can be determined—theory of Carl Jung (1875-1961), Swiss psychiatrist **fraught** [frɔːt] full of **to grasp** to completely understand **unsettled** disturbed **node** Knoten, Knotenpunkt **impenetrability** the quality of being impossible to understand **crackpot** eccentric, crazy **precognitive** knowing s.th. before it will happen **premonition** an early warning of a future event

side, telling myself that I would return to it at some later date. As chance would have it, I never did.

Kitty started her classes at Juillliard in mid-September, and some time toward the end of that first week, I finally heard from Solomon Barber. Almost four months had gone by since Effing's death, and I was no longer expecting him to write. It was not essential in any case, and given the many different responses that seemed possible for a man in his position—shock, resentment, happiness, awe—I could hardly hold it against him for not being in touch. To have spent the first fifty years of your life thinking your father was dead, and then to discover that he had been alive all along, only to learn in that same instant that he was in fact now really dead—I could not even presume to guess how someone would react to a landslide of those proportions. But then Barber's letter showed up in the mail: a gracious and apologetic letter, filled with effusive thanks for all I had done to help his father in the last months of his life. He would welcome the opportunity to talk to me, he said, and if it wasn't asking too much, he wondered if he might not come to New York one weekend that fall. His tone was so polite and tactful, it did not occur to me to say no. As soon as I had finished reading his letter, I wrote back and said that I would be glad to meet him whenever he chose to come.

He flew into New York not long after that—a Friday afternoon in early October, just as the weather was beginning to turn. Once he had checked into his hotel, the Warwick in midtown, he called to tell me that he had arrived, and we arranged to meet in the lobby as soon as I could get there. When I asked him how I would be able to recognize him, he laughed softly into the telephone. "I'll be the biggest person in the room," he said, "you can't miss me. But just in case there's another man my size, I'll be the bald one, the one without a hair on his head."

As I soon discovered, the word "big" hardly did justice to him. Effing's son was immense, monumental in his bulk, a pandemonium of flesh heaped upon flesh. I had never met anyone of his dimensions before, and when I first spotted him sitting on a couch in the hotel lobby, I hesitated to approach him. He was one of those monstrous fat men you

**awe** wonder **to presume** to suppose **landslide** (fig) when a mass of land or rocks falls down a slope; here: a mass of new information **gracious** polite and kind **apologetic** [əˌpɑː.ləˈdʒet.ɪk] saying one is sorry for what one had done wrong **Warwick** Warwick Hotel, an expensive hotel on 54th Street between 5th and 6th Avenue **bald** with no hair on one's head **to do justice to s.th.** to represent s.th. adequately **bulk** big mass **pandemonium** wild confusion **to heap** to pile **to spot** to notice s.th. suddenly that is difficult to see

sometimes pass in a crowd: no matter how hard you struggle to avert your eyes, you can't help gawking at him. He was titanic in his obesity, a person of such bulging, protrusive roundness that you could not look at him without feeling yourself shrink. It was as though his three-dimensionality was more pronounced than that of other men. Not only did he occupy more space than they did, but he seemed to overflow it, to ooze out from the edges of himself and inhabit areas where he was not. Sitting in repose, with his bald behemoth's head jutting from the folds of his massive neck, there was a legendary quality about him, a thing that struck me as both obscene and tragic. It was not possible that the spare and diminutive Effing had fathered such a son: he was a genetic mishap, a renegade seed that had run wild, blossoming beyond all measure. For a moment or two, I almost managed to convince myself that he was a hallucination, but then our eyes met, and his face lit up in a smile. He was wearing a green tweed suit and tan Hush Puppy shoes. The half-spent panatella in his left hand looked no larger than a pin.

"Solomon Barber?" I asked.

"The same," he said. "And you must be Mr. Fogg. I'm honored to meet you, sir."

He had a large and resonant voice that rumbled slightly from the cigar smoke in his lungs. I shook the enormous hand he offered me and sat down beside him on the couch. For several moments neither one of us said anything further. The smile slowly vanished from Barber's face, and his features took on a disturbed, far-off expression. He was studying me intently, but at the same time he seemed lost in thought, as though some important idea had just occurred to him. Then, inexplicably, he closed his eyes and took a deep breath.

**to avert** to look away from s.th. you don't want to see **to gawk** to stare in a stupid way **titanic** gigantic **obesity** quality of being too fat **bulging** sticking out because of being too full **protrusive** sticking outwards **to shrink** to become smaller in size **pronounced** marked, noticeable **to overflow** to flow out of a container, the bank of a river, etc. **to ooze** to flow very slowly **in repose** resting **behemoth** [bɪˈhiːməθ] s.th. or s.o. monstrous **to jut** to stick out farther than the surrounding area **fold** Falte **spare** thin **diminutive** (formal) small or short **mishap** accident, mistake **renegade** (fig.) outlaw, rebel **to blossom** (fig.) to grow well and have flowers **beyond all measure** to a very great size **tan** yellowish-brown **Hush Puppy** (trademark) inexpensive shoes with rubber soles **half-spent** half smoked **panatella** a long slender cigar **resonant** deep and loud **to rumble** to make a long low sound **to vanish** to disappear **features** eyes and mouth **to take on** to begin to have **disturbed** upset, troubled **intently** in a concentrated way, closely

"I once knew someone by the name of Fogg," he said at last. "A long time ago."

"It's not the most common name," I said. "But there are a few of us around."

"This Fogg was a student of mine back in the forties. I had only just started teaching then."

"Do you remember his first name?"

"I remember, yes, but it wasn't a man, it was a young woman. Emily Fogg. She was a freshman in my American history class."

"Do you know where she was from?"

"Chicago. I think it was Chicago."

"My mother's name was Emily, and she came from Chicago. Could there have been two Emily Foggs from the same city at the same college?"

"It's possible, but I don't think it's very likely. The resemblance is too strong. I recognized her the moment you walked into the room."

"One coincidence after another," I said. "The universe seems to be filled with them."

"Yes, it can get quite bewildering at times," said Barber, starting to drift back into his thoughts. Clearly making an effort, he gathered himself together after a few seconds and continued. "I hope you won't be offended by my asking," he said, "but how did you happen to wind up with your mother's maiden name?"

"My father died before I was born, and my mother went back to calling herself Fogg."

"I'm sorry. I didn't mean to pry."

"That's all right. I never knew my father, and my mother has been dead for years."

"Yes, I heard about it not long after it happened. A traffic accident of some kind, I believe. A terrible tragedy. It must have been awful for you."

"She was run over by a bus in Boston. I was just a little boy at the time."

"A terrible tragedy," Barber repeated, closing his eyes once again. "She was a beautiful and intelligent girl, your mother. I remember her well."

**resemblance** similarity in appearance **bewildering** extremely confusing, puzzling **to drift** to wander, to move slowly **gatherered himself together…** here: returned his attention to the matter being dealt with **to offend** to hurt s.o.'s feelings **to wind up with s.th.** to arrive in a situation as a result of s.th. **maiden name** a woman's last name before marriage **to pry** to try to find out the details of s.o.'s private life

Ten months later, when Barber lay dying in a Chicago hospital with a broken back, he told me that he had begun to suspect the truth as early as that first conversation in the hotel lobby. The only reason he didn't come out with it then was that he thought it would frighten me off. He didn't know me yet, and it was impossible for him to predict how I would respond to such sudden, cataclysmic news. He had only to imagine the scene to understand the importance of holding his tongue. A 350 pound stranger invites me to a hotel, shakes my hand, and then, rather than talk about the things I have come to discuss, looks me in the eye and tells me that he is my long-lost father. No matter how strong the temptation, it just wouldn't wash. In all likelihood, I would think he was a madman and refuse to talk to him again. Since there would be plenty of time for us to get to know each other, he didn't want to destroy his chances by provoking a scene at the wrong moment. As with so many of the things in the story I am trying to tell, this turned out to be a mistake. Contrary to what Barber had imagined, there was not much time at all. He trusted in the future to resolve the problem, but then that future never came to pass. That was hardly his fault, but he paid for it nevertheless, as I paid for it along with him. In spite of the results, I don't see how he could have acted any differently. No one could have known what would happen; no one could have guessed the dark and terrible things that lay in store for us.

Even now, I cannot think of Barber without being overwhelmed by pity. If I had never known who my father was, at least I knew that a father had once existed. A child must come from somewhere, after all, and the man who engenders that child is willy-nilly called a father. Barber, on the other hand, knew nothing. He had slept with my mother only once (on a damp, starless night in the spring of 1946), and by the next day she was gone, disappearing from his life for good. He did not know that she had become pregnant, did not know that he had a son, did not know the first thing about what he had accomplished. Given the disaster that followed, it seems only fair that he should have received something for his pains, even if only the knowledge of what he had done. The charwoman had walked in early that morning without knocking, and because she could

**cataclysmic** disastrous **temptation** the desire to do s.th. one knows is bad or wrong **...it just wouldn't wash...** it was unacceptable or unconvincing **in all likelihood** almost certainly **to come to pass** (old fashioned) to happen **to lie in store for s.o.** to be about to happen to s.o. **to engender** to cause to be born **willy-nilly** whether you want to or not **damp** slightly wet **pains** here: suffering for what he went through **charwoman** (BE, old-fashioned) woman who cleans a house

not suppress the shriek that came rushing from her throat, the entire population of the boardinghouse was inside the room before they had a chance to put on their clothes. If it had just been the charwoman, they might have been able to invent a story, perhaps even have wriggled out of it, but as it was, there were too many witnesses against them. A nineteen-year-old freshman in bed with her history professor. There were rules against that kind of thing, and only a dolt would be clumsy enough to get caught, especially in a place like Oldburn, Ohio. He was dismissed, Emily ran back to Chicago, and that was the end of it. His career never rebounded from the setback, but even worse was the torment of losing Emily. It clung to him for the rest of his life, and not a month went by (as he put it to me in the hospital) when he did not relive the cruelty of her rejection, the look of absolute horror on her face when he asked her to marry him. "You've destroyed me," she said, "and I'll be damned if I ever let you see me again." As it turned out, he never did. By the time he managed to track her down thirteen years later, she was already lying in her grave.

From all that I can gather, my mother never spoke to anyone about what had happened. Her parents were both dead, and with Victor traveling around the country with the Cleveland Orchestra, there was nothing that obliged her to mention the scandal. For all intents and purposes, she was just another college dropout, and for a young woman in 1946, that could not have been considered very alarming. The mystery was that even after she learned she was pregnant, she refused to divulge the name of the father. I asked my uncle about it several times during the years we lived together, but he was just as much in the dark as I was. "It was Emily's secret," he said. "I pressed her about it more often than I'd like to remember, but she never even gave me a hint." To give birth to an illegitimate child back in those days was a brave and stubborn thing to do, but apparently my mother never hesitated. Along with everything

**shriek** shrill cry **boardinghouse** a private house where you can pay to eat and sleep **to wriggle out of s.th.** to avoid problems by finding clever excuses **dolt** [doʊlt] stupid person **Oldburn** doesn't exist **to dismiss** to remove s.o. from his/her job **to rebound** here: to return to the way it was before **setback** difficulty that makes a situation worse **torment** mental main, torture **clung to him…** here: remained constantly in his memory **rejection** the refusal of accepting s.o.'s offer **I'll be damned if…** (coll) I most certainly will not… **as it turned out…** as it happened… **obliged her…** forced her…, made her… **for all intents and purposes** for all practical purposes, essentially **to divulge** to give some secret information **to press s.o.** to try very hard to persuade s.o. to do s.th. **stubborn** very determined not to change one's mind

else, I have that to thank her for. A less willful woman would have given me up for adoption—or, even worse, have arranged to have an abortion. It is not a very pleasant thought, but if my mother hadn't been who she was, I might not have made it into the world. If she had done the sensible thing, I would have been dead before I was ever born, a three-month-old fetus lying at the bottom of some garbage can in a back alley.

In spite of his grief, my mother's rejection did not really surprise Barber, and as the years went by, he found it difficult to hold it against her. The wonder was that she had been attracted to him in the first place. He was already twenty-nine in the spring of 1946, and the fact was that Emily was the first woman who had gone to bed with him without being paid for it. Nor had those transactions been anything but few and far between. The risk was simply too great, and once he learned that pleasure could be killed by humiliation, he seldom dared to try. Barber had no illusions about himself. He understood what people saw when they looked at him, and he knew that they were right to feel what they did. Emily had been his one chance, and he had lost her. Hard as it was to accept, he could not help feeling that this was exactly what he deserved.

His body was a dungeon, and he had been condemned to serve out the rest of his days in it, a forgotten prisoner with no recourse to appeals, no hope for a reduced sentence, no chance for a swift and merciful execution. He had reached his full adult height by the time he was fifteen, somewhere between six-two and six-three, and from then on his weight kept mounting. He struggled through his adolescence to keep it below 250, but his late-night binges did not help, nor did diets seem to have any effect. He shrank from mirrors and spent as much time alone as he could. The world was an obstacle course of staring eyes and pointing fingers,

**willful** determined to do what one wants **abortion** Abtreibung **garbage can** (AE) dust bin (BE) **back alley** narrow street behind a building **grief** deep sorrow **transaction** (ironic) business deal, i.e. paid sex **few and far between** not happening very often **humiliation** a situation that makes you feel ashamed of yourself or embarrassed **dungeon** a prison cell under a castle **to serve out** to spend **no recourse to appeals** without the possibility of going to a higher court that may decide differently **sentence** the punishment that a judge gives to a person found guilty **swift** quick **merciful** kind because it ends suffering **six-two** six feet two inches = 1.85 meters **to mount** to increase **binge** short time of excessive drinking and eating **to shrink/shrank/shrank from s.th.** to stay away from s.th. **obstacle course** here: a number of difficulties that must be dealt with to achieve a particular aim

and he was an ambulatory freak show, the balloon boy who waddled through gauntlets of laughter and stopped people dead in their tracks. Books became a refuge for him early on, a place where he could keep himself hidden—not only from others, but from his own thoughts as well. For Barber was never in doubt as to who should be blamed for the way he looked. By entering the words that stood before him on the page, he was able to forget his body, and that, more than anything else, helped to put his self-recriminations in abeyance. Books gave him the chance to float, to suspend his being in his mind, and as long as he paid complete attention to them, he could delude himself into thinking that he had been cut free, that the ropes that held him to his grotesque moorings had been snapped.

He graduated first in his high school class, compiling grades and test scores that astonished everyone in the little town of Shoreham, Long Island. In June of that year he delivered a heartfelt if rambling valedictory in defense of the pacifist movement, the Spanish republic, and a second term for Roosevelt. It was 1936, and the audience in the hot gymnasium clapped loudly for him at the end, even if it did not support his politics. Then, as his unwitting son would do twenty-nine years later, he set off for New York and four years of Columbia College. By the end of that

**ambulatory** (formal) walking **freak show** a deformed person as is shown to curious people in a carneval show to make money **to waddle** to walk slowly from side to side **gauntlet** (fig) a punishment in which the victim is forced to run between two rows of men who hit him as he passes **to stop s.o. dead in his/her tracks** to cause s.o. to suddenly stop walking because of shock or fear **refuge** [ˈref.ju:dʒ] a place that provides protection from danger, cf. the caves in the novel **self-recrimination** the act of blaming yourself for s.th. **in abeyance** (formal) not being used at the moment **to float** to cause to stay on the surface of water, to move slowly about in air **to suspend** to cause to remain hanging **he deluded himself into thinking** he deceived himself so that he thought… **moorings** place, anchor used to keep a ship from moving away **to snap** to break suddenly with a sharp noise **to compile** to get, to acquire **score** (AE) result of a test or exam **heartfelt** strongly felt **rambling** long and not clearly organized **valedictory** [ˌvæl.əˈdɪk.tər.i] (AE) farewell speech delivered by the best student in a graduating class **Spanish republic** at the time the government of the Spanish republic was fighting against the fascists in the Spanish Civil War (1936-1939) **Roosevelt** Franklin Delano Roosevelt (president of the U.S.A. 1933-1945) was re-elected in 1936. He brought about a number of reforms (the New Deal) to pull America out of the Great Depression. **unwitting** not knowing or realizing s.th.

time, he had fixed his weight barrier at 290. Graduate school in history followed, accompanied by a rejection from the army when he tried to enlist. "No fatties allowed," the sergeant said with a contemptuous smirk. Barber therefore joined the ranks of the home front, staying behind with the paraplegics and mental incompetents, the too young and the too old. He spent those years in the history department at Columbia surrounded by women, an anomalous hulk of male flesh brooding in the library stacks. But no one denied that he was good at what he did. His thesis on Bishop Berkeley and the Indians won the American Studies Award for 1944, and afterward he was offered positions in a number of Eastern universities. For reasons he could never quite fathom, he opted for Ohio.

The first year went well enough. He turned out to be a popular teacher, joined the faculty chorus as a baritone, and wrote the first three chapters of a book on Indian captivity narratives. The war in Europe finally ended that spring, and when the two bombs were dropped on Japan in August, he tried to console himself with the thought that it could not happen again. Against all odds, the next year began brilliantly. Between September and January he worked his weight down to three hundred pounds, and for the first time in his life he began to look to the future with some optimism. The spring semester brought Emily Fogg into his freshman history class, a charming, effervescent girl who unexpectedly became smitten with him. It was too good to be true, and

**to fix** to place, to set **graduate school** part of a university where you study to get a master's degree or doctorate after completing four years of study with a lower academic degree **to enlist** to join the army, navy, etc. **comtempuous** [kən'temp.tʃu.əs] showing that you think s.o. doesn't deserve any respect **smirk** a kind of smile that shows you're happy about s.o. else's misfortune **to join the ranks of s.th.** to become a member of s.th. **paraplegic** [ˌper.ə'pli:.dʒɪk] s.o. who cannot use the body below the waist **hulk** large mass **to brood** to keep thinking about s.th. that upsets you **library stacks** the part of a library where the books are stored in shelves **American Studies Award** presumably the one from Columbia Unversity—Numerous other American universities grant this award. **to fathom** to understand s.th., to discover the meaning of s.th. **faculty chorus** a group of the teaching staff that sing together **Indian captivity narratives** stories about people captured by Indians and living with them **two bombs** i.e. the two atom bombs dropped on Japan **to console oneself with s.th.** to try to find comfort for oneself with s.th. after a disappointment or sad event **against all odds** in spite of what seemed impossible **effervescent** very cheerful and lively **to become smitten with s.o.** to fall suddenly in love with s.o.

although he did his best to proceed with caution, it gradually became clear to him that all things were suddenly possible, even the thing he had never dared to imagine before. Then came the boardinghouse, the charwoman bursting into the room, the disaster. The sheer speed of it paralyzed him, left him too stunned to react. When he was called into the president's office later that day, the idea of protesting his dismissal did not even occur to him. He returned to his room, packed his bags, and left without saying good-bye to anyone.

The night train took him to Cleveland, where he checked into a room at the YMCA. His first plan was to throw himself out the window, but after three days of waiting for the right moment, he realized that he lacked the nerve. After that, he made up his mind to give in, to abandon the struggle once and for all. If he did not have the courage to die, he said to himself, then at least he was going to live as a free man. That much was certain. He was no longer going to cringe from himself; he was no longer going to let others determine who he was. For the next four months, he ate his way to the brink of oblivion, gorging himself on cream puffs and doughnuts, on buttery potatoes and gravy-drenched roasts, on pancakes, fried chickens, and hefty bowls of chowder. By the time his rampage was done, he had put on thirty-seven new pounds—but the numbers were no longer important. He had stopped looking at them, and therefore they had ceased to exist.

The larger his body grew, the more deeply he buried himself inside it. Barber's goal was to shut himself off from the world, to make himself invisible in the massiveness of his own flesh. He spent those months in Cleveland learning how to ignore what strangers thought of him, immunizing himself against the pain of being seen. Every morning, he would test himself by walking down Euclid Avenue at rush hour, and on Saturdays and Sundays he made a point of frittering away the afternoon in

**the sheer speed** the very speed **to stun** to surprise, to shock **YMCA** Young Men's Christian Association, an organization that provides cheap hotel rooms, and activities for young people in larger cities **to lack** to not have s.th. you need **to abandon** here: to give up **to cringe from oneself** here: to feel embarrassment about oneself **brink** edge **oblivion** state of not being aware of what's going on around you **to gorge oneself on s.th.** to eat s.th. until you are full **cream puff** a small soft cake with cream in it **drenched** completely covered with a large amount **hefty** large **chowder** thick soup made with clams (Muscheln), potatoes and milk **rampage** angry and destructive behavior **Euclid Avenue** [ˈjuː.klɪd] main shopping street in Cleveland **to fritter away** to waste one's time doing s.th.

Weye Park, exposing himself to as many people as possible, pretending not to hear what the gawkers said, willing their glances to bounce off of him. He was alone now, entirely separate from everyone: a bulbous, egg-shaped monad plodding through the shambles of his consciousness. But the work had paid off, and he no longer feared this isolation. By plunging into the chaos that inhabited him, he had become Solomon Barber at last, a personage, a someone, a self-created world unto himself.

The crowning touch came several years later, when Barber began losing his hair. At first it seemed like a bad pun—a bald man named Barber—but since wigs and toupees were out of the question, he had no choice but to live with it. The beautiful garden on his head gradually withered away. Where thickets of reddish-brown curls had once grown, there was now only blank scalp, a barren expanse of naked skin. He did not like this change in his appearance, but even more disturbing was the fact that it was so thoroughly beyond his control. It pushed him into a passive relation with himself, and that was precisely what he could no longer tolerate. One day, therefore, when the process was about half complete (hair on either side but none on top), he calmly picked up a razor and shaved off what was left. The result of this experiment was far more impressive than he would have thought. He possessed a great stone of a head, Barber found, a mythological head, and as he stood there looking at himself in the mirror, it seemed right to him that the vast globe of his body should now have a moon to go with it. From that day on, he treated this orb with scrupulous care, rubbing creams and oils into it every morning to maintain the proper sheen and smoothness, pampering it with electric massages, making sure that it was always well protected from the elements. He began wearing hats, all sorts of hats, and little by

**Weye Park** doesn't exist—Auster probably means the Wade Oval, a park in Cleveland. **to expose oneself to s.o.** to display or exhibit oneself for others to see **gawker** a person who stares stupidly at s.th./s.o. **bulbous** unpleasantly fat and round **monad** atom, single-celled microorganism, smallest unit in reality (cf. Leibniz) **to plod** to move along slowly with great difficulty **shambles** a place of destruction and disorder **consciousness** Bewusstsein **to plunge into s.th.** to throw oneself into s.th. **personage** important person **world unto himself** (old-fashioned) his own world **crowning touch** an action that makes s.th. complete or perfect **to wither away** to become weak and die, and finally disappear **thicket** a group of bushes and small trees **curl** Locke **barren** (fig) land that is of such poor quality that nothing can grow in it **expanse** very large area **orb** large ball-shaped object like the sun or moon **scrupulous** extreme **sheen** soft shiny appearance **to pamper** to look after s.th. with too much care

little they became the badge of his eccentricity, the ultimate sign of who he was. He was no longer just the obese Solomon Barber, he was the Man Who Wore Hats. It took a certain daring to do what he did, but by then he had learned to take pleasure in cultivating his oddness, acquiring a motley paraphernalia along the way that only enhanced his talent for perplexing others. He wore bowlers and fezes, baseball caps and fedoras, pith helmets and cowboy hats, whatever captured his fancy, without regard to style or convention. By 1957, his collection had grown so large that he once went twenty-three days without wearing the same hat twice.

After the Ohio crucifixion (as he later referred to it), Barber found work at a variety of small, undistinguished colleges in the Midwest and West. What at first he thought would be a temporary exile stretched on for more than twenty years, and by the time it was over the map of his wounds was circumscribed by points in every corner of the heartland: Indiana and Texas, Nebraska and Oklahoma, South Dakota and Kansas, Idaho and Minnesota. He never stayed anywhere for more than two or three years, and while the schools all tended to be alike, the constant movement kept him from being bored. Barber had a great capacity for work, and in the dusty calm of those retreats he rarely did anything else, steadily producing articles and books, attending conferences and delivering lectures, devoting such long hours to his students and courses that he never failed to emerge as the best-liked teacher on campus. His ability as a scholar was not in doubt, but even after the Ohio blemish began to fade, the big schools kept turning him down. Effing had talked about McCarthy, but Barber's only foray into left-wing politics had been as a

**badge** sign, special mark **obese** excessively fat **oddness** quality of being different from what is normal **motley** including things that are different and don't fit together **paraphernalia** assorted articles or equipment **bowler** (BE) round black hat often worn by businessmen in London **feze** [fez] round red hat with a flat top as was worn in Egypt and Turkey **fedora** Filzhut **pith helmet** lightweight hat that was once worn in areas with a hot climate **to capture one's fancy** to suddenly become of interest **crucifixion** (fig) Kreuzigung **undistinguished** not famous or well known **to stretch on** to continue on for a long time **to circumscribe** to draw a line round **heartland** the middle of America **retreat** place one can go to where it's safe and quiet **to devote** to use your time in order to so s.th. **to emerge as** to become known as after a period of time **blemish** (fig) flaw, defect, mark that spoils the appearance of s.th., i.e. the scandal **McCarthy** i.e. Senator Joseph McCarthy **foray** a short attempt at doing s.th.

fellow traveler with the peace movement back at Columbia in the thirties. He had not been blacklisted in any formal sense, but it was nevertheless convenient for his detractors to surround his name with pinkish innuendos, as if that were finally a better excuse for rejecting him. No one would come right out and say it, but the feeling was that Barber would simply not fit in. He was too large, somehow, too rambunctious, too thoroughly unrepentant. Imagine a 350-pound titan lumbering through the Yale quads in a ten-gallon hat. It just wouldn't do. The man had no shame, no sense of decorum. His mere presence would disrupt the order of things, and why court trouble when there were so many candidates to choose from?

Perhaps it was all for the best. By staying on the periphery, Barber could remain who he wanted to be. The small colleges were glad to have him, and because he was not only the fattest professor anyone had ever seen, but also the Man Who Wore Hats, he was mercifully exempt from the petty bickerings and intrigues that plague life in the provinces. Everything about him was so far-flung and extravagant, so flagrantly outside the norm, that no one dared to judge him. He would arrive in late

**fellow traveler** s.o. who sympathizes and supports the ideas of the Communist party without being a member **peace movement** Pacifism and supporting the Communists was fashionable with many intellectuals in America (and Great Britain) as a result of the Depression and the growing threat of fascism in Europe. **to blacklist** to put s.o. on a list of people who should be punished or avoided—During the McCarthy era in the late 1940s and early 1950s many writers and artists in America were blacklisted because of their supposed Communist sympathies, thus making it difficult for them to find work. **in any formal sense** i.e., He was not included in any actual blacklist. **convenient** helpful, suitable for one's needs **detractor** s.o. who criticizes another person to make this other person look bad **pinkish** here: associating with leftist causes **innuendo** [ˌɪn.juˈen.doʊ] an indirect remark that makes s.o. look bad **rambunctious** (AE) full of energy, cheerful in a loud way **unrepentant** not feeling ashamed of one's behavior or beliefs **to lumber** to move in a slow awkward way **Yale** one of the most prestigious and oldest universities—in New Haven, Connecticut **quad** quadrangle—open four-sided area with buildings around it, especially in a university **ten-gallon hat** tall cowboy hat **It just wouldn't do.** It wouldn't be acceptable. **decorum** the correct way to behave **his mere presence** just being there **to court trouble** to do s.th. that causes trouble **exempt from s.th.** freed from the obligation to participate in s.th. **petty** trivial, unimportant **bickering** silly argument, squabbling **far-flung** here: extreme **flagrantly** outrageously, shockingly

summer, all dusty from his days on the road, towing a U-Haul behind his battered, exhaust-belching car. If any students were around, he would promptly hire them to unload his things, paying them an exorbitant price for their work and then treating them all to lunch. That always helped to set the tone. They would see his staggering collection of books, the innumerable hats, and the special writing table that had been built for him in Topeka—the Saint Thomas Aquinas desk, as he called it, with the large semicircle removed from the surface to accommodate his belly. It was hard not to be fascinated: watching him move in that breathless, wheezing way of his, hefting his great bulk slowly from one place to another, continually smoking those long cigars that left ashes all over his clothes. The students made fun of him behind his back, but they were also devoted to him, and for these sons and daughters of farmers and shopkeepers and ministers, he was the closest they would ever come to knowing real brilliance. Inevitably, there were the coeds whose hearts throbbed for him (proving that the mind can indeed be more powerful than the body), but Barber had learned his lesson, and he never fell into that trap again. He secretly loved it when the young girls mooned around him, but he pretended not to understand, acting his part as scholarly curmudgeon, the jovial eunuch who had eaten his way past desire. It was a painful, solitary business, but it gave him a measure of protection, and if that didn't always work, at least he had learned the importance of keeping the shades drawn and the door locked. In all the years of his wanderings, no one ever found fault with him. He overwhelmed them with his singularity, and before his colleagues had a chance to tire of him, he was

**to tow** to pull along with a car or truck **U-Haul** (trademark) an open trailer for transporting goods that can be rented from a company of the same name **battered** old and in bad condition **to belch** to send out a large amount or smoke or air **to set the tone** to establish the general atmosphere **staggering** unbelievable **Topeka** capital of Kansas **Saint Thomas Aquinas** (1225-1274) most important Roman Catholic theologian, who believed knowledge comes from both reason and faith **to accommodate** to allow room for s.th. **to wheeze** to breathe with a whistling sound **to heft** to lift **to be devoted to s.o.** to have great love for s.o. and to be completely loyal **minister** Pfarrer **brilliance** great intelligence **inevitably** it was certain to happen that **coed** ['kou.ed] (AE) female student **to throb** to beat stongly and fast **to moon** to spend one's time constantly thinking about s.o. one loves **scholarly** concerning oneself with serious study **curmudgeon** an old bad-tempered person **solitary** lonely **business** affair **shade** (AE) a covering that call be pulled down over a window **drawn** pulled down **to find fault with s.o.** to find s.th. wrong about a person **singularity** quality of being unique or different

already moving on to the next place, saying his farewells and vanishing into the sunset.

According to what Barber told me, he crossed paths with Uncle Victor once, but in thinking through the details of both their lives, I believe they may have seen each other as many as three times. The first encounter would have been in 1939, at the New York World's Fair. I know for a fact that they both attended, and while the odds are heavily against it, it is certainly possible that they could have been there on the same day. I like to imagine them standing together in front of some exhibit—the Car of the Future, for example, or the Kitchen of Tomorrow—and then bumping into each other by accident and tipping their hats in simultaneous apology, two young men in the prime of life, one fat and the other thin, a phantom comedy team performing their little act for me in the projection room of my skull. Effing was also at the fair, of course, freshly returned from his years in Europe, and there are times when I have placed him in that imaginary scene as well, sitting in an old-fashioned wicker buggy as Pavel Shum pushes him across the grounds. Perhaps Barber and Uncle Victor are standing next to each other when Effing passes by. Perhaps, at just that moment, Effing is shouting some foul-tempered insult at his Russian companion, and Barber and Uncle Victor, stunned by the man's rudeness in public, smile at each other and sadly shake their heads. Little knowing, of course, that this man is the father of one of them and the future grandfather of the nephew of the other. The possibilities for such scenes are limitless, but I generally try to keep them as modest as I can—brief and silent interactions: a smile, a tip of the hat, a mumbled apology. They are more suggestive to me that way, as if by not daring too much, by concentrating on small, ephemeral details, I can trick myself into believing that these things truly happened.

The second encounter would have been in Cleveland, in 1946. This one is perhaps more conjectural than the first, but I distinctly remember walking through Lincoln Park in Chicago with my uncle one day and seeing a gigantic fat man eating a sandwich on the grass. This man reminded Victor of another fat man he had once seen in Cleveland ("back

**to bump into s.o.** to meet s.o. unexpectedly **to tip one's hat** to raise one's hat slightly as a greeting **simultaneous** happening at the same time **in the prime of life** at the time of life when one is strongest and most active **phantom** imaginary **skull** Schädel **wicker buggy** (iron.) wheelchair made of sticks of wood woven together—buggy (AE) = Kinderwagen **foul-tempered** constantly in a bad mood **rudeness** impolite behavior **ephemeral** lasting for only a short time **conjectual** not based on any definite information **distinctly** clearly **Lincoln Park** park on Lake Michigan in Chicago

in the days when I was still with the orchestra"), and although I have no definite proof, I like to think that the man who made such an impression on him was Barber. If nothing else, the dates match up perfectly, since Victor played in Cleveland from 1945 to 1948, and Barber moved to the YMCA in the spring of 1946. As Victor told it, he was eating cheesecake one night in Lansky's Delicatessen, a large, noisy emporium three blocks west of Severence Hall. The orchestra had just finished performing an all-Beethoven program, and he had gone there with three other members of the woodwind section for a late-night snack. From the seat he occupied at the rear of the restaurant, he had an unobstructed view of an obese man sitting alone at a table along the side partition. Unable to turn his eyes away from this enormous, solitary figure, my uncle watched in horror as the man worked his way through two bowls of matzoh ball soup, a platter of stuffed cabbage, a side order of blintzes, three dishes of cole slaw, a basket of bread, and six or seven pickles speared from the bucket of brine. Victor was so awed by this display of gluttony that it stuck with him for the rest of his life, a portrait of pure and unadulterated human unhappiness. "Anyone who eats like that is trying to kill himself," he said to me. "It's the same thing as watching a man starve to death."

The last time they collided was in 1959, during the period when my uncle and I were living in Saint Paul, Minnesota. Barber was doing a stint at Macalester College then, and one evening as he sat in his apartment scanning the used car ads in the back pages of the *Pioneer Press*, his eyes happened to fall on an announcement for clarinet lessons given by one Victor Fogg, "formerly of the Cleveland Orchestra." The name

**delicatessen** a store that sells cooked meat, cheese, and unusual food, often imported—There is no listing for Lansky's Delicatessen in the Yellow Pages of Cleveland between 1943 and 1959. An Auster joke: Meyer *Lansky* (1902-1983) was an American Jewish gangster. **emporium** large store **Severence Hall** the concert hall in Cleveland **woodwind section** Holzbläser **to occupy** here: to sit in **unobstructed** with nothing in the way **partition** thin wall that separates a room into parts **matzoh ball** ['mɑːt.sə] an kind of thin unleavened (ungesäuert) bread made into a ball—This bread is also used for Passover (Passah) in the Jewish religion. **platter** large plate **cabbage** Kohl **side order** food served on a smaller plate with the main meal **blintz** a folded over pancake filled with meat, cheese, fruit, etc. **cole slaw** salad made with uncooked cabbage, onions, sour cream, etc. **brine** water, salt, and other spices used for making pickles **to be awed by s.th.** to feel great wonder and a bit of fear about s.th. **gluttony** the practise of eating too much **unadulterated** complete and total **stint** a fixed period of work **Macalester College** small private college in St. Paul, Minnesota **Pioneer Press** daily paper in St. Paul

ripped through his memory like a lance, and an image of Emily came back to him, more vivid and fragrant than any image he had seen of her in years. She was suddenly inside him again, restored to life by the appearance of her name, and for the rest of that week he could not get her out of his thoughts, wondering what had happened to her, conjuring up the various lives she might have lived, seeing her with a clarity that almost shocked him. The music teacher was probably not related to her, but he didn't see what harm it could do to find out. His first impulse was to call Victor on the phone, but then, after rehashing what he would say, he thought better of it. He didn't want to sound like a fool when he tried to tell his story, stammering incoherences to a bored stranger on the other end of the line. He decided on a letter instead, drafting seven or eight versions before he was satisfied, and then mailed it off in a fit of anguish, regretting what he had done the instant the envelope disappeared into the box. The answer came ten days later, a tight-lipped scribble slanting across a sheet of yellow notepaper. "Sir—" the message read, "Emily Fogg was indeed my sister, but it is my sad duty to inform you that she died in a traffic accident eight months ago. Infinite regrets. Sincerely, Victor Fogg."

When it came right down to it, the letter did not tell him anything he had not known before. Victor had divulged just one fact, and this fact was something Barber had learned for himself long ago: that he would never see Emily again. Death did not change this. It merely confirmed what was already a certainty, reiterated the same loss he had been living with for years. This did not make the letter any less painful to read, but once his crying stopped, he found himself hungering for more information. What had happened to her? Where had she gone and what had she done? Had she been married? Had she left behind any children? Had anyone loved her? Barber wanted facts. He wanted to fill in the blanks and construct a life for her, something tangible to carry around with him: a series of pictures, as it were, a photo album that he could open in his mind and study

**to rip through s.th.** to move violently through s.th. **lance** Lanze **fragrant** having a pleasant smell **to conjure up** here: to imagine **clarity** clearness **to rehash** to rework without any great improvement **to stammer** to speak with many pauses and repetitions because of being nervous **incoherences** thoughts that are badly arranged **to draft** to prepare **in a fit of anguish** in a moment of extreme misery **tight-lipped** not willing to express much **scribble** writing that is difficult to read **slanting** here: moving downwards from left to right **infinite** very many **to reiterate** (formal) to repeat **tangible** able to be felt or touched

at will. He wrote back to Victor the next day. After expressing his heartfelt condolences and sorrow in the first paragraph, he went on to suggest, ever so delicately, how important it would be for him to know the answers to some of these questions. He waited patiently for a response, but two weeks went by without a word. At last, thinking his letter might have been lost, he called up Victor on the telephone. After three or four rings, an operator broke in and told him that the number had been disconnected. This was puzzling, but Barber did not let it daunt him (the man might have been poor, after all, too strapped to pay his phone bill), and so he climbed into his '51 Dodge and drove to Victor's apartment house at 1025 Linwood Avenue. Unable to find Fogg's name among the buzzers on the entranceway, he rang the janitor's bell instead. Several moments later, a small man in a green and yellow sweater shuffled out to the door and told him that Mr. Fogg was gone. "Him and the little boy," the man said, "they just picked up and left about ten days ago." This was a disappointment to Barber, a blow he had not been expecting. But not for one heartbeat did he stop to consider who that little boy was. And even if he had, it would not have made any difference. He would have taken him for the clarinetist's son and left it at that.

Years later, when Barber told me about the letter he had received from Victor, I finally understood why my uncle and I had left Saint Paul so suddenly back in 1959. The whole scene made sense to me now: the flurry of late-night packing, the nonstop drive back to Chicago, the two weeks of living in a hotel and not going to school. Victor could not have known the truth about Barber, but that did not make him any less afraid of what that truth might have been. A father was out there somewhere, and why take a chance on this man who was so curious to learn things about Emily? If worse came to worse, who was to say he wouldn't fight for custody of the boy? It was simple enough to avoid mentioning me when he wrote back after the first letter, but then the second letter came with all those new questions, and Victor realized that he was trapped.

**heartfelt** very strongly felt **condolences** (often plural) expression of sympathy for s.o. in grief **delicately** carefully so as not to hurt anybody's feelings **to daunt s.o.** to discourage s.o. **strapped** having little money at the moment **Dodge** middle priced car that used to be made by Chrysler **Linwood Avenue** a middle-class to upper-class neighborhood in St. Paul **buzzer** i.e. the button at the entrance you push for s.o.'s apartment **to shuffle** to walk very slowly not lifting one's feet **to pick up** to quickly pack up one's belongings **blow** unhappy event, setback **flurry** a sudden quick activity **custody** the legal right to take care of a child

Ignoring the letter would only postpone the problem, for if the stranger was as curious as he seemed to be, he would eventually come looking for us. What would happen then? Victor saw no choice but to abscond, to gather me up in the middle of the night and vanish in a cloud of smoke.

This story was one of the last things Barber told me, and it tore me apart to hear it. I understood what Victor had done, and seeing that devotion spelled out for me, I was caught in a surge of sentiment—aching with regret for my uncle, mourning his death all over again. But at the same time I also felt frustration, bitterness over the years that had been lost. For if Victor had answered Barber's second letter instead of running away, I might have discovered who my father was as far back as 1959. No one was to blame for what happened, but that does not make it any less difficult to accept. It was all a matter of missed connections, bad timing, blundering in the dark. We were always in the right place at the wrong time, the wrong place at the right time, always just missing each other, always just a few inches from figuring the whole thing out. That's what the story boils down to, I think. A series of lost chances. All the pieces were there from the beginning, but no one knew how to put them together.

* * *

None of this came out during that first meeting, of course. Once Barber decided not to talk about his suspicions, the only subject available to us was his father, and we covered that quite thoroughly during the days he spent in town. The first night, he took me to dinner at Gallagher's on Fifty-second Street; the second night, we went out to a restaurant in Chinatown with Kitty; and the third day, Sunday, I joined him for breakfast at his hotel before he caught the plane back to Minnesota. Barber's wit and charm soon made you forget his unfortunate appearance, and the more time I spent with him, the more comfortable I felt. We talked freely almost from the beginning, trading jokes and ideas as we told our stories to each other, and because he was not someone who was afraid of the truth, I was able to talk about his father without censoring

**to postpone** to delay **to abscond** to run away secretly, especially after having done s.th wrong **devotion** strong affection and loyalty **to spell out** to explain in detail and clearly **surge** sudden, large increase in emotion **to mourn** to feel sad about s.o. who has died **to blunder** to move about foolishly **to boil down to s.th.** to be essentially, basically s.th. **Gallagher's** Gallagher's Steak House on 52nd Street near Broadway, an expensive restaurant **to censor** to check s.th. with the purpose of removing anything that is unpleasant

myself, giving the whole story of my months with Effing, the good along with the bad.

As for Barber, he had never known much of anything. His father, they told him, had died out West a few months before he was born, and that seemed plausible enough, since the walls of the house were covered with paintings, and everyone had always said his father was a painter, a specialist in landscapes who had gone on many travels for his art. His last trip was to the deserts of Utah, they said, a godforsaken place if there ever was one, and that was where he had died. But the circumstances of that death were never made clear to him. When he was seven years old, an aunt told him that his father had fallen off a cliff. Three years later, an uncle explained that his father had been captured by Indians, and then, not six months after that, Molly Sharp announced that it had been the work of the devil. She was the cook who fed him all those delicious puddings after school—a florid, red-faced Irishwoman with large gaps between her teeth—and he had never known her to tell a lie. Whatever the cause, his father's death was always given as the reason why his mother had taken to her room. That was how the family referred to his mother's condition, although the fact was that she sometimes left her room, especially on warm summer nights, when she would wander through the corridors of the house, or even walk down to the beach and sit by the water, listening to the small waves wash in from the Sound.

He did not see his mother very often, and even on her good days she had trouble remembering his name. She addressed him as Teddy, or Malcolm, or Rob—always looking him straight in the eye, speaking with the utmost conviction—or else by using strange epithets that made no sense to him: Bally-Ball, Pooh-Bah, and Mr. Jinks. He never tried to correct her when she did this, since the hours spent in his mother's company were too rare to be wasted, and he knew from experience that the slightest

**his father…had died** The theme of the husband abandoning his wife can be found in Auster's novels *The Locked Door, The Leviathan*, as well as Nathaniel Hawthorne's short story *Wakefield*. As a child Auster heard various stories about how his father's father had died. In fact he had been murdered by his grandmother, cf. *Portrait of an Invisible Man* **godforsaken** with nothing interesting or cheerful, desolate **florid** with a rosy colour **gap** an empty space between two objects **to refer to s.th.** to speak about s.th. **Teddy** cf. Theodore (Teddy) Roosevelt (1858-1919), 26th president of the U.S.A. **Malcolm** cf. the man made king of Scotland after Macbeth was defeated and killed in Shakespeare's play **Rob** cf. Rob Roy (1671-1734) Scottish robber **utmost** greatest possible **conviction** an opinion one is sure is correct **epithet** a descriptive word or phrase **Jinks** cf. jinx = bad luck or s.th./s.o. that is the cause of bad luck

quibble could disrupt her mood. The others around the house called him Solly. He did not object to this nickname, for it somehow left his real name intact, as though it were a secret known only to him: Solomon, the wise king of the Hebrews, a man so precise in his judgments that he could threaten to cut a baby in half. Later on, the diminutive was dropped, and he became Sol. The Elizabethan poets taught him that this was an old word for "sun," and not long after that he discovered it was also the French word for "ground." It intrigued him that he could be both the sun and the earth at the same time, and for several years he took it to mean that he alone was able to encompass all the contradictions of the universe.

His mother lived on the fourth floor with a series of companions and helpers, and there were long stretches of time when she did not come down even once. It was a separate realm up there, with the newly built kitchen at one end of the hall and the large, nine-sided room at the other. That was where his father used to paint his pictures, they said, and the windows were built in such a way that when you looked out of them you saw nothing but water. If you stood in front of those windows long enough, he found, pressing your face against the glass, it would begin to feel as though you were floating in the sky. He was not allowed to go up there very often, but from his room on the floor below he could sometimes hear his mother pacing at night (the creak of floorboards under the rug), and every once in a while he was able to distinguish voices: the rumble of conversations, laughter, snatches of songs, bouts of groaning and sobbing. His visits to the fourth floor were dictated by the nurses, and each one laid down a different set of rules. Miss Forrest set aside one hour for him every Thursday; Miss Caxton examined his fingernails before letting him in; Miss Flower championed brisk walks on the beach;

**quibble** small complaint **Solomon** cf. Old Testament: 1 Kings 3:16-27 **diminutive** word formed by adding a suffix like "-ly" to express affection **Elizabethian poet** Auster was probably thinking of "sol" used as the personification of the sun in sonnet 72 from "Idea" by the English poet Michael Drayton (1563-1631)—otherwise "sol" in the sense of sun was not that common in poetry at the time of Elizabeth I. **ground** The French word is related to the English "soil." **to intrigue** to interest s.o. because of being strange and mysterious **to encompass** to include a wide range of things **companion** constant friend **stretch** continuous period **realm** here: world **to pace** to walk slowly back and forth **creak** harsh squeaking noise such as made by wood **rumble** a number of long low sounds **snatch** a short and incomplete part **bout** a moment **to sob** to cry noisily **to lay down** to officially state **Caxton** cf. William Caxton (1442-1491) first English printer **to champion** (iron.) to support a cause **brisk** quick, lively

Miss Buxley served hot chocolate; and Miss Gunderson talked in a voice so low that he couldn't hear what she said. Once, Barber played dress-up with his mother for an entire afternoon, and on another occasion they sailed a toy boat in the pond until it got dark. Those were the visits that stood out most sharply for him, and years later he realized they must have been the happiest hours he spent with her. As far back as he could remember, she had seemed old to him, with her gray hair and unadorned face, the watery blue eyes and downturned mouth, the liver spots on the backs of her hands. There was a slight but constant trembling to her movements, and this probably made her seem even more fragile than she was—nerves flying off in all directions, a woman forever on the verge of collapse. Still, he did not think of her as mad (*unhappy* was the word that usually came to him), and even when she did things that alarmed everyone else, he often felt that she was only pretending. There were a number of crises over the years (a screaming fit when one of the nurses was fired, a suicide attempt, a period of several months when she refused to wear any clothes), and at one point she was sent away to Switzerland for what was called a long rest. Much later, he discovered that Switzerland was merely the polite term for a mental asylum in Hartford, Connecticut.

It was a lugubrious childhood, but not without its pleasures, and far less lonely than it might have been. His mother's parents lived there most of the time, and in spite of his grandmother's penchant for harebrained fads—Fletcherism, Symmes's holes, the books of Charles Fort—she was exceedingly good to him, as was his grandfather, who told him stories about the Civil War and taught him how to hunt for wildflowers. Later on, his Uncle Binkey and Aunt Clara also moved in, and for several years they all lived together in a kind of cantankerous harmony. The crash of 1929

**to play dress-up** to play a children's game in which one dresses as if for a formal occasion or to be s.o. else **unadorned** without make-up **liver spot** dark spots that appear on the skin of older people **fragile** weak **on the verge of** about to **fit** a sudden moment of uncontrollable emotion **mental asylum** [ə'saɪ.ləm] hospital for the mentally ill **Hartford** capital of Connecticut **lugubrious** [lə'guːbri.əs] (formal) sad **harebrained** silly, foolish **fad** s.th. fashionable for a short time **Fletcherism** a method of losing weight by chewing on food for a long time invented by the American Horace Fletcher (1849-1919) **Symmes's hole** the American John C. Symmes (1780-1829) believed there was a hole in the North Pole that went to the center of the earth **Charles Fort** (1874-1932) American writer who collected stories about the bizarre and occult **cantankerous** in a bad mood and complaining all the time **crash of 1929** the collapse of the New York Stock Market on October 29, 1929 that lead to the Great Depression of the 1930s did not destroy them, but certain economies had to be made after that. The Pierce Arrow departed along with the chauffeur, the lease on the New York apartment was allowed to run out, and Barber was not sent to boarding school as everyone had planned. In 1931, a number of works from his father's collection were sold—the Delacroix drawings, the Samuel French Morse painting, and the small Turner that had hung in the downstairs parlor. Still, there was much that remained. Barber was particularly fond of the two Blakelocks in the dining room (a moonlight canvas on the eastern wall and a view of an Indian encampment on the southern), and there were scores of paintings by his father everywhere he turned: the Long Island water scenes, the pictures of the Maine coast, the Hudson River studies, and an entire room of landscapes brought back from an excursion to the Catskills—crumbling farmhouses, otherworldly mountains, enormous fields of light. Barber spent hundreds of hours looking at these works, and in his third year of high school he organized an exhibition that was mounted in the town hall, complete with an essay on his father's work that was distributed free of charge to everyone who came to the opening.

The following year, he spent his nights composing a novel based on his father's disappearance. Barber was just seventeen then, and, trapped in the throes of adolescent tumult, he began to fancy himself an artist, a future genius who would save his soul by pouring his anguish onto paper. He sent me a copy of the manuscript after he returned to Minnesota—not, as he apologetically warned in his cover letter, to show off his juvenile talents (the book had been rejected by twenty-one publishers), but to give me an idea of the extent to which his father's absence had affected his

**Pierce Arrow** luxury car manufactured in the 1920s and 30s **Delacroix** Eugène Delacroix (1798-1863) French artist in the romantic movement **Morse** Samuel (1791-1872) American inventor and painter **Turner** Joseph Turner (1774-1851) foremost English landscape artist in the first half of the 19th century **parlor** (old-fashioned) living room **scores** very many **Hudson River study** study: a small drawing to prepare for a bigger painting—cf. Hudson River School (p. 129), group of landscape artists, 1825-1875, influenced by the romantic movement of Europe **Catskills** Catskill Mountains—group of moutains that are a part of the Appalachians in southeastern New York State **to crumble** to break apart **otherworldly** not connected with the real world **to mount** here: to organize **to be trapped in s.th.** to be in a bad situation one can't escape from **in the throes of** in the middle of **to fancy oneself** to believe oneself to be **anguish** extreme pain or misery **juvenile** youthful, not like an adult

imagination. The book was called *Kepler's Blood*, and it was written in the sensational style of thirties pulp novels. Part Western and part science fiction, the story lurched from one improbability to the next, churning forward with the implacable momentum of a dream. Some of it was dreadful, but for all that I found myself engrossed, and by the time I came to the end, I felt that I had a better idea of who Barber was, that I understood something about what had formed him.

The setting of the book was pushed back by about forty years, with the initial event taking place in the 1870s, but otherwise the story follows almost directly from the few things that Barber had managed to learn about his father. A thirty-five-year-old artist named John Kepler says good-bye to his wife and young son and leaves his Long Island home for a six-month trek through Utah and Arizona, fully expecting, in the words of the seventeen-year-old author, "to discover a land of marvels, a world of wild beauty and ferocious color, a domain of such monumental proportions that even the smallest stone would bear the mark of the infinite." All goes well for the first several months, and then Kepler meets up with an accident similar to the one that had supposedly befallen Julian Barber: he tumbles off a cliff, breaks numerous bones, and lapses into unconsciousness. Upon coming to himself the next morning, he discovers that he cannot move, and because his supplies are inaccessible to him, he resigns himself to starving to death in the wilderness. On the third day, however, just as he is on the point of giving up the ghost, Kepler is rescued by a group of Indians—which echoes another one of the stories that Barber heard as a young boy. The Indians carry the dying man to their settlement, a rock-strewn glen flanked by cliffs on all sides, and in this place rich with the smell of yucca and juniper, they nurse him

**Kepler** Johannes Kepler (1571-1630), German astronomer—considered one of the founders of modern astronomy—confirmed the theory that the earth goes around the sun **thirties pulp novel** poor quality literature printed on cheap paper in the 1930s **to lurch** to suddenly move in different directions **to churn** to move violently **implacable** unwilling to stop or change **engrossed** so interested in s.th. that one doesn't notice anything else **marvel** s.th. that causes wonder **ferocious** here: extremely bright **domain** area, region **to bear the mark** to show the sign **to tumble** to fall quickly **to lapse into unconsciousness** to go into a state of unconsciousness (Bewusstlosigkeit) **inacessible** impossible to obtain **to resign oneself to s.th.** to accept s.th. unpleasant that can't be changed **rock-strewn** with rocks scattered around **glen** an narrow and deep valley especially in Scotland **flanked** here: surrounded **yucca** ['jʌk.ə] small desert plant with pointed leaves **juniper** Wacholder **to nurse** to look after s.o. who is ill

back to health. Thirty or forty people live in this community, roughly an equal number of men, women, and children who walk around with little or nothing on their bodies in the torrid midsummer heat. Scarcely saying a word to him or each other, they watch over him as his strength gradually returns, holding water to his lips and giving him odd-looking foods that he has never tasted before. As his mind begins to clear, Kepler notices that these people do not resemble the Indians from any of the local tribes—the Ute and the Navaho, the Paiute and the Shoshone. They seem more primitive to him, more isolated, more gentle in their manners. On closer inspection, in fact, he concludes that many of them do not have Indian features at all. Some have blue eyes, others have a reddish tint to their hair, and a number of men even have hair on their chests. Rather than accept the evidence, Kepler begins to think that he is still on the brink of death, having imagined his recovery in a delirium of coma and pain. But that does not last long. Little by little, as his condition continues to improve, he is forced to admit that he is alive and that everything around him is real.

"They called themselves the Humans," Barber writes, "the Folk, the Ones Who Came from Far Away. Long ago, according to the legends they told him, their ancestors had lived on the moon. But a great drought took the water from the land, and all the Humans died except for Pog and Ooma, the original Father and Mother. For twenty-nine days and twenty-nine nights, Pog and Ooma walked through the desert, and when they reached the Mountain of Miracles, they climbed to the top and attached themselves to a cloud. The spirit cloud carried them through space for seven years, and at the end of that time they floated down to earth, where they discovered the Forest of First Things and started the world again. Pog and Ooma produced more than two hundred children, and for many years the Humans were happy, building houses among the trees, planting corn, hunting the magic deer, and gathering fish from the water. The Others also lived in the Forest of First Things, and because they were willing to share their secrets, the Humans learned the Vast

**roughly** about **torrid** very hot **Ute** [ju:t] a fierce group of Native Americans in western Colorado and eastern Utah **Navaho** [nɑ:vəˌhoʊ] orginally warlike group of Native Americans originally in northeast Arizona **Paiute** [paɪˈju:t] originally in California and Nevada **Shoshone** [ʃoʊˈʃoʊnɪ] Native Americans originally in California, Utah, Wyoming, Idaho with many subgroups **on closer inspection** examining the matter more closely **tint** a bit of a color **on the brink of** on the verge of **drought** [draʊt] long period of dry weather

Knowledge of the plants and animals, which helped them to feel at home on earth. The Humans returned the Others' kindness with gifts of their own, and for generations the two realms lived in harmony. But then the Wild Men came from the other side of the world, sailing onto the land one morning in their huge wooden boats. For a time the Bearded Ones seemed friendly, but then they marched into the Forest of First Things and cut down many trees. When the Humans and the Others asked them to stop, the Wild Men took out their thunder-and-lightning sticks and killed them. The Humans understood that they were no match for the power of such weapons, but the Others chose to stand and fight. That was the time of the Terrible Farewell. Some of the Humans joined ranks with the Others, a few of the Others joined ranks with the Humans, and then the two families went their separate ways. The Humans left their homes and moved off into the Darkness, traveling through the Forest of First Things until they felt they were beyond the reach of the Wild Men. This happened many times over the course of the years, for no sooner would they build a settlement in some new area of the Forest and begin to feel at home there than the Wild Men would follow. The Bearded Ones always professed friendliness at first, but inevitably they would start cutting down trees and killing the Humans, shouting about their god and their book and their indomitable strength. The Humans therefore continued to wander, always moving westward, always trying to stay ahead of the advancing Wild Men. Eventually, they came to the end of the Forest of First Things and discovered the Flat World, with its interminable winters and brief, hellish summers. From there they moved on to the Land in the Sky, and when time ran out for them there, they descended into the Land of Little Water, a place so parched and desolate that even the Wild Men refused to live there. When the Wild Men appeared, it was only because they were on their way to some other place, and those who happened to stop and build houses were so few and scattered that the Humans could avoid them with little trouble. This was where the Humans had lived since the beginning of the New Time, and it had been going on for so long now that no one could remember what came before."

**to be no match** to not be nearly strong enough **to join ranks with** to become a member of a group **over the course of** during **to profess** to claim s.th. that is very likely false—There are obvious parallels to the colony on Roanoke Island at the end of the 16th century, and what happened later to Native Americans. **indomitable** difficult or impossible to defeat **interminable** seemingly endless **to descend** to move down **parched** dried up **desolate** gloomy, depressing **scattered** spread over a wide area

Their language is incomprehensible to Kepler at first, but within several weeks he has mastered enough to grope his way through a simple conversation. He begins by acquiring nouns, the this and the that of the world around him, and his speech is no more subtle than a child's. *Crenepos* is woman. *Mantoac* are the gods. *Okeepenauk* refers to an edible root, and *tapisco* means stone. With so much to absorb all at once, he is unable to detect any structural coherence to the language. Pronouns do not seem to exist as separate entities, for example, but are a part of a complex system of verb endings that shift according to the age and sex of the speaker. Certain frequently used words have two diametrically opposed meanings—top and bottom, noon and midnight, childhood and old age—and there are many instances in which the meanings of words are altered by the facial expression of the speaker. After two or three months, Kepler's tongue grows more adept at producing the strange sounds of this language, and as the morass of undifferentiated syllables begins to separate into smaller, more definable units of sense, his ear becomes sharper, more finely adjusted to nuance and intonation. Remarkably enough, he begins to think that he can hear traces of English when the Humans speak—not English as he knows it, precisely, but cut-off pieces of it, remnants of English words, a kind of transmogrified English that has somehow slid into the crevices of this other language. A phrase such as Land of Little Water, for example, becomes a single word, Lano-li-wa. Wild Men becomes Wi-me, and Flat World becomes something that resembles the word *flow.* At first, Kepler is inclined to dismiss these parallels as coincidence. Sounds overlap from one language to another, after all, and he is reluctant to let his imagination run away with him. On the other hand, it seems that roughly every seventh or eighth word of the Humans' language follows this same pattern, and when Kepler finally puts his theory to the test by making up words and trying

**to master** to learn a language or skill well **to grope one's way through s.th.** here: to find—with great effort—the right words and expressions **Mantoac** the name given by the Native Americans of the late 16th century on Roanoke Island to spirits **Okeepenauk** the name given by the same Roanoke Island Native Americans to an edible root **to absorb** to read or learn about and understand a large amount of information **coherence** logical connection **entity** a single element **adept at** good at, skilled at **morass** a disordered confusing situation **remnant** what remains of what has been largely used up **to transmogrify** (humorous) to change into s.th. bizarre **crevice** (fig) narrow crack **inclined** tending **to dismiss** to refuse to consider **to overlap** here: to be similar in some respects **to run away with s.o.** to take complete control of s.o. **roughly** approximately

them out on the Humans (words he has not been taught, but which he forms by the same method of paring and decomposition he used to construct the others), he finds himself speaking a number of words that the Humans recognize as their own. Encouraged by his success, Kepler begins to advance certain ideas about the origins of this strange tribe. The legend about the moon notwithstanding, he feels that they must be the product of some prior intermingling of English and Indian blood. "Stranded in the immense forests of the New World," Barber writes, following the thread of Kepler's argument, "perhaps faced with the threat of extinction, a band of early colonists might well have asked admittance into an Indian tribe to ensure their survival against the hostile forces of nature. Perhaps those Indians were the 'Others' who appeared in the legends he had been told, Kepler thought. If so, then perhaps a group of them split off from the main body and headed out West, eventually settling in Utah. Taking this hypothesis one step further, he reasoned that the story of their origins was probably composed after their arrival in Utah, as a way of drawing spiritual comfort from their decision to live in such a barren place. For nowhere in the world, Kepler thought, does the earth look more like the moon than it does here."

It is not until he becomes fluent in their language that Kepler understands why they have saved him. The Humans are diminishing, they explain, and unless they can begin to increase their numbers, the whole nation will disappear into nothingness. Silent Thought, their wise man and leader, who left the tribe the previous winter to live alone in the desert and pray for their deliverance, was told in a dream that a dead man would save them. They would find the body of that man somewhere in the cliffs that surround the settlement, he said, and if they treated it with the proper medicine, the body would come back to life. All these things happened exactly as Silent Thought said they would. Kepler was found, he was resurrected, and now it is up to him to become the father of a new generation. He is the Wild Father who fell from the moon, the Begetter of Human Souls, the Spirit Man who will rescue the Folk from oblivion.

**to pare** to cut the outer layer of s.th. **decomposition** the breaking up of s.th. into separate parts **notwithstanding** (formal) in spite of **prior** previous **to intermingle** to mix together **thread** here: the logical connection between the various parts **extinction** dying out **to ask admittance** (formal) to ask for permission to enter a place **to draw** here: to get **barren** unproductive, bare **to diminish** to become fewer **deliverance** rescue, salvation **to resurrect** to bring back to life **begetter** creator, father **oblivion** state of being completely forgotten

At this point, Barber's writing begins to stumble badly. Without the least pang of conscience, Kepler turns native and decides to stay with the Humans, forever renouncing the thought of returning to his wife and son. Shifting from the precise, intellectual tone of the first thirty pages, Barber indulges himself in a number of long and flowery passages of lascivious sexual fantasies, a teenager's masturbatory lust run wild. The women do not resemble North American Indians so much as Polynesian sex toys, beautiful, bare-breasted maidens who give themselves to Kepler with laughing joyous abandon. It is pure make-believe: a society of prelapsarian innocence populated by noble savages who live in complete harmony with each other and the world. It does not take Kepler long to decide that their way of life is vastly superior to his own. He shucks off the trappings of nineteenth-century civilization and enters the stone age, happily throwing in his lot with the Humans.

The first chapter ends with the birth of Kepler's first Human child, and when the next chapter opens, fifteen years have passed. We are back on Long Island, witnessing the funeral of Kepler's American wife through the eyes of John Kepler, Jr., who is now eighteen years old. Resolving to uncover the mystery of his father's disappearance, the young man sets out the following morning in true epic fashion, determined to devote the remainder of his life to the quest. He travels to Utah, and for the next year and a half he tramps around the wilderness searching for clues. With miraculous good luck (none too plausible as presented by Barber), he finally stumbles upon the Humans' settlement in the rocks. It has never occurred to him that his father could still be alive, but lo and behold, when he is introduced to the bearded chief and savior of this small tribe, which now numbers almost a hundred souls, he

**to stumble** to become unsteady or unsure **pang of conscience** Gewissensbisse **to turn native** to adopt the lifestyle of the natives **to renounce** to give up **to indulge oneself in s.th.** to let yourself do s.th enjoyable that is considered bad **lascivious** [lə'sɪv.i.əs] exciting sexual desire **lust** [lʌst] strong desire for sex **maiden** young unmarried girl **with joyous abandon** in a joyful and careless way without thinking of the consequences **make-believe** fantasy **prelapsarian** (theol) before the fall of Adam and Eve **to shuck off** (AE, coll) to remove, to throw off **trappings** clothing, possessions, etc. that are associated with a particular situation **to throw in one's lot with s.o./s.th.** to join s.o./s.th. and share their fortune **to resolve to do s.th.** to decide firmly to do s.th. **to devote** to use one's time to do s.th. **quest** search **to tramp** to walk long and far **clue** anything that helps to solve a mystery **to stumble upon s.th.** to come across s.th. by chance **lo and behold** Look! **savior** a person who has saved others from danger or harm

recognizes this man as John Kepler. Struck with stupefaction, he blurts out that he is Kepler's long-lost American son, but Kepler, calm and impassive, pretends not to understand him. "I am a spirit man who came here from the moon," he says, "and these people are the only family I have ever had. We will be happy to give you food and lodging for the night, but tomorrow morning you must leave us and continue on your journey." Crushed by this rejection, the son turns his thoughts to revenge, and in the middle of the night he slips from his bed, crawls up to the sleeping Kepler, and plunges a knife into his heart. Before an alarm can be sounded, he runs off into the darkness and disappears.

There is only one witness to the crime, a twelve-year-old boy named Jocomin (Wild Eyes), who is Kepler's favorite son among the Humans. Jocomin chases after the murderer for three days and three nights, but he does not find him. On the morning of the fourth day, he climbs to the top of a mesa for a view of the surrounding countryside and there, just minutes after giving up hope, he encounters none other than Silent Thought, the aged medicine man who left the tribe years before to live as a hermit in the desert. Silent Thought adopts Jocomin and gradually initiates him into the mysteries of his art, training the boy over long and difficult years to acquire the magical powers of the Twelve Transformations. Jocomin is a willing and able student. Not only does he learn how to heal the sick and communicate with the gods, but after seven years of constant work, he finally penetrates the secret of the First Transformation, mastering the forces of his body and mind to such an extent that he can turn himself into a lizard. The other transformations follow in rapid succession: he becomes a swallow, a hawk, a vulture; he becomes a stone and a cactus plant; he becomes a mole, a rabbit, and a grasshopper; he becomes a butterfly and a snake; and then, last of all, conquering the most strenuous of the transformations, he turns himself into a coyote. By now, nine years have passed since Jocomin came to live with Silent Thought. Having taught his adopted son everything he knows, the old man tells Jocomin that the moment has come for him to die. Without uttering another word,

**stupefaction** astonishment **to blurt s.th. out** to say s.th. suddenly without thinking **impassive** not showing any emotion or feeling **crushed** extremely saddened **revenge** Rache **to plunge** to push deeply into s.th. **mesa** a steep flat hill as often found in southwestern U.S.A. **to initiate s.o. into s.th.** to introduce s.o. to special knowledge or skills **to penetrate** to succeed in understanding s.th. **to master** to learn completely or well **lizard** Eidechse **swallow** Schwalbe **hawk** Habicht **vulture** Geier **mole** Maulwurf **strenuous** requiring a great deal of effort

he wraps himself in his ceremonial garments and fasts for three days, at which point his spirit flies out of his body and travels to the moon, the place where the souls of the Humans dwell after death.

Jocomin returns to the settlement and lives there as the chief for a number of years. But hard times have fallen on the Humans, and as drought gives way to pestilence, and pestilence gives way to discord, Jocomin dreams a dream in which he is told that happiness will not return to the tribe until his father's death has been avenged. After consulting with the council of elders the next day, Jocomin leaves the Humans and travels east, going into the world of the Wild Men to search for John Kepler, Jr. He takes on the name of Jack Moon and works his way across the country, eventually coming to New York, where he finds a job with a construction company that specializes in building skyscrapers. He becomes a member of the topmost crew on the Woolworth Building, an architectural marvel that would stand as the tallest structure in the world for close to twenty years. Jack Moon is a superb laborer, undaunted by even the most tremendous heights, and he quickly gains the respect of his co-workers. Outside of his job, however, he keeps to himself and makes no friends. All his spare time is devoted to tracking down his half-brother, and this task takes him nearly two years to accomplish. John Kepler, Jr. has become a prosperous businessman. He lives in a mansion on Pierrepont Street in Brooklyn Heights with his wife and six-year-old son and is driven to work every morning in a long black car. Jack Moon stakes out the house for several weeks, at first intending to kill Kepler

**garments** (formal, often plural) clothing **to fast** to not eat for a while, especially for religious reasons **to dwell** (formal) to live **to give way to s.th.** to be replaced by s.th. **pestilence** a disease that spreads quickly killing many people **discord** quarreling **to avenge** to punish or harm s.o. in return for s.th. bad that this person has done to you **council** a group of people appointed or elected to give advice **elders** the older members of a tribe that are in position of authority **Woolworth Building** completed in 1913 it was at the time the tallest building in the world until 1929 (244 meters) Native Americans traditionally often help to construct skyscrapers as they seem to have no fear of heights. **undaunted** not discouraged even in the face of danger **mansion** large imposing house **Pierrepont Street** [ˈpɪr.pɑːnt] street in Brooklyn Heights with many 19th century houses **Brooklyn Heights** area in Brooklyn on the East River south of the Brooklyn Bridge with many historical buildings from the 19th century; it was and is a fashionable area **to stake out s.th.** to watch a place secretly for a while

pure and simple, but then he decides that he can mete out a more proper vengeance by abducting Kepler's son and carrying him back to the land of the Humans. He does this without being detected, snatching the boy from his nanny one afternoon in broad daylight, and at that point the fourth chapter of Barber's novel comes to an end.

Back in Utah with the boy (who in the meantime has become deeply devoted to him), Jocomin discovers that everything has changed. The Humans have vanished, and their empty houses are devoid of any sign of life. For the next six months he hunts high and low for them, but with no success. At last, realizing that his dream has betrayed him, he accepts the fact that his people are all dead. With grief in his heart, he decides to remain there and look after the boy as his own, all the while hoping for a miracle of regeneration. He renames the boy Numa (New Man) and tries not to lose courage. Seven years go by. He passes on the secrets he learned from Silent Thought to his adopted son, and then, after three more years of steadfast work, he manages to bring about the Thirteenth Transformation. Jocomin turns himself into a woman, a young and fertile woman who seduces the sixteen-year-old adolescent. Twins are born nine months later, a boy and a girl, and from these two children, the Humans will once again populate the land.

The action then shifts back to New York, where we find Kepler, Jr., desperately searching for his lost son. One clue after another leads him nowhere, but then, by pure chance—everything in Barber's book happens by chance—he is put on the trail of Jack Moon, and bit by bit Kepler begins to piece the puzzle together, realizing that his son was taken from him because of what he did to his father. There is no choice for him but to go back to Utah. Kepler is forty years old now, and the hardships of desert hiking are a strain on him, but he doggedly pushes on with his journey, horrified at the thought of returning to the place where he killed his father twenty years before, but knowing that he has no choice, that

**pure and simple** (coll) without any further discussion **to mete out vengeance** (formal) to make s.o. suffer for what this person has done to you **to abduct** to kidnap **to snatch** to seize suddenly **nanny** woman hired to take care of a child **devoted** showing great love and loyalty **devoid of s.th.** completely lacking in s.th. **high and low** everywhere **to betray** here: to not do as expected so that one's trust in s.th. is a disappointment **regeneration** rebirth, renewal **steadfast** determined, constant **fertile** here: able to have children **to be put on the trail of s.o.** to find out where s.o. has been so that you can catch this person **to be a strain on s.o.** to cause s.o. excessive stress or effort **doggedly** [ˈdɑː.gɪdli] determinedly, willfully, obstinately

this is the place where he will find his son. A full moon is poised dramatically in the sky for the last scene. Kepler has come within range of the Humans' settlement and is camped out in the cliffs for the night, holding a rifle in his hands as he watches for signs of activity. On a neighboring outcrop of rocks, not fifty feet away from him, he suddenly sees a coyote standing with its silhouette against the moon. Fearful of everything in this remote and barren territory, Kepler impulsively points his rifle at the animal and pulls the trigger. The coyote is killed with one shot, and Kepler cannot help congratulating himself on the accuracy of his aim. What he does not realize, of course, is that he has just killed his own son. Before he has time to stand up and walk over to the felled animal, three other coyotes leap out at him from the darkness. Unable to defend himself against their attack, he is chewed to pieces within a matter of minutes.

So ends *Kepler's Blood*, Barber's one and only attempt at a work of fiction. Given his age at the time he wrote it, it would be unfair to judge his effort too harshly. For all its shortcomings and excesses, the book is valuable to me as a psychological document, and more than any other piece of evidence, it demonstrates how Barber played out the inner dramas of his early life. He doesn't want to accept the fact that his father is dead (hence Kepler's rescue by the Humans); but if his father is not dead, then there is no excuse for his not having returned to his family (hence the knife that Kepler, Jr., thrusts into his father's heart). But the thought of that murder is too horrible not to inspire revulsion. Whoever thinks such a thought must be punished, and that is precisely what happens to Kepler, Jr., whose fate is worst than any other character's in the book. The whole story is a complex dance of guilt and desire. Desire turns into guilt, and then, because this guilt is intolerable, it becomes a desire to expiate itself, to submit to a cruel and inexorable form of justice. It was no accident, I think, that Barber's later scholarship was devoted to exploring many of the same issues that appeared in *Kepler's Blood*. The lost colonists of Roanoke, the accounts of white men living among Indians, the mythology of the American West—those were subjects that Barber dealt

**poised** not moving, but ready for movement any time **within range** near enough to see or be reached **outcrop** rocks above the surface of the ground **remote** far away from other towns or people **to fell** here: to kill **harshly** severely, strictly **shortcoming** fault **hence** (formal) for this reason **to inspire** to make s.o. feel s.th. **revulsion** a strong and violent reaction because of s.th. unpleasant **to expiate** to accept punishment for s.th. one did wrong with the purpose of showing one will become a better person **to submit to s.th.** here: to accept s.th.willingly **inexorable** that cannot be stopped **scholarship** academic research **to be devoted to s.th.** here: to be concentrated on s.th.

with as a historian, and no matter how scrupulous and professional he was in treating them, there was always a personal motive behind his work, a secret conviction that he was somehow digging into the mysteries of his own life.

In the spring of 1939, Barber had one last opportunity to learn something more about his father, but it did not produce any results. He was a junior at Columbia then, and somewhere around the middle of May, just one week after his hypothetical brush with Uncle Victor at the World's Fair, Aunt Clara called to tell him that his mother had died in her sleep. He took the early morning train out to Long Island, then weathered the sundry ordeals of burying her: the funeral arrangements, the reading of the will, the torturous conversations with lawyers and accountants. He paid off the bills to the home where she had lived for the past six months, signed papers and forms, sobbed intermittently in spite of himself. After the funeral, he returned to the big house to spend the night, realizing that it would probably be the last night he ever spent there. Aunt Clara was the only person left by then, and she was in no condition to sit up talking with him. For the last time that day he patiently went through the ritual of telling her that she was welcome to go on living in the house as long as she liked. Once again, she blessed him for his kindness, standing on tiptoes to kiss his cheek, and once again she returned to the bottle of sherry that she kept hidden in her room. The staff, which had consisted of seven people at the time of Barber's birth, was now down to one—a limping black woman by the name of Haffie Newcombe, who cooked for Aunt Clara and made an occasional stab at housecleaning—and for some years now the place had been collapsing around them. The garden had been left untended since his grandfather's death in 1934, and what had once been a decorous effusion of flowers and lawn was now a tangle of grim, chest-high grass. Inside, cobwebs hung from nearly every ceiling; the chairs could not be touched without emitting stormclouds of dust; mice

**scrupulous** careful and detailed **conviction** strong belief **junior** (AE) a student in the third year in a college or university **brush** brief encounter **to weather** to successfully come through a difficult situation **sundry** (formal) various **ordeal** very difficult situation **tortuous** complicated and confusing **accountant** Buchhalter **intermittently** repeatedly **to bless s.o.** segnen **to limp** to walk with difficulty because of an injured leg **occasional** not happening often **to make a stab at s.th.** to try to do s.th. **untended** not properly taken care of **decorous** in good taste **effusion** here: a seemingly unlimited amount **tangle** confused mass **grim** unpleasant and unattractive **cobweb** Spinnwebe **to emit** to send out

sprinted crazily through the rooms, and Clara, the tipsy, perpetually grinning Clara, did not notice a thing. It had been going on like this for so long now that Barber had ceased to care. He knew that he would never have the courage to live in this house, and once Clara died the same alcoholic death as her husband Binkey, it was all one to him whether the roof caved in or not.

The next morning, he found Aunt Clara sitting in the downstairs parlor. It was not yet time for the first glass of sherry (as a general rule, the bottle was not uncorked until after lunch), and Barber realized that if he was ever going to talk to her, it would have to be now. She was sitting at the deal table in the corner when he entered the room, her tiny sparrow's head bent over a game of solitaire, humming some tuneless, meandering song under her breath. "The Man on the Flying Trapeze," he thought to himself as he approached, and then he came around behind her and put his hand on her shoulder. The body was all bones beneath the woolen shawl.

"Red three on the black four," he said, pointing to the cards on the table.

She clicked her tongue at her own stupidity, merged two piles, and then turned over the card that had been freed. It was a red king. "Thank you, Sol," she said. "I'm not concentrating today. I miss the moves I'm supposed to make and then wind up cheating when I don't have to." She let out a small, tittering laugh and then resumed her humming.

Barber worked himself into the chair opposite Aunt Clara, trying to think of how to begin. He doubted that she had much to tell him, but there was no one else to talk to. For several moments he just sat there and studied her face, examining the intricate network of wrinkles, the white powder caking on her cheeks, the ludicrous red lipstick. He found her

**to sprint** to run very fast for a short distance **tipsy** slightly drunk **perpetually** continuing all the time **to cease to do s.th.** to stop doing s.th. **to cave in** to collapse, to fall inwards **deal table** table made of unfinished wood **sparrow** Spatz **meandering** [mi'æn.dər.ɪŋ] moving along without any particular direction **"The man on the Flying Trapeze..."** Popular song in the 1890s that later was associated with the architect Stanford White (1853-1906) after he was killed by the husband of the woman he was having an affair with. He had sex with her on a swing in his garden. **to click** schnalzen **to merge** to combine, to bring together **move** here: one of many actions in a game **to titter** to laugh nervously in a high voice **to resume s.th.** to start s.th. again after having stopped **to work oneself into s.th.** here: to sit down with a great deal of effort **intricate** complex, with many different parts that fit together **to cake** here: to become dry and harden **ludicrous** absurd

pathetic, poignant. It could not have been easy marrying into this family, he thought, living with his mother's brother for all those years, never having any children. Binkey was a moronic, good-natured philanderer who had married Clara back in the 1880s, less than a week after seeing her perform on the stage of the Galileo Theatre in Providence as the assistant in Maestro Rudolfo's magic act. Barber had always liked listening to the scatterbrained stories she told about her days in vaudeville, and it struck him as odd that the two of them should now be the only people left in the family. The last Barber and the last Wheeler. A girl from the lower classes, as his grandmother had always called her, a dimwitted floozy who had lost her looks more than thirty years ago, and Sir Rotundity himself, the ever-burgeoning boy wonder, born to a madwoman and a ghost. He had never felt more tenderness for Aunt Clara than he did at this moment.

"I'm going back to New York tonight," he said.

"No need to worry about me," she answered, not looking up from the cards. "I'll be just fine here by myself. I'm used to it, you know."

"I'm going back tonight," he repeated, "and then I'm never setting foot in this house again."

Aunt Clara placed a red six on a black seven, scanned the table for a spot to throw off a black queen, sighed with disappointment, and then looked up at Barber. "Oh, Sol," she said. "You don't have to be so dramatic."

"I'm not being dramatic. It's just that this is probably the last time we'll ever see each other."

Aunt Clara still did not understand. "I know it's a sad thing to lose your mother," she said. "But you mustn't take it so hard. It's really a blessing that Elizabeth is gone. Her life was a torment, and now she's finally at peace." Aunt Clara paused for moment, groping for the right word. "You mustn't get silly ideas into your head."

**moronic** not very intelligent **good-natured** kind, not easy to get angry **philanderer** a man who likes to flirt with girls **Providence** capital of Rhode Island, whose capitol was designed by Stanford White **scatterbrained** confused **vaudeville** [ˈvɑːd.vɪl] (AE) music hall entertainment (singing, dancing, jokes) that was popular in the early 20th century **dimwitted** stupid **floozy** a woman with a bad reputation **Sir** (here: ironic) title of nobility given by the British monarch to s.o. who has done s.th. special **rotundity** being fat and round **ever-burgeoning** continuously becoming bigger **tenderness** gentle love **to scan** to examine an area carefully **to throw off** to get rid of **blessing** Segen—s.th that improves one's life **torment** s.th. causing great suffering and pain **to grope for s.th.** to try to find s.th. with great difficulty

"It's not my head, Aunt Clara, it's the house. I don't think I could stand to come here anymore."

"But it's your house now. You own it. Everything in it belongs to you."

"That doesn't mean I have to keep it. I can get rid of it any time I want."

"But Solly...you said yesterday you weren't going to sell the house. You promised."

"I'm not going to sell it. But there's nothing to prevent me from giving it away, is there?"

"It comes to the same thing. Someone else would own it, and then I'd be packed off somewhere to die in a room full of old women."

"Not if I give the house to you. Then you could stay right here."

"Stop talking nonsense. You'll give me a heart attack talking like that."

"It's no trouble transferring the deed. I can call the lawyer today and get things started."

"But Solly..."

"I'll probably take some of the paintings with me, but everything else can stay here with you."

"It's wrong. I don't know why, but it's wrong for you to be talking like this."

"There's just one thing you have to do for me," he said, ignoring her remark. "I want you to make out a proper will, and in the will I want you to leave the house to Hattie Newcombe."

"*Our* Hattie Newcombe?"

"Yes, *our* Hattie Newcombe."

"But Sol, do you think that's right? I mean Hattie...Hattie, you know, Hattie is..."

"Is what, Aunt Clara?"

"A colored woman. Hattie is a colored woman."

"If Hattie doesn't mind, I don't see why it should bother you."

"But what will people say? A colored woman living in Cliff House. You know as well as I do that the only colored people in this town are servants."

"That doesn't change the fact that Hattie is your best friend. As far as I can tell, she's your only friend. And why should we care what people say? There's nothing more important in this world than being good to our friends."

When Aunt Clara realized that her nephew was in earnest, she started to giggle. An entire system of thought had suddenly been demolished by

**deed** Übertragungsurkunde **to giggle** to laugh in a silly way

his words, and it thrilled her to believe that such a thing was possible. "The only bad part is that I have to die before Hattie takes over," she said. "I wish I could live to see it with my own eyes."

"If heaven is all they say it is, then I'm sure you will."

"For the life of me, I'll never understand why you're doing this."

"You don't have to understand. I have my reasons, and there's no need for you to concern yourself with them. I just want to talk over a few things with you first, and then we can consider the matter settled."

"What kind of things?"

"Old things. Things about the past."

"The Galileo Theatre?"

"No, not today. I was thinking about other things."

"Oh." Aunt Clara paused, momentarily confused. "It's just that you always liked to hear me talk about Rudolfo. The way he'd put me in the coffin and saw me in half. It was a good stunt, the best one in the act. Do you remember?"

"Of course I remember. But that's not what I want to talk about now."

"As you wish. There are plenty of old days, after all, especially when you get to be my age."

"I was thinking about my father."

"Ah, your father. Yes, that was a long time ago, too. Indeed it was. Not as long ago as some things, but long enough."

"I know that you and Binkey didn't move into the house until after he disappeared, but I was wondering if you remember anything about the search party that went looking for him."

"Your grandfather made all the arrangements, along with Mr. what's-his-name."

"Mr. Byrne?"

"That's right, Mr. Byrne, the man with the son. They looked for about six months, but they never found anything. Binkey was out there for a while, too, you know. He came back with all sorts of funny stories. He was the one who thought they were killed by Indians."

"He was just guessing, though, wasn't he?"

"Binkey was a great one for telling tall tales. There was never an ounce of truth in anything he said."

"And my mother, did she go out West, too?"

**to thrill** to make s.o. feel excited and happy **for the life of me** as much as I might try **coffin** a long box in which a dead person is buried **an ounce of truth** (ounce = 28 grams) even a little truth

"Your mother? Oh no, Elizabeth was here the whole time. She was hardly…how shall I put it…hardly in any condition to travel."

"Because she was pregnant?"

"Well, that must have been part of it."

"What was the other part?"

"Her mental condition. It wasn't very sound then."

"Was she already crazy?"

"Elizabeth was always what you'd call moody. All sulks one minute, then laughing and singing the next. Even years ago, way back when I first met her. *High-strung* was the word we used for it in those days."

"When did it get worse?"

"After your father didn't come back."

"Did it build up slowly, or did she snap all at once?"

"All at once, Sol. It was a terrible thing to see."

"You saw it?"

"With my own eyes. The whole thing. I'll never forget it."

"When did it happen?"

"The night you…I mean, one night…I don't remember when. One night during the winter."

"What night was that, Aunt Clara?"

"A snowy night. It was cold outside, and there was a big storm. I remember that because the doctor had trouble getting here."

"It was a night in January, wasn't it?"

"It might have been. It often snows in January. But I don't remember which month it was."

"It was January eleventh, wasn't it? The night I was born."

"Oh, Sol, you shouldn't keep asking me about it. It happened so long ago, it doesn't matter anymore."

"It matters to me, Aunt Clara. And you're the only one who can tell me about it. Do you understand? You're the only one left, Aunt Clara."

"You don't have to shout. I can hear you perfectly well, Solomon. There's no need for bullying and rough words."

"I'm not bullying you. I'm just trying to ask the question."

"You know the answer already. It slipped out of my mouth a moment ago, and now I'm sorry it did."

"You shouldn't be sorry. The important thing is to tell the truth. There's nothing more important than that."

**sound** stable, healthy **all sulks** just being in a resentful and angry mood **high-strung** easily upset, nervous **to snap** to become mentally ill **to bully** [ˈbʊl.i] to hurt or persecute a weaker person

"It's just that it was so…so…I don't want you to think I'm making it up. I was in the room with her that night, you see. Molly Sharp and I were both there, waiting for the doctor to come, and Elizabeth was screaming and thrashing so much, I thought the house would fall down."

"What was she screaming?"

"Awful things. Things that make me sick to think about."

"Tell me, Aunt Clara."

"'He's trying to kill me,' she kept shouting. 'He's trying to kill me. We can't let him out.'"

"Meaning me?"

"Yes, the baby. Don't ask me how she knew it was a boy, but that's the way it was. The time was getting close, and the doctor still wasn't there. Molly and I tried to get her to lie down on the bed, to coax her into the proper position, but she wouldn't cooperate. 'Open your legs,' we told her, 'it will ease the pain.' But Elizabeth wouldn't do it. God knows where she found the strength. She kept breaking loose from us and going for the door, shrieking those terrible words over and over again. 'He's trying to kill me. We can't let him out.' We finally wrestled her onto the bed—or I should say that Molly did, with a little help from me—that Molly Sharp was an ox—but once we got her there, she wouldn't open her legs. 'I'm not going to let him out,' she screamed. 'I'll smother him in there first. Monster-boy, monster-boy. I won't let him out until I kill him.' We tried to pry open her legs, but Elizabeth kept squirming away, thrashing and flailing until Molly started slapping her across the face whack, whack, whack, as hard as she could—which angered Elizabeth so much that all she could do after that was scream, just like a baby herself, all red in the face, shrieking and screaming as though to wake the dead."

"Good Lord."

"It was the worst thing I ever saw in my life. That's why I didn't want to tell you."

"Still, I managed to get out, didn't I?"

"You were the biggest, strongest baby anyone had ever seen. More then eleven pounds, the doctor said. A gigantus. I do believe that if you

**to thrash** to move from side to side in an uncontrolled way **to coax** to persuade by pleading **to ease** to relieve, to lessen **to shriek** to scream with a high voice **to wrestle s.o.** to force s.o. into a certain position by holding and pushing this person **to smother** to put s.th. over s.o.'s face so this person can't breathe properly **to pry open** (AE) to force s.th. open **to squirm away** to move one's body away with a twisting movement **whack** the act of hitting s.o./s.th. hard **gigantus** from the Latin *gigas, gigantis*

hadn't been so large, Sol, you never would have made it. You should always remember that. It was your size that brought you into the world."

"And my mother?"

"The doctor finally came—Doctor Bowles it was, the one who died in that car wreck six or seven years ago—and he gave Elizabeth a shot that put her to sleep. She didn't wake up until the next day, and by then she had forgotten everything. I don't just mean the previous night, but everything—her whole life, all the things that had happened to her for the past twenty years. When Molly and I carried you in to let her see her new son, she thought you were her baby brother. It was all so strange, Sol. She had become a little girl again, and she didn't know who she was."

Barber was about to ask her another question, but just then the grandfather clock in the hall began to chime. Aunt Clara cocked her head alertly to one side and listened to the bells, counting out the hours on her fingers. By the time the bells stopped ringing, she had made it up to twelve, and this brought an eager, almost imploring look to her face. "It seems to be noon," she announced. "It wouldn't be polite to keep Hattie waiting."

"Lunchtime already?"

"I'm afraid so," she said, standing up from her chair. "Time to fortify ourselves with a little food."

"You go ahead, Aunt Clara. I'll be along in a minute."

As he watched Aunt Clara walk out of the room, Barber realized that the conversation was suddenly over. Worse than that, he understood that it would never begin again. He had played out his hand at one sitting, and there were no more houses to bribe her with, no more tricks to lure her into talking.

He swept up the cards from the table, shuffled the deck, and then dealt out a hand of solitaire. Solly Tear, he said to himself, punning on his name. He decided to play until he won—and wound up sitting there for

**shot** (AE) an injection **grandfather clock** a tall wooden clock with a long pendulum that stands on the floor **to chime** to strike a bell to indicate the time **to cock** to raise **alertly** attentively, in a way showing that one is ready to notice s.th. **to implore** to ask earnestly, to plead **to fortify oneself** to make oneself stronger **to play out one's hand** (fig) to use up all the good cards one has in a game **to bribe** to offer money to persuade to do s.th., especially s.th. dishonest **to lure s.o. into doing s.th.** to trick s.o. into doing s.th. with the promise of a reward **to sweep up** to pick s.th. up with quick movement **to shuffle** to mix up cards **to deal out** to distribute cards to a player **hand** set of cards that can be given to a player **tear** either in the sense of "Träne" or "Riss" **to pun** ein Wortspiel machen

more than an hour. Lunch was over by then, but that didn't seem very important. For once in his life he wasn't hungry.

We were sitting in the hotel coffee shop having breakfast when Barber recounted this scene to me. It was Sunday morning, and time had nearly run out on us. We drank a last cup of coffee together, and then, as we rode the elevator upstairs to fetch Barber's luggage, he gave me the end of the story. His Aunt Clara had died in 1943, he said. Hattie Newcombe was duly given title to the Cliff House, and for the rest of the decade she lived there in crumbling splendor, reigning over a host of children and grandchildren who inhabited the rooms of the mansion. After she died in 1951, her son-in-law Fred Robinson sold the property to the Cavalcante Development Company, and the old house was promptly torn down. Within eighteen months the estate had been divided into twenty half-acre lots, and on every lot there was a brand-new split-level house, each one identical to the nineteen others.

"If you had known that would happen," I asked, "would you still have given it away?"

"Absolutely," he said, putting a match to his dead cigar and puffing smoke into the air. "I've never had any second thoughts about it. We don't often get the chance to do such extravagant things, and I'm glad I didn't waste the opportunity. When it comes right down to it, giving that house to Hattie Newcombe was probably the smartest thing I've ever done."

We were standing outside in front of the hotel by then, waiting for the doorman to flag down a taxi. When the time came for us to say good-bye, Barber was inexplicably on the verge of tears. I assumed it was a delayed response to the situation, that the weekend had finally been too much for him—but of course I had no idea what he was going through, could not

**to recount** to tell the details of s.th. **duly** in the proper way **to give s.o. title to s.th.** to give s.o. the legal right to own s.th. **to crumble** to break into pieces **splendor** impressive beauty **to reign over** (fig) to rule over **host** a great number **Robinson** cf. Robinson Crusoe **Calvacante** the name of a "soul" in the 6th circle of Dante's (1265-1321) *The Divine Comedy* (It means "singing horse.") **development company** a company that buys land and builds houses on it **estate** large piece of land with a large house on it **acre** 1 acre = 4046.86 square meters **lot** (AE) a piece of land on which a building is built **split-level house** a house that has the floor level of one part about half a storey above or below the floor level of connecting part **to puff** to blow out **second thoughts** doubts **to flag down a taxi** to wave at a taxi driving by as a sign that it should stop and take passengers **delayed** happening later than expected

even begin to imagine the first thing about it. He was saying good-bye to his son, whereas I was merely seeing off a new friend, a man I had met just two days before. The taxi stood there in front of him, its meter ticking out a frantic little rhythm as the doorman loaded his bag into the trunk. Barber made a gesture as if to embrace me in farewell, but then, thinking better of it at the last moment, he awkwardly grabbed hold of my two shoulders and squeezed them tightly.

"You're the first person I've ever told those stories to," he said. "Thank you for being such a good listener. I feel...how shall I put it...I feel there's a bond between us now."

"It's been a memorable weekend," I said.

"Yes, that it's been. A memorable weekend. A weekend to end all weekends."

Barber then maneuvered his enormous bulk into the cab, threw me a thumbs-up sign from the back seat, and disappeared into the traffic. At that moment, I did not think I would ever see him again. We had taken care of our business, explored whatever ground there was for us to explore, and that seemed to be the end of it. Even when the manuscript of *Kepler's Blood* arrived in the mail the following week, I did not feel it was a continuation of what we had started so much as a conclusion, a last little flourish to our encounter. Barber had promised to send it, and I assumed that he was merely being polite. The next day, I wrote back a letter of thanks, reiterating how much I had enjoyed our meeting, and then I lost contact with him, apparently for good.

My Chinatown paradise continued. Kitty danced and studied, and I went on writing and taking walks. There was Columbus Day, there was Thanksgiving, there was Christmas and New Year's Eve. Then, one morning in the middle of January, the telephone rang and it was Barber on the other end of the line. I asked him where he was calling from, and when he said New York, I could hear the excitement and happiness in his voice.

**whereas** but on the other hand **merely** only, simply **to see s.o. off** to say good-bye to s.o. who is departing **meter** Taxameter **frantic** hurried and excited **to embrace s.o.** to put your arms around s.o. as a sign of affection **awkwardly** ineptly, clumsily, not gracefully **bond** s.th. that unites two people **flourish** a decorative detail, a showy gesture **to reiterate** to say again **Columbus Day** national holiday on the second Monday of October **Thanksgiving** national holiday on the fourth Thursday of November

"If you have some free time," I said, "it would be nice to get together again."

"Yes, I'm very much hoping we will. But you don't have to disrupt your schedule for me. I'm planning to be here for a while."

"Your college must give a long break between semesters."

"Actually, I've gone on leave again. I'll be off until next September, and in the meantime I thought I'd have a go at living in New York. I've sublet an apartment on Tenth Street, on the block between Fifth and Sixth Avenues."

"That's a pretty neighborhood. I've walked through it many times."

"Cozy and charming, as the real-estate ads say. I just got in last night, and I'm very pleased with it. You and Kitty will have to come and visit me."

"We'd love to. Just name a day, and we'll be there."

"Capital. I'll ring back later in the week, as soon as I'm settled in. There's a project I want to discuss with you, so be prepared to have your brains picked."

"I'm not sure you'll find much inside them, but you're welcome to whatever there is."

Three or four days later, Kitty and I went to Barber's apartment for dinner, and after that we began to see him often. It was Barber who initiated the friendship, and if he had some ulterior motive in courting us, neither one of us could perceive it. He invited us out to restaurants, to movies and concerts, to accompany him on Sunday drives to the country, and because the man was so filled with good humor and affection, we could not resist him. Wearing those outlandish hats of his wherever he went, cracking jokes left and right, undaunted by the commotion he caused in public places, Barber took us under his wing as though he

**to disrupt** here: to cause an inconvenient change in s.th. **to go on leave** to be absent from work for a period of time with official permission **to have a go at s.th.** to try s.th. **to sublet** [sʌbˈlet] to rent from s.o. who is already renting an apartment **Tenth Street…between 5th and 6th Avenues** There are a number of historical buildings from the 19th century in this street. **cozy** warm and comfortable **real-estate** having to do with a business that buys and sells houses and land **capital** (old-fashioned) excellent **to pick s.o.'s brains** to ask s.o. a lot of questions who is knowledgeable **ulterior** hidden **to court** here: to be very friendly to s.o. because you want s.th. from this person **to perceive** to notice, to observe **outlandish** strange and unusual **to crack a joke** (coll) to tell a joke **undaunted** not discouraged **to take s.o. under your wing** to give s.o. help and protection

meant to adopt us. Since Kitty and I were both orphans, everyone seemed to benefit from the arrangement.

The first night we saw him, Barber told us that Effing's estate had been settled. He had come into a good deal of money, he said, and for once in his life he was not dependent on his job. If things worked out as he hoped they would, he wouldn't have to go back to teaching for another two or three years. "It's my chance to live it up," he said, "and I'm going to make the most of it."

"With all the money that Effing had," I said, "I'd have thought you could retire for good."

"No such luck. There were inheritance taxes, estate taxes, lawyers' fees, expenses I'd never heard of before. That took care of a big chunk. And then there was a lot less to start with than we thought there'd be."

"You mean there weren't millions?"

"Hardly. More like thousands. When all was said and done, Mrs. Hume and I each came out of it with something like forty-six thousand dollars."

"I should have known better," I said. "He talked as though he was the richest man in New York."

"Yes, I do think he was prone to exaggeration. But far be it for me to hold it against him. I've inherited forty-six thousand dollars from someone I never even met. That's more money than I've ever had in my life. It's a tremendous windfall, a boon beyond imagining."

Barber told us that he had been working on a book about Thomas Harriot for the past three years. Ordinarily, he would have expected it to take him two more years to finish it, but now that he no longer had any other obligations, he thought he might be able to complete it by the middle of the summer, just six or seven months away. That brought him to the project he had mentioned to me over the phone. He had only been toying with the idea for a couple of weeks, he said, and he wanted my opinion before he devoted any serious thought to it. It would be some-

**to settle an estate** to legally determine who should get the money and property in the will of s.o. who has died **to live it up** to enjoy oneself and not worry about spending too much money **inheritance tax** a percentage of the estimated value of the property that a person may receive in a will that must be paid to the state **estate tax** a tax that must be paid based on the actual value of the property that a person is to receive in a will **chunk** amount **prone to s.th.** tending to do s.th. **tremendous** great **windfall** a large amount of money that one unexpectedly gets **boon** s.th. very useful or helpful **obligation** legal requirement, duty **to toy with s.th.** to consider, but not very seriously

thing for later, something to tackle once the Harriot book was finished, but if he wound up going ahead with it, then a considerable amount of planning would be required. "I suppose it boils down to one question," he said, "and I don't expect you'll be able to give me an unqualified answer. But under the circumstances, your opinion is the only one I can trust."

We had finished eating dinner at that point, and I remember that the three of us were still sitting around the table, drinking cognac and smoking Cuban cigars that Barber had smuggled back from a recent trip to Canada. We were all slightly drunk, and in the spirit of the moment, even Kitty had accepted one of the huge Churchills that Barber had offered around. It amused me to watch her puffing calmly away at it as she sat there in her *chipao*, but just as funny was the sight of Barber himself, who had dressed up for the occasion by putting on a burgundy smoking jacket and a fez.

"If I'm the only one," I said, "then it must have something to do with your father."

"Yes, that's it, that's it exactly." To punctuate his response, Barber tilted back his head and blew a perfect smoke ring into the air. Kitty and I both looked up at it in admiration, following the O as it quivered past us and slowly lost its form. After a brief pause, Barber lowered his voice a full octave and said: "I've been thinking about the cave."

"Ah, the cave," I repeated. "The enigmatic cave in the desert."

"I can't stop thinking about it. It's like one of those old songs that keeps on playing in your head."

"An old song. An old story. There's no getting rid of it. But how do we know there ever was a cave?"

"That's what I was going to ask you. You were the one who heard the story. What do you say, M. S.? Was he telling the truth or not?"

Before I could gather my wits to answer him, Kitty leaned forward on her elbow, looked to her left at me, looked to her right at Barber, and then

**to tackle s.th.** to deal with s.th. **Harriot** Thomas Harriot (1560-1621) English mathematician and astronomer who wrote a report about his experiences in Virginia in 1685. **to boil down to s.th.** (coll) to be basically, or essentially **unqualified** without any restrictions or conditions **smuggled back** It has been illegal to import most goods into the U.S.A. from Cuba since 1961 because of the communist takeover. **Churchill** large cigar as smoked by Winston Churchill (1874-1965) **burgundy** purplish-red **smoking jacket** a comfortable well-made jacket worn at home **to punctuate** here: to give emphasis to s.th. **to tilt back** to bend back **to quiver** to tremble **enigmatic** puzzling, mysterious **to gather one's wits** to think s.th. through

summed up the whole complicated problem in two sentences. "Of course he was telling the truth," she said. "His facts might not always have been correct, but he was telling the truth."

"A profound answer," said Barber. "No doubt it's the only one that makes sense."

"I'm afraid so," I said. "Even if there wasn't an actual cave, there was the experience of a cave. It all depends on how literally you want to take him."

"In that case," Barber continued, "let me rephrase the question. Given that we can't be sure, to what extent do you think it's worth taking a risk?"

"What kind of risk?" I asked.

"The risk of wasting time," Kitty said.

"I still don't understand."

"He wants to look for the cave," she said to me. "Isn't that right, Sol? You want to go out there and see if you can find it."

"You're very perceptive, my dear," Barber said. "That's precisely what I'm thinking of, and the temptation is very strong. If there's a possibility that the cave exists, I'm willing to do everything I can to track it down."

"There's a possibility," I said. "It might not be a good possibility, but I don't see why that should stop you."

"He can't do it alone," Kitty said. "It would be too dangerous."

"True enough," I said. "No one should climb mountains alone."

"Especially not fat men," Barber said. "But those are details to be worked out later. The important thing is that you think I should do it. Is that right?"

"We could all do it together," Kitty said. "M. S. and I could be your scouts."

"Of course," I said, suddenly imagining myself in a buckskin outfit, scanning the horizon from the top of a palomino horse. "We'll find that bloody cave if it's the last thing we do."

To be perfectly honest, I never took any of this seriously. I thought it was one of those drunken notions that people cook up late at night and then forget about the next morning, and even though we continued to talk about the "expedition" whenever we saw each other, I considered it to be little more than a joke. It was enjoyable to study maps and photo-

**literally** word for word **to rephrase** to express in different words so it's easier to understand **perceptive** quick at understanding **buckskin** soft leather made from deerskin **palomino** a horse of a golden or cream color, with a white mane and tail **notion** idea **to cook up** (coll) to invent

graphs, to discuss itineraries and weather conditions, but playing along with the project was very different from believing in it. Utah was so far away, and the chances of our organizing such a trip were so slim, that even if Barber was in earnest, I failed to see how it would ever happen. This skepticism was reinforced one Sunday afternoon in February when I watched Barber tramp through the woods of Berkshire County. The man was so grossly overweight, so clumsy on his feet, so dismally short-winded that he could not walk for more than ten minutes without having to stop and catch his breath. Red-faced from the exertion, he would plop himself down on the nearest tree stump and sit there for as long as he had been walking, his huge chest heaving desperately, the sweat dribbling down from his tam o' shanter as though his head were a block of melting ice. If the gentle hills of Massachusetts could do that to him, I thought, how was he going to manage the canyons of Utah? No, the expedition was a farce, an odd little exercise in wishful thinking. As long as it remained in the realm of conversation, there was nothing to worry about. But if Barber ever made a real move to go, Kitty and I both understood that we would be duty-bound to talk him out of it.

Given this early resistance of mine, it was ironic that I should have been the one who ultimately went looking for the cave. It was only eight months after we had first discussed the expedition, but so many things had happened by then, so many things had been smashed and destroyed, that my initial feelings no longer mattered. I went because I had no choice. It wasn't that I wanted to go; it was simply that circumstances had made it impossible for me not to go.

Kitty discovered that she was pregnant in late March, and by the beginning of June I had lost her. Our whole life flew apart in a matter of weeks, and when I finally understood that the damage was beyond repair, I felt as if my heart had been cut out of me. Until then, Kitty and I had

**itinerary** [aɪˈtɪn.ə.reri] plan of travel, route **slim** very small **to reinforce** to give added strength **Berkshire County** mountainous area in western Massachusetts **grossly** extremely **clumsy** awkward **dismally** awfully **shortwinded** unable to breathe properly even after a little exercise with the body **exertion** strong physical effort **to plop oneself down on s.th.** to sit on s.th. heavily **stump** bottom part of a tree still in the ground after the tree has been cut down **to heave** to move up and down with strong movements **to dribble** to flow in small drops **tam o' shanter** a Scottish woolen cap with a small wool ball on top **gentle** not steep **farce** here: ridiculous project **realm** area **duty-bound** obliged, having the duty **ultimately** finally, in the end **to smash** to break violently into pieces

lived together in supernatural harmony, and the longer it went on, the less likely it seemed that anything could come between us. Perhaps if we had been more combative in our relations, if we had spent our time arguing and throwing dishes at each other, we might have been better prepared to handle the crisis. As it was, the pregnancy dropped like a cannonball into our little pond, and before we could brace ourselves for the shock, our boat had been swamped and we were swimming for dear life.

It was never a question of not loving each other. Even when our battles were at their most intense and tearful, we never recanted, never denied the facts, never pretended that our feelings had changed. It was just that we no longer spoke the same language. As far as Kitty was concerned, love meant the two of us, and that was all. A child had no part in it, and therefore whatever decision we made should depend exclusively on what we wanted for ourselves. Even though Kitty was the one who was pregnant, the baby was no more than an abstraction for her, a hypothetical instance of future life rather than a life that had already come into being. Until it was born, it did not exist. From my point of view, however, the baby had begun to exist the moment Kitty told me she was carrying it inside her. Even if it was no larger than a thumb, it was a person, an inescapable reality. If we went ahead and arranged for an abortion, I felt it would be the same thing as committing murder.

All the reasons were on Kitty's side. I knew that, and yet it hardly seemed to make a difference. I shut myself up in a stubborn irrationality, more and more shocked by my own vehemence, but powerless to do anything about it. She was too young to be a mother, Kitty would say, and while I recognized this as a legitimate statement, I was never willing to concede the point. Our own mothers were no older than you are now, I would answer, obstinately yoking together two situations that had nothing to do with each other, and then we would suddenly be at the crux of the problem. That was fine for our mothers, Kitty would say, but how could she go on dancing if she had a baby to take care of? To which I would answer, smugly pretending that I knew what I was talking about, that I would take care of the baby. Impossible, she would say, you can't

**supernatural** here: extraordinary **combative** ready to fight or argue **pond** Teich **to brace yourself for s.th.** to prepare yourself for s.th. unpleasant **to be swamped** to be filled with water **for dear life** with the greatest effort so as not to die **to recant** to deny what one had said **vehemence** [ˈviː.ə.mənts] **to concede the point** to admit that the argument is good **obstinately** stubbornly, in a way refusing to change one's mind **to yoke together** to bring together **smugly** in a way showing that one is very satisfied with oneself

deprive an infant of its mother. There's a tremendous responsibility in having a child, and it has to be taken seriously. One day, she said, she very much wanted us to have children, but it wasn't the right moment, she just wasn't ready for it yet. But the moment has come, I would say. Like it or not, we've already made a baby, and now we have to deal with things as they are. At which point, exasperated by my thickheaded arguments, Kitty would inevitably start to cry.

I hated to see those tears come out of her, but not even tears could make me give in. I would look at Kitty and tell myself to let go of it, to put my arms around her and accept what she wanted, but the harder I tried to soften my feelings, the more inflexible I became. I wanted to be a father, and now that the prospect was before me, I couldn't stand the thought of losing it. The baby was my chance to undo the loneliness of my childhood, to be part of a family, to belong to something that was more than just myself, and because I had not been aware of this desire until then, it came rushing out of me in huge, inarticulate bursts of desperation. If my own mother had been sensible, I would shout at Kitty, I never would have been born. And then, not pausing to let her respond: If you kill our baby, you'll be killing me along with it.

Time was against us. We had only a few weeks in which to make a decision, and each day the pressure grew worse. No other subject existed for us, and we talked about it constantly, arguing back and forth into the middle of the night, watching our happiness dissolve in an ocean of words, in exhausted accusations of betrayal. For all the time we spent at it, neither one of us budged from our original position. Kitty was the one who was pregnant, and therefore it was up to me to persuade her, not the other way around. When I finally saw that it was hopeless, I told her to go ahead and do what she had to do. I had no desire to punish her any further. Almost in the same breath, I added that I would also pay for the operation.

The laws were different back then, and the only way a woman could obtain a legal abortion was for a doctor to certify that having the baby

**to deprive s.o. of s.th.** to take s.th. away from s.o. that is needed or wanted **exasperated** very upset **thickheaded** (coll) stupid **inarticulate** not expressed clearly **to dissolve** (fig) to mix with a liquid and become part of it **accusation** saying s.o. is guilty of doing s.th. wrong **betrayal** being disloyal, breaking a promise **to budge** to change one's opinion **in the same breath** at the same moment **legal abortion** Auster is describing the situation *before* 1970. Until the Supreme Court decision of 1973 *Roe v. Wade* the states could decide how to deal with abortion. New York State had already liberalized abortion in 1970: women could have an abortion as long as it was performed by a doctor and within the first 24 days of the pregnancy.

would endanger her life. In New York State, interpretations of the law were broad enough to include "mental endangerment" (meaning the woman might try to kill herself if the baby was born), and therefore a psychiatrist's report was considered just as valid as a physician's. Because Kitty was in perfect physical health, and because I did not want her to have an illegal abortion—my fears about that were immense—she had no choice but to look for a psychiatrist who would be willing to accommodate her. She eventually found one, but his services were not cheap. Coupled with the bills from St. Luke's Hospital for the abortion itself, I wound up spending several thousand dollars to destroy my own child. I was nearly broke again, and when I sat by Kitty's bed in the hospital and saw the drained and agonized look on her face, I could not help feeling that everything was gone, that my whole life had been taken away from me.

We went back to Chinatown together the next morning, but things were never the same again. We had both managed to convince ourselves that we could forget what had happened, but once we tried to return to our old life, we discovered that it was no longer there. After the miserable weeks of talk and quarreling, we both lapsed into silence, as though we were afraid to look at each other now. The abortion had been more difficult than Kitty had thought it would be, and in spite of her conviction that she had done the right thing, she could not help thinking it was wrong. Depressed, battered by what she had been through, she sulked around the loft as though in mourning. I understood that I should be comforting her, but I could not muster the strength to overcome my own hurt. I just sat there and watched her suffer, and at a certain point I realized that I was enjoying it, that I wanted her to pay for what she had done. That was the worst moment of all, I think, and when I finally saw the ugliness and cruelty that were inside me, I turned against myself in horror. I couldn't go on. I couldn't bear to be who I was anymore. Every time I looked at Kitty, I saw nothing but my own contemptible weakness, the monstrous reflection of what I had become.

**valid** legally acceptable **physician** doctor **to accomodate s.o.** to do s.o. a favor, to be willing to help s.o. **coupled with** together with **St. Luke's Hospital** hospital near Columbia University **drained** very tired and without any energy **agonized** suffering great mental pain **to lapse into silence** to stop talking **battered** worn, shattered, tired and shocked **to sulk around** to walk around silent and resentful because s.o. wrong has been done to one **in mourning** feeling grief or sadness because s.o. had died **to muster** to gather, to try to find **contemptible** not worthy of being at all respected

I told her that I needed to go away for a while to sort things out, but that was only because I did not have the courage to tell her the truth. Kitty understood, however. She didn't have to hear the words to know what was going on, and when she saw me packing my things the next morning and getting ready to leave, she begged me to stay with her, she actually went down on her knees and begged me not to go. Her face was all contorted and wet with tears, but I had become a block of wood by then, and nothing could stop me. I put my last thousand dollars on the table and told Kitty to use it while I was gone. Then I walked out the door. I was already sobbing by the time I made it down to the street.

**to sort things out** to deal with a problem and find a solution **to contort** to twist s.th. so that it does not have its normal shape

# 7

Barber put me up in his apartment for the rest of the spring. He refused to let me help him with the rent, but with my funds nearly down to zero again, I found myself a job almost at once. I slept on the couch in the living room, woke up every morning at six-thirty, and spent my days hauling furniture up and down flights of stairs for a friend who ran a small moving business. I hated the work, but it was sufficiently exhausting to numb my thoughts, at least in the beginning. Later on, when my body became more accustomed to the routine, I discovered that I wasn't able to fall asleep without first drinking myself into a stupor. Barber and I would sit up talking until around midnight, and then I would be left alone in the living room, faced with the choice of staring up at the ceiling until dawn or getting drunk. It generally took a full bottle of wine before I was able to shut my eyes.

Barber could not have treated me better, could not have been more thoughtful or sympathetic, but I was in such a sorry state that I hardly noticed he was there. Kitty was the only person who was real for me, and her absence was so tangible, so overpoweringly insistent, that I could think of nothing else. Every night began with the same ache in my body, the same breathless, throbbing need to be touched by her again, and before I could register what was happening, I would feel the assault along the inside of my skin, as though the tissues that held me together were

**to haul** to transport **flight of stairs** a set of stairs between two floors **to numb my thoughts** to make me forget the pain of my thoughts **stupor** state of no longer being able to use one's senses because of alcohol or drugs **tangible** so close to reality, so clear **insistent** so difficult to ignore **throbbing** here: strongly emotional, heartfelt **assault** attack **tissue** [ˈtɪʃ.uː] group of similar cells in the body

about to explode. This was deprivation in its most sudden, most absolute form. Kitty's body was a part of my body, and without it there beside me, I did not feel that I was myself anymore. I felt that I had been mutilated.

After the ache, images would begin to march through my head. I would see Kitty's hands reaching out to touch me, I would see her bare back and shoulders, the curve of her buttocks, her smooth belly bunching together as she sat on the edge of the bed and slipped on her panties. It was impossible to make these pictures go away, and no sooner did one present itself than it would spawn another, reviving the smallest, most intimate details of our life together. I could not remember our happiness without feeling pain, and yet I persisted in seeking out this pain, oblivious to the damage it caused me. Every night, I would tell myself to pick up the phone and call her, and every night I would battle against the temptation, summoning every bit of self-hatred to keep me from doing it. After two weeks of torturing myself in this way, I began to feel that I had been set on fire.

Barber was distressed. He knew that something awful had happened, but neither Kitty nor I would tell him what it was. At first, he took it upon himself to act as go-between, talking to one of us and then going to the other to report on the conversation, but for all his shuttling back and forth, he never made any progress. Whenever he tried to get the secret out of us, we would each give him the same answer: I can't tell you; go ask the other. Barber was never in doubt that Kitty and I were still in love, and our refusal to do anything about it bewildered and frustrated him. Kitty wants you to come back, he would say to me, but she doesn't think you ever will. I can't go back, I would answer. There's nothing I want more, but it can't be done. As a last-ditch strategy, Barber even went so far as to invite each of us out to dinner at the same time (without mentioning that the other would also be there), but his plan was foiled when Kitty caught sight of me entering the restaurant. If she had turned the corner just two seconds later, the scheme might have worked, but as it

**deprivation** s.th. that one needs and is suddenly taken away **to bunch together** to tighten, to become pressed together **to spawn** to produce **to persist** to insist on going on with s.th. in spite of difficulties **oblivious** unaware of, not thinking about **to summon** to gather, to make a great effort to get **distressed** troubled, upset **to take it upon oneself to do s.th.** to decide to do s.th. without having been asked to do so **go-between** a person who takes messages from one person or group to another because they do not want to meet with each other **to shuttle** to travel frequently between two places **to bewilder** to puzzle, to confuse **last-ditch** done as a last desperate attempt **to foil** to stop from happening

was, she was able to avoid the trap, and instead of going in to join us, she simply turned around and went home. When Barber asked her about it the next morning, she told him that she didn't believe in tricks. "It's up to M. S. to make the first move," she said. "I did something that broke his heart, and I wouldn't blame him if he never wants to see me again. He knows I didn't do it on purpose, but that doesn't mean he has to forgive me."

After that, Barber backed off. He stopped carrying messages between us and let things follow their own dismal course. Kitty's last statement to him was typical of the courage and generosity I had always found in her, and for months and even years afterward I could not think of those words without feeling ashamed of myself. If anyone had suffered, it was Kitty, and yet she was the one who shouldered the responsibility for what had happened. If I had possessed even the smallest fraction of her goodness, I would have run to her on the spot, prostrated myself before her, and begged her to forgive me. But I did nothing. The days passed, and still I could not find it in myself to act. Like a wounded animal, I curled up inside my pain and refused to budge. I was still there, perhaps, but I could no longer be counted as present.

Barber had failed in his role as Cupid, but he continued to do everything he could to save me. He tried to get me interested in my writing again, he talked to me about books, he coaxed me into going to movies, to restaurants and bars, to lectures and concerts. None of this did much good, but I was not so far gone that I did not appreciate the effort. He worked hard at it, and inevitably I began to wonder why he was putting himself out for me in this way. He was going great guns on his book about Thomas Harriot, crouching over his typewriter for six or seven hours at a stretch, but the moment I entered the house, he always seemed ready to drop everything, as if my company were more interesting to him than his own work. This puzzled me, for I knew I was dreadful company just then, and I failed to see how anyone could enjoy it. For lack of any other ideas, I began to speculate that he was a homosexual, thinking that

**to back off** to stop taking part in s.th. **dismal** miserable, gloomy **fraction** Bruchzahl **on the spot** immediately **to prostrate oneself** to lie down flat on the ground with the face downwards as a sign of submission **to curl up** to fold one's body together into a curve **counted as present** i.e., fully aware of one's surroundings **Cupid** the Roman god of love **to coax s.o. into s.th.** to patiently try to persuade s.o. to do s.th. he/she doesn't want to do **to put oneself out for s.o.** to make a great effort to help s.o. else **to go great guns** (coll) to do s.th. quickly and successfully **to crouch over** to bend over **at a stretch** without stopping **dreadful company** an awful guest to do s.th. with

perhaps he was too excited by my presence to concentrate on anything else. It was a logical guess, but there was nothing to it—just one more stab in the dark. He made no moves on me, and I could tell from the way he looked at women in the street that all his desires were confined to the opposite sex. What was the answer, then? Perhaps loneliness, I thought, loneliness pure and simple. He had no other friends in New York, and until someone else came along, he was willing to take me as I was.

One night in late June, we went out together for beers at the White Horse Tavern. It was a warm, sticky night, and as we sat at a table in the back room (the same one that Zimmer and I had often sat at in the fall of 1969), Barber's face began oozing rivulets of sweat. Mopping himself with an oversized checkered handkerchief, he drank down his second beer in one or two gulps and then suddenly pounded his fist on the table. "It's too bloody hot in this city," he announced. "You stay away from it for twenty-five years, and you forget what the summers are like."

"Wait until July and August," I said. "You haven't seen anything yet."

"I've seen enough. If I hang around here much longer, I'll have to start walking around in towels. The whole place is like a Turkish bath."

"You could always take a vacation. Lots of people go away during the warm weather. The mountains, the beach, you could go anywhere you want."

"There's only one place I'm interested in. I think you know where it is."

"But what about your book? I thought you wanted to finish it first."

"I did. But now I've changed my mind."

"It can't just be the weather."

"No, I need a little break. For that matter, so do you."

"I'm fine, Sol, really I am."

"A change of scenery would do you good. There's nothing to hold you here anymore, and the longer you stay, the worse off you are. I'm not blind, you know."

"I'll get over it. Things will start turning around soon."

"I wouldn't bet on it. You're stuck, M. S., you're eating yourself alive. The only cure is to get away from it."

**stab in the dark** a guess without any idea what the result might be **to make a move on s.o.** here: to show any sexual interest **to be confined to s.th.** to be limited to s.th. **sticky** warm and humid **to ooze** to cause to flow slowly **rivulet** a very small stream **to mop** to wipe or clean as if with a mop **checkered** kariert **gulp** act of swallowing a large amount quickly **to hang around** to stay somewhere with no purpose **cure** means of restoring one's health

"I can't just quit my job."

"Why not?"

"I need the money, for one thing. For another, Stan depends on me. It wouldn't be fair to walk out on him like that."

"Give him a couple of weeks' notice. He'll find someone else."

"Just like that?"

"Yes, just like that. I know you're a pretty strong young fellow, but somehow I don't see you working as a furniture mover for the rest of your life."

"I wasn't planning to make a career of it. It's what you'd call a temporary situation."

"Well, I'm offering you another temporary situation. You can be my assistant, my trailblazer, my right-hand man. The deal comes with room and board, free supplies, and any petty cash you feel you might need. If these terms don't satisfy you, I'm willing to negotiate. What do you say to that?"

"It's summer. If you think New York is bad, the desert is even worse. Our bodies would fry if we went out there now."

"It's not the Sahara. We'll buy ourselves an air-conditioned car and go in comfort."

"Go where? We don't have the faintest idea of where to begin."

"Of course we do. I'm not saying that we'll find what we're looking for, but we know the general area. Southeastern Utah, beginning with the town of Bluff. It can't do us any harm to try."

We went on with the discussion for several more hours, and little by little Barber wore down my resistance. For every argument I gave him, he came back with a counterargument; for each negative I proposed, he proposed two or three positives. I don't know how he managed to do it, but in the end he made me feel almost happy that I had surrendered. Perhaps it was the sheer hopelessness of the venture that clinched it for me. If I had thought there was the slightest possibility of finding the cave, I doubt that I would have gone, but the idea of a useless quest, of setting out on a journey that was doomed to failure, appealed to my sense of things at that

**temporary situation** (euph) a job for a short time **trailblazer** here: first person to go through an undiscovered area and is then followed by others **room and board** a place to live and food **petty cash** small amount of money **terms** conditions **to negotiate** to discuss terms for an agreement **faintest** slightest **to wear down s.o.'s resistance** to cause s.o.'s resistance to become weaker **sheer** complete **venture** project with risks **to clinch it for s.o.** to finally make s.o. decide to do s.th. **to be doomed to failure** to be certain not to be successful

moment. We would search, but we would not find. Only the going itself would matter, and in the end we would be left with nothing but the futility of our own ambitions. This was a metaphor I could live with, the leap into emptiness I had always dreamed of. I shook hands with Barber on it and told him to count me in.

We perfected our plan over the next two weeks. Instead of traveling straight through, we decided to begin with a sentimental detour, stopping off in Chicago first and then heading north to Minnesota before we picked up the road to Utah. It would take us a thousand miles out of our way, but neither one of us considered that a problem. We were in no rush to get there, and when I told Barber that I wanted to visit the cemetery where my mother and uncle were buried, he did not raise any objections. Since we were going to be in Chicago, he said, why not veer a bit further off course and go on up to Northfield for a couple of days? He had some odds and ends of business to take care of, and in the meantime he could show me the collection of his father's paintings and drawings in the attic of his house. I didn't bother to mention to him that I had avoided those paintings in the past. In the spirit of the expedition we were about to embark on, I said yes to everything.

Three days later, Barber bought an air-conditioned car from a man in Queens. It was a red 1965 Pontiac Bonneville with only 47,000 miles on the odometer. He fell in love with its flashiness and speed and didn't haggle much over the price. "What do you think?" he kept saying to me as we looked it over. "Is this a chariot or what?" We had to replace the muffler and the tires, the carburetor needed adjusting, and the rear end was dented, but Barber's mind was made up, and I didn't see any point in

**futility** uselessness of s.th. because there is no chance of success **to count s.b. in** to include s.b. **detour** a route that is longer than the usual route **to raise an objection** to state that one disapproves of s.th. **to veer off course** to change directions from the planned route **Northfield** small town in southeast Minnesota **odds and ends** various unimportant matters **attic** the rooms under the roof **spirit** state of mind, the way one feels **to embark on s.th.** to begin a project **Queens** borough of New York City to the east of Manhattan **Pontiac Bonneville** large medium priced car made by General Motors **odometer** instrument that shows how many miles a car has been driven **flashiness** impressiveness that many would consider cheap **to haggle** to argue with s.o. to get the lowest price **chariot** wagon with two wheels pulled by one horse as used by the Romans and Greeks **muffler** Auspufftopf **carburetor** Vergaser **dented** damaged so there is a hollow area on the surface

trying to talk him out of it. For all its flaws, the car was a snappy little piece of machinery, as he put it, and I supposed it would serve as well as any other. We took it out for a trial spin, and as we crisscrossed the streets of Flushing, Barber lectured enthusiastically on Pontiac's rebellion against Lord Amherst. We shouldn't forget, he said, that this car was named after a great Indian chief. It will add another dimension to our trip. By driving this car out West, we'll be paying homage to the dead, commemorating the valiant warriors who rose up in defense of the land we stole from them.

We bought hiking books, sunglasses, backpacks, canteens, binoculars, sleeping bags, and a tent. After putting in another week and a half at my friend Stan's moving business, I was able to retire with a good conscience when a cousin of his showed up in town for the summer and agreed to take my place. Barber and I went out for a last dinner in New York (corned beef sandwiches at the Stage Deli) and returned to the apartment by nine o'clock, planning to turn in at a reasonable hour so we could get an early start the next morning. It was early July, 1971. I was twenty-four years old, and I felt that my life had come to a dead end. As I lay on the couch in the darkness, I heard Barber tiptoe into the kitchen and call Kitty on the phone. I couldn't make out everything he said, but apparently he was telling her about the trip. "Nothing is sure," he whispered, "but it might do him some good. Maybe he'll be ready to see you again by the time we get back." It wasn't hard for me to guess who he was referring to. After Barber returned to his room, I turned on the light and uncorked another bottle of wine, but alcohol seemed to have lost its power over me. When Barber came in to wake me at six o'clock the next morning, I don't think I had been asleep for more than twenty or thirty minutes.

**for all its flaws** in spite of its defects **snappy** smart, attractive **trail spin** (coll) a short drive to test a car **to crisscross** to drive in many different directions that cross each other **Flushing** lower middle-class area of Queens **to lecture** to give a talk about a particular subject **Pontiac's rebellion** (1720?-1769) chief of the Ottawa Indians, who led a rebellion against the British (1763-1766) **Lord Amherst** (1717-97) Jeffrey, 1st Baron Amherst. British general who defeated the French in Canada (1758-60)—governor general of British North America (1761-63) **to pay homage to s.o./s.th.** to show respect and honor for s.o./s.th. **to commemorate** to honor the memory of s.o./s.th. **valiant** brave, courageous **canteen** small container for carrying s.th. to drink **Stage Deli** delicatessen in Manhattan on 7th Avenue near 53rd Street **to turn in** to go to bed **to come to a dead end** to arrive at a point where no further progress is possible **to refer to** to speak about

We were on the road by quarter to seven. Barber drove, and I sat in the shotgun seat, drinking from a thermos of black coffee. For the first two hours, I was only half conscious, but once we hit the open countryside of Pennsylvania, I slowly emerged from my torpor. From then until we reached Chicago, we talked without interruption, taking turns at the wheel as we passed through western Pennsylvania, Ohio, and Indiana. If most of what we said escapes me now, it was probably because we kept shifting from one subject to another, in much the same way that the landscape kept disappearing behind us. We talked for a while about cars, I remember, and how America had been changed by them; we talked about Effing; we talked about Tesla's tower on Long Island. I can still hear Barber clearing his throat, as we left Ohio and crossed into Indiana, getting ready to deliver a lengthy speech on the spirit of Tecumseh, but no matter how hard I try, I cannot bring back a single sentence of it. Later on, when the sun began to go down, we spent more than an hour enumerating our preferences in every area of life we could think of: our favorite novels, our favorite foods, our favorite ballplayers. We must have come up with more than a hundred categories, an entire index of personal tastes. I said Roberto Clemente, Barber said Al Kaline. I said *Don Quixote*, Barber said *Tom Jones*. We both preferred Schubert over Schumann, but Barber had a weakness for Brahms, which I did not. On the other hand, he found Couperin dull, whereas I could never get enough of *Les Barricades Mystérieuses*. He said Tolstoy, I said Dostoyevsky. He said *Bleak House*, I said *Our Mutual Friend*. Of all the fruits known to man, we both agreed that lemons smelled the best.

**shotgun seat** seat in the middle next to the driver where a shotgun (Schrotflinte) is often fastened to the dashboard (Armaturenbrett) **half conscious** not completely aware of one's surroundings **to hit** (coll) to arrive at **to emerge from s.th.** to come out of s.th. **torpor** state of inactivity **to escape s.o.** to not be able to remember **spirit** mind, way of thinking **to enumerate** to list **index** a systematic or alphabetic list of subjects **Roberto Clemente** (1934-1872) Puerto Rican baseball player **Al Kaline** (1934-) baseball player active in the 1950s, 1960s and early 1970s **Don Quixote** [kɪ'hoʊ.ti] novel about a man crazed in the mind who believes he is a knight and must redress all the wrongs in the world—by the Spanish writer Miguel de Cervantes (1547-1616) **Tom Jones** picaresque novel about a foundling by the English writer Henry Fielding (1707-1754) **Couperin** (1668-1733) Francois Couperin, French composer **dull** boring **Les Barricades Mystérieuses** harpsichord (Cembalo) piece by Couperin **Tolstoy** (1828-1910) Lev Tolstoy, major Russian novelist **Dostoyevsky** (1821-1881) Fyodor Dostoyevsky, Russian novelist—has had a great influence on modern literature. **Bleak House** novel about an illegitimate girl by the English writer Charles Dickens (1812-1870) **Our Mutual Friend** another novel by Charles Dickens

We slept in a motel on the outskirts of Chicago. After eating breakfast the next morning, we drove around at random until we found a flower shop, where I bought identical bouquets for my mother and Uncle Victor. Barber was strangely subdued in the car, but I attributed that to exhaustion from the previous day's drive and did not dwell on it. We had some trouble finding Westlawn Cemetery (a couple of wrong turns, a long detour that took us in the opposite direction), and by the time we drove through the gate, it was close to eleven o'clock. It took us another twenty minutes to find the graves, and when we stepped out of the car into the broiling summer heat, I remember that neither one of us said a word. A crew of four men had just finished digging a grave for someone several plots down from my mother and uncle, and we stood by the car in silence for a minute or two, watching the gravediggers as they loaded their shovels into the back of their green pickup truck and drove off. Their presence was an intrusion, and both Barber and I tacitly understood that we had to wait until they disappeared, that we couldn't do what we had come for unless we were alone.

After that, things happened very fast. We walked across the road, and when I saw the names of my mother and uncle on the small stone markers, I suddenly found myself fighting back tears. I had not been expecting such a violent response, but once it hit me that the two of them were actually lying there under my feet, I couldn't stop myself from shaking. Several minutes went by, I think, but that is only a guess. I can't see much more than a blur, a few isolated gestures in the fog of recollection. I remember putting a stone on top of each marker, and every now and then I manage to catch a glimpse of myself on all fours, frantically plucking out weeds from the tangled grass that covered the graves. Whenever I look for Barber, however, I am unable to bring him into the picture. This suggests to me that I was too distraught to notice him, that for the interval of those few minutes I had forgotten he was there. The

**outskirts** here: area just outside the border of a city **at random** without following any prearranged plan **bouquet** [boʊˈkeɪ] **subdued** passive, quiet **to attribute s.th. to s.th.** to say that a situation is caused by s.th. **to dwell on s.th.** to speak about s.th. for a long time **detour** a longer route than the usual one **broiling** extremely hot **plot** a piece of land in a cemetary that is reserved for a particular family **intrusion** an unwelcome visit **tacitly** understood without being directly said **stone marker** small gravestone **blur** s.th. one cannot see clearly **...stone on top...** It is a Jewish custom to place a stone on a gravestone in remembrance of the dead person. **frantically** hurriedly and nervously **weed** wild flower growing where it is not wanted **tangled** twisted together in an untidy mass **distraught** so upset and worried that one cannot think clearly

story had begun without me, so to speak, and by the time I entered it myself, the action was already far advanced, the whole thing was flying out of control.

Somehow or other, I was standing next to Barber again. The two of us were side by side in front of my mother's grave, and when I turned my head in his direction, I saw that tears were pouring down his cheeks. Barber was sobbing, and when I heard the choked and miserable sounds that were coming out of his mouth, I realized that they had been going on for some time. I believe I said something at that point. What's the matter, or why are you crying, I can't recall the exact words. But Barber didn't hear me in any case. He went on staring at my mother's grave, weeping under the immense blue sky as if he were the only man left in the universe.

"Emily..." he finally said. "My darling little Emily...Look at you now...If only you hadn't run away...If only you'd let me love you...Sweet, darling, little Emily...It's all such a waste, such a terrible waste..."

The words tumbled out of him in a spasm of breathlessness, an onrush of grief that splintered into fragments as soon as it touched the air. I listened to him as though the earth had begun to speak to me, as though I were listening to the dead from inside their graves. Barber had loved my mother. From this single, incontestable fact, everything else began to move, to totter, to fall apart—the whole world began to rearrange itself before my eyes. He hadn't come out and said it, but all of a sudden I knew. I knew who he was, all of a sudden I knew everything.

For the first few moments, I felt nothing but anger, a demonic surge of nausea and disgust. "What are you talking about?" I said to him, and when Barber still did not look at me, I shoved him with my two hands, jolting his massive right arm with a hard and belligerent smack. "What are you talking about?" I repeated. "Say something, you big bag of guts, say something or I'll smash you in the mouth."

**choked** unclear because one is unable to breathe properly because of strong emotions **to tumble out** to fall out violently **spasm** sudden burst **onrush** a strong fast forward movement **to splinter** to break into small sharp pieces **incontestable** impossible to deny **to totter** to move insteadily from side to side **surge** sudden increase in feeling **disgust** a strong unpleasant feeling that makes one almost sick **to shove** to push in a careless way **to jolt** to make s.o./s.th. move in a sudden rough way **belligerent** ready to fight, aggressive **smack** a sharp blow or slap with s.th. flat **bag of guts** big piece of flesh (guts = the stomach and the internal organs around it)

Barber turned to me then, but all he could do was shake his head back and forth, as if trying to tell me how useless it would be to say anything. "Jesus God, Marco, why did you have to bring me here?" he said at last. "Didn't you know this would happen?"

"Know!" I shouted at him. "How the hell was I supposed to know? You never said a thing, you liar. You tricked me, and now you want me to feel sorry for you. But what about me? What about me, you fucking hippopotamus!"

I vented my rage like a madman, screaming my lungs out in the hot summer air. After a few moments, Barber began to back off, staggering away from my assault as though he couldn't stand it anymore. He was still weeping, and his face was buried in his hands as he walked. Blind to everything around him, he lurched down the row of graves like some injured animal, howling and sobbing as I continued to scream at him. The sun was at the top of the sky by then, and the whole cemetery was shimmering with a strange, pulsing glare, as if the light had grown too strong to be real. I saw Barber take a few more steps, and then, as he came to the edge of the grave that had been dug that morning, he began to lose his balance. He must have stumbled on a stone or a depression in the ground, and suddenly his feet were collapsing under him. It all happened so fast. His arms shot out from his sides, desperately flapping like wings, but he had no chance to right himself. One moment he was there, and the next moment he was falling over backward into the grave. Before I could start running to him, I heard his body land at the bottom with a sharp thud.

In the end, it took a crane to lift him out of there. When I first looked down into the hole, I couldn't tell if he was dead or alive, and with nothing to grab onto along the sides, I felt it would be too risky to hazard a descent. He was lying on his back with his eyes shut, utterly motionless.

**hippopotamus** Nilpferd **to vent** to express without controlling oneself **to back off** to move backwards **to stagger** to walk unsteadily almost falling **to lurch** to move suddenly forwards or sideways **to shimmer** to shine unsteadily with a soft light **to stumble on s.th.** to hit s.th. with one's foot so that one falls **depression** an area that is lower than the surrounding area **to flap** to move up and down as the wing of a bird **to right oneself** to get oneself back into the right position **falling... into the grave** cf. the Greek tragedy *Oedipus Rex* and Sigmund Freud's *Oedipus Complex*—There is a similar scene in Franz Kafka's *The Trial.* Auster felt no love for his father because of his father's emotional coldness. His father had seen his mother kill his father. Cf. Auster's *Portrait of an Invisible Man* **thud** sound made by a heavy object falling on a surface **to hazard** to risk **descent** the process of moving down **utterly** completely

I thought I might fall on top of him if I tried to climb down, so I rushed back to the gatehouse in the car and asked the attendant to phone for help. An emergency squad was on the scene within ten minutes, but they soon found themselves faced with the same dilemma that had thwarted me. After some dithering, we all linked hands and managed to lower one of the paramedics down to the bottom. He announced that Barber was alive, but other than that the news wasn't good. Concussion, he told us, perhaps even a fractured skull. Then, after a short pause, he added: "The guy's back might also be broken. We gotta be awful careful getting him out of here."

It was six o'clock by the time Barber was finally wheeled into the emergency room of Cook County Hospital. He was still unconscious, and for the next four days he showed no signs of coming back to life. The doctors operated on his back, put him in traction, and told me to cross my fingers. I didn't leave the hospital for the next forty-eight hours, but when it became apparent that we were in for a long haul, I used Barber's American Express card to check into a nearby motel, the Eden Rock. It was a gruesome, bottom-dollar place, with smudged green walls and a lumpy bed, but I did no more than sleep there. Once Barber woke up from his coma, I spent eighteen or nineteen hours a day at the hospital, and for the next two months that was my entire world. I did nothing else but sit with him until the moment he died.

For the first month, it was by no means clear that things would end so badly. Girdled in a huge plaster cast that was suspended from pulleys, Barber hovered in midair as though defying the law of physics. He was immobilized to such a degree that he could not turn his head, could not

**attendant** person employed to look after and guide visitors **emergency squad** team of people trained for emergencies **to thwart** to prevent s.o. from doing s.th., to frustrate **to dither** to be unable to do s.th. because one is unable to make a decision **to link** to join **paramedic** person trained to help a doctor **concussion** Gehirnerschütterung **gotta** (slang) have got to **Cook County Hospital** public hospital in Chicago **unconscious** bewusstlos **in traction** im Streckverband **to cross one's fingers** i.e. to hope for the best **apparent** obvious **to be in for a long haul** to have to wait for a long time before s.th. is over **Eden Rock** The motel never existed. **gruesome** horrible, ghastly **bottom-dollar** (coll) the cheapest possible **to smudge** to smear, to spread over a surface **lumpy** with parts that are soft and parts that are hard **to girdle** to cover tightly **plaster cast** Gipsverband **to suspend** here: to hold up **pulley** ['pul.i] Flaschenzug **to hover** to remain suspended in one place in the air **to defy** to refuse to obey, to resist

eat without having tubes put down his throat; but for all that, he made progress, he seemed to be recovering. More than anything else, he told me, he was glad the truth had finally come out. If lying in a cast for a few months was the price he had to pay, he felt it was worth the trouble. "My bones might be broken," he said to me one afternoon, "but my heart is finally on the mend."

Those were the days when the story spilled out of him, and with nothing else for him to do but talk, he wound up giving me an exhaustive and meticulous account of his whole life. I heard every detail of his romance with my mother, I heard the depressing saga of his sojourn in the Cleveland YMCA, I heard the story of his subsequent travels through the heartlands of America. It probably goes without saying that my burst of anger against him in the cemetery had long since evaporated, but even though the evidence left little room for doubt, something in me hesitated to accept him as my father. Yes, it was certain that Barber had slept with my mother one night in 1946; and yes, it was also certain that I had been born nine months later; but how could I be sure that Barber was the only man she had slept with? The odds were against it, but it was nevertheless possible that my mother had been seeing two men at the same time. If so, then perhaps it was the other man who had made her pregnant. This was my only defense against total belief, and I was reluctant to let go of it. As long as a sliver of skepticism remained, I would not have to admit that anything had happened. This was an unexpected response, but looking back on it now, I feel that it makes a peculiar kind of sense. For twenty-four years, I had lived with an unanswerable question, and little by little I had come to embrace that enigma as the central fact about myself. My origins were a mystery, and I would never know where I had come from. This was what defined me, and by now I was used to my own darkness, clinging to it as a source of knowledge and self-respect, trusting in it as an ontological necessity. No matter how hard I might have dreamed of finding my father, I had never thought it would be possible. Now that I had found him, the inner disruption was so great that my first impulse

**but for all that** in spite of everything **on the mend** healing **...spilled out of him...** was rapidly told by him **exhaustive** very thorough **meticulous** very precise about details **sojourn** short stay **subsequent** happening afterwards **to evaporate** here: to disappear **...the odds were against it...** ...it was unlikely that... **to let go of it** to reject, to not accept **sliver** (fig) a very small thin piece **to embrace** here: to accept fully **enigma** mystery, puzzle **to cling to s.th.** to hold on tightly to s.th. **ontological** having to do with the branch of philosophy that deals with the nature of existence

was to deny it. Barber was not the cause of the denial, it was the situation itself. He was the best friend I had, and I loved him. If there was any man in the world I would have chosen to be my father, he was the one. But still, I couldn't do it. A shock had been sent through my entire system, and I didn't know how to absorb the blow.

Weeks went by, and eventually it became impossible for me to close my eyes to the facts. With his body held rigid in its white plaster cast, Barber could not eat any solid food, and it wasn't long before he started to lose weight. This was a man who was accustomed to gorging himself on thousands of calories a day, and the abrupt change in his diet caused an immediate and noticeable effect. It takes hard work to maintain such a mountainous excess of blubber, and once you slacken your consumption, the pounds drop off quite rapidly. Barber complained about it at first, and several times he even wept from hunger, but after a while he began to see this enforced starvation as a blessing in disguise. "It's an opportunity to accomplish something I've never been able to do before," he said. "Just think of it, M. S. If I can keep going at this rate, I'll shed a hundred pounds by the time I get out of here. Maybe even a hundred and twenty. I'll be a new man. I'll never have to look like myself again."

The hair grew back along the sides of his scalp (a mixture of gray and ruddy brown), and the contrast between those colors and the color of his eyes (a dark, gunmetal blue) seemed to set off his head with a new clarity and definition, as though it were gradually emerging from the undifferentiated air that surrounded it. After ten or twelve days in the hospital, his skin turned a deathly white, but with this pallor came a new thinness to his cheeks, and as the bloat of fat cells and puffy flesh continued to subside, a second Barber came up to the surface, a secret self that had been locked inside him for years. It was a stunning transformation, and once it was fully underway, it unleashed a number of remarkable side-effects. I hardly noticed at first, but one morning after he had been in the hospital for about three weeks, I looked at him and saw something familiar. It was

**blow** shock **rigid** in a set position **to gorge oneself** to eat a lot in a greedy way **blubber** too much fat **to slacken** to reduce **consumption** the amount one eats and drinks **to enforce** to make s.o. obey a rule or law **a blessing in disguise** s.th. which seems to be bad at first, but later is found to be good **to accomplish s.th.** to achieve s.th. **at this rate** at this speed **to shed** to lose **ruddy** having a reddish color **gunmetal** gray **to set s.th. off** to make s.th. more distinctive **pallor** pale condition **bloat** swelling **puffy** swollen **to subside** to gradually decrease **stunning** very surprising **to unleash** to suddenly let loose, to release

just a momentary flash, and before I could identify the thing I had seen, it was gone. Two days later, something similar occurred, but this time it lasted long enough for me to sense that the area of recognition was located somewhere around Barber's eyes, perhaps even in the eyes themselves. I wondered if I hadn't noticed a family resemblance with Effing, if something about the way Barber glanced at me just then had not reminded me of his father. Whatever it was, this brief moment was disturbing, and I was unable to shake myself free of it for the rest of the day. It haunted me like a fragment from some unremembered dream, a flicker of intelligibility that had risen up from the depths of my unconscious. Then, the very next morning, I finally understood what I had been seeing. I entered Barber's room for my daily visit, and as he opened his eyes and smiled at me, his face all languid with the painkillers in his blood, I found myself studying the contours of his eyelids, concentrating on the space between the brows and the lashes, and all of a sudden I realized that I was looking at myself. Barber had the same eyes I did. Now that his face had shrunk, it was possible for me to see it. We looked like each other, and the similarity was unmistakable. Once I became aware of this, once the truth of it was finally thrown up against me, I had no choice but to accept it. I was Barber's son, and I knew it now beyond a shadow of a doubt.

For the next two weeks, everything seemed to go well. The doctors were optimistic, and we began looking forward to the day when the cast would be removed. Some time in early August, however, Barber suddenly took a turn for the worse. He came down with an infection of some kind, and the medicine they gave him produced an allergic reaction, which pushed up his blood pressure to crisis levels. Further tests revealed a diabetic condition that had never been diagnosed before, and as the doctors went on probing him for further damage, new diseases and problems kept being added to the list: angina, incipient gout, circulatory trouble, God knows what else. It was as though his body simply couldn't

**flash** here: sudden image **resemblance** similarity **disturbing** upsetting **to shake oneself free of s.th.** to get rid of s.th., to forget **to haunt** to continuously come back to mind **flicker** (fig) a very short brightness of light **intelligibility** s.th. that can be understood **languid** without energy or spirit **lashes** the hairs at the end of the eyelids **to take a turn for the worse** to become worse **to come down with s.th.** (coll) to become ill with s.th. **to probe s.o.** to examine **angina** [æn'dʒaɪ.nə] pains in the chest because of problems with the heart **incipient** just starting to happen **gout** Gicht **circulatory trouble** Kreislaufstörung

take it anymore. It had been through too much, and now the machinery was breaking down. His defenses had been weakened by the enormous weight loss, and there was nothing left for him to fight with, his blood cells refused to mount a counterattack. By the twentieth of August, he told me that he knew he was going to die, but I wouldn't listen to him. "Just sit tight," I said. "We'll have you out of here before they throw the first pitch of the World Series."

I didn't know what I felt anymore. The strain of watching him fall apart left me numb, and by the third week of August I was walking around in a trance. The only thing that mattered to me at that point was to keep up an impassive front. No tears, no bouts of despair, no lapses of will. I exuded hope and confidence, but inwardly I must have known how impossible the situation really was. This was not brought home to me until the very end, however, and I learned it only in the most roundabout way. I had gone into a diner for a late-night supper. One of the specials that evening happened to be chicken pot pie, a dish I had not eaten since I was a small boy, perhaps not since the days when I was still living with my mother. The moment I read those words on the menu, I knew that no other food would do for me that night. I gave my order to the waitress, and for the next three or four minutes I sat there remembering the apartment in Boston where my mother and I had lived, seeing for the first time in years the tiny kitchen table where the two of us had eaten our meals together. Then the waitress came back and told me they were out of chicken pot pies. It was nothing at all, of course. In the large scheme of things, it was a mere speck of dust, an infinitesimal crumb of antimatter, and yet I suddenly felt as though the roof had caved in on me. There were

**to mount** to plan, to prepare, to start on a course of action **just sit tight** just wait and see what happens **first pitch** when the first ball in the first game is thrown to the batter in the (baseball)World Series in October **strain** worry, stress **numb** unable to think or feel anything **to keep up an impassive front** to try to give the appearance of being without any emotion or feeling **bout** short period of some kind of suffering **lapse of will** lack of the will to do anything **to exude** to make apparent **confidence** here: feeling that everything will work out **to bring home to s.o.** to make clear to s.o. **in a roundabout way** indirectly **diner** (AE) a small cheap restaurant **chicken pot pie** a stew with vegetables and chicken covered with a crust of pasty **dish** a particular kind of prepared food **in the large scheme of things** seen as the way things happen in general **mere speck** simply a very small piece **infinitesimal** [ˌɪn.fɪ.nɪˈtes.ɪ.məl] extremely small **crumb** (fig) small piece of bread or cake **antimatter** matter made of antiparticles—exists in very small amounts, cf. quantum physics **to cave in on s.o.** to collapse on s.o.

no more chicken pot pies. If someone had told me an earthquake had just killed twenty thousand people in California, I would not have been more upset than I was at that moment. I actually felt tears forming in my eyes, and it was only then, sitting in that diner and wrestling with my disappointment, that I understood how fragile my world had become. The egg was slipping through my fingers, and sooner or later it was bound to drop.

Barber died on September fourth, just three days after this incident in the restaurant. He weighed only 210 pounds at the time, and it was as though half of him had already disappeared, as though once the process had been set in motion, it was inevitable that the rest of him should disappear as well. I wanted to talk to someone, but the only person I could think of was Kitty. It was five o'clock in the morning when I called her, and even before she answered the phone, I knew that I wasn't calling just to tell her the news. I had to find out if she was willing to take me back.

"I know you're asleep," I said, "but don't hang up until you've heard what I have to say."

"M. S.?" Her voice was muffled, groggy with confusion. "Is that you, M. S.?"

"I'm in Chicago. Sol died about an hour ago, and there wasn't anyone else I could talk to."

It took me a while to tell her the story. She wouldn't believe me at first, and as I continued to give her the details, I understood how improbable the whole thing sounded. Yes, I said, he fell into an open grave and broke his back. Yes, he really was my father. Yes, he really died tonight. Yes, I'm calling from a pay phone at the hospital. There was a short interruption as the operator broke in to ask me to deposit more coins, and when the line opened again, I could hear Kitty sobbing on the other end.

"Poor Sol," she said. "Poor Sol and poor M. S. Poor everyone."

"I'm sorry I had to tell you. But I wouldn't have felt right if I hadn't called."

"No, I'm glad you did. It's just so hard to take. Oh God, M. S., if you only knew how long I've been waiting to hear from you."

"I've made a mess of everything, haven't I?"

**to wrestle with s.th.** to deal with s.th. difficult **bound** likely **to hang up** to stop talking on the phone by putting the receiver down **muffled** not clear because there is s.th. in the way **groggy** very tired, weak **pay phone** (AE) a public phone using coins or a card **operator** person who works for a telephone company who takes care of phone calls or helps when there are problems **to deposit** to put into s.th., to insert into s.th.

"It's not your fault. You can't help what you feel, no one can."

"You didn't expect to hear from me again, did you?"

"Not anymore. For the first couple of months, I didn't think about anything else. But you can't live like that, it's not possible. Little by little, I finally stopped hoping."

"I've gone on loving you every minute. You know that, don't you?"

Once more, there was a silence on the other end, and then I heard her start to sob again—wretched, broken sobs that seemed to suck the breath out of her. "Jesus Christ, M. S., what are you trying to do to me? I don't hear from you since June, and then you call me up from Chicago at five o'clock in the morning, tear my guts out with what happened to Sol—and then you start talking about love? It's not fair. You don't have the right to do that. Not now."

"I can't stand being without you anymore. I tried to do it, but I can't."

"Well, I tried to do it, too, and I can."

"I don't believe you."

"It was too hard for me, M. S. The only way I could survive was to make myself just as hard."

"What are you trying to tell me?"

"It's too late. I can't open myself up to that anymore. You nearly killed me, you know, and I can't risk anything like that again."

"You've found someone else, haven't you?"

"It's been months. What did you want me to do while you were halfway across the country trying to make up your mind?"

"You're in bed with him now, aren't you?"

"That's none of your business."

"You are, aren't you? Just tell me."

"As a matter of fact, I'm not. But that doesn't mean you have any right to ask."

"I don't care who it is. It doesn't make any difference."

"No more, M. S. I can't stand it, I can't take another word."

"I'm begging you, Kitty. Let me come back."

"Good-bye, Marco. Be good to yourself. Please be good to yourself."

And then she hung up.

I buried Barber next to my mother. It took some doing to get him into Westlawn Cemetery, a lone Gentile in a sea of Russian and German Jews, but given that the Fogg family plot still had room for one more person,

**wretched** [ˈretʃ.ɪd] miserable **to tear s.o.'s guts out with s.th.** (coll) to make s.o. feel miserable because of s.th. **Gentile** a person who is not a Jew

and given that I was technically the head of the family and therefore the owner of that land, I eventually got my way. In effect, I buried my father in the grave that had been destined for me. Considering all that had happened in the past few months, I felt it was the least I could do for him.

After the conversation with Kitty, I needed every distraction from my thoughts that I could find, and in lieu of anything else, the business of funeral arrangements helped to carry me through the next four days. Two weeks before his death, Barber had summoned the last bits of his remaining strength to turn his assets over to me, and so I had enough money to work with. Wills were too complicated, he said, and since he wanted me to have everything in any case, why not simply give it to me now? I tried to talk him out of it, knowing that this transaction was the ultimate acceptance of defeat, but I didn't want to press too hard. Barber was barely hanging on by then, and it wouldn't have been fair to stand in his way.

I paid the hospital bills, I paid the mortuary, I paid for a gravestone in advance. To officiate at the burial service, I called up the rabbi who had presided over my bar mitzvah eleven years before. He was an old man now, well past seventy, I think, and he did not remember my name. I'm retired, he said, why don't you ask someone else? No, I said, it has to be you, Rabbi Green, I don't want anyone else. It took some persuading, but I finally wrangled him into doing it for twice his normal fee. This is highly unusual, he said. There are no usual cases, I answered. Every death is unique.

Rabbi Green and I were the only people at the funeral. I had thought of notifying Magnus College of Barber's death, thinking that some of his colleagues might want to attend, but then I decided against it. I wasn't up to spending the day with strangers, I didn't want to talk to anyone. The rabbi agreed to my request not to deliver a eulogy in English, confining

**in effect** in fact **destined** intended **distraction** s.th. that helps s.o. to forget the worries **in lieu of anything else** because there was nothing else **to summon** to make a great effort to use s.th. **to turn one's assets to s.o.** to legally give s.o. one's money and property **transaction** business agreement **ultimate** last, final **to press s.o.** to try hard to persuade s.o. **to hang on** here: to continue to live **mortuary** a building where dead bodies are kept until burial **to officiate** to conduct a religious ceremony **to preside over s.th.** to be in charge of s.th. **bar mitzvah** [ˈmɪts.və] Jewish ceremony to celebrate a (usually 13-year-old) boy becoming a full member of the religious community **to wrangle s.o. into doing s.th.** (AE) to persuade s.o. to do s.th. by argument **to be up to s.th.** to be in the mood to do s.th. **to deliver a eulogy** [ˈjuːlə.dʒi] to give a speech in which one praises s.o., especially s.o. who has died

himself to a recitation of the traditional Hebrew prayers. My Hebrew had all but vanished by then, and I was glad I wasn't able to understand what he said. It left me alone with my thoughts, which was all I finally wanted. Rabbi Green considered me insane, and during the hours we spent together, he kept as much distance between us as possible. I felt sorry for him, but not enough to do anything about it. All in all, I don't think I said more than five or six words to him. When the limousine deposited him in front of his house after the ordeal, he reached out and shook my hand, patting my knuckles softly with his left palm. It was a gesture of consolation that must have been as natural to him as signing his name, and he hardly seemed to notice he was doing it. "You're a very disturbed young man," he said. "If you want my advice, I think you should go to a doctor."

I had the chauffeur drop me off at the Eden Rock Motel. I didn't want to spend another night in that place, so I immediately began packing up my things. It took no more than ten minutes to finish the job. I cinched my bag shut, sat down on the bed for a moment, and gave the room a last look around. If accommodations are provided in hell, I said to myself, this is what they would look like. For no apparent reason—that is, for no reason that I was aware of at the time—I curled my hand into a fist, stood up, and punched the wall as hard as I could. The thin beaverboard panel gave way without a struggle, bursting open with a dull cracking noise as my arm shot through it. I wondered if the furniture was just as flimsy and picked up a chair to find out. I smashed it down on the bureau, then watched in happiness as the whole thing splintered to bits. To complete the experiment, I took hold of one of the severed chair legs in my right hand and proceeded to go around the room, attacking one object after another with my make-shift club: the lamps, the mirrors, the television, whatever happened to be there. It took only a few minutes to destroy the place from top to bottom, but it made me feel immeasurably better, as

**to deposit s.o. somewhere** here: to drive s.o. somewhere where he/she can get out **ordeal** unpleasant experience **to pat** to hit s.th. lightly with an open hand **knuckle** Fingerknöchel **palm** Handfläche **disturbed** emotionally troubled **to cinch shut** (AE) to pull tightly to close s.th. **accommodations** a place to stay or live **apparent** obvious **to curl** to roll **to punch** to hit s.th. hard with one's fist **beaverboard** Hartfaserplatte **panel** flat piece of wood **dull** not loud **to crack** to break so lines appear **flimsy** not well-made and easily broken **to splinter** to break into thin sharp pieces **severed** cut off, broken off **to proceed to do s.th.** to continue with s.th. already started **make-shift** make for the moment because nothing else is available **immeasurably** extremely so that it cannot be measured

though I had finally done something logical, something truly worthy of the occasion. I did not stand around long to admire my work. Still breathing hard from the exertion, I scooped up my bags, ran outside, and drove away in the red Pontiac.

I kept on going for the next twelve hours. Night fell as I crossed into Iowa, and little by little the world was reduced to an immensity of stars. I became hypnotized by my own loneliness, unwilling to stop until my eyes wouldn't stay open anymore, watching the white line of the highway as though it was the last thing that connected me to the earth. I was somewhere in central Nebraska when I finally checked into a motel and went to sleep. I remember a din of crickets in the darkness, the thump of moths crashing against the screen window, a dog barking faintly in a far corner of the night.

In the morning, I understood that chance had taken me in the right direction. Without stopping to think about it, I had been following the road to the west, and now that I was on my way, I suddenly felt calmer, more in control of myself. I would do what Barber and I had set out to do in the first place, I decided, and knowing that I had a purpose, that I was not running way from something so much as going toward it, gave me the courage to admit to myself that I did not in fact want to be dead.

I did not think I would ever find the cave (until the very end, that was a foregone conclusion), but I felt that the act of looking for it would be sufficient in itself, an act to annihilate all others. I had more than thirteen thousand dollars in my bag, and that meant there was nothing to hold me back: I could keep on going until every possibility had been exhausted. I drove to the end of the flat plains, spent a night in Denver, and then pushed on to Mesa Verde, where I lingered for three or four days, climbing around the massive ruins of a dead civilization, reluctant to tear myself away from it. I had not imagined that anything in America could be so old, and by the time I crossed into Utah, I felt that I was beginning

**exertion** great physical effort **to scoop up** to pick up with the open hand **din** loud confused noise **cricket** Grille **thump** dull sound when s.th. hits a surface **moth** Nachtfalter **faintly** very softly **foregone conclusion** the result is certain even if it hasn't happened yet **sufficient in itself** enough when just doing it **to annihilate** [aˈnaɪ.ə.leɪt] to destroy completely **exhausted** here: considered or made use of **flat plains** area in the middle of the U.S.A. between the Mississippi and the Rocky Mountains—the Great Plains **Mesa Verde** [vɜːrd] area with ancient Native American ruins—the tribes that lived there are known as the cliff dwellers—now a museum **to linger** to stay somewhere a little longer because one doesn't want to leave

to understand some of the things that Effing had talked about. It was not so much that I was impressed by the geography (everyone is impressed by it), but that the hugeness and emptiness of the land had begun to affect my sense of time. The present no longer seemed to bear any of the same consequences. Minutes and hours were too small to be measured in this place, and once you opened your eyes to the things around you, you were forced to think in terms of centuries, to understand that a thousand years is no more than a tick of the clock. For the first time in my life, I felt the earth as a planet whirling through the heavens. It wasn't big, I discovered, it was small—it was almost microscopic. Of all the objects in the universe, nothing is smaller than the earth.

I found myself a room at the Comb Ridge Motel in the town of Bluff, and for the next month I spent my days exploring the surrounding countryside. I climbed up rocks, prowled the craggy interstices of canyons, put hundreds of miles on the car. I discovered many caves in the process, but none of them bore the marks of habitation. Still, I was happy during those weeks, almost buoyant in my solitude. To avoid unpleasant encounters with the people of Bluff, I kept my hair cut short, and the story I gave them about being a graduate student in geology seemed to quell any suspicions they might have had about me. With no plans other than to continue my search, I could have gone on for many more months in this way, eating breakfast every morning at Sally's Kitchen and then tramping off into the wilderness until dark. One day, however, I drove farther afield than usual, going past Monument Valley to the Navaho trading post at Oljeto. The word meant "moon in the water," which was enough to attract me in itself, but someone in Bluff had told me that the people who ran the trading post, a Mr. and Mrs. Smith, knew as much

**...bear any of the same consequences...** didn't seem to have the effect it normally had **to whirl through s.th.** to move along spinning **Comb Ridge** group of mountains to the southwest of Bluff; there has never been a motel of this name **to prowl** to move about quietly as if hunting **craggy** with steep masses of rock, very uneven **interstice** [ɪn'tɜːr.stɪs] small space or crack between two things close together **many caves** e.g. the Grand Gulch Primitive Area to the west, which contains the remains of Native American civilizations **in the process** here: while hiking **to bear the marks of s.th.** (formal) to show signs of s.th. **buoyant** ['bɔɪ.ənt] cheerful **solitude** state of being alone **graduate student** a student studying beyond the first degree, e.g. studying for a doctorate **to quell** to reduce **Sally's Kitchen** has never existed **farther afield** farther away **Oljeto** Ol = moon, jeto = water; trading post founded by an American explorer in 1908 25 km to the northwest of Monument Valley—There really was a Mrs. Smith at the time.

about the history of the country as anyone else for miles around. Mrs. Smith was Kit Carson's granddaughter or great-granddaughter, and the house she lived in with her husband was filled with Navaho blankets and pottery, a museumlike collection of Indian artifacts. I spent a couple of hours with them, drinking tea in the coolness of their dark living room, and when I finally found the moment to ask them if they had ever heard of a man named George Ugly Mouth, they both shook their heads and said no. What about the Gresham brothers? I asked. Had they ever heard of them? Oh sure, said Mr. Smith, they was that gang of outlaws that disappeared about fifty years ago. Bert and Frank and Harlan, the last of the Wild West train robbers. Didn't they have a hideout somewhere? I asked, trying to cover up my excitement. Someone once told me about a cave they lived in, way up in the mountains I think it was. I believe you're right, said Mr. Smith, I heard some talk about it once myself. Supposed to be in the neighborhood of Rainbow Bridge. Do you think it would be possible to find it? I asked. It might have been, Mr. Smith muttered, it might have been, but you wouldn't get nowhere looking for it now. Why is that? I asked. Lake Powell, he answered. The whole country out there is underwater. They flooded it about two years back. Unless you've got some deep-sea diving equipment, you ain't likely to find much of anything.

I gave up after that. The moment Mr. Smith spoke those words, I knew there would be no point in going on. I had always known that I would have to stop sooner or later, but I had never imagined it happening so abruptly, with such devastating finality. I was just getting started, just warming up to my task, and now there was nothing left for me to do. I drove back to Bluff, spent a last night in the motel, and checked out the

**Kit Carson** Christopher ("Kit") Carson (1809-1868) explorer, guide, Indian fighter, and Civil War general—a western hero for Americans; a murderer for Native Americans **pottery** objects made of baked clay **artifacts** hand-made objects of historical interest **hideout** a hiding place used by outlaws **Rainbow Bridge** in Glen Canyon on Lake Powell: said to be the longest natural bridge in the world—considered holy by Native Americans; according to a Park Ranger there are and were no caves in the immediate area of Rainbow Bridge **Lake Powell** artificial lake to supply the surrounding area with water and electricity in southeast Utah/northeast Arizona created by damming the Colorado River in 1963. The lake didn't become completely filled up until 1979. There has been a lot of opposition to this lake by environmentalists. The lake was named after the explorer John Wesley Powell (already discussed). **devastating** destructive **finality** the quality of coming to a conclusion that cannot be changed **to warm up to s.th.** to become excited or interested in s.th.

following morning. From there I went to Lake Powell, wanting to get a firsthand look at the water that had destroyed my beautiful plans, but it was hard to feel much anger against a lake. I rented a motorboat and passed the whole day cruising over the water, trying to think of what to do next. It was an old problem for me by then, but my sense of defeat was so enormous that I failed to think of anything. It was not until I returned the boat to the rental shack and started looking for my car that the decision was suddenly taken out of my hands.

The Pontiac was nowhere to be found. I searched everywhere for it, but once I realized that it wasn't in the spot where I had parked it, I knew that it had been stolen. I had my knapsack with me and fifteen hundred dollars in traveler's checks, but the rest of the money had been in the trunk—over ten thousand dollars in cash, my entire inheritance, everything I owned in the world.

I walked up to the top of the road, hoping to hitch a ride from someone, but no cars stopped for me. I cursed them all as they passed, shouting obscenities as each one sped by. Evening was coming on, and when my bad luck continued on the main highway, I had no choice but to blunder off into the sagebrush and find a place to spend the night. I was so stunned by the disappearance of the car, I never even thought of reporting it to the police. By the time I woke up the next morning, shivering against the cold, it struck me that the theft had not been committed by men. It was a prank of the gods, an act of divine malice whose only object was to crush me.

That was when I started walking. I was so angry, so insulted by what had happened, that I stopped holding out my thumb to ask for rides. I walked the whole of that day, from sunup to sundown, walking as though I meant to punish the ground beneath my feet. The next day, I did the same thing again. And the day after that. And then the day after that. For the next three months, I continued walking, slowly working my way west, stopping off in little towns for a day or two and then moving on, sleeping in open fields, in caves, in ditches by the side of the road. For the first two weeks, I was like someone who had been struck by lightning. I

**to cruise** to sail along slowly **rental** for renting **shack** building primitively built **to hitch a ride** to try to get a free ride by standing at the road with one's thumb up **to blunder off** to walk away in a confused or unsteady way **sagebrush** plant with white flowers that grows in the dry areas of southwestern U.S.A. **to shiver against the cold** to tremble because of the cold **prank** trick, joke **malice** the desire to do harm **to crush s.o.** to defeat **ditch** a long narrow hole dug along a road to drain away the water

thundered inside myself, I wept, I howled like a madman, but then, little by little, the anger seemed to burn itself out, and I settled into the rhythm of my steps. I went through one pair of boots after another. By the end of the first month, I gradually began talking to people again. A few days later, I bought a box of cigars, and every night after that I smoked one in honor of my father. In Valentine, Arizona, a chubby waitress named Peg seduced me in an empty diner at the edge of town, and I wound up staying with her for ten or twelve days. In Needles, California, I twisted my left ankle and couldn't walk on it for a week, but otherwise I walked without interruption, heading toward the Pacific, borne along by a growing sense of happiness. Once I reached the end of the continent, I felt that some important question would be resolved for me. I had no idea what that question was, but the answer had already been formed in my steps, and I had only to keep walking to know that I had left myself behind, that I was no longer the person I had once been.

I bought my fifth pair of boots in a place called Lake Elsinore on January 3, 1972. Three days later, all ragged with exhaustion, I climbed over the hills into the town of Laguna Beach with 413 dollars in my pocket. I could already see the ocean from the top of the promontory, but I kept on walking until I was all the way down to the water. It was four o'clock in the afternoon when I took off my boots and felt the sand against the soles of my feet. I had come to the end of the world, and beyond it there was nothing but air and waves, an emptiness that went clear to the shores of China. This is where I start, I said to myself, this is where my life begins.

I stood on the beach for a long time, waiting for the last bits of sunlight to vanish. Behind me, the town went about its business, making familiar late-century American noises. As I looked down the curve of the coast, I saw the lights of the houses being turned on, one by one. Then the moon came up from behind the hills. It was a full moon, as round and yellow as a burning stone. I kept my eyes on it as it rose into the night sky, not turning away until it had found its place in the darkness.

**to settle into s.th.** to get used to s.th. and for that reason continue to do it **Valentine** town in northwest Arizona near Las Vegas **chubby** a bit fat that is still attractive **to seduce** to persuade s.o. to have sex with you **Needles** town in southeast California **ankle** Fußknöchel **borne along** (fig) carried along **to resolve** to find the answer to s.th. **Lake Elsinore** town to the east of Los Angeles, cf. Elsinore the site of Shakespeare's *Hamlet* **ragged** ['ræg.ɪd] completely worn-out, in a poor condition **Laguna Beach** town on the Pacific ocean south of Los Angeles **promontory** a high point of land that goes out into the sea

# ADDITIONAL MATERIAL

## 1. Views of America

...We are entered into covenant with Him for this work [...] We must be knit together in this work as one man. We must entertain each other in brotherly affection, we must be willing to abridge ourselves of our superfluities, for the supply of others' necessities [...] For we must consider that we shall be as *a city upon a hill*. The eyes of all people are upon us, so that if we shall deal falsely with our God in this work we have undertaken, and so cause Him to withdraw His present help from us, we shall be made a story and a by-word through the world...

In *A Model of Christian Charity* written by John Winthrop (1588-1649, Puritan leader) on board the Arabella before the settlement of the Puritan colony in Massachusetts, *1630*

America, you have it better than our continent, the old one.

Johann von Goethe, *1831*

...The practice of Americans leads their minds to other habits, to fixing the standard of their judgment in themselves alone. As they perceive that they succeed in resolving without assistance all the little difficulties

**convenant** a legal contract, cf. Hebrews 8:8 **this work** i.e. this new settlement **to knit** to join closely together **to entertain** (archaic) to treat, to deal with **affection** love and caring **to abridge oneself** to reduce **superfluity** something not needed **city upon a hill** cf. Matthew 5:14 **byword** here: well-known as a bad example **to perceive** to notice

which their practical life presents, they readily conclude that everything in the world may be explained, and that nothing in it transcends the limits of the understanding...

[...] vegetables and fish are served before the meat, the oysters for dessert. In a word barbarism [...]

The whole society seems to have melted into the middle class...

Alexis de Tocqueville (1805-1859) French politician and historian, in *Democrary in America, 1840*

There is no room in this country for hyphenated Americanism [...] The one absolutely way of bringing this nation to ruin [...] would be to permit it to become a tangle of squabbling nationalities.

Theodore Roosevelt (1858-1919, 26th American president) in a speech given in 1915

So we beat on, boats against the current, borne back ceaselessly into the past.

last line of *The Great Gatsby*, by F. Scott Fitzgerald (1896-1940, American writer), *1924*

To live for the moment is the prevailing passion—to live for yourself, not for your predecessors or posterity.

From: *The Culture of Narcissism* by Christopher Lasch, W.W. Norton & Company, Inc. New York, *1978*, p. 5

The United States can [...] be seen as a country always on the move from a shabby today, which many consider a betrayal of the Founding Fathers' designs and lofty hope, to a radiant tomorrow. It has been compared to a man on a bicycle who falls if he stops pedaling and moving ahead.

*The Europeans*, by Luigi Barzini, Simon and Schuster, New York, *1983*, p. 230

**to transcend** to go beyond or outside of **oyster** Auster **hyphenated** mit Bindestrich, e.g. German-American **tangle** here: a chaotic mixture **to squabble** to constantly argue **borne** carried **ceaselessly** without a pause **prevailing** accepted at the moment **predecessor** s.o. who lived before you **posterity** future generations **betrayal** Verrat **Founding Fathers** those who helped to write the American Constitution in 1787 **design** plan, intention **lofty** of very high moral quality **radiant** (fig) bright

...Smile [in America] and others will smile back. Smile to show how transparent, how candid you are. Smile if you have nothing to say. Most of all, do not hide the fact that you have nothing to say nor your total indifference to others. Let this emptiness, this profound indifference shine out spontaneously in your smile. *Give* your emptiness and indifference to others, light up your face with the zero degree of joy and pleasure, smile, smile, smile...Americans may have no identity, but they do have wonderful teeth.

Jean Baudrillard, *America*, Verso, London, New York, 1988, p. 34

America is the original version of modernity. We [Europeans] are the dubbed or subtitled version. America ducks the question of origins; it cultivates no origin or mythical authenticity; it has no past and no founding truth. Having known no primitive accumulation of time, it lives in a perpetual present. Having seen no slow, centuries-long accumulation of a principle of truth, it lives in perpetual simulation, in a perpetual present of signs. It has no ancestral territory. The Indians' territory is today marked off in reservations, the equivalent of the galleries in which America stocks its Rembrandts and Renoirs. But this is of no importance—America has no identity problem. In the future, power will belong to those peoples with no origins and no authenticity who know how to exploit that situation to the full.

ibid, p. 76

Nothing can astound an American.

Jules Verne (1828-1905, French novelist) in
*From the Earth to the Moon* (1865)

**candid** frank and honest **to dub** to replace the language spoken in a film with voices in another language **to duck** (coll) to avoid **perpetual** permanent **Rembrandts and Renoirs** Rembrandt (1606-1669), Dutch painter, Renoir (1841-1919), French painter **to exploit** to make the best use of s.th. for one's own advantage **to astound** to surprise

## 2. The American Dream: One and Many

Few terms are defined in so many different ways or bandied about more loosely than "The American Dream." To some people, the term is a joke, an object of satire, derision, or contempt, a made-in-America label for a congeries of chauvinistic clichés mouthed by jingoists like the orator in e.e. cummings' poem, "next to of course God america i." To others, it merely signifies self-determined success, wealth, the "good life" of modish clothes, sports cars, and hot tubs—in a word, the latest thing touted by Madison Avenue. And to still others, less scornful or frivolous, it denotes a unique set of social and moral ideals. The United States may not be in many respects quite so exceptional as it believes itself to be. Nevertheless, the fact remains, as Lionel Trilling once remarked, that it is the "only nation that prides itself upon a dream and gives its name to one." Thus it is no accident that one recent bestseller challenged Americans to restore the Dream, while another asked them to reconsider whether its best aspirations have been fulfilled. Best aspirations? What are they? In short, what is the American Dream?

The framers of the Declaration of Independence stated many of the Dream's basic assumptions in 1776 when they asserted that "all men are created equal, that they are endowed by their Creator with certain unalienable Rights, that among these are Life, Liberty and the pursuit of Happiness." In *Letters from an American Farmer* (1782), Hector St. John de Crèvecoeur enlarged this vision by describing the new republic as a place where a man could abandon "all his ancient prejudices and manners," act "upon new principles," and be "rewarded by ample subsistence." Indeed, to Crèvecoeur the hopes that Philip Freneau and Hugh Henry Brackenridge had poetically expressed in "The Rising Glory of

**to bandy about** to mention frequently **derision** remarks that show one doesn't take s.th. seriously **congeries** collection **to mouth** to say s.th. one doesn't really believe or understand **jingoist** chauvinist **orator** a person who makes a formal speech **E.E. Cummings** (1894-1962) American poet **hot tub** tub (Wanne) filled with hot water in which one relaxes **to tout** to praise s.th. so that people buy it **to denote** to mean **Trilling** (1905-1975) American critic **framers** here: those who prepared and wrote the Constitution **assumption** s.th. thought to be true without proof **to assert** to declare **to endow** (formal) to give **unalienable** cannot be taken away **pursuit** the striving after s.th. **Crèvecoeur** (1735-1813) French immigrant who wrote insightful essays about colonial America **ample** more than sufficient **Frenau** (1752-1832) American poet **Brackenridge** (1748-1816) American writer

America" (1771), that the nation-to-be would constitute a new Paradise, were already virtually fulfilled: America was "the most perfect society now existing in the world."

According to Charles I. Sanford, however, "perhaps the most impressive early statement of the American Dream" was made in 1823 by Hugh Swinton Legaré. Delivering a Fourth of July speech in Charleston, South Carolina, Legaré declared that America's goal was nothing less than to establish a democratic Utopia of liberty, prosperity, and public virtue. Others, the most expansive of whom was Walt Whitman, aspired to similar goals in the decades following. Yet the term "American Dream" itself is of relatively recent coinage. One of the first to popularize it was the historian James Truslow Adams. In *The Epic of America* (1931), he referred to "that dream of a land in which life should be better and richer and fuller for every man, with opportunity for each according to his ability or achievement." Adams believed that this dream might be "the greatest contribution" that the United States has "made to the thought and welfare of the world." His very phrasing also suggested, probably inadvertently, what others had suspected: that America is not just the home of the Dream but the Dream itself.

Although the foregoing descriptions capture some of the ideals—equality, liberty, prosperity, opportunity, public virtue—commonly associated with the American Dream, they omit others which have been equally influential. Furthermore, their very reliance on abstractions reduces complexity to a misleading simplicity. For the Dream is and always has been comprised of many dreams; no single vision has ever totally dominated the American imagination. As even Ralph Ellison's novel, *Invisible Man* (1952), puts it, "America is woven of many strands; I would recognize them and let it so remain...Our fate is to become one, and yet many—This is not prophecy, but description." Echoing the national motto—*E Pluribus Unum*—Ellison's narrator here not only

**Sanford** American historian alive at the time of this article **Legaré** (1797-1843) American lawyer and public figure **public virtue** morality in government **expansive** eloquent **Whitman** (1819-1892) American poet **to aspire** to work towards achieving s.th. **coinage** (fig) a newly invented word or phrase **Adams** (1878-1949) American historian **epic** here: long history **very phrasing** the manner of expression used here **inadvertently** unintentionally **foregoing** (formal) what has just been mentioned **to omit** to leave out **very reliance** extreme dependence **Ellison** (1914-1994) Afro-American writer **to weave, wove, woven** weben, flechten **strand** Faden **E Pluribus Unum** (Latin) from many, one

expresses both the unity and the diversity of American society; he implicitly acknowledges the complex, sometimes paradoxical nature of the Dream which that society has reflected and perpetuated. Whatever unity it possesses is delicate, its diversity undeniable. [...]

None of those strands is more persistent than a belief in new beginnings. This belief exemplifies better than any other the optimism—some would call it the naivety—of Americans and the fundamental reason why rhetoric about the Dream caught on in the United States. From their inception, American self-images reflected the idea that the past did not bind one irrevocably. Fresh starts could be made, tomorrow promised to be better than today, and progress seemed always to be possible. To speak of the American Dream, therefore, became one appealing way to epitomize the many principles and experiences that reinforced those hopes in American life. Individuals and groups have, of course, disagreed markedly as to the contents and priorities emphasized in their particular versions of the Dream, thus sparking controversies that make the American Dream not only an ideal to rally around but also a convenient target for criticism. The net result is that debates about the Dream infuse American identity so much that they are unlikely to cease.

From *The American Dream* by Robert H. Possum and John K. Roth, London: British Association for American Studies 1986, pp. 5-7.

**to acknowledge** to accept the truth of s.th. **delicate** easily damaged **persistent** continuing to exist in spite of difficulties **rhetoric** speeches or writing that should sound convincing **to catch on** to become popular **inception** beginning **irrevocably** in such a way that no changes can be made **to epitomize** to serve as a summary or typical example **markedly** noticeably **to spark** to cause **to rally around s.th.** to use as a source of inspiration or encouragement **convenient** easily available **to infuse** to fill with a certain quality **to cease** to stop

## 3. The Significance of the Frontier in American History

by Frederick Jackson Turner (1861-1932), American historian

[...] American social development has been continually beginning over again on the frontier. This perennial rebirth, this fluidity of American life, this expansion westward with its new opportunities, its continuous touch with the simplicity of primitive society, furnish the forces dominating American character. The true point of view in the history of this nation is not the Atlantic coast, it is the Great West. [...]

[...] The American frontier is sharply distinguished from the European frontier—a fortified boundary line running through dense populations. The most significant thing about the American frontier is, that it lies at the hither edge of free land. [...] Our early history is the study of European germs developing in an American environment. Too exclusive attention has been paid by institutional students to the Germanic origins, too little to the American factors. The frontier is the line of most rapid and effective Americanization. The wilderness masters the colonist. It finds him a European in dress, industries, tools, modes of travel, and thought. It takes him from the railroad car and puts him in the birch canoe. It strips off the garments of civilization and arrays him in the hunting shirt and the moccasin. [...] In short, at the frontier the environment is at first too strong for the man. He must accept the conditions which it furnishes or perish, and so he fits himself into the Indian clearings and follows the Indian trails. Little by little he transforms the wilderness, but the outcome is not the old, Europe, not simply the development of Germanic germs [...]. The fact is, that here is a new product that is American. At first, the frontier was the Atlantic coast. It was the frontier of Europe in a very real sense. Moving westward, the frontier became more and more American. [...] Thus the advance of the frontier has meant a steady movement away from the influence of Europe, a steady growth of independence on American lines. And to study this advance, the men who grew up under these conditions, and the political, economic, and social results of it, is to study the really American part of our history [...]

**perennial** occurring again and again **fluidity** constant change, flexibility **to furnish** to provide **to fortify** to protect militarily **hither** closer, towards onself **germs** i.e. culture, civilization **Germanic** i.e. Western European **industries** various types of occupations **modes** means **birch** Birke **to strip off** to take off **garment** clothing **to array** to dress **to perish** to die in a terrible way **clearing** area of land without trees in the middle of a forest **on American lines** in the American tradition

From the conditions of frontier life came intellectual traits of profound importance. The works of travelers along each frontier from colonial days onward describe certain common traits, and these traits have, while softening down, still persisted as survivals in the place of their origin, even when a higher social organization succeeded. The result is that to the frontier the American intellect owes its striking characteristics. That coarseness and strength combined with acuteness and inquisitiveness; that practical, inventive turn of mind, quick to find expedients; that masterful grasp of material things, lacking in the artistic but powerful to effect great ends; that restless, nervous energy; that dominant individualism, working for good and for evil, and withal that buoyancy and exuberance which comes with freedom—these are traits of the frontier, or traits called out elsewhere because of the existence of the frontier. Since the days when the fleet of Columbus sailed into the waters of the New World, America has been another name for opportunity, and the people of the United States have taken their tone from the incessant expansion which has not only been open but has even been forced upon them. He would be a rash prophet who should assert that the expansive character of American life has now entirely ceased. Movement has been its dominant fact, and, unless this training has no effect upon a people, the American energy will continually demand a wider field for its exercise. But never again will such gifts of free land offer themselves. [...] each frontier did indeed furnish a new field of opportunity, a gate of escape from the bondage of the past; and freshness, and confidence, and scorn of older society, impatience of its restraints and its ideas, and indifference to its lessons, have accompanied the frontier. [...] And now, four centuries from the discovery of America, at the end of a hundred years of life under the Constitution, the frontier has gone, and with its going has closed the first period of American history.

From the speech given in 1893 by Frederick Jackson Turner "The Significance of the Frontier in American History," pp. 81, 82, 84, 85 in *A Nineteenth Century American Reader*, M. Thomas Inge, editor, U.S. Information Agency, Washington, D.C., 1987.

**trait** characteristic **coarseness** Grobheit **acuteness** ability to think clearly **inquisitiveness** eagerness to ask questions **expedient** s.th. found to solve a problem in an urgent situation **grasp** understanding **to effect great ends** to achieve great goals **withal** besides, together with this **buoyancy** cheerfulness because one believes one call solve problems easily **exuberance** high spirits, vitality, cheerful energy **to call out** here: to put into practice **tone** here: guiding principle **incessant** continuous, never stopping **rash** not taking the time to think carefully about s.th. **to assert** to declare or state to be true **to cease** to stop **bondage** dependent on s.th. so that one's freedom is limited

## 4. Letters from an American Farmer

In this great American asylum the poor of Europe have by some means met together, and in consequence of various causes; to what purpose should they ask one another what countrymen they are? Alas, two thirds of them had no country. Can a wretch who wanders about, who works and starves, whose life is a continual scene of sore affliction or pinching penury, can that man call England or any other kingdom his country? A country that had no bread for him, whose fields procured him no harvest, who met with nothing but the frowns of the rich, the severity of the laws, with jails and punishments; who owned not a single foot of the extensive surface of this planet? No! Urged by a variety of motives, here they came. Everything has tended to regenerate them: new laws, a new mode of living, a new social system; here they are become men: in Europe they were as so many useless plants, wanting vegetative mold, and refreshing showers; they withered, and were mowed down by want, hunger, and war; but now by the power of transplantation, like all other plants they have taken root and flourished! Formerly they were not numbered in any civil lists of their country except in those of the poor; here they rank as citizens. By what invisible power has this surprising metamorphosis been performed? By that of the laws and that of their industry...

What then is the American, this new man? He is either a European or the descendant of a European, hence that strange mixture of blood which you will find in no other country. I could point out to you a family whose grandfather was an Englishman, whose wife was Dutch, whose son married a French woman, and whose present four sons have now four wives of different nations. He is an American, who, leaving behind him all his ancient prejudices and manners, receives new ones from the new mode of life he has embraced, the new government he obeys, and the new rank he holds. He becomes an American by being received in the broad lap of our great Alma Mater. Here individuals of all nations are melted into a new

**alas** unfortunately **wretch** a person in a miserable situation **sore** very difficult, serious **affliction** a condition of pain or suffering **pinching** painful **penury** extreme poverty **frown** disapproving look on one's face **severity** harshness, strictness **to urge** to drive, to strongly motivate **to regenerate** to help s.th./s.o. to become strong again **vegetative mold** earth that helps plants to grow healthily **to wither** to become small and dry and die **to mow down** to cut down with a machine **civil list** list of inhabitants prepared by the authorities **to rank** to have the status of s.th. **hence** thus **to embrace** to accept eagerly **lap** Schoß **Alma Mater** Latin: here: mother who provides you with a plentiful life

race of men, whose labors and posterity will one day cause great changes in the world. Americans are the Western pilgrims, who are carrying along with them that great mass of arts, sciences, vigor, and industry which began long since in the East; they will finish the great circle.

The Americans were once scattered all over Europe; here they are incorporated into one of the finest systems of population which has ever appeared, and which will hereafter become distinct by the power of the different climates they inhabit. The American ought therefore to love this country much better than that wherein either he or his forefathers were born. Here the rewards of his industry follow with equal steps the progress of his labor; his labor is founded on the basis of nature, self-interest; can it want a stronger allurement? Wives and children, who before in vain demanded of him a morsel of bread, now, fat and frolicsome, gladly help their father to clear those fields whence exuberant crops are to arise to feed and to clothe them all, without any part being claimed either by a despotic prince, a rich abbot, or a mighty lord. Here religion demands but little of him: a small voluntary salary to the minister, and gratitude to God; can he refuse these? The American is a new man, who acts upon new principles; he must therefore entertain new ideas, and form new opinions. From involuntary idleness, servile dependence, penury, and useless labor, he has passed to toils of a very different nature, rewarded by ample subsistences—This is an American.

From *Letters from an American Farmer* (published in 1782) by J. Hector St. John Crèvecoeur (1735-1813, French born writer and agriculturist, who lived in New York for many years)

**posterity** future generations **vigor** vitality **great circle** refer to the concept of *translatio imperii*, the idea, since the Middle Ages, of the passing of civilization from the East to the West **to scatter** (fig.) throw about in many different directions **wherein** in which place **industry** here: hard work **labor** work **allurement** s.th. that is attractive or appealing **morsel** small piece **frolicsome** merry **whence** (archaic) from where **exuberant** here: growing in great amounts **abbot** head of a settlement of monks **to entertain** to think about, to consider **involuntary** not intentional **idleness** lack of work, inactivity **servile** like a servant or slave **penury** extreme poverty **toils** hard work **ample** abundant, plenty of **subsistences** food, clothing, land, a place to live

## 5. Facing West from California's Shores

Facing west from California's shores,
Inquiring, tireless, seeking what is yet unfound,
I, a child, very old, over waves, towards the house of maternity, the land of migrations, look afar,
Look off the shores of my Western sea, the circle almost circled;
For starting westward from Hindustan, from the vales of Kashmere,
From Asia, from the north, from the God, the sage, and the hero,
From the south, from the flowery peninsulas and the spice islands,
Long having wander'd since, round the earth having wander'd.
Now I face home again, very pleas'd and joyous,
(But where is what I started for so long ago?
And why is it yet unfound?)

In *Leaves of Grass* by Walt Whitman (1860)

**to inquire** to ask for information **tireless** here: never stopping **maternity** state of being or becoming a mother **circle** cf. the hermeneutic circle **Hindustan** India **vale** (old-fashioned) valley **the north** western Europe **the God** the Christian God that Europeans explorers believed gave them the right to explore and conquer new continents **sage** a wise and experienced person, here: possibly Christopher Columbus or Marco Polo **the hero** possibly Ferdinand Magellan (1480-1521) **flowerly peninsulas** (peninsular = Halbinsel) southeast Asia, such as Malaysia **spice islands** islands in eastern Indonesia

## 6. Walden

...I went to the woods [to live alone at Walden Pond in Massachusetts] because I wished to live deliberately, to front only the essential facts of life, and see if I could not learn what it had to teach, and not, when I came to die, discover that I had not lived.

[...] I learned at least, by my experiment, that if one advances confidently in the direction of his dreams, and endeavors to live the life which he has imagined, he will meet with a success unexpected in common hours. He will put some things behind, will pass an invisible boundary; new, universal, and more liberal laws will begin to establish themselves

**deliberately** concentrating on the purpose **to front** to be confronted with **to endeavor** to try **common hours** everyday life

around and within him; or the old laws be expanded, and interpreted in his favor in a more liberal sense, and he will live with the license of a higher order of beings. In proportion as he simplifies his life, the laws of the universe will appear less complex, and solitude will not be solitude, nor poverty poverty, nor weakness weakness. If you have built castles in the air, your work need not be lost; that is where they should be. Now put the foundations under them…

Why should we be in such desperate haste to succeed, and in such desperate enterprises? If a man does not keep pace with his companions, perhaps it is because he hears a different drummer. Let him step to the music which he hears, however measured or far away…

From *Walden* (1845) by Henry David Thoreau (1817-1862),
American writer and philosopher.

## 7. The West as seen by Lasch

In the nineteenth-century American imagination, the vast continent stretching westward symbolized both the promise and the menace of an escape from the past. The West represented an opportunity to build a new society unencumbered by feudal inhibitions, but it also tempted men to throw off civilization and to revert to savagery. Through compulsive industry and relentless sexual repression, nineteenth-century Americans achieved a fragile triumph over the id. The violence they turned against the Indians and against nature originated not in unrestrained impulse but in the white Anglo-Saxon superego, which feared the wildness of the West because it objectified the wildness within each individual. While celebrating the romance of the frontier in their popular literature, in practice Americans imposed on the wilderness a new order designed to keep impulse in check while giving free rein to acquisitiveness. Capital accu-

**menace** s.th. that is dangerous **unencumbered** not hindered **inhibition** a feeling of worry or embarrassment that stops you from doing what you want to do **to tempt** in Versuchung führen **to revert to s.th.** to go back to a former practice **savagery** uncivilized behavior **compulsive** difficult to stop or control **industry** working hard **relentless** continuing without stopping **repression** keeping an impulse under control **id** according to Freud, the mass of primitive instincts in a person's mind **unrestrained** not held back **superego** according to Freud, the conscience **to objectify** to make it possible for a person to experience s.th. in him-/herself **to keep in check** to limit, to control **to give**

mulation in its own right sublimated appetite and subordinated the pursuit of self-interest to the service of future generations. In the heat of the struggle to win the West, the American pioneer gave full vent to his rapacity and murderous cruelty, but he always envisioned the result—not without misgivings, expressed in a nostalgic cult of lost innocence—as a peaceful, respectable, churchgoing community safe for his women and children. He imagined that his off-spring, raised under the morally refining influence of feminine "culture," would grow up to be sober, law-abiding, domesticated American citizens, and the thought of the advantages they would inherit justified his toil and excused, he thought, his frequent lapses into brutality, sadism, and rape.



**free rein to s.th.** to allow s.th. a lot of freedom **acquisitiveness** eagerness to acquire things **capital accumulation** making money and becoming rich **to sublimate** according to Freud: to direct the energy of a primitive impulse into activities that are considered to be socially more acceptable **to subordinate** to place in a lower position than s.th. else **to give full vent to s.th.** to do s.th. without any limits **rapacity** greed, taking everything you want with violence **to envision** to think of s.th. possible for the future **misgiving** feeling of doubt **off-spring** children **to refine** here: to make more civilized **sober** having a serious attitude towards life **law-abiding** obeying the law **toil** hard work **lapse** a short return to a lower moral state **rape** Vergewaltigung

## 8. New Frontier and Great Society

In 1960, Democrat John F. Kennedy was elected president. Young, energetic and handsome, Kennedy promised to "get the country moving again"; to forge ahead toward a "New Frontier." But one of Kennedy's first foreign policy ventures was a disaster. In an effort to overthrow the Communist dictatorship of Fidel Castro in Cuba, Kennedy supported an invasion of the island nation by a group of Cuban exiles who had been trained by the Central Intelligence Agency (CIA). In April 1961, the exiles landed at the Bay of Pigs and were almost immediately captured.

**John F. Kennedy** (1917-1963) 35th President of the U.S.A. **to forge ahead** to move forward in a powerful way **venture** an undertaking with risks **Fidel Castro** Cuban head of state (1926-) **CIA** agency founded in 1947 to gather intelligence outside the U.S.A. **Bay of Pigs** bay on the south coast of Cuba

In October 1962, observation planes discovered that the Soviet Union was installing nuclear missiles in Cuba, close enough to strike American cities in a matter of minutes. Kennedy imposed a blockade on Cuba and prepared an invasion force. Soviet Premier Nikita Khrushchev finally agreed to remove the missiles, in return for an American promise not to invade Cuba.

In April 1961, the Soviets scored another triumph in space: Yuri Gagarin became the first man to orbit the Earth. President Kennedy responded with a pledge that the United States would land a man on the moon before the end of the decade. In February 1962, John Glenn made the first American orbital flight, and he was welcomed home as a hero—much as Charles Lindbergh had been celebrated 35 years earlier after he made the first nonstop solo flight across the Atlantic. It took $24 thousand million and years of research, but Kennedy's pledge was fulfilled in July 1969, when Neil Armstrong stepped out of the Apollo 11 spacecraft onto the surface of the moon.

In the 1960s, Martin Luther King, Jr. led a nonviolent campaign to desegregate southern restaurants, interstate buses, theaters and hotels. His followers were met by hostile police, violent mobs, tear gas, fire hoses and electric cattle prods. The Kennedy administration tried to protect civil rights workers and secure voting rights for southern blacks. In June 1963, Governor George Wallace of Alabama symbolically stood at the doors of the all-white state university to prevent the admission of two black students, but the federal government forced him to give way. Speaking that evening, President Kennedy demanded the enactment of a tough federal civil rights law.

On November 22, before Kennedy could achieve that goal, he was assassinated in Dallas, Texas. Kennedy was not a universally popular president, but his death was a terrible shock to the American people.

The new president, Lyndon Johnson, the vice president under Kennedy who succeeded to the office on the death of the president, passed the Civil Rights Act of 1964, which outlawed racial discrimination in public accommodations and in any business or institution receiving

**to impose** to officially order **Khrushchev** (1894-1971) head of the Soviet government 1958-1964 **to score** to win, to gain **Gagarin** (1934-1968) **to orbit** to travel around **pledge** promise **Glenn** (1921-) **Lindbergh** (1902-1974) **Armstrong** (1930-) **King** (1929-1968) **cattle prod** a stick normally used to push cattle along **Wallace** (1919-1998) **admission** permission given to s.o. to become a member of s.th. **to give way** to no longer show opposition **enactment** the act of making a proposal into law **Johnson** (1908-1973) **accommodations** (AE) hotel rooms, restaurants

federal money. Johnson was elected to a new term with widespread popular support in 1964. Encouraged by a great election victory, Johnson pushed through Congress many social programs: federal aid to education, the arts and the humanities; health insurance for the elderly (Medicare) and for the poor (Medicaid); low-cost housing and urban renewal. The Voting Rights Act of 1965 finally enabled all black Americans to vote. Discrimination in immigration was also ended: National origins quotas were abolished, allowing a great increase in entry visas for Asians.

Although most Americans had by now achieved affluence, Michael Harrington's book *The Other America* (1962) identified persistent pockets of poverty—in urban slums, in black neighborhoods and among the poor whites of the eastern Appalachian mountains. President Johnson responded with his "War on Poverty," which included special preschool education for poor children, vocational training for school dropouts and community service jobs for slum youths.

With all these programs, Johnson aimed to build his "Great Society"—an America where equality of opportunity and a high quality of life would be enjoyed by all. And in 1965, there was every reason to be optimistic about the future of the nation. All forms of legal race discrimination had been eliminated, poverty was declining, and Americans were more prosperous and better educated than ever before. Only three years later, the "Great Society" lay in ruins, wrecked by the Vietnam War.

## Vietnam War

American involvement in Vietnam did not begin with President Johnson. When Communist and nationalist rebels fought French colonialism in Indochina after World War II, President Truman sent military aid to France. After the French withdrew from Southeast Asia in 1954, President Eisenhower dispatched American advisers and aid to help set up a democratic, pro-Western government in South Vietnam. Under President Kennedy, thousands of military officers trained South Vietnamese soldiers and sometimes flew Vietnamese warplanes into combat.

In August 1963, two American destroyers sailing in the Gulf of Tonkin reported attacks by North Vietnamese torpedo boats. Some of

**urban renewal** improvement of poor areas in a city **affluence** having plenty of money **Harrington** (1928-1989) American socialist **persistent** continuing to exist although not desirable **pocket** small area **vocational training** training that teaches you a skill for a certain job **Truman** (1884-1982) 33rd President of the U.S.A. **to dispatch** to send **combat** fighting in a war **Gulf of Tonkin** area of water between China and Vietnam

those reports may have been in error, but President Johnson launched air strikes against North Vietnamese naval bases in retaliation. The first American combat soldiers were sent to Vietnam in March 1965. By 1968, 500,000 American troops had arrived. Meanwhile, the Air Force gradually stepped up B-52 raids against North Vietnam, first bombing military bases and routes, later hitting factories and power stations near Hanoi. But this massive application of military force succeeded only in devastating Vietnam.

Demonstrations protesting American involvement in this undeclared and, many felt, unjustified war broke out on college campuses across the United States. There were some violent clashes between students and police. In October 1967, 200,000 demonstrators demanding peace marched on the Pentagon in Washington.

At the same time, unrest in the cities also erupted, as younger and more militant black leaders were denouncing as ineffectual the nonviolent tactics of Martin Luther King. King's assassination in Memphis, Tennessee, in 1968, triggered race riots in over 100 cities. Business districts in black neighborhoods were burned, and 43 people were killed—most of them black.

Ever increasing numbers of Americans from all walks of life opposed the involvement of the United States in the War in Indochina, and in the 1968 election, President Johnson faced strong challenges from two antiwar Democrats, Senators Eugene McCarthy and Robert Kennedy, brother of President John F. Kennedy. On May 31, facing a humiliating defeat at the polls and a seemingly endless conflict in Vietnam, Johnson withdrew from the presidential race and offered to negotiate an end to the Vietnam War. Robert Kennedy was assassinated at the end of the primary campaign, and the voters narrowly elected Republican Richard Nixon. As president, Nixon appealed to "Middle America"—the "great silent majority" who were unhappy with violence and protest at home.

**to launch air strikes** to allow air attacks to start **in retaliation** an action against s.o. who has done s.th. bad to you **to step up** to increase **B-52** a large bomber plane **raid** attack **application** use **to devastate** to heavily destroy **clash** short fight **the Pentagon** the headquarters of the military **unrest** violent protest **to erupt** to start suddenly **to denounce** to strongly criticize **assassination** murder for political reasons **to trigger** to cause violent events to happen very quickly **riot** violent behavior by a large crowd **walks of life** of different professions or social classes **McCarthy** (1916-) **Robert Kennedy** (1925-1968) **to humiliate** demütigen **polls** here: the presidential primary elections **Richard Nixon** (1913-1994) 37th president of the U.S.A. **"Middle American", "silent majority"** i.e. the middle class

In Indochina, Nixon pursued a policy of "Vietnamization," gradually replacing American soldiers with Vietnamese. But heavy bombing of Communist bases continued, and in the spring of 1970 Nixon sent American soldiers into Cambodia. That action caused the most massive and violent campus protests in the nation's history. During a demonstration at Kent State University in Ohio, National Guardsmen killed four students.

Then, as the American people perceived that the war was being ended, the situation quite suddenly changed: Quiet return to the nation's colleges and cities. By 1973, Nixon had signed a peace treaty with North Vietnam, brought American soldiers home, and ended conscription. Students began rejecting radical politics and generally became more oriented toward individual careers. Many blacks were still living in poverty, but many others were finally moving into well-paid professions. The fact that many big cities—Cleveland, Newark, Los Angeles, Washington, Detroit, Atlanta—had elected black mayors contributed to the ending of urban riots.

From *History: 1929 to The Present* by Jonathan Rose. In the pamphlet series "About the United States," The United States Information Agency 1986.

**National Guardsman** a member of the National Guard (military reserve units) **to perceive** to think of s.th. in a certain way **conscription** making young men join the armed forces, the draft **to reject** to no longer accept **Newark** city in northeastern New Jersey where Paul Auster was born

## 9. Some Notes on Paul Auster's Life

born of Samuel and Queenie Auster in Newark, New Jersey on February 3, 1947
Samuel Auster was the son of Jewish immigrants from eastern Europe
father owned a number of buildings in a poor area of Jersey City
sister 31/2 years younger was to have serious mental problems
parents' marriage unhappy and ended in divorce
father unable and unwilling to have a close and loving relationship with his son
as a high school student developed an interest in literature through books left in storage by his uncle Allen Mandelbaum
was a good baseball player and became well acquainted with the sport
after high-school graduation traveled to Europe, Italy, Spain, Paris, Ireland

from 1965 to 1969 attended Columbia University and experienced the political unrest at Columbia University

B.A. 1969 in comparative literature, M.A. with an emphasis on Renaissance literature in 1970

able to escape military service in Vietnam because of a high lottery number [draft system used in the late 1960s]

was able to work on a tanker that sailed along the Atlantic—through the connections of his stepfather

1971-1974 lived in Paris with his girlfriend Lydia Davis, often close to poverty

after 1974 lived in New York earning very little money doing translations of French writers with Lydia Davis and publishing articles in literary magazines

married Lydia Davis on October 6, 1974—marriage would end in divorce

published collection of poetry *Facing the Music* in 1980

after death of father in January 1979 was temporarily without financial worries because of an inheritance from his father

in 1980 moved to Brooklyn

met his new wife Siri Hustvedt in 1981 and quickly married

*The Art of Hunger*, a collection of essays, published in 1982

*City of Class* published in 1985—praised by critics—followed by *Ghosts* in 1986 and *The Locked Door* in 1987—the three novels known as *The New York Trilogy* are very much influenced by postmodernism

lecturer at Princeton University 1986-1990

dystopia *The Country of Last Things* published in 1987—Auster begins to use a more conventional form of narration

novel *Moon Palace* published in 1989

novel *The Music of Chance* published in 1990 and made into a movie in 1993

two films *Smoke* (based on an Auster Christmas story) and *Blue in The Face* (with sketches by Auster) released in 1995

*The Leviathan* published in 1992 followed by *Mr. Vertigo* (considered his most entertaining novel) in 1994

*Timbuktu* published in 1999—most critics are disappointed—as a result Auster becomes something of a recluse [person who prefers to live in solitude]

Auster has plans for more movies and novels

ironically Auster is more popular and better known in Europe, especially France and Germany

## 10. Interview with Paul Auster

[...]

**Larry McCaffery**: At one point in *Moon Palace*, Marco Fogg says that art's purpose is "penetrating the world and finding one's place in it". Is that what writing does for you?

**Paul Auster**: Sometimes. I often wonder why I write. It's not simply to create beautiful objects or entertaining stories. It's an activity I seem to need in order to stay alive. I feel terrible when I'm not doing it. It's not that writing brings me a lot of pleasure—but not doing it is worse.

**Sinda Gregory**: Your books have always relied more on chance and synchronicity to move their plots forward than the sorts of causality found in most fiction: this is even more apparent in your two new novels, *Moon Palace* and *The Music of Chance*. Is this foregrounding of chance a result of your own sense of how life operates (your "personal philosophy")? Or does it have more to do with your sense that this approach has interesting aesthetic applications?

**PA**: From an aesthetic point of view, the introduction of chance elements in fiction probably creates as many problems as it solves. I've come in for a lot of abuse from critics because of it. In the strictest sense of the word, I consider myself a realist. Chance is a part of reality: we are continually shaped by the forces of coincidence, the unexpected occurs with almost numbing regularity in all our lives. And yet there's a widely held notion that novels shouldn't stretch the imagination too far. Anything that appears "implausible" is necessarily taken to be forced, artificial, "unrealistic". I don't know what reality these people have been living in, but it certainly isn't my reality. In some perverse way, I believe they've spent too much time reading books. They're so immersed in the conventions of so-called realistic fiction that their sense of reality has been distorted. Everything's been smoothed out in these novels, robbed of its singularity, boxed into a predictable world of cause and effect. Anyone with the wit to get his nose out of his book and study what's actually in front

**to penetrate** here: to fully understand **The Music of Chance** novel published in 1990 after *Moon Palace* **to foreground** to especially make use of s.th. **application** using s.th. for a special purpose **to come in for s.th.** to have to be faced with s.th. **abuse** here: very harsh criticism **numbing** emotionally shocking or depressing **notion** idea, opinion **to stretch** here: to use too much of s.th. **immersed** so completely involved **to distort** to twist out of shape, to deform **to smooth out** to remove all difficulties or problems **singularity** fact of being different, uniqueness **to box s.th. into s.th.** (fig) to force s.th. into a certain limited space

of him will understand that this realism is a complete sham. To put it another way: truth is stranger than fiction. What I am after, I suppose, is to write fiction as strange as the world I live in.

**LM**: I'd say your books don't use coincidence in an effort to "smooth things over" or to create the usual realist's manipulated illusion that everything can be explained. Your books seem more fundamentally "about" mystery and coincidence, so that these operate almost as governing principles that are constantly clashing with causality and rationality.

**PA**: Precisely. When I talk about coincidence, I'm not referring to a desire to manipulate. There's a good deal of that in bad eighteenth- and nineteenth-century fiction: mechanical plot devices, the urge to tie everything up, the happy endings in which everyone turns out to be related to everyone else. No, what I'm talking about is the presence of the unpredictable, the utterly bewildering nature of human experience. From one moment to the next, anything can happen. Our life-long certainties about the world can be demolished in a single second. In philosophical terms, I'm talking about the powers of contingency. Our lives don't really belong to us, you see—they belong to the world, and in spite of our efforts to make sense of it, the world is a place beyond our understanding. We brush up against these mysteries all the time. The result can be truly terrifying—but it can also be comical. [pp. 116-122]

[...]

**SG**: Earlier in the interview you referred to yourself as basically an "intuitive writer" in terms of the way your writing process operates. Maybe we could discuss the relationship between your conscious intentionality versus your intuition by talking about the way a specific image in your work develops. For instance the moon image in *Moon Palace* appears in dozens of different contexts that occasionally dovetail or coalesce into groupings—Barber's legends of the Indians (with their origins on the moon), the way the Utah desert is described as a lunar landscape, the fortune cookie that says, "The sun is the past, the earth is the present, the moon is the future" (and which turns out to be a quote from Tesla

**wit** intelligence **sham** s.th. false, a fake **to smooth things over** to make problems seem less important **to clash** to be in conflict with s.th. **device** special method to achieve s.th. **urge** strong impulse **utterly** completely **bewildering** puzzling, confusing **contingency** chance, uncertainty **to brush against s.th.** to come in contact with s.th., to come across s.th. **in terms of** if one considers **to dovetail with s.th.** to fit neatly with s.th. else **to coalesce** to unite or come together in one body or mass, to blend

[Nikola Tesla, 1856-1943, Serbian born American inventor, eccentric and poet]), the restaurant named "Moon Palace," and so on. Is the unfolding of these connections and resonances the product of conscious design or happy accident?

**PA**: If you think about any one thing long enough or hard enough, it's going to begin to reverberate for you. Once that happens, waves are emitted, and those waves travel through space and bounce off other things, which in turn emit their own waves. It's an associative process, and if you stick with it conscientiously enough, large portions of the world will eventually be touched by your thoughts. It's not really a question of accident or design. This is my way the mind works. It just happens, but you have to be watching attentively for it to go on happening. Pick any object in front of you—a coffee cup, or a box of cigars, or a telephone—and try to think about where it comes from. Within ten minutes, you're onto any number of other things—geology, history, labor problems, biology. God knows what—a whole range of subjects. "To see the world in a grain of sand." [a quote from the English poet William Blake and the American poet Walt Whitmann]. If you're capable of doing that, imagine how much can be seen in the moon!

**LM**: There's also a certain sense in which those elaborate connections and metaphorical associations being developed grow naturally out of the kind of sensibility you project for Fogg.

**PA**: Precisely. Fogg is a bookish young man, an intellectual, and he has a penchant for this kind of thing. It's something he inherits from his Uncle Victor, a man who is constantly searching the world for hidden connections. The moon imagery comes from Fogg—I wasn't trying to impose it on him. At the same time, remember, he's telling the story of his youth from the distance of middle age, and he often pokes fun at himself. He's looking back on the way he used to think, the way he used to interpret the world. It's one of the many follies of his adolescence, a symptom of the madness of those times. But Fogg is a unique case. Other characters I've written about have none of these tendencies; they don't indulge in such elaborate mental gymnastics. Nashe, for example, the hero of *The*

**to unfold** to reveal more and more **design** planning **to reverberate** to echo, here: to bring about a great number of connecting ideas **to emit** to send out **conscientiously** taking great care **elaborate** complex **to project** to plan **penchant** a strong liking for s.th. **to inherit** to receive from s.o. especially from one's family before you **to impose on s.o.** to force on s.o. **to poke fun at s.th./s.o.** to make fun of s.th./s.o. **folly** foolish action or mistake **to indulge in s.th.** to let yourself do s.th. you enjoy

*Music of Chance*, has nothing in common with Fogg. He's a much more straightforward kind of person, and consequently the book he appears in is a much simpler story.

**LM**: Let's go back for a second to your comment about seeing the world in a grain of sand. What made it seem so much a part of what you were doing in the novel? And how did this fit in with the "follies" of Fogg's adolescence?

**PA**: The moon is many things all at once, a touchstone. It's the moon as myth, as "radiant Diana, image of all that is dark within us;" the imagination, love, madness. At the same time, it's the moon as object, as celestial body, as lifeless stone hovering in the sky. But it's also the longing for what is not, the unattainable, the human desire for transcendence. And yet it's history as well, particularly American history. First there's Columbus, then there was the discovery of the West, then finally there is outer space: the moon as the last frontier. But Columbus had no idea that he'd discovered America. He thought he had sailed to India, to China. In some sense, *Moon Palace* is the embodiment of that misconception, an attempt to think of America as China. But the moon is also repetition, the cyclical nature of human experience. There are three stories in the book, after all, and each one is finally the same. Each generation repeats the mistakes of the previous generation. So it's also a critique of the notion of progress. And if America is the land of progress, what are we to make of ourselves then? And so on and so on and so on. Fogg wends his way among all these ideas, this pinball machine of associations, struggling to find a place for himself. By the end of the book I think he manages to get somewhere. But he only reaches the beginning, the brink of his adult life. And that's where we leave him—getting ready to begin. [pp. 149-152]

[…]

From *The Red Notebook* by Paul Auster, Faber and Faber, London 1995.

**straightforward** simple, uncomplicated **to fit in with s.th.** to be suitable for s.th. **touchstone** s.th. used as a standard or test **radiant** shining **Diana** Roman goddess of the moon and the hunt **celestial body** star or planet, anything that can be seen shining in the sky **to hover** to stay in one place in the air or sky **longing** strong desire to have s.th. **unattainable** cannot be had or achieved **embodiment** an example or expression of an idea **misconception** mistaken view or opinion **to wend one's way through s.th.** to travel through **pinball machine** Flipper(automat) **brink** edge, border